Drag 'n' Drop CGI

Enhance Your Web Site
Without Programming

Bob Weil

and

Chris Baron

ADDISON-WESLEY DEVELOPERS PRESS

An Imprint of Addison Wesley Longman, Inc.

Reading, Massachusetts • Harlow, England • Menlo Park, California
Berkeley, California • Don Mills, Ontario • Sydney
Bonn • Amsterdam • Tokyo • Mexico City

The authors acknowledge with thanks the following software contributions: WS-FTP from Ipswich, Inc. and ThumbsPlus (PC) from Cerious Software. ColorHexer, and Append-It, Copyright © 1997 Shazron Abdullah, http://www.toptown.com/hp/canuck. cgi-lib.pl 2.14, Copyright © 1996 Steven E. Brenner. All rights reserved. The cgi-lib.pl homepage is at http://www.bio.cam.ac.uk/cgi-lib/. Tera Term, Copyright © 1994–1996 Takashi Teranishi. NetObjects Fusion version 2.0 for Windows. The smart way to build Web sites. PerlShop and Adverware are trademarks of Arpanet Corp. CGIWrap is written by Nathan Neulinger <nneul@umr.edu>. For more information, see http://www.umr.edu/~cgiwrap/. WingFlyer, Copyright © 1996–1997 James D. Borror. Anarchie, Copyright © Peter N. Lewis and distributed by Stairways Software Pty Ltd. Anarchie is shareware: if you continue to use it, you must pay for it.

Many of the designations used by manufacturers and sellers to distinguish their products are claimed as trademarks. Where those designations appear in this book, and Addison Wesley Longman, Inc. was aware of a trademark claim, the designations have been printed in initial capital letters or all capital letters.

The authors and publisher have taken care in preparation of this book, but make no expressed or implied warranty of any kind and assume no responsibility for errors or omissions. No liability is assumed for incidental or consequential damages in connection with or arising out of the use of the information or programs contained herein.

Library of Congress Cataloging-in-Publication Data

Weil, Bob.
    Drag 'n' drop CGI: enhance your web site without programming/
  Bob Weil and Chris Baron.
      p. cm.
    ISBN 0-201-41966-1
    1. CGI (Computer network protocol)   2. Web sites—Design.
  I. Baron, Chris. II. Title. III. Title: Drag and Drop CGI.
  TK5105.565.W445 1997
005.2'768—dc21   97–16884
                                                 CIP

Sponsoring Editor: Ben Ryan
Project Manager: John Fuller
Production Coordinator: Maureen A. Hurley
Cover design: Square One Design
Text design: Octal Publishing, Inc.
Set in 10 point Sabon by Octal Publishing, Inc.

1 2 3 4 5 6 7 8 9—MA—0100999897

First printing, July 1997

Addison Wesley Longman, Inc. books are available for bulk purchases by corporations, institutions, and other organizations. For more information please contact the Corporate, Government, and Special Sales Department at (800) 238-9682.

Find A-W Developers Press on the World Wide Web at: http://www.aw.com/devpress/
Find the authors' company, Holland Marketing, Inc., on the World Wide Web at:
http://www.hollandmkt.com

This book is dedicated with love to our wives:
Marya Weil and Laura Baron

Contents

· · · · · · · · · · · · ·

Acknowledgments   xv

Chapter 1   Taking Your Internet or Intranet Web Site
to the Next Level   1

Why You Need This Book 1

    The Three-Year Roller Coaster Ride 2
    How to Turn Circumstances to Your Advantage 3
    Why We Wrote This Book 4
    Our Target Audience 5
    Our Choice of Programs 5
    Gain Without Pain: How We've Organized This Book 6
    Conventions Used in This Book 8
    Caveats 10
    Some Copyright Stuff 10
    So Let's Enhance, Already! 10

Chapter 2   The Nonprogrammer's Guide to the Web,
CGI, and Programming Languages   11

How the World Wide Web Works 11

    Protocol Shmotocol 14
    Client versus Server 15

HTTP: Your Good and Faithful Servant 17

A Really Short Introduction to Web Programming Languages 20

    Perl 20
    Java 21
    Javascript 21

Holy Wars: A Word About Operating Systems 22

Chapter 3   The Nonprogrammer's Toolbox   25

Getting Down to Business 26

Your ISP or SA Is Your Friend—Really 26

The ISP/SA Questionnaire 28

Editing Script Code 33

Getting the Files on the Server—FTP to the Rescue 33

    How FTP Works 34
    WS_FTP for Windows-based Computers 35
    Anarchie for MacOS-based Computers 39

Tell Me About Telnet. 44

    Telnet for Windows 95/NT. 46
    Tera-Term for Windows 3.1 48
    NCSA Telnet for the MacOS 50

Using What You've Learned—Your First CGI Script 52

    Configuration 53
    Detailed FTP Uploading Procedures 57
    Detailed Telnet Procedures 59

Chapter 4   Giving Your Visitor a Hint (or Two) Using Javascript   65

Why You Would Want to Use This Script 66

Introduction to the *hint* Script 67

Configuring and Installing the hint Script 71

    Step 1: Configuration 71
    Step 2: Installation 74

Using the *hint* Script in Your Pages 74

Chapter 5   Counting Visitors to Your Web Site with Perl   79

Why You Would Want to Use This Script 80
    Hits versus Visits 81
Introduction to the *vcount.cgi* Script 82
    How *vcount.cgi* Works 83
Configuring and Installing *vcount.cgi* 85
    Step 1: Configuration 85
    Step 2: Installation 89
Using the *vcount.cgi* Script in Your Pages 91

Chapter 6   Fun with Scrolling Text Using Javascript   97

Why You Would Want to Use This Script 98
Introduction to the *scroller* Script 99
    How the *scroller* Script Works 101
Configuring and Installing the scroller Script 102
    Step 1: Configuration 103
    Step 2: Installation 105
Using the *scroller* Script in Your Pages 105

Chapter 7   Automating Graphics Changes on Your Web Site with Perl   109

Why You Would Want to Use This Script 110
Introduction to the *pid.cgi* Script 110
    How *pid.cig* Works 111

Configuring and Installing *pid.cgi* 113
  Step 1: Configuration 113
  Step 2: Installation 116
Using the *pid.cgi* Script in Your Pages 117
  Example 1: Roll Them Bones 117
  Example 2: A Timely Greeting 119

Chapter 8 Remote Controls for All Occasions Using Javascript 125

Why You Would Want to Use This Script 126
Introduction to the *remote* Script 127
  How the *remote* Script Works 127
Configuring and Installing the *remote* Script 130
  Step 1: Configuration 130
  Step 2: Installation 131
Using the *remote* Script in Your Pages 131

Chapter 9 Processing and Responding to Interactive Forms Using Perl 137

Why You Would Want to Use This Script 138
Introduction to the *formp.cgi* Script 138
  Security Concerns 139
  How the *formp.cgi* Script Works 139
Configuring and Installing the *formp.cgi* Script 145
  Step 1: Configuration 145
  Step 2: Installation 151
Using the *formp.cgi* Script in Your Pages 153

Chapter 10   Example Form-Processing Applications Using Perl   159

Why You Would Want to Use This Script 160

A Request-for-Information Form 161

How the Form Works 163

A Guest Book 166

How the Form Works 168

An On-line Test Form 170

How the Form Works 172

Chapter 11   Client-side Form Validation with Javascript   177

Why You Would Want to Use This Script 178

Introduction to the *formv* Script 179

How the *formv* Script Works 179

Configuring and Installing the *formv* Script 181

Step 1: Configuration 182

Step 2: Installation 186

Using the *formv* Script in Your Pages 186

Checking a Single Field 187

Checking an Entire Form 190

Putting It All Together 190

Chapter 12 A Perl-based Web Site Search Engine 195

Why You Would Want to Use This Script 196

Introduction to the *ICE* Scripts 197

How the *ICE* Scripts Work. 198

Configuring and Installing the *ICE* Scripts. 202

Step 1: Configuration 203

Step 2: Installation 210

Using the *ICE* Scripts in Your Pages 212

Advanced *ICE* Configuration 214

Chapter 13 A Perl-based On-line Store System—Part 1: Installation 223

What You Need to Install This Script 224

Introduction to On-line Store Systems 225

Overview of the *PerlShop* System 228

Configuring and Installing *PerlShop* 231

Step 1: Directory Configuration 231

Step 2: Script Configuration 232

Step 3: Installation 250

Secure Server Setup 251

Up Next. 253

Chapter 14 A Perl-based On-line Store System—Part 2: Setting Up the Store 255

Where We Are Now 256

How *PerlShop* Processes Pages 256

Server-Independence Tags 258

Entering the Store 259

Creating the Catalog Pages 262

    Single-item Selection Form 263
    Multi-item Selection Form 269
    Selection Form Tag Order 273

Navigating the Store 274

The Built-in Search Engine 275

"Driving" the Shopping Cart 276

Customizing the Script 279

    The *PerlShop* Logo 280
    Page Header 281
    Shopping-Cart Contents 281
    Order Form 281
    Confirmation Message 281
    Shipping Rates Page 282
    Button and Menu Bar 282
    Search Page 282

Up Next 282

Chapter 15   A Perl-based On-line Store System—Part 3: Processing Orders and Security   285

Where We Are Now 286

The Payment and Shipping Process 286

Ordering Process Outputs 292

    The Customer File 293
    The Order File 294
    The Invoice 295

Increasing Store Security 297
 Add *index.html* Files 298
 Relocate the Store Directories. 299
 Using *cgiwrap*. 300
Encryption. 303
 Pretty Good Privacy (PGP) 304
 Modifying *PerlShop* to Use PGP. 304

Chapter 16   What's Next   307

What (We Think) We've Given You. 307
 Becoming a Script Hacker: Is It for You? 307
Where to Now?. 309
 Making Sure Your Web Site Makes Sense. 310
 Targeting Your Audience 311
 A Solution: Focus Groups and Usability Testing. 312
Visit Our Drag 'n' Drop Web Site 313
Some Great Books to Look For 314
 Javascript Books. 314
 Perl Books 314
 Perl CGI Books. 314
 Books on Web Site Design 315
 Books on Internet Marketing 315
A Short List of Web Resources 316

Appendix A   Some Notes on Perl for Nonprogrammers   317

Do I Need to Read This If I Don't Want to Be a Perl Programmer? 318
A Bit about Perl Programs 318

Perl Data. 319
    Numeric 319
    String. 319
    Array. 320
Perl Code 322
    Variables 323
    Operators 323
    Conditionals 324
    Statements. 324
    Subroutines and Libraries 327
    Regular Expressions 328
    Functions. 329
    Special Variables 330

Appendix B   A UNIX Command Reference for Non-nerds   333

Introduction to UNIX. 334
Common Shell Commands 335
    Path Name Conventions 336
    Command Format Conventions. 336
    Directory and File Commands. 337
UNIX Permissions 339
How to Find Things and Get Help 341
Miscellaneous Commands 343
Some Useful Programs 343
Conclusion 344

Appendix C   What's on the CD-ROM   347

The CD-ROM Directories 348

The Root Directory 348
The /questionnaire Directory 348
The /scripts Directory.. 348
The /tools Directory.. 349
The /nettools Directory....................................... 349
The /commercial Directory.................................... 350
CD Warranty 350

Index   351

Acknowledgments

Many people have contributed to this book in one way or another. It would be impossible to name them all here, but the authors must touch on the most important co-conspirators. Mentioning them chronologically probably makes the most sense.

If Bob could make a really long list, it would begin with his reading tutor, Mrs. Mahon, who got through to a 9 year-old that it was fun to read and write. About 30 years later (in 1994), Bill Allen, publisher of *3D Artist* magazine, gave an inexperienced animator the chance to write a software product review. Reading that substandard bit of hack prose, Mary Treseler of Addison Wesley Longman found that it had some promise. The authors further thank Kim Fryer (a former editor at Addison Wesley Longman) for giving their book idea a receptive ear the following year.

Closer to home (*at* home, as a matter of fact), Bob wishes to thank his incredible wife Marya and children Lisa and Nicholas for supporting and believing in him as he worked on a book that never seemed to get finished. Bob's mother, Helen, instilled a love of learning and a willingness to take chances that he hasn't outgrown. His dad, Robert, showed him that technology could be comprehended—and even made interesting. He also read this book from cover to cover, offering much salient criticism of the evolving copy. Bob's parents encouraged him to write, and they didn't judge his work too harshly, even when it would have been well-deserved.

Finally, this book would not have been written if Bob had not been "downsized" out of corporate America. The Orange County Register gave him the opportunity (and briefly, the funding) to start his own business in 1995, with the fledgling Web as its focus.

Chris wishes to thank his wife Laura and the boys—Michael, Patrick, Daniel, Mario, George, and John-Paul—for their love and patience. They gave up many hours, meals, conversations, and games so this book could be written. Chris also wishes to thank Bob Weil for suggesting in 1995 that a career might be found somewhere in this crazy thing called the World Wide Web.

The Byzantine Catholic monks of the Holy Resurrection Monastery in Barstow, California contributed prayers and encouragement throughout the process. A call to the monks helped break more than one writer's block with a little help from "upstairs." The crew at Addison-Wesley Developers Press could not have been better to work with: Kim Fryer, of course, who grasped our concept early on and pushed it through the selection committees; Ben Ryan, our editor; Maureen Hurley (and previously,

Erin Sweeney) on the production side; and last, but certainly not least, Laura Michaels whose inspired copyediting filled us with awe and made the book much better.

Chris would also like to thank the U.S. Air Force for giving him an education, the chance to develop some really cool software, and the opportunity to spend some truly enormous amounts of money.

Finally, Bob and Chris both wish to thank their company, Holland Marketing, Inc. (www.hollandmkt.com), of Tustin, California, for providing us some breathing space between exciting Internet marketing projects to work on this book.

Bob Weil
Chris Baron
June 1997

Chapter 1

Taking Your Internet or Intranet Web Site to the Next Level

Why You Need This Book

This book is for people who have built an Internet, intranet, or extranet Web site and are now asking themselves, "What do I do for an encore?" If one or more of the following statements apply to you, then you need this book:

- You know HTML, and you've put together a Web site or two. Now you want to create a page with a little something extra that the next guy doesn't have.

- You want or need to add some of the more advanced features and functions you've seen on other (perhaps competitive) Web sites, and you'd like to do that without having to become either a programmer or a UNIX expert.

- You've seen mysterious things called Common Gateway Interface (CGI) scripts, Java, and Javascript bandied about in the trades. You know these are the tools needed to add interactive, next-generation features to your site, but you aren't a programmer and you don't have the time and/or the inclination to become one.

- You've searched in vain for a book written in plain English (not nerd-speak) that tells you just what you need to know to get the job done. You don't want hundreds of pages on programming syntax, networking theory, design lessons, or the whole history of the World Wide Web.

- You want a selection of complete, tested, full-function applications that offer a wide range of features—not examples or components. You want them presented in a cookbook format that says, *do this, this, and this, and here's what you can expect for your efforts.*

1

This book should also appeal to businesspeople getting ready to take their companies on-line, but who have some healthy skepticism about doing business on the Web. Rest assured, there are a lot more like you out there. Much of the wired world is wrestling with these issues:

- "Why are we on the Internet?"
- "How do we cost-justify our expenditures?"
- "How can we use this thing to reduce expenses, sell products, and/or service customers?"

Unfortunately, there are no easy answers to these and the other questions that soon follow. It doesn't help that corporate objectives and expectations for an Internet presence have undergone countless changes over the last three years.

The Three-Year Roller Coaster Ride

In 1995, it seemed that everybody had to get on-line. Personal users discovered just how easy it is to create a Web page. Consequently, the Web exploded with millions of home pages featuring pictures of cats and babies and links to more of the same, ad nauseam. For businesses, the battle cry went something like this: "@#*?! [expletive of your choosing]. All of our competitors have Web sites! We've got to get on-line, too! You [boss points to unsuspecting subordinate], get us a Web site by Friday!" And so another Webmaster was conscripted.

Far from developing a coherent Internet marketing strategy, many companies simply converted their existing print brochures to HTML with little thought about exactly what they wanted their site to accomplish. Money appeared to be no object as huge "brochureware" corporate Web sites sprang into being. Although they were not bound by the "publish once" realities of print media, many of these sites were not updated in any significant way for months at a time.

In 1996, clipart-laden personal home pages were still alive and well (if unvisited), but many executives (rightly) questioned the unbudgeted expense of joining the on-line party. They started to ask for some return on investment (ROI). However, cost justification of an on-line presence proved difficult to produce. On-line commerce models were—and still are—evolving, and not many companies were consistently earning money from their Web sites. Many large and small companies shuttered their Web sites at this stage or completely revamped them into what has been called "second-generation" Web sites.

These second-generation Web sites tried to sell the company's products or services on-line, generally with little success. At this stage, many corporate sites ballooned, full of oversized graphics, gratuitous Shockwave movies, RealAudio, and "talking head" downloadable video files of the company's founder. As often as not, these elements were not integrated with the site design or the marketing message (if one was present). As in 1995, there was little systematic effort to keep site content current or to invite visitor interaction in a meaningful way.

"The year of the Internet shakeout" is most likely how 1997 will be remembered. Just as many smaller ISPs (Internet Service Providers) and Web design firms will likely vanish, so, too, will a number of typical first- and second-generation Web sites. Companies will either completely rethink their Web presence, let their current site gather digital dust, or depart the new medium altogether. These last two alternatives will obviously have an impact on anyone whose career is in any way linked to the company Web site.

How to Turn Circumstances to Your Advantage

Don't misunderstand us. There's still plenty of opportunity to have your Web site counted among the Web's success stories—whether it's a personal, small business, or Fortune 500 site. Unfortunately, there are no "elder statesmen" with all the answers because no one's done it all before. Think about how long (most of) you have been involved with the Internet. Odds are, you can reckon this time in months. In what other discipline can you go from the Internet equivalent of semiliteracy to electronic publisher in just a few months? The Internet has yet to see its first William Randolph Hearst or Rupert Murdoch, which means there continue to be tremendous opportunities for the rest of us until they arrive—and even after.

How can you meet or anticipate management objectives for your company Web site? And once those objectives are identified, how do you harness this new medium in service of them? *The simple answer is, see your site as a weapon in the battle to gain market share for your company.*

Hair Saver

This isn't intended to be a marketing book, so we can't pretend to tell you how to integrate your Web site into your corporate marketing effort. (Chapter 16, "What's Next," lists several books you may want to investigate.) We do recommend, however, that you find a prominent ally or champion on the marketing side of the company. This is especially true if you are working in the information services part of your organization. Like it or not, the future of your Web site will be driven not by the people providing the tools, but by the part of the company that is responsible for positioning your products or services in the marketplace and for growing the bottom line. And it goes (almost) without saying that flashy technology alone won't amount to anything. It must work in service of company objectives.

Here are some of the important steps to take when developing a successful Web presence strategy:

1. Clearly understand the marketing direction of your company.
2. Stay current with "enabling" Internet technologies.
3. Identify those technologies that can most effectively align your site with corporate marketing objectives.
4. Incorporate the appropriate technologies into your site to effectively deliver your message.
5. Measure your success in connecting with your current and potential customers.
6. Refine your strategy accordingly.

None of this is easy, and we can help you only with items two and four. Many of you reading this book don't have the time, resources, or knowledge to program all the features of a third-generation Web site. (Characteristics of a third-generation site include the creation of customized visit experiences, and the use of cutting-edge technology to encourage visitor interaction with the site.) For that reason, we've developed some ready-made tools for your use and customization in reaching these objectives.

Why We Wrote This Book

Think of this book as a "fast-food menu" for Internet, intranet, and extranet Web site developers. For those of you with modest technical aspirations, the programs we've included can be used "as is" with only minor configuration required. For the more technically adroit, they can serve as a foundation for even more sophisticated applications.

Our objective in writing this book is to provide you with self-contained, prepackaged, ready-made enhancements—called **scripts**—that you can quickly add to your Web site without taking the time and effort required to learn how to program. Although you may have to make some changes to a configuration file or modify some variables in the scripts, this is still a far cry from serious programming (and will not qualify you to wear a pocket protector).

We wanted the scripts to be relatively easy to configure, install, and modify, yet fully functional and diverse enough in scope to satisfy your beginning-, intermediate-, and advanced-level needs. And we wanted them to run on the widest possible array of server and browser platforms.

The result is nine scripts from which to select. They range from the utilitarian (a visit counter for your site) to the incredibly useful (a full-featured, on-line sales system), all of which can be easily modified to reflect your Internet marketing strategy. And to help you see how they can solve your real-world problems, we begin each script chapter with a few ideas on how you can put them to use.

Our Target Audience

This book is for the savvy (although not necessarily technical) reader who may not have the time or skill set to enhance his or her Web pages "from scratch." These are the people who are responsible in some way for a Web site, whether for personal use or as part of a business. It doesn't matter whether they report to Marketing, MIS, or even Finance. They may or may not be called Webmasters, but their phones ring when someone has a question about (or problem with) the Web site. Chances are they have received no special training for their new role, although they typically have some knowledge of HTML and they understand the process of creating, maintaining, and updating a Web site. Most important, they're willing to learn new things in order to achieve their goals. While the majority of readers who pick up this book will not be programmers, even the "techies" in the audience will find a number of useful scripts that they can use and modify.

Our Choice of Programs

The world of the Web changes about three times as fast as the rest of the already fast-moving technical world. It's easy to get into a rut and use last week's cool effect and find that it's already showing its age. Although your first inclination may be to impress your visitors, the real goal is to engage them so that they find their stay rewarding and they return later.

In this book, we stayed away from programs that are merely flashy, since these tend to date quickly. Still, some of the programs we've chosen can be used to great dramatic effect. Examples are the Javascript scrolling text display in Chapter 6, "Fun with Scrolling Text Using Javascript," and the Javascript remote control window described in Chapter 8, "Remote Controls for All Occasions Using Javascript." We felt it was crucial to include programs that could continue to be a solid resource for our readers well into the future (well, at least for the next several years). These include such Web stalwarts as sophisticated interactive form validation using Javascript (Chapter 11, "Client-side Form Validation with Javascript"), a robust Web site search engine in Perl (Chapter 12, "A Perl-based Web Site Search Engine"), and a complete on-line store sporting a shopping-cart style user-interface (Chapters 13–15, "A Perl-based On-line Store System").

There are a number of valuable books on the market that offer "Learn *XX* in *YY* Days" lessons. Unlike these texts, our primary goal has been to develop or select applications that

- solve real-world problems,

- represent complete, rather than partial or merely "demonstrator," applications,

- have a robust feature set, and

- can be immediately used by novice and experienced users alike.

We make no pretense of trying to teach you a programming language. You're reading this book because you want sophisticated applications that you can quickly put to use on your Web site, with minimal hassle.

Gain Without Pain: How We've Organized This Book

This book starts with three introductory chapters to bring the novice up to speed on the basics:

Chapter 1: Taking Your Internet or Intranet Web Site to the Next Level. The chapter you're reading now.

Chapter 2: The Nonprogrammer's Guide to the Web, CGI, and Programming Languages. This chapter gives a cursory (but essential) overview of Internet communications and how Common Gateway Interface (CGI) scripts work their magic. We also provide details on the Perl and Javascript programming languages we've chosen to use and the differences in Web server operating systems.

Chapter 3: The Nonprogrammer's Toolbox. This extensive chapter may be skipped by true Internet cognoscente, although it could prove helpful as a review. We've included a detailed questionnaire you can work through with your ISP or System Administrator (SA) to determine the server-based resources that are available for your use, along with the necessary details of how your ISP/SA's Web server is set up. We explain how to edit the code we've provided and how to integrate the software into your pages. We also describe how to upload these programs from Mac and Windows platforms by using the software we've included on the CD-ROM.

The next 12 chapters serve up the "meat and potatoes" of the book. They cover nine specific capabilities that you can add to your Web site without programming. In fact, we don't even include the full source code in each chapter. Instead, we focus on showing you how to configure each program for your server and how to customize each to fit into *your* Web site. The complete source code is on the accompanying CD-ROM. As the book progresses, the software increases in complexity and functional sophistication. Unless you are already experienced in configuring and uploading CGI programs, we recommend that you work through the book from the beginning. You should at least read the first three chapters before trying to use one of the programs described in the later ones.

Chapter 4: Giving Your Visitor a Hint (or Two) Using Javascript. This chapter shows you how to create status-line messages and pop-up windows containing short messages that appear for a visitor as he or she moves through your site.

Chapter 5: Counting Visitors to Your Web Site with Perl. In this chapter, you customize a simple Perl program that allows you to count the number of visitors to your home page (or any other page or pages on your site).

Chapter 6: Fun with Scrolling Text Using Javascript. This chapter shows you how to add a scrolling, ticker-tape-style message to the browser status line or a form field. We've included a couple of brand-new-to-the-Web variations not available elsewhere.

Chapter 7: Automating Graphics Changes on Your Web Site with Perl. This chapter introduces a program that allows you to swap images in and out on your site either randomly or by using time- and date-based criteria. (Advanced users can modify this program to replace whole sections of HTML as well.)

Chapter 8: Remote Controls for All Occasions Using Javascript. You've seen them on a few sophisticated and urbane Web sites—the little directory windows that pop up alongside your browser window. We show you how to create this handy little tool, which can be used in many novel ways.

Chapters 9 and 10: Processing and Responding to Interactive Forms Using Perl and **Example Form-Processing Applications Using Perl.** Form processing has been, and will remain, a major functional requirement on Web sites that interact with visitors. Chapter 9 deals with configuration and installation of the basic script. Chapter 10 presents three sample applications covering concepts immediately usable on your site: a request-for-information form, a simple guest book, and an on-line test form.

Chapter 11: Client-side Form Validation with Javascript. This chapter covers methods for validating the accuracy and completeness of data input by your visitor, down to the field level. Forms may be evaluated field-by-field either as they are filled in or just prior to the form's submission. This program works well in tandem with the form-processing program covered in Chapters 9 and 10.

Chapter 12: A Perl-based Web Site Search Engine. This chapter offers a high-powered Web site search engine that returns hyperlinks to every location on your site where the selected word or string appears.

Chapters 13, 14, and 15: A Perl-based On-line Store System. These chapters show you how to install and configure a sophisticated on-line store complete with on-line credit card processing and support for secure commerce Web servers.

Chapter 16: What's Next. This chapter offers some suggestions on how to keep the goals of your Web site in sync with your needs and how to evaluate it after you go live. Also presented is information about where to look if you'd like to learn more about enhancing your Web pages.

The three appendices fill in some detail you'll find helpful as you work through the chapters:

Appendix A: Some Notes on Perl for Nonprogrammers. This appendix gives you some basic information about the Perl programming language and how it works.

Appendix B: A UNIX Command Reference for Non-nerds. This appendix covers the most common UNIX commands and concepts.

Appendix C: What's on the CD-ROM. This appendix describes the goodies we've placed on the CD-ROM. Naturally, all the scripts and configuration files covered in this book are included, as well as several utilities to make your on-line life easier. There also are several Web-based resources that you can turn to for further learning or for additional software. The CD-ROM supplies hyperlinks to some of these, one of which is the *Drag 'n' Drop CGI* Web site (*http://www.hypertising.com/DnDCGI/*).

Conventions Used in This Book

There are several conventions used in this book that are intended to make it easy to use. Each script chapter is generally divided into the following sections:

Features of the Script. A bulleted list of the basic script features, benefits, and capabilities.

What You Need to Use This Script. The resources required to implement the script, such as the Perl version number, type of server access, and so on.

Why You Would Want to Use This Script. As anyone in marketing will remind you, *features* become *benefits* only when they solve real-world problems. We've developed each of these scripts as a complete solution you can immediately put to work on your site. We introduce each chapter with a few ideas about how you might put each script to use.

Introduction to the Script. A description of how the script works, in general terms, including the theory of operation, presented in layman's terms.

Using the Script in Your Pages. Examples and instructions on how to use the functions of the script in your Web pages.

Configuration and Installation. How to configure and install the script and a high-level explanation of how it accomplishes its magic.

What We've Covered. A concluding list that summarizes the specific script features presented in the chapter.

Appendices differ somewhat in that they begin with **What You'll Find in This Appendix** and **What You Won't Find in This Appendix**. Since we're not attempting to teach Perl, Javascript, or UNIX, this helps keep our objectives in clear focus.

To break the flow of individual chapters, and to share our occasional flashes of insight, we also created the following categories of comments:

Hot Tip

True to its name, these notes usually offer some additional insider technique, concept, or "heads up" that may assist you in more effectively putting a script to work for you.

Amazing Factoid

These notes highlight some interesting tangent that we just had to pursue. They're usually not essential to your mastery of the script, but we promise they will be relevant to the subject being discussed. And we hope they might even be interesting bits of information and, dare we say, in some way useful.

Hair Saver

These notes directly relate to the associated section of the chapter and offer technical advice on how to avoid grief, hair-pulling, and other forms of midnight madness.

Nerd Note

These notes are much like Amazing Factoids, except that they will primarily interest techies and would-be techies. If you have aspirations to becoming a Web programmer extraordinaire, or you're just looking to pick up some technical tidbits with which to impress your friends, you will want to read these.

Caveats

The nice thing about Latin is that most people don't know it very well. And *caveat* sounds a lot better than *beware*. But, we can't emphasize how important it is to "be wary" as you make changes to your Web site. Test any changes you make with all the browsers that are likely to be used by visitors to your site. If this isn't practical, at least test the site using the current versions of the predominant browsers. (As of this writing, Microsoft *Internet Explorer* and Netscape *Navigator* are the most popular Web browsers.) Testing is critical; sometimes the same browser, even with an identical version number, performs differently on different operating systems.

We try to touch on these crucial issues throughout the book. Of course, most of them apply only to the browsers available as we write. So, don't take anything for granted. Test your Web site thoroughly as you develop it, and view it on multiple browsers. Don't get caught with a Web site few people can appreciate.

Some Copyright Stuff

We've written most of the scripts contained in this book, and they are copyrighted by us. That simply means that you can't resell them, give them away, use, or include our code in scripts you distribute without our permission. Having purchased the book, you're welcome to use each script as many times as you like and modify it as you see fit. We simply ask that wherever you use the script, you include the copyright notice that appears at the start of each script. The same applies to the two scripts that we included but did not write (the Web site search engine and the on-line shopping system). We'd appreciate it!

So Let's Enhance, Already!

We hope this book will offer you a number of ways to easily enhance your Internet or intranet Web site without programming. If even one of the scripts proves useful, it will save you hours (perhaps days) of searching the Internet for the appropriate script and configuring it to meet your needs. As they say in those late-night TV commercials: "Now what would you pay?" We think you'll easily recover the purchase price of a set of Ginsu steak knives (or of this book) by implementing even the simplest script we offer.

With that, let's start enhancing your Web site. Please place your seat backs and tray tables in the upright and locked position, fasten your seat belt low and tight across your lap, and prepare for takeoff!

Chapter 2

The Nonprogrammer's Guide to the Web, CGI, and Programming Languages

How the World Wide Web Works

Predictably, every book in any way associated with the World Wide Web, CGI programming, or the Internet in general has to have a diagram showing the logical relationship between the Web server, the Web browser, and the Internet. Figure 2.1 presents our version of this obligatory illustration.

This diagram helps explain some important distinctions between the major components of the Web environment. Many people don't have a clear understanding of what each component shown in Figure 2.1 does or how the components fit together to create the wonderful invention/industry/revolution called the World Wide Web.

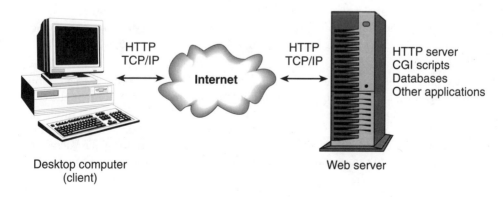

Figure 2.1 *Obligatory World Wide Web topology diagram*

Since most people are familiar with a desktop computer, we'll start there. The desktop computer provides the interface between the user and the Web. The Web browser software is responsible for communicating with other computers over the network (either the global Internet or an internal network called an intranet, or both). The Web browser is also responsible for displaying HTML text, graphics, sound, and other types of multimedia data. The Web browser is known as the client because it is the program that uses the data sent from a server (see Figure 2.1). This mode, where the browser simply displays data received from the network, works very well for a large percentage of the data available on the Web today. However, the data are essentially static. The user cannot interact with them beyond viewing. Further, the processing power of the desktop computer is left untapped. Early in the history of the Web, it became clear that the static "view-only" mode would not be sufficient. The capacity for greater interactivity was needed.

To address this need, several methods have been introduced to send not only static data but actual computer programs to the desktop machine. These include the Java and Javascript programming languages. With Java, you can create small applications called "applets" that can run on any computer that supports Java. Javascript was developed by Netscape to embed simple programs within Web pages. We discuss Java and Javascript in more detail later in the chapter. Both Netscape *Navigator* and Microsoft *Internet Explorer* browsers have Java and Javascript support built in. The result is that the leading Web browser software can both display static data and execute graphical interactive programs, received from the network, on the desktop computer.

Server is a term used to identify both a computer and a software program. Some computers are called *servers* because they are responsible for answering requests for data or computations from other computers. This can be confusing sometimes. The computer stores HTML pages, graphics, and other data in a central location. When a Web browser requests data, the Web server software (known as the HTTP server or HTTP daemon [See Nerd Note on the following page]) answers the request—that is, it "serves" the data—over the network. In this mode, no processing of the data is done by the server; it simply sends the requested files. However, data other than HTML and graphics data is often stored on the server. To serve data from an application such as a database management system, a special interface program called a *gateway* is used.

The final part of the diagram in Figure 2.1 is the network itself. Contrary to a famous vendor slogan that "the network is the computer," no processing is done by the computers and wires that make up the network (Internet or Intranet). You can think of the network as an ad hoc series of interconnected computers, phone lines, and cables that transport data back and forth between the server and the desktop. The details of how this is done aren't important for our purposes here. What is critical to understand is that the computers connected to the network communicate using strictly defined rules called *protocols*.

Nerd Note

Web server programs and other types of server programs are known as *daemons* within the computer world because of their resemblance (at least to nerds) to those spirit servants of medieval wizards of the same name. The early UNIX gurus liked to think of themselves as wizards in the arcane art of computers. Computer daemons are specialized programs that run invisibly in the background and do the master's bidding.

Amazing Factoid

The Internet started in 1969 as a research project sponsored by the United States Advanced Research Projects Administration (ARPA) and was originally known as the ARPAnet. The ARPAnet was a Cold War project intended to help the United States build a high-speed data network capable of functioning after a nuclear attack. The goal was to design a network architecture and communications protocols that could keep operating after sustaining losses of up to 50 percent of the connected computers. This meant there could be no single "master" computer controlling the network, since it could be one of the 50 percent destroyed. All the computers on the network had to act as equals and be partially responsible for routing the data to its destination.

The original ARPAnet was used only for research. Commercial activity was forbidden due to the government-funded nature of the project. Other networks lacking this restriction soon sprang up between businesses and universities both in the United States and in other countries. When these networks connected with each other and to the ARPAnet, the global Internet was formed. The United States government has since ended its sponsorship of the ARPAnet project, and the Internet has evolved into a vehicle for on-line business and global communications. The decentralized nature and other attributes that made the original ARPAnet able to survive a nuclear attack also make possible today's chaotic, unregulated, global Internet. Computers connect and disconnect from the Internet by the thousands every hour. Through all this activity, the data keeps flowing—all despite the fact that no one is "at the helm." ARPAnet's legacy lives on. So don't say nothing good ever came out of the Cold War.

Protocol Shmotocol

A **protocol** is a strictly defined set of rules regarding how two entities (in this case, computers) communicate. A good protocol is flexible enough to handle a variety of data, yet rigid enough that system designers can depend on its working successfully if they follow the protocol to the letter.

The Internet communicates by using the Transmission Control Protocol (TCP) and Internet Protocol (IP), commonly known as TCP/IP. Together these protocols define how the computers connected to the Internet (and intranets for that matter) communicate to transfer data. TCP allows two computers to establish a "connection" for a data transfer. During the exchange, TCP breaks down the data into small chunks called *data packets,* numbers them, and sends them over to IP for transmission to the other computer. The IP protocol is the delivery mechanism that knows how to get data packets from one computer to another. To make sure the right data gets to the right computer, all computers attached to a TCP/IP network (such as the Internet) have a unique identification number, or IP "address."

Nerd Note

An IP address is made up of a 32-bit binary number. It looks like this to the computer:

11001100010001111001010100011001

People usually work with IP addresses as four 3-digit numbers separated by periods, like this:

204.071.149.025

Each 3-digit number can range from 0 to 255, and each represents 8 bits of the IP address. Most often, the first three numbers represent the address of a network or domain, and the last represents an individual computer within the network. You will occasionally see an IP address in a Web or FTP Uniform Resource Locator (URL).

IP addresses are allocated in blocks of a minimum of 256 addresses for each domain. This is done even if fewer addresses are needed. The result is that many of the available IP addresses are wasted. Even worse, in the early days of the Internet many domains were allocated in blocks of 65,536 or even 16,777,216 addresses for large companies, the military, or other purposes, thus even more addresses were wasted. This means that there are far fewer than the 4,294,967,296 ($256 \times 256 \times 256 \times 256$) addresses implied by the 32-bit size of the IP address. This is one of the major problems in the current IP addressing scheme. Various plans have been proposed to reallocate the existing addresses in a more efficient manner and/or to create a new 128-bit address (3.4×10^{38} addresses!). However, these plans would all involve massive amounts of effort to reprogram all the millions of computers that currently have an IP address. Any global program that aims to change the existing IP address structure will be a major undertaking indeed.

At the far end, TCP checks for errors or missing data packets and reassembles the packets into the data item. If any data is lost along the way, TCP requests a retransmission of the lost packet(s). The details of how TCP/IP works are beyond the scope of this book. However, you can think of TCP/IP as a reliable data communication method that allows computers to exchange data without needing specific knowledge of each other's location or the connections between them.

TCP/IP provides the foundation for many different applications to exchange data using higher-level protocols built on top of TCP/IP. The following protocols are of particular interest here:

- **HTTP** (Hypertext Transport Protocol). The protocol used by Web servers and Web browsers the world over.

- **CGI** (Common Gateway Interface). The protocol that defines how Web servers execute and exchange data with external programs. This protocol is called a gateway interface because CGI scripts were originally envisioned to act as gateways between the Web server and a database management system or other application. Programs using this protocol are called CGI applications or scripts.

- **SMTP** (Simple Mail Transport Protocol). Used to send electronic mail. Probably the most used Internet service.

- **MIME** (Multipurpose Internet Mail Extensions). An extension of the SMTP protocol that allows multiple types of data (commonly known as *attachments*) to be included along with plain text in e-mail; for example, binary images files or ZIP archives. The MIME protocol is also used by HTTP servers and browsers and by CGI scripts.

- **FTP** (File Transfer Protocol). Used to send files between computers. We discuss FTP extensively in Chapter 3, "The Nonprogrammer's Toolbox."

- **Telnet**. Supports character terminal sessions across a TCP/IP network. We discuss Telnet extensively in Chapter 3, "The Nonprogrammer's Toolbox."

- **DNS** (Domain Name Service). Uses a network of servers to translate a text name like *microsoft.com* into an IP address. DNS is actually a huge distributed database of names and IP addresses stored on thousands of computers worldwide. It allows computers (and people) to find the IP address of any computer on the Internet without knowing where the computer is, whether it exists at all, or how it is connected.

TCP/IP and HTTP are the two protocols that form the foundation of the Web. The features and limitations of these protocols will affect you directly as you progress from simple HTML into the world of CGI programming.

Client versus Server

TCP/IP doesn't recognize different classes of computer. All computers connected to a TCP/IP network are technically equal, and can both send and receive data. (So your desktop PC is, in the eyes of TCP/IP at least, equivalent to a giant Cray supercomputer.) A computer can act as both a client and a server. Your Web server computer acts as an HTTP server when answering requests from Web browsers. The same computer might also act as a client when accessing a large database server using a CGI script. You could run an HTTP server daemon on your desktop machine and it would act as both an HTTP client (with your browser) and a Web server as well.

Processing of data may take place both on the server computer (*server-side processing*) and on the client computer (*client-side processing*). To help interface with servers, the HTTP protocol defines a method of calling server-side programs called the Common Gateway Interface (CGI). This protocol defines how requests are sent from the client and how data returned from a CGI program are relayed to the browser. CGI programs are commonly called *scripts* because they were originally intended to be a simple list of commands (i.e., a script) acting as a "gateway" between the Web server and other applications, such as a database management system. As CGI has evolved, however, many scripts have come to do all their own processing, and they don't interface with any other applications. (These should properly be called CGI *applications*, but the name script has stuck.)

CGI is ideal, for example, when numerous clients need to access data located on a central server, since distributing large databases isn't practical. However, because the server is only a single computer, it may become overwhelmed by large numbers of accesses to CGI-based Web pages. Also, with CGI the processing power of the client computers, often as powerful or more powerful than the HTTP server, is not used at all.

Client-side processing, on the other hand, does the processing on the client computer. Client-side processing makes use of the high speed processor and graphical display available on most desktop computers to provide the friendly graphical user interfaces (GUIs), animation, and sound people have come to expect from their desktop applications. In response to a client request, the server sends the requested program to the client, which executes it. Since many different types of computers running all kinds of operating systems connect to the Web, some kind of processor and operating system independent language is needed. However, once the platform-independence problem is overcome, client-side processing makes possible many applications that can't be run on the server side. The Java language, developed by Sun Microsystems, provides the first really practical platform-independent client-side programming language. Later in the chapter, we say more about Java and a similarly named, but only distantly related, language called Javascript.

At the time of this writing (mid-1997), client-side applications are still in their infancy. Java programs are just beginning to make serious inroads on the Web, and many remain little more than toys or demonstrations. For the near term (and who talks confidently about the Internet in the long term?), server-side CGI scripts will continue to play a major role in managing interactive processes on the Web.

HTTP: Your Good and Faithful Servant

Since this book is about adding functionality to Web pages, we should take a brief look at how the HTTP protocol works. An understanding of how the game is played is what separates those who are at the mercy of the technology from those who are its masters.

We begin our story on a day just like any other day. A desktop computer user, wanting to get the latest scores in the fast-paced Final-four of curling, selects the bookmark for *The Curling World Mega-site* on her Web browser. As you know, locations on the Web are identified by a URL, whose format should be very familiar to you. The URL for our mythical *Curling World* site might look like this:

```
http://www.curling-world.com/final-four.html
```

This URL contains everything the Web browser needs in order to request the Web page from the server. `http://` indicates to the browser that this location will be read using the HTTP protocol. `www` is the name of the Web server computer located within the `curling-world.com` domain. The single slash followed by the filename— `final-four.html`—says to request the *Curling World* computer to send the file *final-four.html* from the base-level HTML document directory, known as the server *root*. Here are the major steps in the process of fetching a Web page:

1. The browser on the desktop computer requests the IP address of *curling-world.com* from its DNS server. The DNS server searches its local database for the address of *curling-world.com*. If it finds the address, it returns the address. If it does not, it requests the address from the next higher-level DNS server. This continues until finally the address is found and returned to the requesting desktop computer.

2. Once the desktop computer's browser has the *curling-world.com* IP address, it sends out via TCP/IP an HTTP GET request (a text message requesting the other computer to send a file). See the next Nerd Note if you're curious what a GET request looks like.

3. The TCP software on the desktop computer creates a data packet containing the GET request and attaches the IP address. IP takes the packet and sends it out onto the Internet where it passes through many other computers en route to its destination.

4. The IP software on the curling-world server receives the packet and lobs it to TCP, which verifies it. The request for data is then forwarded to the Web server. Neither TCP or IP cares what is in the packet.

5. The Web server has been sitting and waiting for requests. When it receives the GET request, it leaps into action. It checks whether the requested file (HTML page or graphic, multimedia file, etc.) exists. If so, the server creates an HTTP response header and sends the header back to the requesting browser along with the HTML file. TCP and IP perform their respective roles again in the reverse direction. If the file doesn't exist, the server returns an HTTP response header indicating an error.

6. The browser checks the response header status code in the server's reply. If everything is OK, the browser starts to process the HTML. It reads through the HTML file and sends additional GET requests for any images, sounds, or other files embedded in the page. Then the browser renders the HTML along with its graphical images and calls the appropriate player for any multimedia files attached to the page. Client-side programs written in Java or Javascript may also execute at this time. If an error is indicated by the status code in the response header, an error message is displayed on the browser.

7. If a CGI script is the target of an HTTP GET request, the server recognizes this from the directory and/or file extension of the file requested. To satisfy the request, the server executes the CGI script and passes to the script any associated data from the HTTP request (such as form data or a search string) along with extra information about the requesting computer retrieved from the HTTP request header. The CGI script is responsible for generating the HTTP `Content/type:` line in the header along with any HTML text or graphical image data sent back to the browser (see Nerd Note below). Instead of transferring an existing file to the browser, the server transfers the data output from the CGI script.

Each time the user clicks a hyperlink, this process starts again for the new page.

Nerd Note

For the curious, the HTTP GET request looks like this:

```
GET /final-four.html HTTP/1.0
Accept: www/source
Accept: text/html
Accept: image/gif
... (lots more like this deleted)
User-Agent: Mozilla-Windows95/3.01
From: cbaron@hypertising.com
```

> **The HTTP reply from the server looks like this:**
>
> ```
> HTTP/1.0 200 OK
> Date: Friday, 03-January-1997 10:13:27 GMT
> Server: NCSA/1.4.2
> MIME-version: 1.0
> Content-type: text/html
> Content-length: 1534
>
> <HTML>
> <HEAD><TITLE>Curling World's Final Four Up-to-the-minute Status
> Page</TITL>
> ... (the rest of the HTML file follows)
> ```

From the Web server's point of view, each request for an HTML page, a graphical image, or a video clip is a separate and unrelated request. The Web server doesn't keep track of where the pages are going or what browser has previously requested a particular image. In fact, neither the browser nor the server maintains any knowledge of prior requests or the state of the other system. This is known as a *stateless protocol*. This feature allows the Web server program to be small and fast enough to handle thousands of requests per hour. However, your role as a Web developer is somewhat complicated by the stateless nature of HTTP for these reasons:

- Tracking user movement through a site becomes hard because all the page requests are unique to the server.

- Links to other sites don't register on the server at all because the browser simply sends an HTTP request to the other server, imparting no information to the originating server. Hence, evaluating the success of advertising links is a challenge.

- Shopping-cart programs and multimove games have to use a variety of tricks to maintain the state of a player's data. (Our Holland Marketing, Inc. Web site at http://www.hollandmkt.com features a good example of such a game.) The basic HTTP protocol doesn't provide a way of associating one set of actions (like clicking a "buy-this" link) or the submission of a fill-in form (e.g., for payment and shipping information) with any other.

CGI is the Web developer's salvation for these and other problems. CGI scripts allow a program external to the Web server to perform actions on the HTTP requests. CGI scripts can insert data into an HTML page, create custom user tracking logs, access databases to record user actions or requests, and even generate entire pages complete with graphics. CGI scripts provide access to data stored on the Web server, but some functions are best done using the power of the client computer, and some decisions about the layout or content of the page can best be made using the knowledge of the client browser that a client-side program can access. Thus, client-side scripts, such as those created using Javascript, complement and enhance CGI scripts.

To address a wide range of needs we've included both client-side and server-side scripts in this book.

A Really Short Introduction to Web Programming Languages

Over the years, many computer programming languages have been developed. Usually the features of the language make them espesially well suited to a particular type of programming task. The languages we discuss in this section—Perl, Java, and Javascript—are well suited to Web-related programming. Each language fills a particular niche in the Web programming world: Perl excels at small programs that tie different applications and data sources together, and Java and Javascript were both developed explicitly to function well within a Web page. In this section we'll give you some background on each language and explain in more detail the role played by each.

Perl

Perl (Practical Extraction and Report Language) is, without a doubt, the king of the CGI languages. A trip to the Internet section of your local bookstore will reveal many books about using Perl for CGI programming. (Even though our book is most likely in the same section, we give you the benefits of Perl *without* your having to learn programming.)

Perl was originally developed around 1986 to support system administration on UNIX machines. It contains many functions for accessing files and manipulating text. It also contains powerful searching and pattern-matching capabilities. Perl has been used for many different purposes on all kinds of systems, but its powerful text-handling features are what make it a natural choice for processing the CGI data, which is ASCII text based. Another factor influencing Perl's CGI popularity were the early Webmasters, mostly UNIX system administrator types, who were already familiar with Perl and probably had it running on the UNIX machines that became the first Web servers. The rest, as they say, is history. Perl has been ported to nearly every operating system and hardware platform. It has evolved continuously ever since its creation by the addition of new features and improved performance. It has from the start been freely available, which no doubt hasn't hurt its popularity. For the server-side scripts included in this book, Perl was really the only choice.

The next most popular CGI languages are C and/or C++. These languages surpass the performance of Perl in many areas. However, they suffer from a lack of built-in text processing functions and have a more complex development process than Perl does. Visual Basic is a language with a small but enthusiastic following on Microsoft Windows–based Web servers. Unfortunately (or thankfully, depending on your point of view), Visual Basic is not portable to UNIX-based systems, which still dominate the Web server world, especially among commercial ISPs.

Java

On the client side, the Java programming language has generated tremendous excitement among pundits, programmers, and software development companies in the last couple of years. The computer nerds of the world are excited by the advanced capabilities of the language such as built-in networking and extensive security features. Java is designed to run on many different operating systems and environments using the same code. No modifications are required to run the identical code on a Macintosh, Windows 95 PC, or Silicon Graphics workstation. Small Java programs called *applets* can be embedded in HTML pages and can provide Web pages with an interactive GUI that can include sound and animation. This marriage of client-side Java processing with server-delivered HTML promises great things in the future of the Web. Slowing the growth of Java, however, is its rather complex structure. Java can function as a server-side CGI-like language as well as a client-side language. It gives a promise of portability that equals that of Perl, with the added benefit of built-in security. Moreover, it requires additional development software, as well as more programming knowledge and money, to get a program working in Java than it does in Perl.

At present, only a few variations of UNIX, along with MS-Windows NT and 95, can run Java on the server side. So most of Java's platform independence is still more promise than reality. We predict, along with the pundits, that Java will become much more important as a server-side language in the future.

Javascript

The Netscape *Navigator* browser is, at the time of this writing, the dominant Web browser in the world. *Navigator's* market share and deployment across many different operating systems have allowed Netscape to propagate a proprietary client-side language called Javascript as a de facto standard. Javascript is a client-side scripting language that functions only within pages displayed on a Web browser. No additional development software is needed to write Javascript programs—Javascript code is simply inserted into the HTML file. *Navigator's* market-leading status has also proven to be a strong incentive to the other major browser—Microsoft *Internet Explorer*—to support Javascript. This development has ensured that Web pages written using Javascript will work for most visitors to your site.

Javascript was designed explicitly to enhance HTML pages and provide easy control of Java applets. Java on the other hand is a full applications programming language that can function quite well without being anywhere near a Web browser or the Internet. Beyond the similar names, and a somewhat similar language format, the two languages aren't really related. As a point of reference, all the client-side scripts included in this book are written in Javascript.

Holy Wars: A Word About Operating Systems

When we started this book, we had a grand vision of our readers running these scripts on all operating systems, Web servers, and client computers. After all, Perl runs on all these operating systems, every Web server claims to support the CGI specification, and Netscape and Microsoft offer browsers for almost every possible client operating system, right? Sadly, we found that reality is a little less rosy. While Perl does run on just about every operating system, there are vast differences in how the operating systems do things, and the Perl implementation for a given machine tends to reflect these differences. Java isn't available on most UNIX and non-Windows PCs, and the effort required to make a C program run well on a variety of systems is "non-trivial," as programmers like to say. Even had Perl been truly platform-independent, there are differences in how server-side programs are executed by the various Web servers. Unlike UNIX, Windows PCs don't really support the concept of scripts defining their own language, and the Macintosh doesn't have an easy way to access a text command line.

We finally accepted the fact that giving the detailed level of installation and configuration instructions that we hoped to do for all the various operating systems would have put this book right up there with the Yellow Pages in length. We realized we had to reduce the server-side environments we supported. Our research showed that UNIX-based machines comprise the vast majority of Web servers in the world. Windows NT-based servers are gaining in popularity, but mostly within corporate internal networks (intranets and extranets). Macintosh, Amiga, Atari-ST, Plan 9, VMS, Timex-Sinclair, and all those other operating systems make up a very small percentage of the Web server world. Plus (a short pause while we don flame-proof clothing), UNIX-based systems are better suited for Web servers in general, and for server-side CGI scripts in particular. All the major Web server software was originally developed for UNIX, and Perl and other scripting languages were developed on and run best under UNIX. Also, the multiuser and security features of UNIX systems have been in place for many years, thus making UNIX systems much more robust for connecting to the wild and wooly Internet as opposed to modified single-user operating systems like Windows or MacOS. Don't misunderstand us—the other operating systems can do everything UNIX systems can do. However, you have to jump through more hoops to make things work and basically trick the operating system into acting like UNIX. We simply couldn't support all the variations these other systems introduce and still provide the level of instruction we felt was needed for a book of this type.

For those of you still with us, the next chapter covers finding the right ISP and gathering all the information and tools you need to run the scripts presented in Chapters 4 through 15 of the book.

What We Covered in Chapter 2

- The basics of how the World Wide Web works
- A bit about the TCP/IP protocol set that makes the Internet go
- Details on how HTTP works within the Web
- The differences between client-side and server-side scripts
- A little about the various script languages in use on the Web today
- Why only UNIX server systems are covered in this book

Chapter 3

The Nonprogrammer's Toolbox

What We Cover in This Chapter

- How to determine if you can run CGI scripts on your Web server and some advice about what to do if you can't
- What script code looks like and what software you need to edit it
- Uploading the script to your Web server with FTP and Telnet
- How to use a script in your Web pages

Getting Down to Business

In this chapter, we show you how to find out if your ISP or SA allows you to run CGI scripts. Then, we gather the data you'll need to configure and install the scripts in this book (and others you may obtain from the Internet). If your ISP or SA won't allow CGI scripts, you can still use the Javascript scripts (since they run on the user's machine). We also give you details on editing the scripts and show you how to use common Internet tools to upload and activate the scripts on your server.

In the following explanations, we assume you're familiar with HTML and have previously created at least a few Web pages.

Your ISP or SA Is Your Friend—Really

As part of your decision to use CGI scripts in your Web pages, you need to realize that your relationship with your ISP or SA is going to change. When you were a simple user with a nice quiet Web site, there was really not too much you could do to cause him or her problems. About the worst you could do was run a super-popular site and bog down the Web server with a large volume of hits. But since most ISPs charge for data transfers, so this may not trouble him or her much.

Running CGI scripts, on the other hand, is a whole different ball game. Unlike HTML pages, CGI scripts are actual programs running on the Web server. They can use significant amounts of processor time and memory, and they can introduce security holes into the system that could be used by hackers to cause the ISP or SA some serious headaches. Support for CGI users is also more time consuming and difficult than support for normal Web users because their questions are more involved and require a higher level of knowledge on the part of ISP support personnel or the SA. In general, allowing users to run CGI scripts on a public Web server is a pain in the rear for ISPs and SAs.

You can see why many ISPs and SAs don't allow user CGI scripts on a public shared Web server. Some offer a central library of approved CGI scripts for all users. Others are willing to suffer the loss of a small number of customers in exchange for a lighter load on the server and reduced administrative headaches. If your ISP is one of these (we'll tell you how to find out shortly), please respect their decision. Don't verbally abuse them. You can certainly ask them to reconsider their policy or request that an exception be made in your case. We haven't had much luck getting ISPs to change their policies, but it never hurts to ask. Most company SAs don't have to worry about losing customers, so getting them to cooperate is a slightly different challenge that we'll also touch on later in the chapter.

If your ISP simply won't cooperate, you'll have to find one that does. The Internet is still a relatively free market, and you can find ISPs who will provide CGI capability. If you live within local-calling distance of a major city, you will almost certainly be able to find an ISP who offers CGI access. If not, you can get a low-cost shell or Web-only account on a national or international provider in addition to your dial-up ISP. You access this type of account through your current provider using the FTP and Telnet tools we describe later in this chapter. Since this second account doesn't require dial-up access (modems and phone lines are a major expense for ISPs), the monthly cost will likely be quite reasonable. At the time of this writing, these accounts are available in the United States for $15 per month and up. Several companies specialize in offering Web space to Internet users. These have networks of large Web servers connected to very high-speed Internet connections. They usually offer personal and business level accounts with different amounts of disk storage, CGI capability, and monthly Web traffic allowances.

If you are connected to a company LAN or intranet and your SA won't allow CGI scripts on the Web server, you have a slightly different problem. You can't just close your account and go to a different provider. Like ISPs, most company SAs are tremendously busy people with much more to do every day than they can possibly get done. A request to reconfigure the Web server in a way that can potentially cause more problems will probably not be met with joy. Your best approach is to present your SA with a specific business-related function you'd like to implement, such as a Request-for-Information form or a search function for your Web pages. Once CGI capability is activated, you'll be free to add other functions as needed. This is likely to work better than simply requesting that CGI capability be turned on for you to play with. Getting some management support for your idea may do wonders for the cooperation you get from your SA. Also, many managers are excited by the idea of implementing Internet technology on the internal network (it's all the rage in management magazines).

In the next section, we give you some specific questions to ask your ISP or SA so as to get the information you'll need to run the CGI scripts presented in this book. Before we get into that, however, you should contact your ISP or SA to see if you can run CGI scripts from your account on the Web server. The important thing to ask is whether you are allowed to run *user-written* CGI scripts from within your Web account. You can usually reach your ISP at an e-mail address that looks like *support@myisp.com*. Once you've obtained an account that will let you run CGI scripts, the questions in the next section will provide the details you'll need to know in order to configure and run your scripts.

The ISP/SA Questionnaire

The ISP/SA questionnaire is on the CD-ROM in the /*questionnaire* directory. You should send it to your ISP or SA once you have received approval to run scripts and are ready to start using them. Then you generally won't have to bother them again with system-specific details about running CGI scripts. We give you everything else you need.

You may want to read through this section before you send the questionnaire to your ISP or SA. We provide you some background on each question and help you answer the inevitable "why-do-I-need-to-know-that?" questions. You'll also sound much more knowledgeable about CGI programming if you've read this section. Users who sound like they know what they are doing are more likely to get what they ask for, since the likelihood of their screwing up the system and/or needing a lot of hand-holding is much lower.

Here is the introduction to the questionnaire:

ISP/System Administrator CGI Questionnaire

To provide some functional enhancements to my Web pages, I would like to use some CGI and SSI scripts I've gotten from the book *Drag 'n' Drop CGI: Enhance Your Web Site Without Programming.* These are fully tested commercial-quality scripts that I would like to use in my Web pages. To give me the configuration information I need, please fill out the following questionnaire. With the information you provide here, I should be able to configure, install, and run the scripts with minimal additional assistance.

Here we ask politely for the ISP's or SA's assistance. The bit about getting the scripts from a book is intended to make the ISP/SA a little more comfortable with the quality of the script code. Note, SSI refers to Server-Side Includes. (See Chapter 5, "Counting Visitors to Your Web Site with Perl," for more details on what SSI is and how it works in a Web page.)

1. Am I allowed to run user-written CGI programs from my Web account space on this server?

This question is crucial. If the ISP or SA says no (or even "hell no!"), you'll have to either get an account with another ISP or convince your management to change the SA's position. There may be very good reasons for them to turn you down. In any case, it's their responsibility to keep the server running; they are the ones who will "take the heat" if it crashes.

2. If not, can I submit CGI programs to you for approval and then run them, perhaps from a common directory? If that's not possible, can you recommend a provider who does allow CGI access?

This option is not ideal, since it requires that you submit the scripts to the ISP or SA for testing and installation in a common directory. You will have to do this for every change you make in the script. This will become tiring for both you and your ISP/SA if you plan to do very much CGI work. However, it may be an acceptable last resort with an intransigent SA. ISP users will probably want to get an account with a more accommodating ISP.

3. Does this system have a Perl interpreter installed? If so, what version(s) of Perl are available? If not, would you consider installing Perl?

This is another important question. All of the server-side scripts we present in this book are written in Perl. If your ISP or SA's Web server runs any variation of UNIX, you are quite likely to have Perl installed. If it is running Windows NT, you can find a source for Perl/NT among the resource links on the CD-ROM.

4. If the Web server runs UNIX, what is the script comment line to make a Perl script file execute? (e.g., *#!/usr/bin/perl*) If NT, how do I call a Perl CGI script from my Web pages?

UNIX command scripts can tell the system which language they use by including a special comment line at the top of the script. In this case, you're asking how to tell the system to execute the script as a Perl program. Users running on Windows NT will have a different procedure to get the system to execute the Perl script. Each NT Web server does it a little differently.

5. What, if any, are the required filename extensions for CGI programs (e.g., *.cgi, .pl, .bin*)?

For security purposes, many Web servers require a special file extension on CGI scripts. This provides a little protection against running other types of programs (such as system commands) from the Web server and allows all parties to keep track of which programs are intended for use as CGI scripts. This is a configurable item within the Web server, so you need to find out how the server is set up.

6. Are my scripts required to reside in a special directory? If so, what is it called (e.g., *cgi-bin, cgi, htbin*)? Are there any directory names I can't use?

For security purposes, some Web servers restrict CGI programs to special directories. In this way, other executable programs cannot be run directly by the Web server software. On UNIX systems, all directories with CGI scripts need to have what is known as "world read" and "world execute" file permissions. This means that anyone who has access to the Web server computer can read and/or execute files in this directory. UNIX systems allow you to restrict who can see (read), write (change, delete, rename, or move), and execute (open a directory or run a program) each file and directory. See Appendix B for more details.

7. What operating system does the Web server use?

Most of the CGI scripts in this book were chosen because they can run on Windows NT and common UNIX variants. Your knowing which operating system the server uses is useful if you happen to encounter any of the system-specific differences in Perl that sometimes pop up.

8. Can I use the SSI *#exec* command on this Web server?

Two of the scripts in this book—the visit counter (Chapter 5, "Counting Visitors to Your Web Site with Perl") and the programmable image display script (Chapter 7, "Automating Graphics Changes on Your Web Site with Perl")—use the SSI Web server facility. Some ISPs and SAs don't like SSI because it can be a security risk and it increases somewhat the load on the Web server. There are many SSI commands, but the one you're interested in causes a script to execute whenever a page containing the command is sent to a Web browser. Usually, CGI commands require you to click a hyperlink or press a button to get them to execute.

9. Do I need to change anything to activate the SSI feature (e.g., modify a .htaccess file)?

Some Web servers have CGI and SSI turned off by default. To turn it on for a certain directory, you need a special file, commonly called *.htaccess*. This special file tells the Web server what to do with various file types and whether to allow CGI or SSI scripts to run in this directory. Sometimes your ISP or SA will create this file for you. You also can either create it yourself or copy it from another directory. Your best bet is to get your ISP or SA to give you a proper *.htaccess* file, if their Web server needs one.

10. Do my HTML files need a special extension to use SSI (e.g., *.shtml*)?

Processing SSI files requires more effort on the Web server's part, so many servers require a special file extension for HTML files that contain SSI commands. This allows the server to avoid unnecessary processing on files that don't contain the SSI commands. Typically, files with extensions of *.htm* or *.html* are plain HTML files, while *.shtml* or *.stm* files may contain SSI. This behavior is set in the Web server configuration files, so you ask the ISP or SA how their server is configured.

11. What is the absolute path to my root Web directory (e.g., */home/users/user-name/public_html/*)?

You need to know the path to your HTML (and CGI) files to use the Perl scripts in this book. Since you may not have directly accessed your Web directory before via FTP or Telnet, you ask the ISP/SA to provide that directory's absolute path. We assure you that by the time you finish this book, you'll have this location memorized.

12. What should my URL look like to access my Web pages (e.g., *http://www.myisp.net/~username/page.html*)?

You probably already know the answer to this one, but just in case you've switched to a new provider, ask.

13. Which, if any, Perl CGI function modules or libraries are installed in the default Perl library path (e.g., *cgi-lib.pl* and *CGI.pm*)? Which, if any, are installed elsewhere?

The form processing script presented in Chapter 9, "Processing and Responding to Interactive Forms Using Perl," uses a Perl function library called *cgi-lib.pl*. While we include *cgi-lib.pl* on the CD-ROM, having the library already installed will save you some time and configuration. Other scripts you download from the Internet (after you get good at configuring and installing scripts) may require other function libraries, so this information will come in handy for future reference.

14. Does the Web server have a *sendmail* command installed? If so, what is the path (e.g., */usr/sbin/sendmail*)? If not, is an equivalent SMTP mail sending command available, and what is its path? If the syntax is different from *sendmail*'s, what do I change (from a *sendmail* script) to send mail from a CGI script using this command?

Both the form processing script and the on-line store script send e-mail as one of their functions. *sendmail* is the standard UNIX utility that allows you (or another program) to send electronic mail by entering text from the keyboard. Almost all UNIX systems have *sendmail* installed as a basic part of the operating system. Instead of *sendmail*, Windows users need to use a Windows program that does essentially the same thing. We give details on using *sendmail* in Chapters 9 and 10 and Chapters 13–15.

15. Do I have FTP access to this account? If not, how do I upload my Web pages and scripts to the server?

Almost all ISPs will allow FTP access to user accounts if they allow you to upload HTML pages. We don't know of a single one that doesn't, but just to be sure, you should ask. People with LAN or intranet accounts may have other ways of storing files on the Web server that don't involve FTP. Often these users can directly save their files to the Web server disk by using one of the network file systems available. This saves much time over using an FTP client, so don't feel like you're missing out if you don't need to use FTP.

16. Do I have Telnet access to this account? If not, how do I change file permissions on my script files (e.g., use the FTP client *chmod* command)?

This question applies only to UNIX users. In Appendix B, we explain UNIX permission system and why you need to change permissions on script files. In brief, if you want UNIX to run a program, you need to tell the system that the program is executable by setting the "execute" file permissions. This is commonly done by logging on to the UNIX system using a Telnet client. This client acts like a text-based terminal (similar to MS-DOS or an MS-DOS window in Windows), where you can enter commands from the keyboard to change the file permissions and do other things with your files. The newer FTP clients include a command to let you change the file permissions directly without using a Telnet client. We cover both FTP and Telnet clients later in the chapter. Windows NT users don't have to worry about this because Windows uses file extensions, such as *.exe* or *.bat*, to determine if and how a file should be executed.

17. What host name should I use to access my Web account via FTP and/or Telnet? (e.g., *www.myisp.net* or *bucky.wiznet.net*)?

You need to know the name of the host computer your ISP or SA is using as a Web server in order to access them with Telnet and FTP clients. Often the machine is called "www," but in many instances an alias is used. (Web servers don't *have* to be named "*www*"—that's just the convention.) Users with virtual domains will definitely have their name aliased, since no machine with their domain name actually exists. Frequently, you can use the alias with FTP and Telnet clients, but it's still best to ask the ISP or SA.

18. What are my username and password for this machine when using FTP and/or Telnet (i.e., are they the same as for PPP login)?

To access your files with either an FTP or a Telnet client, you need to know your username and password. Often this is the same as your dial-up SLIP/ PPP username and password. Lucky LAN and intranet users with network disk access to the Web server won't need this, but ISP users almost certainly will.

That's all there is to the ISP/SA questionnaire. Send it off to your ISP or SA when you are ready to start installing scripts. It should take them only a few minutes to complete. Armed with the information from your questionnaire, and this book, you will have everything you need to become a CGI powerhouse.

Editing Script Code

To configure and customize this set of scripts, you need only a simple text editor such as MS-Windows *Notepad* or the MacOS *TeachText* that come standard with your operating system. No expensive and complicated compilers, linkers, debuggers, and other development tools are required. Perl programs are compiled when they execute (at what computer guys call *runtime*), and Javascript scripts are contained within HTML pages. Thus, all the script code is stored in plain text files. Your HTML editor can be used to create plain ASCII files (unless it's part of a Web development system like Microsoft *FrontPage* or Adobe *SiteMill*). Word processing programs such as Microsoft *Word* or *WordPerfect* will also work as long as you save your file in plain text format.

Amazing Factoid

> The nice thing about using CGI scripts is that the hard part of creating network applications is already done. The Web server provides the network server communications, and the Web browser provides the user interface. These two areas consume much, if not most, of the code for stand-alone client-server applications. By using Web technology, you have access to a robust, high-performance client-server communications method with a flexible graphical user interface. Couple this with the simple (but powerful) CGI programming protocol, and you can see why Web-based and intranet applications are taking the world by storm.

The next section shows you how to get a file onto the Web server using FTP. Check question 15 on your ISP/SA questionnaire for the proper method of moving your scripts onto the server. If you aren't using FTP, or you already know all about FTP, you can skip the next section. We won't be presenting anything directly concerning CGI scripts until the section after that.

Getting the Files on the Server—FTP to the Rescue

The problem of how to transfer files between computers using different operating systems and different file formats was encountered early in the primordial Internet.

The universally adopted solution is the File Transfer Protocol (FTP). FTP defines how computers can send and receive files in a platform and operating system independent way using a TCP/IP network. As with its much younger cousin, HTTP, any computer that can talk FTP can exchange files with any other computer that knows FTP. Also like HTTP, FTP requires that one of the computers act as a server and one as a client. Since TCP/IP and FTP have been around for eons (in computer time), all the server operating systems you're likely to encounter during your Internet travels will have FTP server software available (although some may have it disabled). All common desktop computer operating systems have several FTP clients available. Commercial ISPs that allow users to upload their Web pages and CGI scripts usually use FTP, since it is the simplest way to allow user file uploads in a relatively secure fashion.

How FTP Works

At the start of the FTP dialog between two computers, the client logs on to the server to create an FTP **session**—the active connection between you and the server. FTP always requires a username and almost always requires a password in order to initiate a session. The special username *anonymous* along with an e-mail address as a password is commonly used to allow anyone access to public files on many Internet FTP servers.

Amazing Factoid

When you access an *ftp://* *URL* in your Web browser, you are actually logging on using a username of *anonymous.* The browser does all the communication with the FTP server for you. All you have to do is point and click. Yet another reason to love your Web browser.

Once accepted as a valid user, the client FTP software initiates all transfers, requesting that files either be downloaded from the server to the client's machine or sent from the client (uploaded) and stored on the server. You can both upload and download files in a single FTP session. One thing to keep in mind (since FTP requires a log-on type connection): Most servers set a fixed number of simultaneous FTP sessions. To keep people from hogging the available sessions all day long, the server may terminate (*time-out*) a session if it's idle (sending no requests) for more than a couple of minutes. You may encounter this while working on your CGI scripts. You may have your FTP session time-out, for example, while you puzzle your way through a script checking for missing quotes. Simply log on again with your FTP client, and you'll be back in business.

We've included FTP clients for Macintosh, Windows 3.1, and Windows 95/NT on the CD-ROM (the CD-ROM also provides hyperlinks to several important Internet-related software archive sites). For computers running MacOS, the software is located in the */tools/anarchie* directory. For those using Windows, it is located in the */tools/wsftp* directory. If you don't have an FTP client already installed, you'll need to install one before you can continue. *Readme* files in the respective directories will give you instructions on installing the software for your operating system.

It is possible to use your Web browser to upload files via FTP. Netscape *Navigator* and several other browsers allow file uploads using both FTP and the less common HTTP (less common for file uploads that is). Check your browser documentation to see if this feature is supported. Some of the popular Internet how-to and HTML programming books also explain how to do nonanonymous FTP sessions with a Web browser.

Be sure to read the license agreement for the software and agree to the terms and conditions before you use it. Note, this software is shareware. We urge you to pay the nominal shareware license fee for the software you use regularly. By complying with the shareware license terms you will not only be doing the right thing by being honest, but you'll also encourage and support all the hard-working software authors who make such great software available.

The instructions in the next two sections are essentially identical for Mac and Windows, with only minor variations because of the differences in the clients. No unique information is presented in the section for a given client software, so you can safely read only the section that applies to you and skip the other.

WS_FTP for Windows-based Computers

The FTP software we include for Windows is called *WS-FTP Limited Edition*, published by Ipswich Software. It is simple to use and works well on all Windows-based computers and nearly all Internet file servers. After you use the version that is on the CD-ROM for a while, you may want to check around to see if a newer version is available. The author is continually making improvements to it.

The instructions in the following paragraphs are not intended to give you a complete course in using this software. We give you only a quick overview of how to start an FTP session and how to transfer files. For more complete information on all the software's features, check the excellent help documentation that comes with it.

You'll need your completed ISP/SA questionnaire to set up your FTP connection with your ISP's or SA's Web server the first time. After that, you can save the session information and log on to the server with a single mouse click.

Before you try to log on, you should have your Internet or LAN connection up and running. Start your PPP session or initiate your connection to your LAN in the normal way. Once you're connected, start *WS_FTP* by double-clicking its icon. You

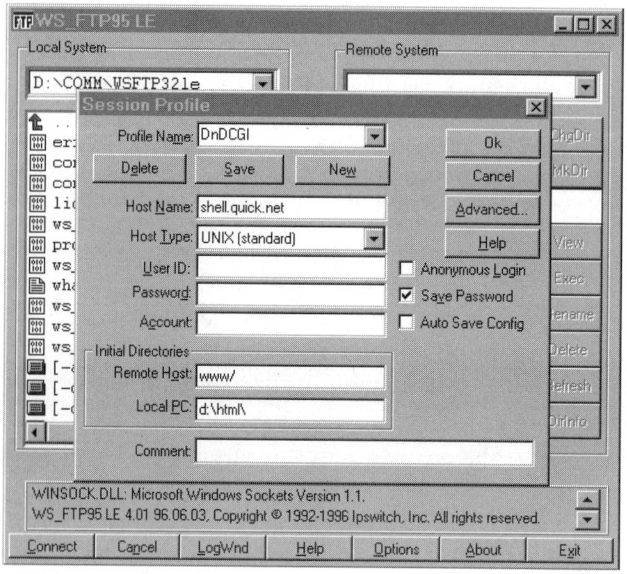

Figure 3.1 WS-FTP *start-up screen display*

should see something like Figure 3.1 on your screen. Note, we're showing screen grabs from the Windows 95/NT version of the software, since that's the operating system we use. The Windows 3.1 version will look a little different, but it operates in the same way.

To create a session, fill in the Host Name, User ID, and Password fields. You can find this information on your ISP/SA questionnaire in questions #17 and 18. Complete the Host Type field with the type of operating system your ISP or SA's Web server uses (question 7). If in doubt, use UNIX (standard) or Windows NT, unless you have a very unusual Web server. The Initial Directories box lets you define the initial directory for both the client and server machines (question 11). Check the Save Password box and give your connection a descriptive name in the Profile Name field. Finally, click Save to store the profile for the next time you wish to access this server (simply choose the profile from the list in the drop-down menu). Click OK to initiate the FTP log on. You can watch the connection progress in the small text area at the bottom of the window.

Once you are logged on to the server, you will see a directory listing of the local disk on the left side and the remote disk on the right of the main window. To move to a different directory on the local or remote machine, either double-click the directory icon you'd like to change to or click the ../ line at the top of the list to move up a directory level.

To transfer a file to the Web server, first select the type of file transfer you want. Use ASCII transfers for Perl code, text data files, and HTML and use binary transfers for images and other binary files. Select the file or files you want to transfer by highlighting them in the local directory window. Click the arrow pointing to the remote directory (to the right) to transfer the files.

Hot Tip

> You can have *WS_FTP* automatically choose the transfer mode by selecting the Auto checkbox (see Figure 3.2). When this is checked, all file types not pre-associated with *WS-FTP* as text files are transferred using binary mode. The text file extensions we use in this book are *.pl, .cgi, .dat, .cnf, .htm,* and *.html.* To register these, click Options on the bottom of the window and then click ASCII Extensions. Add these extensions to the list, and you'll be able to automate your file transfers.

You can monitor the progress of your transfer by watching the area at the bottom of the window. When your transfer has completed, *WS_FTP* will reload the remote directory listing so that you can verify that your files were all transferred. Figure 3.2 shows the main *WS_FTP* window with our cursor poised on the right-facing arrow button to initiate a file transfer to an early version of the *Drag 'n' Drop CGI* Web site.

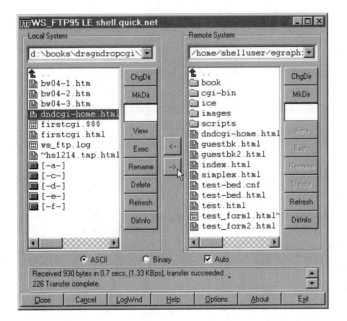

Figure 3.2 *The main* WS_FTP *window*

The same procedure applies to downloading files, except that you highlight the file(s) on the remote system and use the left-facing arrow button to transfer them to your local machine. That's really all there is to transferring files with *WS_FTP*.

Hair Saver

> During the transfer of ASCII files, the file size may change slightly as it moves from the local machine to the remote machine due to the different end-of-line characters used by different operating systems. Some computers use two characters (DOS/ Windows mostly) to indicate the end of a line; others (UNIX and Mac) use only one. (FTP will take care of converting to and from the remote format for you.) In contrast, binary files will be the same size on both the local and remote machines.

Here are a couple of other functions you probably will need to perform:

- Create a directory on the server
- Delete files on the server
- Change file permissions

This last function is important when dealing with CGI files because of the way the UNIX file system controls access to files (see Appendix B). Windows NT users won't need to change file permissions.

WS_FTP can create and delete directories on both the local and remote systems. To create a remote directory, simply click `Mkdir` on the `Remote System` side of the main window and enter the directory name in the popup dialog. *WS_FTP* will create the directory and reload the remote file listing so that you can admire your work. To delete remote files or directories, highlight them with the mouse and click `Delete`. Answer "`Yes`" to the popup dialog, or, to delete multiple files and directories, answer "`Yes to All`."

To change the permissions on a remote UNIX file, select the file with a single click and then right-click in the directory listing pane. You'll get a pop-up menu like that shown in Figure 3.3. Select the `chmod` option, and you'll be able to set the file permissions in the dialog window shown in Figure 3.4.

Appendix B features an extensive discussion of UNIX file permissions. We also cover them later in the chapter when we continue with our example CGI script. Users without Telnet access to their Web accounts can do just about everything they'll need to by using *WS_FTP*. All the scripts in this book can be installed and set up on a UNIX Web server using the features available in *WS_FTP*.

WS_FTP has many other options and nice features to make your FTP sessions more automated and efficient. Read all about them in the excellent on-line help files.

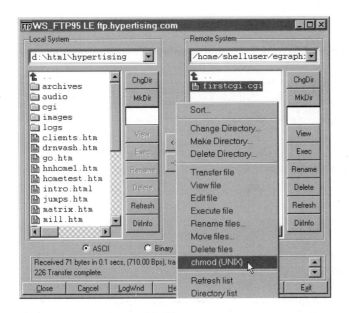

Figure 3.3 *Changing host file permissions with* WS_FTP

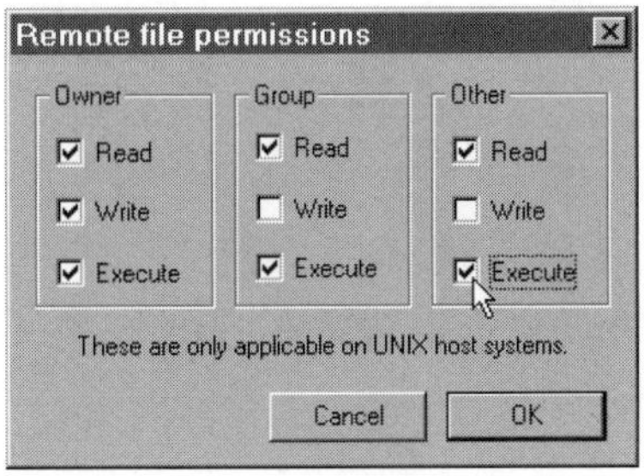

Figure 3.4 WS_FTP *remote file permission dialog*

Anarchie for MacOS-based Computers

The FTP software we include for MacOS is called *Anarchie*, published by Stairways Software. *Anarchie* is actually a combination FTP and Archie client. Archie is a protocol that allows you to search multiple FTP servers for files with names matching a search string. As a means of finding files, it has largely been replaced by the Web and its search engines, but Archie can still be useful in some cases. We don't discuss the

Archie features of *Anarchie* here, but you may find it useful if you get a lot of your software via FTP. *Anarchie* is shareware, so you should pay the shareware fee if you use it regularly. Check the license agreement for usage and payment terms.

The instructions in the following paragraphs are not intended to give you a complete course in using this software. We give you only an overview of how to start an FTP session and to transfer files. For more complete information on all the features of the software, check the help documentation that comes with the software. You'll need your completed ISP/SA questionnaire to set up the FTP connection to your ISP's or SA's Web server the first time. After that, you can save the session information and log on to the server with a single mouse click.

Before you try to log on, you should have your Internet or LAN connection up and running. Start your PPP session or initiate your connection to your LAN in the normal way. Once you're connected, start *Anarchie* by double-clicking its icon. *Anarchie* is part of a suite of related Internet software, and it wants you to run something called the "Internet Config extension." You can run this if you like, but we ignored it without any ill effects on our test system. (Note, some program options require this to be running.) When you start *Anarchie*, you'll see the two dialogs shown in Figure Figure 3.5 on your screen. Just indicate your indifference by clicking I Don't Care followed by Cancel to start *Anarchie* as a stand-alone program. If you want to use the Internet extension, you should read the documentation that comes with the software before you install it.

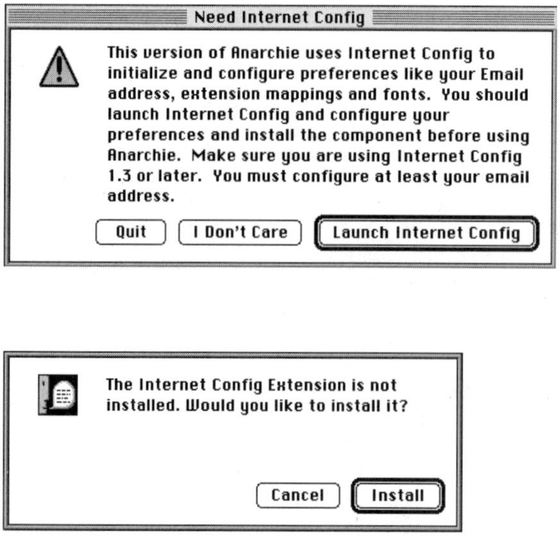

Figure 3.5 Anarchie *start-up screen dialogs*

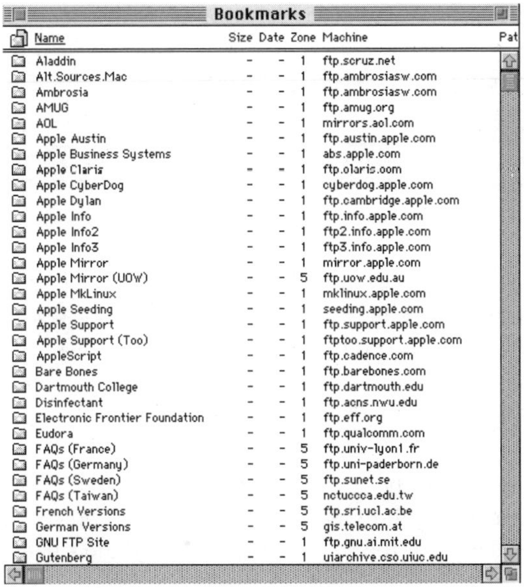

Figure 3.6 Anarchie *FTP site list*

Once you get past the Internet Config dialogs, you'll see a large list of FTP site bookmarks that *Anarchie* has preloaded, as shown in Figure 3.6.

Since your Web site FTP location isn't likely to be in there, select FTP... from the FTP menu. In the dialog shown in Figure 3.7, you supply the needed information to connect to your server. Fill in the Server, Path, Username, and Password fields and leave the other boxes as is.

You can find this information on your ISP/SA questionnaire, (see questions 17 and 18). In the Path field, you define the initial directory on the server machine. The

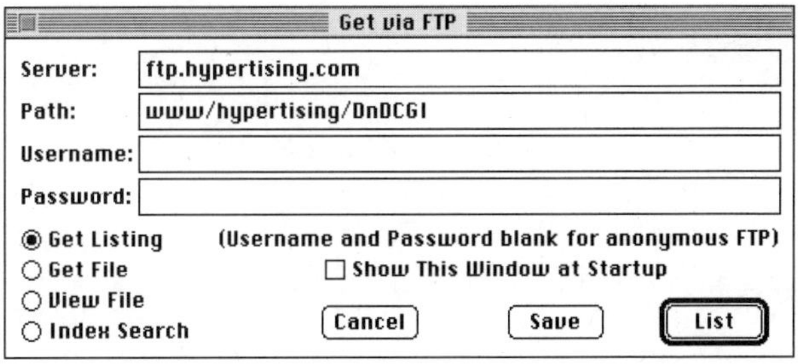

Figure 3.7 Anarchie *connection dialog*

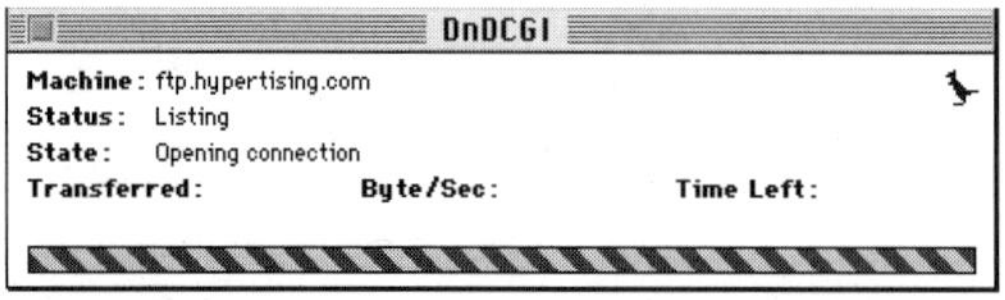

Figure 3.8 Anarchie *progress dialog*

server path should be taken from the answer to question 11. Sometimes the FTP server will put you part way down that path. If it does, enter the remaining part of the path to your Web files in the Path field, as we did in Figure 3.7. In any case, if you put the full path, you'll get to the right directory. Click List to initiate the FTP log on. The progress of all *Anarchie* communications with the server can be seen in the dialog shown in Figure 3.8.

Once you are logged on, you will see a listing of the remote directory in a new window (see Figure 3.9). To view the contents of a subdirectory, double-click the directory name. *Anarchie* will then retrieve a listing of the files in the directory and open another window. The old directory window remains open, so switching between directories is as simple as popping the correct window to the front.

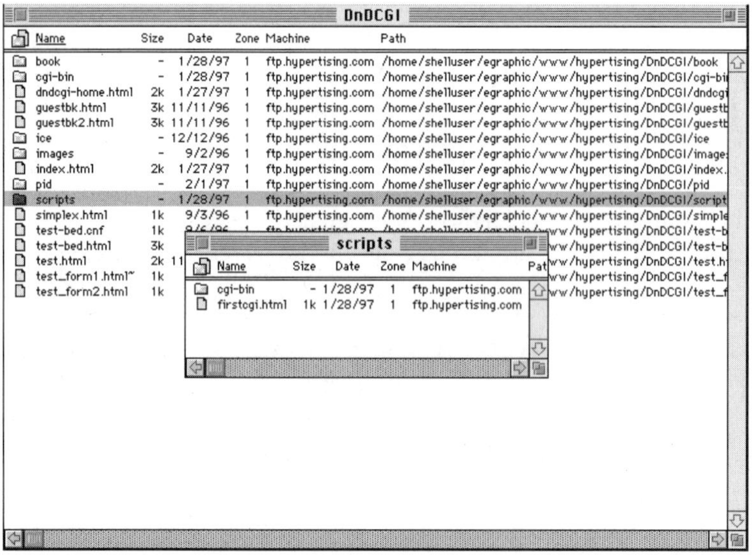

Figure 3.9 Anarchie *FTP directory windows*

Hot Tip

To save a new bookmark for your server and directory, click the window containing the directory you'd like to bookmark (e.g., your root HTML directory or your *cgi-bin* directory) and choose `Save Bookmark...` from the `File` menu.

To transfer a file to the Web server, first set the file type by choosing the appropriate option in the FTP menu. Use text transfers for script code, HTML files, and configuration files; use binary mode for image files and ZIP or other archives. Select `Put...` from the FTP menu and use the standard Mac file dialog to choose the file you wish to upload. Click `Open` to start the transfer. Again, you'll see the progress dialog shown in Figure 3.8. When your upload is finished, *Anarchie* will update the directory window to show your new file on the server.

Downloading files consists of exactly the same procedure, except you double-click the file(s) on the remote directory window to save the files to your local machine. Transferring files using *Anarchie* is really that simple.

Hair Saver

During the transfer of text files, the file size may change slightly as it moves from the local machine to the remote machine due to the different end-of-line characters used by different operating systems. Some computers use two characters (DOS/Windows mostly) to indicate the end of a line; others (UNIX and Mac) use only one. (FTP will take care of converting to and from the remote format for you.) In contrast, binary files will be the same size on both local and remote machines.

Here are a couple of other functions you probably will need to perform:

- Create a directory on the server
- Delete files on the server
- Change file permissions

This last function is important when dealing with CGI files because of the way the UNIX file system controls access to files (see Appendix B). Windows NT users don't need to change file permissions.

To create a remote directory with *Anarchie*, choose `New Directory` from the FTP menu and enter the name of the directory in the dialog. Again, after completing the

```
┌─────────────────────────────────────────────┐
│ ═══════════ Send Command ═══════════          │
├─────────────────────────────────────────────┤
│ Command: │ SITE CHMOD 755 firstcgi.cgi │      │
│                                               │
│          ( Cancel )      ( Send )             │
└─────────────────────────────────────────────┘
```

Figure 3.10 *Changing host file permissions with* Anarchie

operation, *Anarchie* will update the remote directory listing to show your new directory. To delete remote files or directories, highlight them with the mouse and choose
Delete from the FTP menu.

To change the permissions on a remote UNIX file, you need to manually enter the
FTP command. *Anarchie* doesn't have a nice permission dialog like some of the Windows clients. Make sure the file you want to change permissions for is highlighted in
the top window. Choose Send FTP Command... from the FTP menu and fill in the
dialog as shown in Figure 3.10.

The *site* command tells the FTP server that a system-specific command is coming.
chmod is the standard UNIX command for changing file permissions. 755 is the permission string that sets read, write, and execute permissions for the owner of the file
(you) and read and execute permissions for everyone else for the file. Appendix B features an extensive discussion of UNIX file permissions. We also cover them a bit
more later in the chapter when we continue with our example CGI script. Not all
FTP servers will allow this command. If you get an error from the server, you will
need to change permissions using Telnet (as described in the next section).

Users without Telnet access to their Web accounts need not worry. All the scripts in
this book can be installed and set up on a UNIX Web server using the features available in *Anarchie*.

Anarchie has a few other options and features to make your FTP sessions more automatic and efficient. You can read all about them in the on-line help files.

Tell Me About Telnet

Telnet is a communications protocol that lets remote users interact with a host computer over a TCP/IP network. The host computer communicates with the client as if
it were a terminal attached to one of the host's serial ports (in the case of the Internet,
with a *really* long cable). The interface is text based, and the client software emulates
one of a number of actual character terminal devices (a.k.a. *dumb terminals*).

Nerd Note

> Character terminal devices came to be called "dumb terminals" because they consist of only a keyboard, a text-based screen display, and a communications port. They have no processing power of their own and don't do much unless they are connected to a host. An analog in the graphical interface world is an X-term, short for X Windows terminal. This is a slightly smarter dumb terminal. It has a larger graphic display, a mouse, and a TCP/IP communications port. Graphical X Windows display commands are generated by the host and sent to the X-term over a TCP/IP network. The X-Term, like the dumb terminal, has no local processing power beyond drawing something on the screen. X-terms never really caught on because the cost of a full workstation (basically adding a hard disk and operating system software) was only slightly more than that of an X-term.
>
> The current ballyhoo over "network computers" and "thin clients" will sound awfully familiar to those of you who were around during the similar ballyhoo over X-terms.

While dumb terminals have been disappearing in favor of low-cost PCs, the Telnet protocol is still the standard way to access a remote host over a TCP/IP network. There are a couple of reasons for this. First, Telnet is very common among the UNIX-based systems that still dominate the Internet server world. Second, the communication bandwidth and host processing power required are very low. This is compatible with both end users linked via modem and with Web server hosts who have other things to do than talk to Telnet users.

We're telling you all this because as you get into the world of CGI, you'll occasionally need to manipulate files or run programs on your Web server "by hand." A good FTP client such as *WS_FTP* or *Anarchie,* along with a cooperating FTP server, can do almost everything necessary with your CGI scripts and data files. But for the times when FTP clients can't, Telnet is there for you.

The Telnet user interface is similar to that of the DOS window available in MS-Windows. For Mac users who scorn such things, think of it as similar to a dial-up bulletin board system. You enter commands with the keyboard, and the host computer sends back its response in text form for display by your Telnet software. In this way, you can complete all of your file manipulation chores. You can also run host-based commands that aren't available on your desktop machine.

Since an example is worth at least a couple of thousand words, in the next section we show you how to connect to a remote host using either the Telnet client bundled with Windows 95/NT or the ones we've included on the CD-ROM (for Windows 3.1 and MacOS). As with the FTP instructions given previously, the comments for each client will essentially be repeated, so you can skip over the sections covering operating systems you don't use.

Telnet for Windows 95/NT

You may not know it, since it's not well documented, but Windows 95 and NT have a Telnet client built into the operating system. It is installed when you add TCP/IP functionality (along with several other TCP/IP utilities). If you have a different vendor's implementation of TCP/IP, they will almost certainly include a Telnet client (and other utilities as well). Check the vendor documentation to see what it is called.

The Microsoft Telnet client, called *telnet.exe,* is located in your main *windows* directory (probably on your C: drive). To use it, open up the Windows Internet *Explorer* and drag the icon for Telnet onto the desktop and/or into the Start menu to create a shortcut. As with the FTP programs discussed previously, you should have your network connection up and running before trying to connect to the remote computer using Telnet. (It works better that way.)

To start Telnet, double-click its icon. After the program has loaded, you should see a window like that shown in Figure 3.11.

To log on to the server, follow these steps:

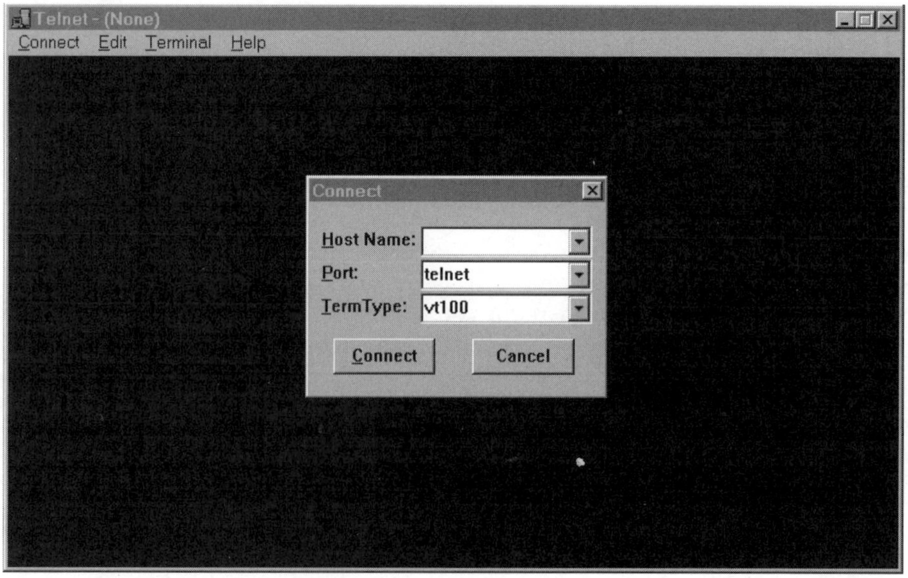

Figure 3.11 *Starting Windows Telnet*

1. Choose `Remote System...` from the `Connect` menu.

2. Enter your host name in the `Host Name` field; that information is in question 18 on your ISP/SA questionnaire. This will probably be the same as your FTP host name. Telnet will remember this host and fill in the `Host Name` field for you the next time you run it.

3. Click `Connect` to start the connection. You will see the welcome text and log on prompt from the host within a few seconds.

4. Enter your username and password when prompted by the host, pressing Enter after each, and you'll be granted access to the system.

Hot Tip

To have Telnet automatically connect to your favorite host, you can edit the properties for the Telnet shortcut and add the host name after the command in the `Target` field of the Shortcut tab. That is, you change

`c:\windows\telnet.exe`

to

`c:\windows\telnet.exe myhost.com`

Once logged on, you'll be able to navigate through the remote server file system and manipulate your files using the command shell for the operating system your ISP or SA's server is running. Figure 3.12 shows the welcome text displayed by QuickNet International, the ISP at which our business Web server is located. See Appendix B for more on common UNIX commands and how to use them.

That's really all there is to connecting to a remote host via Telnet. Once you learn a few commands, you may prefer to use Telnet in combination with your FTP client. Both can have an active connection at the same time, so it's easy to switch between them during your script installation and setup sessions. You can get the full details on the features of Windows Telnet by reading the associated help file. Windows Telnet will be quite sufficient for the amount of Telnet you'll need to do for this book. If you find it too limited, you can find fancier Telnet clients with more features on the Internet. Check the CD-ROM for our hyperlinked list of Internet resource locations or investigate your favorite on-line Windows software archives.

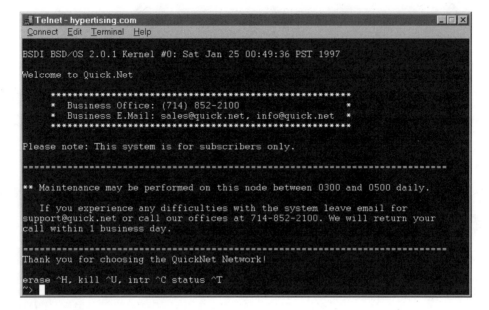

Figure 3.12 *Telnet connected to a remote host*

Tera-Term for Windows 3.1

Users of Windows 3.1 and Windows for Workgroups don't have it quite as nice as users of Windows 95 and NT do. While later versions of Windows have a Telnet client installed as part of the TCP/IP installation, users of Microsoft TCP/IP will need to install a third-party Telnet client. Most third-party TCP/IP vendors for Windows 3.1 include a Telnet client, so you may not have to install one. Confirm this in your vendor documentation. Just in case, your ever-thoughtful authors have provided a Telnet client on the CD-ROM for your version of Windows. Called *Tera-Term,* it is published by Takashi Teranishi in Japan. He was kind enough to let us include his software on our CD-ROM. *Tera-Term* is freeware, so if you like it please drop him an e-mail (see the Tera-Term documentation for the address). *Tera-Term* is located in the *tools/teraterm/* directory. Follow the instructions in the *readme.txt* file in the directory to install the software.

To start *Tera-Term,* double-click its icon. After the program has loaded, you should see a window like Figure 3.13.

To log on to the server, follow these steps:

1. Choose Remote System... from the Connect menu.

2. Enter your host name in the Host field; this information is at question 18 on your ISP/SA questionnaire. This will probably be the same as your FTP host

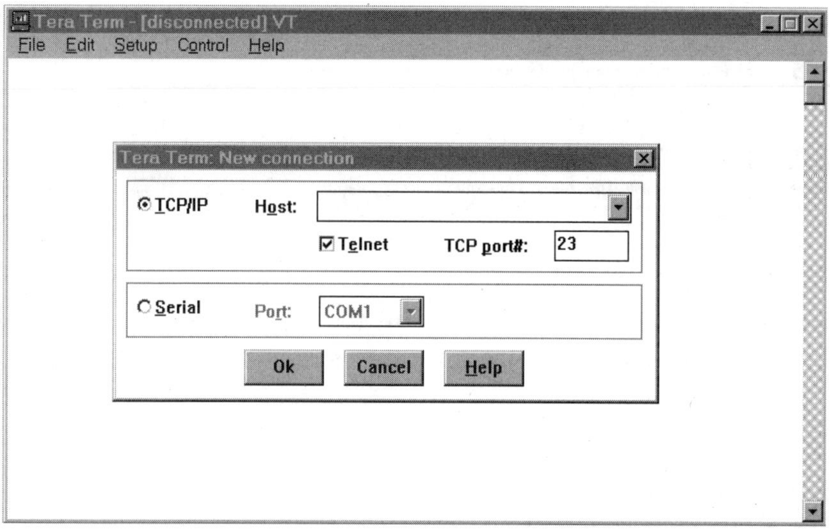

Figure 3.13 *Starting* Tera-Term

name. *Tera-Term* will remember this host and fill in the Host field for you the next time you run it. Leave the other settings in the window at their default values.

3. Click OK to start the connection. You will see the welcome text and log on prompt from the host within a few seconds.

4. Enter your username and password when prompted by the host, pressing Enter after each, and you'll be granted access to the system.

Once logged on, you'll be able to navigate through the remote server file system and manipulate your files using the command shell for the operating system your ISP's or SA's server is running. Figure 3.14 shows the welcome text displayed by QuickNet International, the ISP at which our business Web server is located. See Appendix B for more on common UNIX commands and how to use them.

That's really all there is to connecting to a remote host via Telnet. Once you learn a few host commands, you may prefer to use Telnet in combination with your FTP client. Both can have a connection active at the same time, so it's easy to switch between them during your script installation and setup sessions. You can get the full details on the features of *Tera-Term* by reading the help file. *Tera-Term* will be quite sufficient for the amount of Telnet you'll need to do for this book. However, if you don't like it, you can find other Telnet clients on the Internet. See the CD-ROM for the hyperlinked Internet resource listing.

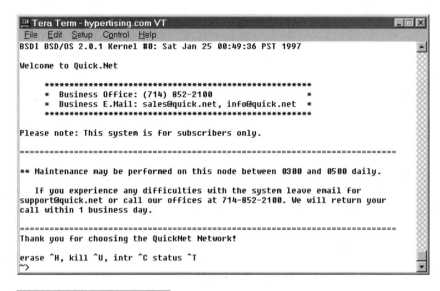

Figure 3.14 Tera-Term *connected to the remote host*

NCSA Telnet for the MacOS

Users of MacOS and Apple's MacTCP TCP/IP will need to install a third-party Telnet client. Most third-party TCP/IP vendors for MacOS include a Telnet client, so you may not have to install one. Check your vendor documentation to be sure. Just in case, your ever-thoughtful authors have provided a Telnet client on the CD-ROM. Called *NCSA Telnet*, it was originally published by the National Center for Supercomputing Applications (NCSA) at the University of Illinois. These are the same Web pioneers who created the *Mosaic* Web browser and the NCSA Web server. *NCSA Telnet* has recently been placed in the public domain by NCSA, so we were free to include it on our CD-ROM. It is located in the *tools/ncsa-telnet/* directory. To install the software, follow the instructions in the *readme.txt* file in the same directory.

To start *NCSA Telnet*, double-click its icon or alias. After the program has loaded, you'll see a window like that depicted in Figure 3.15.

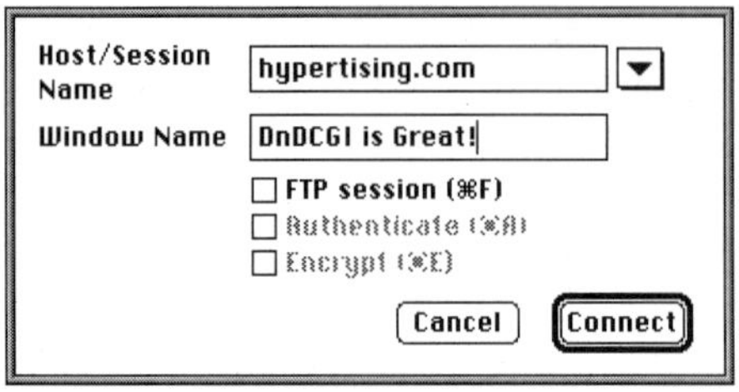

Figure 3.15 *Starting* NCSA Telnet

To log on to the server, follow these steps:

1. Enter your host name in the Host/Session Name field; this information is in question 17 on your ISP/SA questionnaire. It will probably be the same as your FTP host name.

2. Click the "connect" button to initiate the connection. You will see the welcome text and log on prompt from the host within a few seconds.

3. Enter your username and password when prompted by the host, pressing Enter after each, and you'll be granted access to the system.

Once logged on, you'll be able to navigate through the remote server file system and manipulate your files using the command shell for the operating system your ISP or SA's server is running. Figure 3.16 shows the welcome text displayed by QuickNet International, the ISP at which our business Web server is located. See Appendix B for more on common UNIX commands and how to use them.

If you want *NCSA Telnet* to remember this host the next time you run it, choose Preferences... from the Edit menu and select Sessions to get a list of stored sessions. Click New and fill in the dialog as shown in Figure 3.17. You need to enter only the alias and the host name in the specified fields. Leave the other settings in the window at their default values. Click OK to save the session parameters.

That's really all there is to connecting to a remote host via *NCSA Telnet*. Once you learn a few host commands, you may prefer to use Telnet in combination with your FTP client. Both can have a connection active at the same time, so it's easy to switch between them during your script installation and setup sessions. You can get the full details on the features of *NCSA Telnet* by reading the help file. It will be quite sufficient for the amount of Telnet you'll need to do for this book. However, if you don't like it, you can find other Telnet clients on the Internet. The CD-ROM features a hyperlinked reference list of Internet resources.

```
=========== DnDCGI is Great! ===========
BSDI BSD/OS 2.0.1 Kernel #0: Sat Jan 25 00:49:36 PST 1997

Welcome to Quick.Net

*****************************************************
 *  Business Office: (714) 852-2100               *
 *  Business E.Mail: sales@quick.net, info@quick.net  *
*****************************************************

Please note: This system is for subscribers only.

=====================================================================
** Maintenance may be performed on this node between 0300 and 0500 daily.

   If you experience any difficulties with the system leave email for
support@quick.net or call our offices at 714-852-2100. We will return your
call within 1 business day.

=====================================================================
Thank you for choosing the QuickNet Network!

erase ^H, kill ^U, intr ^C status ^T
~>
```

Figure 3.16 NCSA Telnet *connected to the remote host*

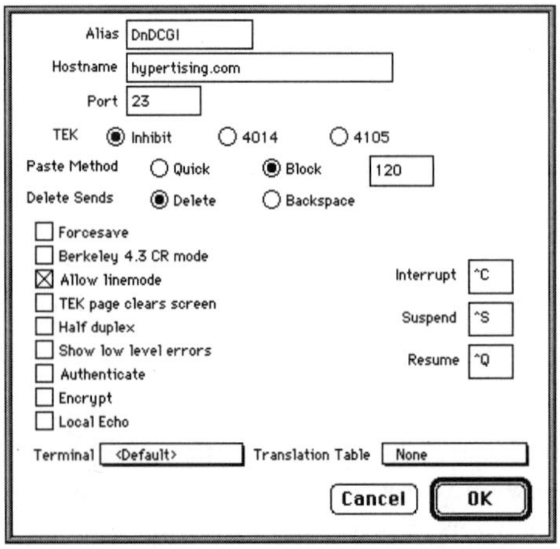

Figure 3.17 *Storing session parameters in* NCSA Telnet

Using What You've Learned—Your First CGI Script

Now that you know how to use all the tools, it's time to get down to the real stuff and create your first CGI program. We've included this script on the CD-ROM for your convenience, but we recommend that you go through the entire process of creating and editing a program at least once. As one of our university professors used to say, "You don't really know something until you've done it enough to be terrible at it." You can, of course, continue on to become a terrific CGI programmer if you desire. Chapter 16 will give you some pointers on that score.

Enough philosophizing. Here's the code for your first CGI script. It's a pert little beauty. We call it simply *firstcgi.cgi*. It is shown in Listing 3.1.

Listing 3.1	Your first CGI program—*firstcgi.cgi*

```perl
#!/usr/bin/perl
# a little test cgi program
$color='black';
$cgi_arg = $ENV{'QUERY_STRING'};
if ($cgi_arg =~ /color=(.*)/) { $color = $1; }
$date = localtime(time);
print <<__END__;
Content-type:  text/html
<HTML><HEAD><TITLE>The time is now</TITLE></HEAD>
<BODY><H3>The time is now:</H3>
```

```
<FONT COLOR="$color">
<CENTER><H1>$date</H1></CENTER>
</FONT></BODY></HTML>
__END__
```

For those of you who decide not to enter the script by hand, it's located on the CD-ROM in the */scripts/firstcgi* directory. The file is called *firstcgi.cgi* The rest of you should start up your editor of choice and enter the lines in Listing 3.1 exactly as shown.

Hair Saver

> Be sure each single quotation mark and double quotation mark has a mate; bachelor quotation marks are a terrible thing to see in a CGI script and cause much frustration and heartache. So we remind you often to check your quotation marks. Perl is very picky about such details; it will complain bitterly and refuse to cooperate if you don't play by its rules. Trust us. If you learn to be obsessive about making sure your quotation marks always have a mate, your CGI-life will be much more satisfying.

Once you've entered the lines and checked the quotation marks a couple of times, you should save the file to a convenient directory. If you're editing with a word processor such as Microsoft *Word*, be sure to save the file as a plain text file, not as a word processor file. We usually create a master CGI directory and then create a subdirectory or a folder for each script. Putting all the files associated with each script in an individual subdirectory helps keep things organized.

What does this script do? It allows the user to display the current local time (local to the server) in a variety of colors. Not a really vital function for most people, but it does accomplish our objective—that is, to be a practice script. The script is called from a hyperlink with an optional color parameter that it uses (if present) in the HTML page it returns to the browser. The returned page displays the current time and date in the chosen color or in black if the color parameter is missing. At the bottom of the script file, you can see the HTML code that the script produces. A little later in the chapter, we give you the HTML code for a page that demonstrates our little script in use.

With the script file safely stored on disk, you're at the point where you'll normally start working with the other scripts in the book. We give you the basic script for each chapter on the CD-ROM.

Configuration

Using the configuration procedures and instructions we present, you'll prepare it for use on your ISP or SA's Web server. You'll also customize the script as necessary to meet your needs. So let's get the script ready to run on the server.

The most important thing to configure for UNIX-based servers is the very first line of the script:

```
#!/usr/bin/perl
```

This line tells the UNIX computer

- that the file is a script program,
- to run the program called *perl* in the */usr/bin* directory, and
- to pass the script file to *perl* for execution.

You can read more about this feature of UNIX in Appendix B, if you're curious. (People with Windows NT servers won't need to configure this line. Windows uses the file associations, based on the file extension, to figure out which program to call when running a script.) To further configure the line for your ISP or SA's Web server, look at question 4 in your ISP/SA questionnaire. Your ISP or SA should have either given you the path and filename for Perl on your system, if you're using UNIX, or told you how to set up to run a Perl script, if the Web server runs Windows or another operating system. Edit the script file to match your ISP or SA's instructions. That's all you'll need to do to configure this particular script. (More complex scripts will require additional configuration. Typically, you'll need to tell the script the location of various data files by changing a couple of Perl variable definitions. If this sounds scary, don't worry—we walk you through it.)

Following the model used later in the book, we point out the areas in the script you can edit to customize the script output to match your Web site's look and feel. In this script, the HTML code returned to the browser is produced by this section of code at the bottom of the script:

```
print <<__END__;
Content-type:  text/html
<HTML><HEAD><TITLE>The time is now</TITLE></HEAD>
<BODY><H3>The time is now:</H3>
<FONT COLOR="$color">
<CENTER><H1>$date</H1></CENTER>
</FONT></BODY></HTML>
__END__
```

The first line

```
print <<__END__;
```

tells Perl to print out everything in the following lines just as it appears in the script until it reaches the end-of-string marker (__END__) to the right of the << signs, but not including the semicolon. This feature of Perl is called a *here document*, for historical UNIX reasons we won't go into.

Nerd Note

"here documents" are common in Perl CGI scripts for just the purpose we're using it for, namely, to print out a large block of predefined text. The alternative is to have a series of individual print statements such as

```
print "<HTML><HEAD>";
print "<TITLE>My Script</TITLE>";
print "</HEAD><BODY>";
```

etc.

Individual statements are much more error prone because any missing quotation marks or semicolons will cause an error in your script.

Now, whenever you see a long series of print statements in a script, you can say with confidence: "I'd use a 'here document' for that."

The first line of the "here document" block, which is part of the HTTP header, looks like this:

```
Content-type: text/html
```

and tells the browser what type of data is coming. Don't edit this line or remove the blank line after it. Both are necessary for the browser to properly recognize the script output as an HTML page.

Perl obediently prints the lines of text, scanning for embedded Perl variable names as it goes. When Perl finds a variable name within the text, it replaces that name with the variable's current value. In this script, we use two variables in our HTML output—$color and $date—that represent, respectively, the color of the text and the server's local date and time. The $color parameter is passed to the script from the calling HTML page. The $date parameter is calculated by Perl from the server's system clock. To change the text or formatting, you can edit this HTML just as you would any HTML page.

Amazing Factoid

> One of the really nifty things about the CGI programming specification is the easy way it gives script programmers to return data to the Web browser. All the script has to do is print out lines of text, just as if they were going to appear on a terminal. The Web server captures this output and sends it to the browser. The script never has to deal with TCP/IP or any of the complicated communication necessary for the server computer to talk to the browser computer.

Once you've configured the script to run on your ISP or SA's Web server and made any initial changes to the HTML output section, save the script to disk again.

Listing 3.2 gives an example of an HTML page that calls the script.

Listing 3.2	HTML code to call *firstcgi.cgi*

```html
<HTML>
<HEAD>
   <TITLE>My First CGI</TITLE>
</HEAD>

<BODY>

<H3>This page will let you test the firstcgi.cgi script from Chapter 3</H3>
<P> Click one these links and see what happens.
Use the "back" function to return to this page.
<UL>
   <LI>
     <A HREF="http://www.hypertising.com/DnDCGI/scripts/cgi-bin/firstcgi.cgi">
     No arguments</A>
   <LI>
     <A HREF="http://www.hypertising.com/DnDCGI/scripts/cgi-bin/firstcgi.cgi?color=red">
     Red</A>
   <LI>
     <A HREF="cgi-bin/firstcgi.cgi?color=blue">Blue</A>
   <LI>
     <A HREF="cgi-bin/firstcgi.cgi?color=FF00FF">Fucsia (uses a hexadecimal color)</A>
</UL>

<HR>
<P>Here's a form that lets you choose your own color!<BR>
Just enter the color name or hexadecimal color code (don't use the # sign) you want to
see.
This form calls the same script as the links above.
<FORM ACTION="cgi-bin/firstcgi.cgi" METHOD="GET">
Color: <INPUT TYPE="TEXT" NAME="color" SIZE=20 MAXLENGTH=20> <BR>
```

```
<P><INPUT TYPE="SUBMIT" VALUE="What time is it oh colorful one?">

</FORM></BODY></HTML>
```

Enter the HTML in the listing into your text or HTML editor. You can test the page with your browser to see how it looks. The hyperlinks call the script; however, since the response page is generated by the script, the form won't work until you get it onto a machine running an HTTP server. The path to the CGI script in the hyperlinks and the `ACTION="cgi-bin/firstcgi.cgi"` field will need to be customized to match your ISP or SA's Web server. CGI scripts, like images and other HTML files, can be called using absolute or relative addresses. Check the answer to question 6 on your ISP/SA questionnaire to see if your CGI scripts have to go in a particular directory. If so, adjust the links in this file to match the questionnaire. If not, place them in the *cgi-bin* directory that we'll show you how to create during the following installation steps. Once you are happy with the file, save it to disk.

Detailed FTP Uploading Procedures

Now's the time to use all your new knowledge of FTP and Telnet to install the script on the Web server.

We walk through this process step by step to make sure we don't lose anyone. It's important that you understand this procedure so that you can use it with the rest of the scripts in the book.

1. Connect to the Internet or your LAN using your normal procedure.

2. Start your FTP client and enter the proper host name (see question 18 on your completed ISP/SA questionnaire). Start the connection process. If you can't log on, observe the resulting error message carefully. Usually the server error message will tell you what the problem is. You may have entered the host name incorrectly, or the Web server may not be available. (Some Web servers limit how many FTP users can be logged on at one time.) If after double-checking the host name, username, and password entries from the ISP/SA questionnaire you still can't connect, you'll need to contact your ISP or SA. It's impossible for us to present solutions to every conceivable problem in this book.

3. After you are successfully logged on, compare the path to the current directory (displayed in the window) with the directory for your Web files (see question 11 on the ISP/SA questionnaire). You will probably have to change to the directory where the Web server expects to find HTML files. To do this, follow the procedure described earlier for your FTP client. The FTP client will bring up a listing of the files in that directory. Keep changing directories until you are at the proper directory for your HTML files.

4. Once you have the correct directory listed in the remote directory window, you are ready to upload *firstcgi.html* to the server. Locate the file on the local machine you wish to transfer or choose Put... from the FTP menu for *Anarchie* and select the *firstcgi.cgi* file. Click the arrow or OK to start the transfer.

   When the transfer is complete, the remote directory listing will refresh and you'll see *firstcgi.html* sitting happily on the server.

5. From the answer to question 6 on the ISP/SA questionnaire, obtain the name of the directory in which your CGI scripts reside. Check the remote file listing to see if that directory already exists. If not, you'll need to create it. If your ISP doesn't have any naming restrictions, just use the name *cgi-bin* for your CGI script directory (that's the name we use throughout this book). If you do need to create the directory, follow the directions given previously for your client.

6. Enter the CGI directory by double-clicking the directory name.

7. Transfer the *firstcgi.cgi* file to the Web server and verify that it is in the proper directory.

8. If your server is UNIX-based, you need to change the file permissions for the script file to include the "execute" bit, as we discussed in the FTP instructions earlier in the chapter. This is necessary to get the Web server to recognize your script for what it is, and not just as another text file.

   To change the permissions, use the *chmod* command (right-click the remote directory list in *WS_FTP* or select Send FTP Command... from the FTP menu in Anarchie). Change the permissions to include Read, Write, and Execute for the Owner and Read and Execute for the Group and All categories (CHMOD 755). In general, only the owner (this means you) should have write permission for Web server files. If you get an error when you attempt to execute the command, your FTP server software doesn't support this function. You will have to change the file permissions manually using Telnet. We describe how to do this later in the chapter.

9. If your *chmod* command was successful, you can verify the file permissions by looking at the extended directory information. Click Dirinfo on the Remote System side of the *WS_FTP* window. *Anarchie* doesn't allow you to see the remote file permissions, so you'll have to either trust that they are correct or check them from the Telnet client.

   If you've successfully uploaded both files, created the CGI directory, and changed the file permissions for *firstcgi.cgi*, you're done! You can skip over the Telnet session (in the next subsection) and come back to it later, if needed.

This is the procedure you'll follow for every CGI script in the book (although you create the CGI directory only once). If you encounter problems that you can't resolve with our instructions, ask for help from your ISP or SA. And please send us an e-mail with your experiences so that we can improve the Frequently Asked Questions list on the book's Web site. (Check the book's Web site, *http://www.hypertising.com/DnDCGI/,* for the e-mail address.)

Hair Saver

> Be sure you save your file from within your editor before you upload it. This is especially important if you're repeatedly making changes and uploading them to the server for testing. We have ripped out more than a few hairs (Bob is nearly bald!) wondering why the changes we made to a file weren't present after the upload. We had made the changes in the editor but didn't save them to disk before we transferred the file. Yet another example of why programmers die young and why attention to detail is important in the CGI biz.

Hot Tip

> Part of what makes the Internet great is the spirit of mutual helpfulness you (generally) find there. When you have a problem and ask for help, the chances are pretty good that someone will help you out. (The only unspoken rule is that you read all the associated documentation and really try to solve the problem yourself before asking your question. Failing to do so can result in getting "flamed"—the Internet equivalent of a rebuke.) In general, if you give at least as much as you get from the Internet, it will continue to be a pleasant place in which to work and play.

Detailed Telnet Procedures

In this section, we cover only the procedures you need to follow if you can't complete the entire script upload and installation process with your FTP client. Telnet differs from FTP in that there is no fixed set of functions that you can perform with a Telnet client. You are actually interacting directly with the host computer, so you can do basically anything you need to with your files and directories. To make full use of the power of the Web server's operating system, you should learn about the commands and functions that are available. Appendix B has more information on common UNIX commands. Mac users not familiar with a command-line environment (and who will be using a Windows NT server) would do well to get an introductory book on MS-DOS, since as a Telnet user, you'll be interacting with the host computer at essentially the MS-DOS level.

The following procedure assumes you were able to upload the *firstcgi.html* and *firstcgi.cgi* files to their proper directories on the server using FTP.

1. If not already connected to the Internet or your LAN, start that connection.

2. Start your Telnet client and connect to the Web server as described in the previous subsection.

3. Log on to the server using your username and password (see question 18 of your ISP/SA questionnaire). If the server won't let you log on, contact your ISP or SA for the proper username and password. Note that UNIX computers are case sensitive; one letter in the wrong case will look like an incorrect entry to the system. So be sure to get the case of both exactly right. To avoid rejection due to typing mistakes, it's best to store your username and password in the client program and have it automatically log on for you.

4. Use the *cd* command to change your working directory to the location of your HTML files. For UNIX servers:

   ```
   cd /path/to/html/files
   ```

   For Windows servers:

   ```
   cd c:\path\to\html\files
   ```

   where *path/to/html/files* in both cases is the path specified in question 11.

5. For UNIX servers, enter the command

   ```
   ls
   ```

   For Windows servers, enter the command

   ```
   dir
   ```

   You should see the *firstcgi.html* file listed along with any other files you may have uploaded in the directory.

6. *cd* to the CGI directory you created in the previously given FTP procedure as follows:

   ```
   cd cgi-bin
   ```

   or to whatever you named the directory. This command works in both Windows and UNIX.

7. For UNIX servers, enter the following command to change the file permissions on *firstcgi.cgi*:

   ```
   chmod 755 firstcgi.cgi
   ```

   Note that this is necessary and possible only on UNIX computers. Figure 3.18 shows this sequence on the Telnet screen.

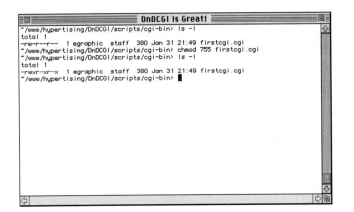

```
                        DnDCGI Is Great!
~/www/hypertising/DnDCGI/scripts/cgi-bin> ls -l
total 1
-rw-r--r--   1 egraphic   staff   380 Jan 31 21:49 firstcgi.cgi
~/www/hypertising/DnDCGI/scripts/cgi-bin> chmod 755 firstcgi.cgi
~/www/hypertising/DnDCGI/scripts/cgi-bin> ls -l
total 1
-rwxr-xr-x   1 egraphic   staff   380 Jan 31 21:49 firstcgi.cgi
~/www/hypertising/DnDCGI/scripts/cgi-bin> █
```

Figure 3.18 *Setting file permissions with Telnet*

See Appendix B for more on what this command does. For now, just enter it as written.

8. Run a quick test of the script by entering the following command.

On UNIX:

```
./firstcgi.cgi
```

On Windows:

```
perl firstcgi.cgi
```

The script should run and print out HTML code similar to the following:

```
~/www/hypertising/DnDCGI/scripts/cgi-bin> ./firstcgi.cgi
Content-type:  text/html
<HTML><HEAD><TITLE>The time is now</TITLE></HEAD>
<BODY><H3>The time is now:</H3>
<FONT COLOR="black">
<CENTER><H1>Fri Jan 31 21:30:16 1997</H1></CENTER>
</FONT></BODY></HTML>
~/www/hypertising/DnDCGI/scripts/cgi-bin>
```

If you get a "No such file or directory" error similar to this:

```
~/www/hypertising/DnDCGI/scripts/cgi-bin> ./firstcgi.cgi
bash: ./firstcgi.cgi: No such file or directory
~/www/hypertising/DnDCGI/scripts/cgi-bin>
```

you will need to contact your ISP or SA for the proper location of Perl. Edit the first line of the script on your desktop machine to match the location of Perl and upload the file again to the server using FTP (UNIX only). You won't need to change the file permissions again as long as you use the same filename (i.e., overwrite the old version) when you upload the file.

If you get errors from Perl similar to the following:

```
~/www/hypertising/DnDCGI/scripts/cgi-bin> ./firstcgi.cgi
Bad name after QUERY_STRING:: at ./firstcgi.cgi line 6.
~/www/hypertising/DnDCGI/scripts/cgi-bin>
```

or

```
~/www/hypertising/DnDCGI/scripts/cgi-bin> ./firstcgi.cgi
syntax error at ./firstcgi.cgi line 10, near "print"
Execution of ./firstcgi.cgi aborted due to compilation errors.
~/www/hypertising/DnDCGI/scripts/cgi-bin>
```

then you have errors in your code. Observe the error message and try to figure out what the problem is. Note the line number mentioned and look carefully at your script for a missing quotation mark or semicolon. After you correct any problems, upload the script again using FTP. Be sure to save your file from the editor before uploading, or you won't make much progress.

Once the script is running, the installation of your first CGI script is complete. Congratulations!

To test the script in action, load the *firstcgi.html* page with your browser. It should look like that shown in Figure 3.19.

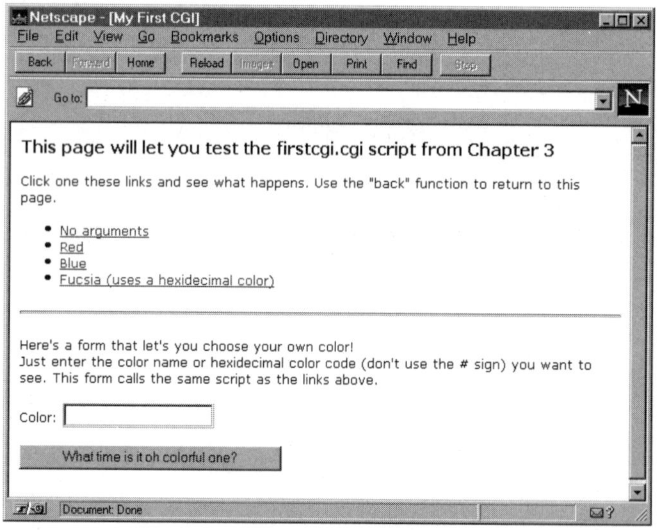

Figure 3.19 *Browser output of* firstcgi.html

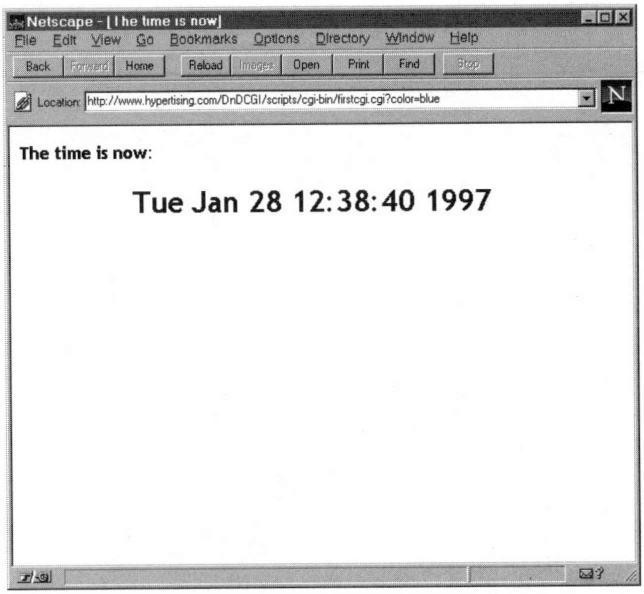

Figure 3.20 *Browser output of the* firstcgi.cgi *script*

Click one of the hyperlinks on the top of the page or enter a color (name or hexadecimal value) in the Color field and click the form button. The script will generate a page that looks like that shown in Figure 3.20, using the color you specified for the date and time.

We encourage you to experiment with the HTML page and the script. Change a few things and see what happens. Try adding the variables at different locations in the HTML output. Practice uploading files to the server. Create several different versions of the script and upload them. The more familiar you are with using the tools, the easier it will be for you to install the more complex scripts presented later in this book.

You've now successfully installed, configured, and run a CGI script. You're ready to proceed with the rest of the scripts in this book.

What We Covered in Chapter 3

- How running CGI scripts changes your relationship with your ISP or SA

- The infamous ISP/SA questionnaire that gives you all you need to know about your Web server in order to run CGI scripts

- An introduction to FTP and Telnet clients for Windows and MacOS

- Detailed procedures for uploading and configuring a CGI script using FTP and Telnet

- Using the *firstcgi.cgi* script in a Web page

*C*hapter *4*
Giving Your Visitor a Hint (or Two) Using Javascript

Features of the *hint* Script

- Displays either status line text or text in a window when the mouse moves over a hyperlinked text or graphic (or portion of a graphic) or when the user tabs to or clicks in a form field

- May be dismissed by a button, after a specific time has elapsed or when the cursor moves off the link

What You Need to Use This Script

- HTML or text editor

- Netscape version 2.02 or greater or Microsoft Internet Explorer version 3.0 or greater (to test scripts locally)

The *hint* script is the first (and easiest) of the three Javascript scripts presented in this book. You'll be able to put it to use quickly. We're big believers in instant gratification, and this is our way of making you feel good about buying this book. As the old hair tonic commercials touted: "Results in just minutes!"

Unlike the Perl scripts we'll get into later in the book, Javascripts are embedded within the HTML page. A Javascript is set off from the surrounding HTML by two HTML tags that tell your browser that a script is contained within them. This tag appears at the start of the block:

```
<SCRIPT LANGUAGE="Javascript">
```

and this tag is used at the conclusion of the block:

```
</SCRIPT>
```

It's necessary to specify the script language in the opening script tag, since other scripting languages (such as Microsoft's VBscript) are also supported by some browsers.

We like to put our script blocks at the beginning of the page so that they load into memory before the HTML page. This ensures that all functions are available to the user by the time the page has loaded enough content for them to begin interacting with it. Loading even long scripts first will not noticeably slow the loading of your Web page.

Several Javascript scripts may be used on a single HTML page and as a complement to Perl scripts, as you'll see in Chapter 8, "Remote Controls for All Occasions Using Javascript."

Before jumping into the chapter, you may want to use your browser to open *hint.htm*, found in the */scripts/hints/* directory on the CD-ROM. Spend a few minutes with the file to get a clear idea of the functions included in the *hint* script.

Why You Would Want to Use This Script

This might seem a sacrilege considering today's passion for all things interactive, but books have very definite virtues that multimedia such as the Internet are hard-pressed to duplicate. Visual and tactile cues tell the reader whether they are near the beginning or end of a book. A chapter title, page numbers, the thickness of the read versus the unread portions of the book between his/her fingers—all of these provide the reader with continuous navigational clues. Also, an index and table of contents are standard features of most books and can almost always be found in their familiar places.

A writer knows with some certainty that a reader will read the current page and then proceed to the next. This makes the presentation, development, and summary of content and analysis comparatively easy. When was the last time you needed context-sensitive help for a book?

On the other hand, how many times in the last week have you found yourself meandering through the pages of a Web site, trying to find what you were looking for? Many a large, content-rich site, however well organized, is overwhelming at first look. Without the comforting tactile clues mentioned previously, many of us still don't have the visual "memory" to easily find our way around larger Web sites. The penchant some page designers have for creating inscrutable navigation icons doesn't help matters.

Wouldn't it be nice if, when you're feeling especially overwhelmed, a little help message popped up as you passed your cursor over a particular hyperlink? Like anything else, pop-up windows and status line prompts can quickly become tiring and even annoying. But used sparingly, such hints can help guide visitors through your site. When invoked, hints can be used to do the following:

- Suggest reasons to go in a particular direction by selecting specific hyperlinks.
- Provide more information about the destination of a particular link.
- Prompt the user to type a particular piece of information into a form field.

It's always a good idea to have potential users review your site before taking it online. Their feedback can give you a good idea of where organizational changes in the site are appropriate and some recommendations on where to place hints on your pages.

Introduction to the *hint* Script

Two types of hints are included in this single Javascript. All of the features of both hint methods are loaded with the page so that you can use either or both, depending on your requirements.

The first hint places a stationary text message in the browser window status line for a time period you specify (see Figure 4.1).

The second hint option displays the message in a little window (see Figure 4.2). You can set this window to close after a specified time interval or allow the visitor to dismiss it with a click of the button (see Figure 4.3). Netscape browsers can also detect when the mouse moves off of the link, and use that event to close the window.

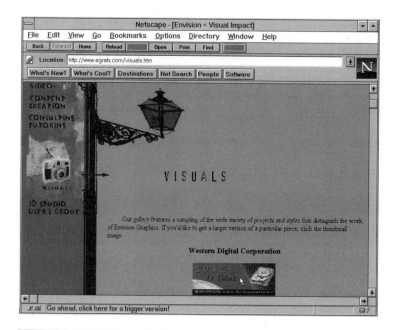

Figure 4.1 *Browser output of the Envision Graphics Web site showing cursor on a hyperlink and text in status line*

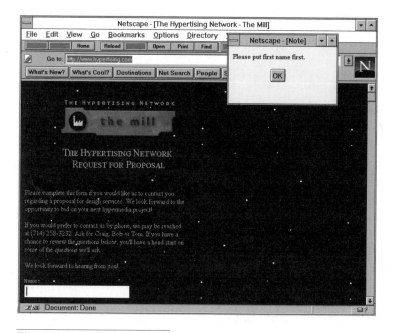

Figure 4.2 *Browser output of the Hypertising Network Web site showing window hint with dismiss button*

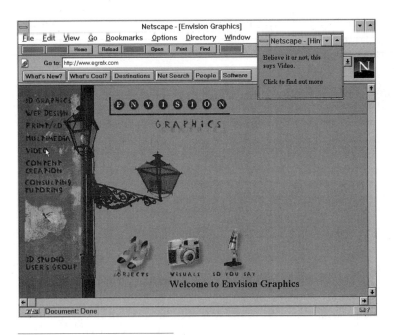

Figure 4.3 *Browser output of the Envision Graphics Web site showing timed hint window*

Amazing Factoid

The window created by the *hint* script is actually a diminutive *Netscape* browser window, not a native windowing system dialog box. All the menu bars and other browser stuff have been turned off, however, for its lean-and-mean role. How do they do it? Javascript is integrated tightly into the browser architecture. This is because it was specifically developed by Netscape for use within a Web browser. Since Javascript was always intended to be a browser scripting language, it incorporates features to allow the creation of browser windows and to contol the appearance of those windows by turning on or off the various "decorations" normally found in the browser.

Although a number of companies have professed the desire to support Javascript, Microsoft *Internet Explorer* 3.0 is the first browser besides Netscape *Navigator* that can (more or less) properly display a Javascript-enhanced page. It sure does help the Javascript cause that *Navigator* and Internet *Explorer* dominate 88 percent of the browser market. Keep in mind that the remaining 12 percent of browsers (including versions of *Netscape* before 2.0 and *Internet Explorer* before 3.0) have no idea what to do with a Javascript when they see one. We can only hope that they will ignore it and that you've designed your page with this in mind.

Our script allows you to specify the size, title, background color, and dismiss button text (in this case, "OK") of the hint window. Unfortunately, you don't get to decide where the window is placed, and there's no way to make it stay on top of other windows in the user's workspace.

The *hint* script responds to Javascript **events.** An event is something that occurs to change the state of the browser or the HTML document. Typical Javascript events include clicking a form button, clicking a hyperlink, or resizing the browser window. An event of interest to *hint* occurs whenever a user does one of the following:

- Moves the cursor onto a hyperlinked graphic, client imagemap area, or hypertext link—called an `onMouseOver` event.

- Moves the cursor off a hyperlinked graphic or hypertext—called an `onMouseOut` event. (This does not work with the Microsoft Internet *Explorer* 3.01 browser.)

- Clicks in or tabs to a particular input field of a form—called an `onFocus` event.

The `onMouseOver` and `onMouseOut` events are pretty self-explanatory. The `onFocus` event means that a particular field in a form has received the focus of the program's attention (i.e., when the user begins typing in it) until the user clicks or tabs to somewhere else on the page.

Special Javascript functions called "event handlers" are executed in the Javascript code whenever one of the above events occurs. Event handlers are the workhorses of Javascript. Always on the prowl for user actions, event handlers allow Javascript to react immediately to user actions (as defined by the script writer) without communicating with the server on which the page resides.

To better understand the concept of event handlers, look at the following snippet of Javascript:

```
<A HREF="home.html" onMouseOver="return hint('Go back to the home page');">
Home Page</A>
```

The `onMouseOver=` HTML parameter is used to tell Javascript to watch for `MouseOver` events. In plain English, this means that when the mouse moves over the text or image that links to *home.html* (the event), the Javascript (`hint`) function is executed by the browser, and the message "Go back to the home page" appears in the status line. (The word *return* is necessary to override the usual browser status line display, which normally shows the full URL for the linked page.)

Configuring and Installing the *hint* Script

Each Javascript script in this book features a configuration block near the top of the file to allow you to customize its behavior to meet your needs. In the following steps, we show you how to modify values in the block to make the script do your bidding (step 1) and then how to install the final script in your page (step 2).

Step 1: Configuration

The *hint* Javascript code is in the file *hint.txt* in the */scripts/hints* subdirectory on the CD-ROM. This is not a complete working example, only the Javascript code. To use it, you need to paste this file into an HTML document.

The following script configuration block is located near the top of the script, following some copyright information. After configuring each variable to your liking, you can cut and paste or import the entire script into an existing HTML Web page.

Start by loading *hint.txt* into your favorite HTML or text editor. The configuration block is shown in Listing 4.1, with some demonstration values.

Listing 4.1	The default *hint* script configuration block before editing

```
/*
     ******************************************************
     Configuration Block
     ******************************************************
*/
     hintdelay = 2000;      // time to display hint in 1000/ths of a second
     winhintdelay = 1500;   // same for window hints
     closebuttontext = "Gotcha Dude!"; // text for the close button on button hints
     hwinwidth = 200;       // width of the hint window
     hwinheight = 120;      // height of the hint window
     hwintitle = "Hint!";   // title of the hint window
     hintbg = "#FFFF80";    // nice balloon help yellow
/*
     ******************************************************
     End of Configuration Block
     ******************************************************
*/
```

The block contains a list of variables that you can define as you wish. We designed the *hint* script so that you don't have to make any changes to the script itself. The remainder of the Javascript (not shown) contains the actual Javascript program code.

Note, the text located between the /* and */ and after the // characters are called **comments.** Comments are ignored by the program when it runs. They are added by the programmer to help explain what is happening in a given line or section of code.

As you can see, we've commented the configuration block thoroughly. Let's look at each line so that you can see exactly what we're doing in this example. Line 1

```
hintdelay = 2000;   // time to display hint in 1000/ths of a second
```

tells the status line hint how long to display, in milliseconds. The default delay is 2 seconds. These times are not very precise and can vary among browsers. Line 2

```
winhintdelay = 1500; // same for window hints
```

indicates the delay for window hints, in this case, about $1\frac{1}{2}$ seconds. Line 3

```
closebuttontext = "Gotcha Dude!"; // text for the close button on
button hints
```

defines the text that will appear on the button that dismisses the hint window. Lines 4 and 5

```
hwinwidth = 200;    // width of the hint window
hwinheight = 120;   // height of the hint window
```

set the dimensions for the hint window, in pixels. You will want to test these values, since the window will have scrollbars if the message defined in the HTML is too long to fit. Line 6

```
hwintitle = "Hint!"; // title of the hint window
```

provides the title of the hint or prompt window. The last line

```
hintbg = "#FFFF80"; // nice balloon help yellow
```

determines the background color of the window, expressed as a hexadecimal value. (For those HTML editors that can't supply this value, we've included a shareware hexadecimal color code generator in the */nettools/colorhex/* directory on the CD-ROM.) If yellow doesn't appeal to you, replacing the number in parentheses with #FFFFFF will change it to a more neutral white. You can also use color names such as black and red.

Hot Tip

Listing 4.1 is your first bit of Javascript code. Not really that frightening, is it? The long, made-up words along the left-hand margin are called *variables;* for example, `hintdelay` and `hintbg`. The variables' values are defined on the other side of the equals sign; for example, `hintdelay = 2000`. We could have called these variables anything we wanted (like chocolatemousse, shortbread, or carrots), but it always makes sense to choose names that more or less describe what they do.

Another common-sense programming habit: use comments liberally to describe what each function and variable does. In Javascript, comments always appear after `//` characters or between the `/*` and `*/` character combinations (if they extend past a single line). If you make a change to the Javascript code, you should always use a comment to remind yourself and explain to posterity what you've done.

Hair Saver

All languages (English included) need the right syntax (statement format) to be properly understood. Javascript syntax includes parentheses, apostrophes, and periods. These marks tell Javascript where one program statement ends (the semi-colon) and what is a text string versus a Javascript function or variable name (the double quotation marks).

A program statement is a basic unit of computer programming. Each program statement performs one distinct action.

Some rules to keep in mind when editing your Javascript scripts:

1. Make sure to leave the parentheses and quotation marks intact whenever you change a value.

2. Within a comments section that begins with //, don't hit Return. Instead let the line wrap on its own. Remembering these simple steps will save you much grief.

That's all there is to it! Save the Javascript file under a new name (like *myhintjs.txt*). Now all you have to do is edit your HTML page to call the script functions and then cut and paste the whole Javascript at the head of the page.

Amazing Factoid

> The most recent browser usage statistics show Microsoft *Internet Explorer* slowly gaining market share against Netscape *Navigator.* As of March 1997, one source (Intersé) shows Netscape with 57 percent of the market and Microsoft with as much as 31 percent of the market. (The remaining 12 percent is divided among other browsers.) These numbers pose some serious issues for content creators on the Internet, since each browser implements both HTML and Javascript support differently. However, Microsoft's stated intention to do everything that Netscape does (and then some) will probably lead to a more standardized implementation of Javascript in Internet *Explorer.*

Step 2: Installation

To install your Javascript script in a Web page, follow these steps:

1. Launch your favorite HTML editor and text editor.

2. Open the modified Web page that will be receiving the "Javascript transplant." Save it under a new name, such as *homepagetest.htm.*

3. In the text editor, open the file *myhintjs.txt* that you modified earlier in this chapter and select all the copy (or use the `insert file` function of your editor).

4. Insert your cursor just after the `<HTML><HEAD>` line (and after lines that begin with the `<META:>` tag, if any) and before the `<BODY>` tag. Paste the Javascript script into the Web page.

5. Save the file again.

That's all there is to it.

Using the *hint* Script in Your Pages

To edit your HTML file, open your favorite editor. Decide which type of hint you want to include on your page, and then follow the simple instructions below. Save the modified HTML file under a new name in the same directory as the Javascript file you modified in Step 1.

Status Line Hint

With this line, you call a status line hint, which is invoked by an `onMouseOver` event:

```
<A HREF="yourlinkhere.htm" onMouseOver="return hint('This is the hint message');"></A>
```

Replace the copy between the first set of apostrophes with your hint message and the link reference inside the first set of quotation marks with the hypertext or image link you want to trigger the hint.

Window Hint, with Dismiss Button

You add this line to invoke a hint window, with a dismiss button:

```
<A HREF="page3.html" onMouseOver=
"winHint('this is a window hint. Close with the button, and click the link to jump to Page 3', 'button');">button</A>.
```

Place your hint message inside the first set of single quotation marks, and put the word *button* inside the second set of single quotation marks. This tells the script to create a dismiss button on the window.

Window Hint, with a Timer

To add a window hint that departs after a specified period of time, add this line:

```
<A HREF="page4.html" onMouseOver="winHint('This is a window hint. Wait a second and it will close by itself. Click the link to jump to Page 4', 'timer');">timer</A>.
```

Insert the hypertext or image link reference within the first set of double quotation marks to call the hint window. Replace the text within the first set of single quotation marks with your hint message. Remember, the length of time the window hangs around is controlled by the `winhintdelay` variable in the configuration block of the script.

Window Hint That Closes with `onMouseOut`

Add this line to your HTML to create a window that closes as soon as the mouse moves off the hyperlink:

```
<A HREF="page1.html" onMouseOver="winHint('This is another hint. It will close when you move your mouse off the link. Click the link to go to Page 1','mouse');" onMouseOut="unWinHint();">mouse off</A>.
```

Replace the link reference between the first set of double quotation marks with the hypertext or image link you want to trigger the hint. Replace the text between the first set of single quotation marks with your hint message. (As we mentioned earlier in the chapter, the `onMouseOut` event doesn't work with *Internet Explorer* 3.01, so use it with caution.)

Status Line Hint for a Form Field

To call a status line hint when a user enters or tabs to a form field, add the following line to your page:

```
Name: <INPUT TYPE="TEXT" NAME="name" onFocus="hint('This is a form
hint');">
```

Replace the copy between the single quotation marks with your hint message. *Note:* To create a window instead (as shown in Figure 4.2), replace `"hint` with `"winHint`. To provide a button to exit the hint, use `onBlur` to add a `button` parameter after the message string.

Once you've made the necessary changes to the HTML file, save the final result.

If the hints don't work as expected, the problem is likely to be what programmers like to call a *syntax error* (in fact, programmers like to call any error a syntax error, since the term causes most people's eyes to glaze over). Reopen the modified Web page and study the HTML around where you inserted the Javascript and modified HTML. The most likely errors are pasting the script between a tag and one of its brackets (shown below as `here`):

```
<HEAD^here... > or <^here... BODY>
```

The other likely error is a missing single quotation mark in the `onMouseOver` call. The format *must* be

```
onMouseOver="hint('a hint', 'timer');"
```

Note the placement of quotation marks, semicolon, and parentheses in the code. The single and double quotation marks can't be mixed, and the other punctuation must be as shown. A similar problem may exist in the configuration block, so this should be checked as well.

You should now be up and running with the *hint* script. Have fun adding hints to your pages, but don't go overboard. Moderation is always the best policy.

What We Covered in Chapter 4

- How to add text hints to the browser status line and pop-up window hints to your Web pages
- An introduction to modifying a canned Javascript configuration file to meet your needs
- How to choose a particular hint function to add to your Web page
- How to modify HTML tags to call Javascript functions
- General procedures on how to incorporate customized Javascript functions into your page

Chapter 5

Counting Visitors to Your Web Site with Perl

Features of the *vcount.cgi* Script

- Stores visit counts for one or a thousand pages in a single file
- Can present page counts as text or graphics
- Supports hidden page counts
- Allows custom HTML tags before and after each digit of the count
- Provides a count summary page
- Allows the page counts to be reset via a hyperlink for easy administration

What You Need to Use This Script

- Perl version 4 or 5 on your Web server
- The capability to execute Server-Side Include scripts
- An FTP client
- A Telnet client
- A text editor

You've probably seen Web sites with those little counters saying you're the 333,123th visitor since January 15 of some unspecified year. Sometimes the graphics for the numbers are pretty cool and go well with the page. At other times they look plain ugly. In this chapter, we give you all the tools you need to make cool counters with the best of them. And since you may not want to to tell the whole world how many (or how few) visitors you've had, you can just as easily set up a hidden "stealth" counter, a counter that no one else knows is there.

Why You Would Want to Use This Script

In 1995, nobody had a budget for a Web site, but everyone who wanted to get onto the Web found the dollars somewhere. By budget time in 1996, accounting got into the act. They started asking to see some cost justification for company Web sites. Hit counts from server logs were a place to start, but they don't tell you much (unless "lots of hits" is what you want to hear). Visit counts give a more precise indication of the traffic to your Web site—but numbers never tell the whole story. If you're asked to justify the Web site on a sales-per-visit basis, you might want to know if the marketing department is asked to show an increase in sales for each brochure mailing they produce (they probably aren't). At this stage of the Internet game, very few companies are making money on the Web. This is changing in 1997, but for now, ROI for a Web site is more a matter of mind share than market share.

You can combine visit counts with useful information massaged from your server logs using commercial software like *Webtrends* (see the e.g. Software site at http://www.webtrends.com). Also, there are several commercial services, such as NetCount and I/Pro, that can make your visit counting still more sophisticated. Beware: The art of visit analysis (Internet "visitorship"?) has not reached the level of sophistication you'll find in the analysis of magazine and newspaper readership or of TV viewership.

Hot Tip

If you need a really huge number in order to impress the boss (or your mom) with your site traffic, by all means use *hits*. If you want to impress the marketing manager with the new Web site's conversion rate (sales per advertising contact), it's better to use the actual visit count, which will be lower.

Hits versus Visits

Exactly how do visit counters work? In Chapter 2, we described how the HTTP protocol is used by Web browsers to request HTML pages, graphics, and other objects from the Web server and to call CGI programs.

When visitors access your page from their browsers, a complex series of requests and responses passes between the browser and the Web server. The browser sends an HTTP GET request for each item on the HTML page. These items include the HTML text, GIF graphics, and even executable programs or data files. Each of these requests is recorded by the Web server in its access log, and each request counts as a hit. This means that if your page has ten graphics and a link to your latest company newsletter in *.zip* format, you could get 12 hits (1 for the HTML, 10 for the graphics, and 1 for the *.zip* file, if the visitor decides to download it) each time a single person visits that page on your site. The effect is multiplied if the visitor views multiple pages. So all those sites claiming thousands or millions of *hits* per day are actually getting far fewer *visits*.

In contrast to the hit logs kept by the Web server, visit counters are CGI programs that execute each time the page is fetched from the server and that increment a counter value which is stored in a file on the server. Since the program increments the counter just once each time the page is accessed, you get a more accurate count of how many visitors that page has actually received. This is probably more useful information than a raw hit count because it tells you how many *people* have visited your site.

Amazing Factoid

> A Web-surfing robot gathering data for search engines will also count as a visit, but such visits should be a small percentage of your total. Also, repeat visitors and pressing the `Refresh` page button on a Web browser will generate visit counts.

This script automatically increments a counter each time one of your pages with the *vcount.cgi* SSI command embedded in it is sent out by the server. Check your ISP/SA questionnaire to see if your Web server supports SSI. If it doesn't, another counter script called *Count* (by Muhammed Muquit; see the links section of the CD-ROM) is an excellent alternative, although it is a bit more complicated to set up and install. Now might also be a good time to review Chapter 3 and try out a few of the techniques we give you there to persuade your ISP or SA to consider allowing the use of SSI.

Introduction to the *vcount.cgi* Script

The *vcount.cgi* script is a Perl program that uses a technique called Server-Side Includes (SSI). The SSI feature was added to Web servers for just the type of thing you'll be doing with *vcount.cgi*—using a script to trigger some action automatically and include the output of the command in the Web page, without requiring the user to click a hyperlink or submit a form. The SSI command is stored in the HTML page as a specially coded comment. The server scans the HTML file and executes any SSI commands it finds before sending the page back to the browser. The anatomy of an SSI command is shown in Figure 5.1.

You can see that this is a valid HTML comment. However, to Web servers that support SSI, it says, "Process the line and execute a program." The *exec* command directs the Web server to execute a program specified in the command's parameter and insert the program's output into the HTML data sent to the browser.

Hair Saver

The SSI command must be placed in the `<BODY>` section of the HTML file and follow the SSI format exactly in order for the server to recognize it as an SSI command and not just an HTML comment. Be sure you don't put any spaces in the first `<!--#exec` sequence, or the server won't recognize the command. This is the first thing to check if your SSI script doesn't work.

Some servers require a special file extension for files with SSI commands. Generally this is `.shtml`, which stands for "smart HTML." These picky servers won't scan the file for SSI commands unless the file has the proper extension. Check your ISP/SA questionnaire to see if you need a special extension on your HTML files in these circumstances.

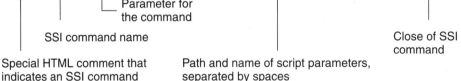

Figure 5.1 *The anatomy of an SSI command*

Nerd Note

> There are many other SSI commands besides `exec`. Most HTML how-to books and references list them. SSI commands are easy to use and don't require writing a script. They do somewhat slow the server that is fetching your page, but unless you're creating a very high traffic site, don't sweat it.

How *vcount.cgi* Works

Basically, *vcount.cgi* works by storing a set of counter numbers and their associated page names in a file on the Web server. Whenever a page is fetched by a browser with an SSI command embedded in the HTML, the server runs the *vcount.cgi* script and increments one of the counts (see Figure 5.2). Parameters following the script name tell the script what to do. Here is the command syntax for the *vcount.cgi* script:

```
<!--#exec cmd=cgi-path/vcount.cgi command [pagename [gr]] -->
```

where `command` is followed by one of the following parameters listed below:

- `page name`. A page name can be the name of the HTML file such as *index.html* or a descriptive name like "HomePage" or "WhatsNew." This name is stored in the data file and used to reference the appropriate counter number. Don't put spaces in the name and don't use < or >. A command containing only the page name will increment the count for that page but not display anything.

- `disp`. If there is no page name following `disp`, the script displays the count for all pages. If there is a page name, it increments and displays the count for that page name. If `gr` follows the page name, then graphical digit images, as specified in the script, are used for each digit in the count. Otherwise text is used.

- `reset`. This resets all counters to zero and stores the date and time when the counts were reset in the counter file. *Hint:* Don't put this one on your high-traffic pages.

The square brackets [ ] in this command syntax are not actually inserted into the command when it's used. They are programmer notation to indicate that what appears between them is optional. Items not in square brackets are required. Thus *vcount.cgi* must have a `command` parameter, but the `pagename` and `gr` parameters are optional.

Here are some examples of valid command lines for the *vcount.cgi* script.

1. `<!--#exec cmd="/cgi-bin/vcount.cgi People" -->`

   This command increments the count for the `People` page and does not return anything for display. This is the hidden count feature. (Note the leading / character. We used an absolute path to the script, as you might have to do if your ISP or SA stores all the CGIs in a central location.)

2. `<!--#exec cmd="../all-cgis/vcount.cgi disp" -->`

   This command displays all the counts for each page in a nice table format along with the current time and the time of the last reset. The CGI script is stored one directory level up from the document, which contains the SSI command in it, in a directory called *all-cgis*.

3. `<!--#exec cmd="cgi-bin/vcount.cgi disp index.html" -->`

   This command increments the count for the page called index.html and returns the count as text. You can place the text within any HTML tags you like, such as `<CENTER>` or `<STRONG>`, or within a `<TABLE>`. Probably the most common CGI location is a subdirectory called *cgi-bin* below the one containing the HTML pages.

4. `<!--#exec cmd="cgi/vcount.cgi disp Products gr" -->`

   This command uses `disp` and `pagename` (products), with `gr` following the page name. This causes the script to insert a series of `<IMG SRC="digit_path/digit#.gif">` lines in the page, where `digit-path` is the location of the digit images relative to the HTML page (not to the *vcount.cgi* script). `digit#.gif` will be the appropriate digit name for each of the digits from 0 to 9, that is, *one.gif, two.gif,* and so on. You can use any image you like for the digit images, but images that look something like a number will obviously make the most sense to your visitors. We've included a digit image set on the CD-ROM, in the */scripts/vcount/digits/* directory, so that you can try the graphic display feature of the script. The CGI location is similar to that in the previous example, but the directory is named *cgi*.

5. `<!--#exec cmd="my-cgi/vcount.cgi reset" -->`

   This command resets all the counters for each page and stores the current date and time in the counter file.

6. `<A href="cgi-bin/vcount.cgi?reset">reset counter</A>`

   This is a second way to access the script so that you can manually reset the counters using a hyperlink. This hyperlink command format works only for the `reset` parameter. You can put this on a password-protected page or simply on a page with no links to it from the rest of your site, whose name only you know. We commonly use this second method when using hidden page counts. Our counter summary page uses the `disp` parameter alone to print the table of page counts. We include a hyperlink to reset the counters. As long as the stats are not really secret, you won't need tight security. But in either case you don't want people messing with the counters.

Configuring and Installing *vcount.cgi*

Now we'll configure and install the *vcount.cgi* script. Soon all this terminology we've used will become second nature to you, and your peers at the office will look at you with renewed awe and respect.

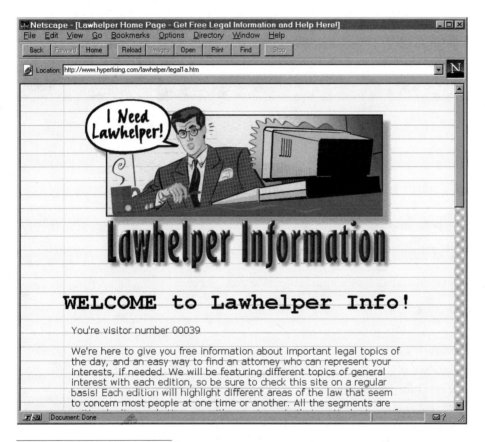

Figure 5.2 *Browser output of a text visit counter using vcount.cgi on the Lawhelper Web site*

Step 1: Configuration

Load the *vcount.cgi* script from the CD-ROM into your favorite text editor. The script is located in the *scripts/vcount/* directory. To configure the script for your ISP's or SA's Web server, you need to edit the configuration block and set the values of several variables that the script needs in order to operate on the server. Before you do that, however, you need to modify the first line of script:

```
#!/usr/bin/perl
```

to match the location of your server. Check question # 4 of the ISP/SA questionnaire if you don't have the location memorized yet.

The configuration block is located near the top of the file following the copyright information. Listing 5.1 shows the configuration block as it appears in the file, before editing.

Listing 5.1   *Vcount.cgi* **configuration block**

```
#################### vcount.cgi Configuration Block ####################

# $cntfile
# where you want to store the page counts
# use the path to your Web directory from your questionnaire
# then put it in a directory accessible by the Web server i.e.
# in a file or sub-directory beneath where your home page resides
# remember UNIX uses / and NT uses \
# example: $cntfile = "/home/shelluser/cbaron/www/cgi/pgcount";
$cntfile = "";

# $digit_dir
# path to the directory containing the digit images
# be sure to put a / or \ on the end
# example: $digit_dir = "images/digits/";
$digit_dir = "";

# $pre_digit
# a string to print before each digit of the count
# this is optional
# example: $pre_digit = "<TD>"; (to put it in a table)
$pre_digit = "";

# $post_digit
# the mate to the above to print after each count digit
# also optional as above
# example: $post_digit = "</TD>";
$post_digit = "";

# $length
# how many digits you want to include in your counter
# optional if you don't want extra zeros leave commented out
# example $length = 10 # gives 0000000001 as your first count
# $length = 5;

######################### End Configuration Block #########################
```

Nerd Note

The Perl language identifies a variable by the first character in its name. A dollar sign ($) indicates a *scalar* (single value) variable, which can be a string of characters or a number. Arrays of scalars indexed by number are designated by an "at" (@) character. A special type of array indexed by a string (called *associative*) is designated by the percent character (%). This makes it easy to spot Perl variables. A common point of confusion is that Perl uses the identifying character (usually a $) of what you want to *get out* of an array when you access it in your program. Look through the Perl code for the various scripts on the CD-ROM to see the different types of variables in action. If this stuff appeals to you, Chapter 16 has some suggestions for how to move on to programming guru-hood yourself.

First, you need to name your counter file. This file will hold all the counts for your pages, along with the date and time of the last counter reset. The name *pgcount*, or just *counts*, is fine. You also need to specify the path to this file as part of the $cntfile variable. Check your ISP/SA questionnaire for the absolute path to your Web documents. You can put the counter file in a different directory than your HTML files if you like to keep things tidy. We generally put data files in the *cgi* script directory. So, for example,

- if you like the name *pgcount*,
- if the path to your Web directory is */home/users/username/www/*, and
- you've decided to put the counter file in the *cgi* subdirectory,

then you would edit the script to make the $cntfile line look like that in Figure 5.3. Note, the actual counter file does not exist yet. It will be created the first time you run the *vcount.cgi* script.

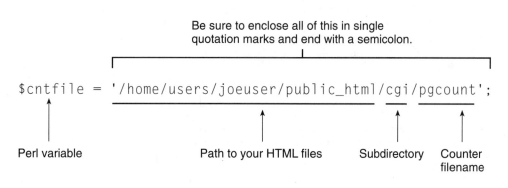

Figure 5.3 *An example configuration for the* $cntfile *variable*

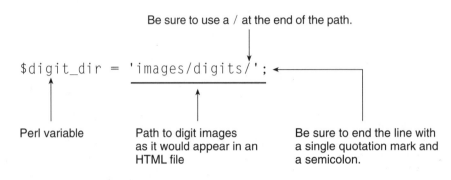

Be sure to use a / at the end of the path.

```
$digit_dir = 'images/digits/';
```

Perl variable

Path to digit images
as it would appear in an
HTML file

Be sure to end the line with
a single quotation mark and
a semicolon.

Figure 5.4 *How* vcount.cgi *uses the* $digit_dir *variable*

Next you configure the $digit_dir variable. This variable specifies the directory in which the images for each digit from 0 to 9 are stored. These are used only with the gr parameter. If you don't plan to use graphical counters, you can skip this section. This variable differs from $cntfile in that you specify a directory rather than a file-name. We generally use a special */digits* subdirectory below the main images directory to hold the number images. The script does not actually read the files named in $digit_dir; it simply uses the path stored in the variable to create the <IMG> tag, which is inserted into your HTML page. Use relative or absolute paths here as you would for the other images in your HTML pages. Figure 5.4 shows how the *vcount.cgi* script uses $digit_dir to form the <IMG> tag.

Hair Saver

The path you specify in $digit_dir must be relative to the page on which the counter images will appear. If you have lots of pages in different directories, you must use an absolute path like */~yourname/images/digits/* (note leading / slash) or */images/digits/.* The directory specified should be whatever comes after the *.com, .net, .edu, .org,* or *.mil* part of your server name in your home page URL. For example, if Joe User's personal home page URL is *http://www.isp.net/~juser/*, the absolute path to an images directory under his root Web directory would be */~juser/ images/.*

The other items in the configuration block are optional. The $pre_digit and $post_digit variables were intended to let you put <TD> and </TD> tags around each text digit or <IMG> tag that is sent to the browser. Some other values might be <STRONG><EM> in $pre_digit and </EM></STRONG> in $post_digit for a really noticeable counter. Font size and color are another possibility, as is the dreaded <BLINK> tag. You get the idea.

The $length variable sets the minimum number of digits in the displayed page counts. Zeros are placed in front of the count as necessary to satisfy this parameter.

This completes the configuration of the *vcount.cgi* script. Be sure to save the modified script file in a convenient directory. We usually create a *cgi* subdirectory on our desktop machines under the directory in which we store the HTML files for a particular Web project.

Step 2: Installation

To install the script, you need to upload the script file and the digit images, if you're using them, to your Web server by using FTP. Then you use Telnet to set the script file permissions so that the Web server can execute the program.

If necessary, review Chapter 3 on how to upload a file using FTP and then fire up your FTP client. Upload the copy of the *vcount.cgi* script which you edited in Step 1 into your *cgi* or *cgi-bin* directory. (Change the file permissions to add the execute permission.)

Once you've got the script on the server, you need to do the same for the digit images if you're going to use graphical counters. Create a directory if you want to keep the digit images by themselves (optional) and upload all the digit images for the style you've chosen. You can always overwrite them with a different style later if you find or make one you like better. The digit images should be uploaded using the binary mode of the FTP software, since they are GIF files. These files don't need their permissions changed.

Good job. You're almost done.

Hair Saver

The UNIX file system is case sensitive, unlike Windows and MS-DOS. And while Windows NT and 95 support uppercase and lowercase characters in filenames, they ignore the case when accessing a file. To make things even dicier, spaces are valid characters in Win NT/95 and Mac filenames, while UNIX generally does not allow spaces in filenames. If you get broken image icons or errors from the Web server for pages or scripts that loaded fine on your local machine, check the case of the filenames. Also, some FTP clients will change the case of filenames during the upload; some, especially Windows 3.1, will upload the files in all uppercase. Make sure the file references in your HTML files and scripts reflect this or use the rename function of your FTP client to rename the files after they are on the server. To ensure that CGI scripts work properly, we use all lowercase names and no spaces for filenames in our HTML files and scripts.

The only step remaining is to test the script. Log on to the Web server with your Telnet software and navigate to the *cgi* directory as described in Chapter 3. Type the following:

```
vcount.cgi disp Home
```

Depending on the $length parameter you set in the script, you should see this:

```
1
```

or

```
00001
```

If you get Perl errors, you have made a mistake in configuring the script. Check the configuration block carefully for missing quotation marks and semi-colons. Once you've corrected the error on your local machine, upload the script file with your FTP client again, using the same filename so that the new file will overwrite the old file on the server. You won't need to change the file permissions again because the new version of the file will inherit them from the old. Next, type

```
vcount.cgi disp
```

and you should see something like this:

```
<TABLE BORDER=2><TR><TH colspan=2>Count Started on Sun Jun 30
0:23:34 1996
</TH></TR>
<TR><TH>Page</TH><TH>Visits</TH></TR>
<TR><TD>Home</TD><TD>1</TD>
</TABLE>
```

Next, verify the disp name gr option by entering

```
vcount.cgi disp Home gr
```

You should get something like this:

```
<IMG SRC="images/digits/two.gif">
```

or this:

```
<IMG SRC="images/digits/zero.gif">
<IMG SRC="images/digits/zero.gif">
<IMG SRC="images/digits/zero.gif">
<IMG SRC="images/digits/zero.gif">
<IMG SRC="images/digits/two.gif">
```

again depending on the $length variable. Finally, check the reset parameter by entering:

```
vcount.cgi reset
```

You should get a response like this:

```
<HTML><BODY>Counts Reset</BODY></HTML>
```

You can check that the counts are actually reset by trying the disp parameter again.

This completes the installation of the *vcount.cgi* script. Fun and easy, wasn't it? Congratulations, you are now a certified UNIX hacker trainee.

Using the *vcount.cgi* Script in Your Pages

Adding the *vcount.cgi* script to your Web pages is pretty simple. We present three basic models to start you thinking.

Example 1: A Text Visit Counter

Listing 5.2 shows an HTML page with the SSI call to *vcount.cgi*. Input this page using your favorite HTML editor or simple text editor and then save it. Upload the page to the Web server using FTP and then load it into your browser.

Listing 5.2	HTML file with a simple call to *vcount.cgi*

```
<HTML>
<!-- A simple example using the vcount.cgi counter script -->
<HEAD>
<TITLE>vcount.cgi test page #1</TITLE>
</HEAD>
<BODY>
<H1>A Test Page for vcount.cgi</H1>
<P>stuff here…
<HR>
<P>This page has been accessed:
<!--#exec cmd="cgi/vcount.cgi disp Test" -->
times.
</BODY></HTML>
```

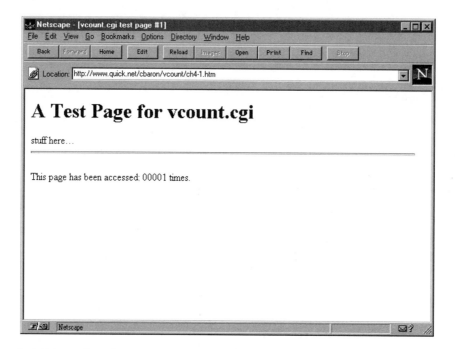

Figure 5.5 *Browser output from the* vcount.cgi *script*

Remember to modify the SSI command to match the location of the script. Also, you may need to put a special file extension on your HTML file (such as *.shtml*) in order for the server to scan it for SSI commands. The UNIX *mv* (move) command is used to rename files on the server. From a Telnet session, you use it as follows:

```
mv index.htm index.shtml
```

Note, you can't preview SSI commands with your browser on your desktop machine because the SSI commands are executed by the Web server. To a browser, they look like comments and are ignored.

If you've correctly installed and configured the script, you should see a page that looks like Figure 5.5 in your browser.

Example 2: A Graphical Digit Visit Counter

If you have a case of graphical-counter envy, The next example (see Listing 5.3) will cure you. Input this page using your editor, and then save it. After uploading it to the server, load it into your browser.

Listing 5.3   **HTML to produce a graphical page count**

```
<HTML>
<!-- An example showing graphics output from -->
<!-- the vcount.cgi counter script -->
<HEAD>
<TITLE>vcount.cgi test page #1</TITLE>
</HEAD>
<BODY>
<H1>A Test Page for vcount.cgi</H1>
<P>This page has been accessed:
<TABLE BORDER=2 CELLPADDING=0 CELLSPACING=0><TR>
<!--#exec cmd="cgi/vcount.cgi disp Test gr" -->
</TR></TABLE>
times.
</BODY></HTML>
```

Your page should now have a stunning graphical counter, as depicted in Figure 5.6.

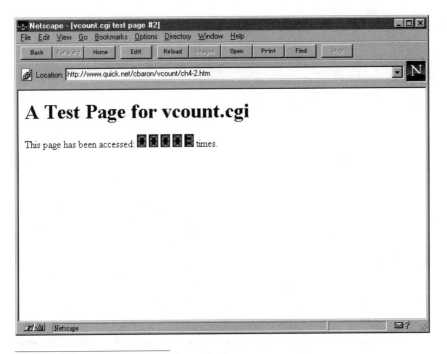

Figure 5.6 *Browser output of graphical page count*

As noted in the configuration section, you can place the digits into a table or other HTML structure by using the pre_image and $post\_image$ variables to store strings that will be output before and after the <IMG> tag. In this example, we used pre_image="<TD>"; and $post\_image$="</TD>"; to put each image into an HTML table cell.

Example 3: A Visit Counter for Multiple Pages

For our final example, we show how we often set up our clients' pages with hidden counters and a summary page with a reset link. Since this is for Webmaster consumption only, we don't need to make it look very fancy. To try it, make a couple of pages with SSI calls using just the page name, excluding the disp parameter, as in the first examples earlier in the chapter:

```
<!--#exec cmd="cgi-bin/vcount.cgi ThisPage" -->
```

You are now counting visits in stealth mode. Listing 5.4 shows an HTML file that will display a summary of all the counts for all the pages on which you've run the script, along with a hyperlink to reset the counters. If desired, input the HTML code that appears in Listing 5.4, save it, and then upload it to your Web server.

Listing 5.4   HTML file showing count summary and counter reset link

```
<HTML>
<!-- An example showing summary output from -->
<!-- the vcount.cgi counter script -->
<!-- Drag 'n Drop CGI          -->
<!-- by Bob Weil and Chris Baron -->
<HEAD>
<TITLE>vcount.cgi counter summary page</TITLE>
</HEAD>
<BODY>
<H1>A Count Summary via vcount.cgi</H1>
<P>Here are the current counts for your pages:<BR>
<CENTER>
<!--#exec cmd="cgi/vcount.cgi disp" -->
</CENTER>
<P> Click
<A HREF="cgi-bin/vcount.cgi?reset">here</A> to reset the counters.
</BODY></HTML>
```

From the browser, you can print the summary page. Keep it to admire. Or take it to the boss when you ask for a raise. Figure 5.7 shows the output in the browser.

That's all there is to the *vcount.cgi* script. If your server supports SSI, it may be all you need for counting visitors to your site.

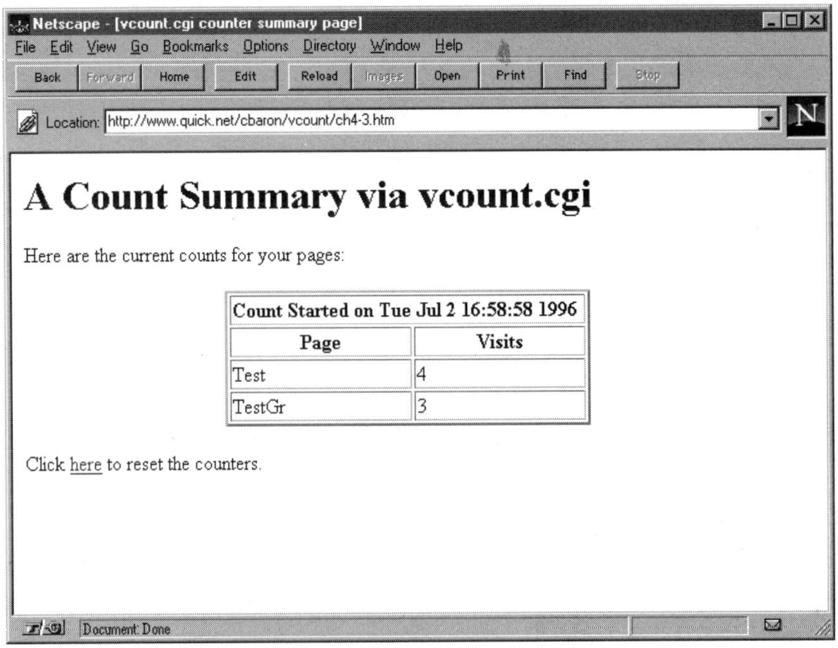

Figure 5.7 *Browser output showing count summary table and counter reset link*

What We Covered in Chapter 5

- The difference between hits and visits
- How visit counters work
- Server Side Includes
- How *vcount.cgi* works
- Customizing the script for your needs
- Installing and testing the script
- Linking the script to your HTML pages

Chapter 6

Fun with Scrolling Text Using Javascript

Features of the scroller Script

- Displays up to three types of scrolling text, delivering copy either as a stream, word-by-word, or letter-by-letter.
- Allows text to appear in either the status line text or a form field.
- Scrolling speed is adjustable.
- Scrolling may be continuous or may be halted by the visitor by using a button or hyperlink.
- Scroll script easily integrates with the *hint* script in Chapter 5, if desired.

What You Need to Use This Script

- HTML or text editor
- Netscape Navigator version 2.02 or greater or Microsoft Internet Explorer version 3.0 or greater (to test scripts locally)

You already know that several Javascript scripts may be used on a single HTML page. The *scroller* script has been specifically written so that it works well with the *hint* script presented in Chapter 5. An additional bit of code in the script keeps the *scroller* script from stepping on the *hint* script as it sends its output to the browser status line.

Find the *scrollerjs.htm* file in the */scripts/scroll/* directory of the CD-ROM and load it into your browser. You can use this page as a test bed to familiarize yourself with the features of the script and sneak a peak at the code (using the *Netscape* Document Source option from the View menu).

Why You Would Want to Use This Script

Sometimes you need to share some late-breaking news or quickly convey information about the latest release of your product with visitors to your site. Although a fancy Shockwave movie, big bold static type, or even the dreaded blinking text, would certainly do the trick, there are several distinct benefits to using scrolling text:

- Scrolling text doesn't require you to change your page design.
- Scrolling text can be added, updated, or easily removed.
- Scrolling text catches the eye without a lot of fanfare and gets along well with all the other fancy stuff you have happening on your page.
- People are accustomed to thinking that scrolling text contains timely and important information that is worthy of immediate attention.

To help your scrolling script get noticed, we've added two more options to the standard method of scrolling the entire message across the screen. The first scrolls the message in word-by-word, and the second, letter-by-letter. Maybe we lead sheltered lives, but we haven't seen the last two scrolling display options presented or used anywhere else on the Internet. You saw it here first!

Amazing Factoid

Why does scrolling text draw attention? Maybe it comes from the enduring old-movie memories of ticker tape spewing out the latest news and stock prices. Or maybe it's the hunter in all of us—our eyes automatically track anything that moves. Whatever the reason, the three options for scrolling text that we offer here can help you spark a glimmer of interest in that newest of creatures, the Web surfer. There is a certain subtlety and immediacy to scrolling text. But like most effects described on these pages, it should be used sparingly. Scrolling text is something that should change periodically (probably more often than the Web pages themselves) in order for people to continue noticing it when they return to your site. To increase the impact of your message, you should keep scrolling text short so that your visitors quickly understand what you are trying to convey. Keep in mind that regardless of the device that first snags their attention, it will still be the content of your site that holds your visitors' interest and keeps them coming back.

Introduction to the *scroller* Script

The *scroller* script, once added to your Web page, makes available two types of scrolling text: scrolling text in the browser status line and scrolling text in a form field. The width of the form field for the scrolling text can be set as desired, although you'll probably want to set it to no wider than 80 percent of the window size. This effectively accommodates other information that might share the status bar. Keep in mind that the width of the browser status line is dictated by the width of the browser window.

For these two types of scrollers, the script offers you three options to present your message:

1. As a single stream. The entire text continuously scrolls. An example of this is shown in Figure 6.1.

2. Word-by-word, until all the words are on-screen. The script then pauses for a moment and begins again. (Consider this option only if your message consists of fewer than 50 characters, including spaces, so that the entire message will fit on a 640 × 480 screen at one time.) An example of this mode is depicted in Figure 6.2.

3. Letter-by-letter, until the entire text is on-screen. The script then pauses for a moment and begins again. (As with the second option, this option is effective only if your message is less than 50 characters, including spaces, thus allowing the entire message to be on-screen at once.) An example of this is shown in Figure 6.3.

With each option, the message will continue to replay indefinitely or until your visitor clicks an optional "Stop This Infernal Scrolling, Already!" or similar button or hyperlink. Since all the features of both scrollers are loaded with your page, you can choose the one you prefer to use in a given situation and easily change it later.

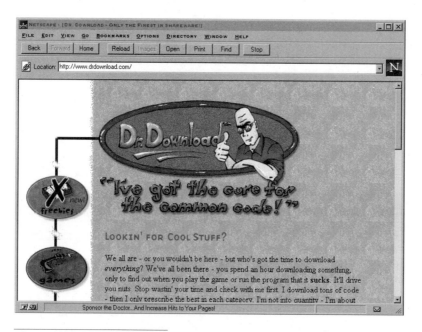

Figure 6.1 *Browser output of the Dr. Download Web site showing scrolling text in status line*

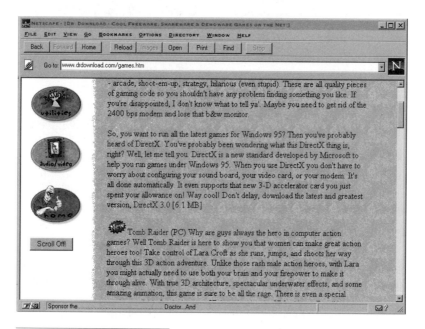

Figure 6.2 *Browser output showing word-by-word scrolling status line*

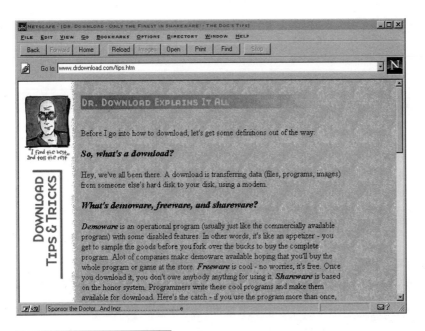

Figure 6.3 *Browser output showing letter-by-letter scrolling status line*

Figures 6.1–6.3 show the three different scrolling methods in use on our Dr. Download shareware site (*http://www.drdownload.com/*). We use the scrolling, in addition to animated GIFs, to help draw attention to new downloads we add to the pages. However, scrolling text is like anything else—if you're not in the mood for it, it can get on your nerves. So we've supplied our visitors with a button they can use to shut off the scrolling.

Figure 6.4 shows the Dr. Download games page with a scrolling message in a form field. Since the form field scrolls with the page, it's easy to place your scrolling message near the copy you want to highlight. The optional STOP button will halt both the status line and form field scrolling methods.

How the *scroller* Script Works

The code enabling the operation of the *scroller* script is very staightforward. Javascript provides a function to define a text string as the message displays on the browser status line. A second function allows the script to insert a string into a form input field. By rapidly writing a slightly different string into the given area, the program creates the illusion of a smoothly scrolling message. A short time delay is needed between each iteration to keep the message from scrolling too quickly on fast computers. The different scrolling styles are created by changing the way the sequence of text strings is calculated.

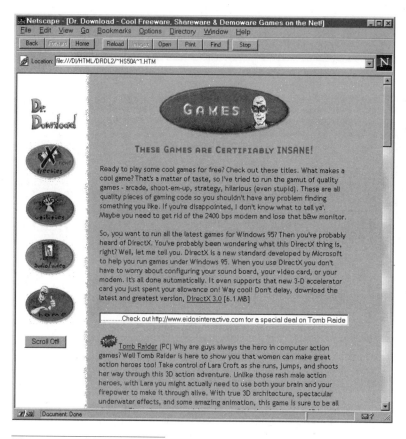

Figure 6.4 *Browser output showing the form field scrolling method*

Configuring and Installing the *scroller* Script

You'll find the *scroll.txt* file in the */scripts/scroll/* subdirectory on the CD-ROM. This file contains the configuration block and Javascript code that create all the scrolling functions presented in this chapter. As with the *hint* script in Chapter 4, "Giving Your Visitor a Hint (or Two) Using Javascript," you will need to paste this code into an HTML file in order to use it.

Step 1: Configuration

On start-up, the *scroller* script reads a configuration block that sets the initial values for the individual scrolling functions defined later in the script. Load *scroll.txt* into your favorite HTML or text editor and find the configuration block. It's located near the top of the file following the copyright information. The values you set in the configuration block shown in Listing 6.1 are valid with both the status line and form field scrolling functions. As with the *hint* script, you start by editing this block.

Listing 6.1   The default *scroller* script configuration block before editing

```
/*
    ****************************************************
    Configuration Block
    ****************************************************
*/
    var spacer =
"..............................................................
.......................";// if you like dots
//  var spacer =
"
                        ";// spaces between words/chars
    var speed = 100; // scrolling speed smaller numbers are faster
/*
    ****************************************************
    End of Configuration Block
    ****************************************************
*/
```

To make your life easier, we wrote the *scroller* script so that you don't have to change the script itself. Instead, you do all the configuration in the configuration block. As with the *hint* script, you call the scroll functions you decide to use later on in the HTML portion of your Web page.

Let's look at each line of the configuration block so that you can better understand exactly what you're doing. Lines 1 through 3:

```
var spacer =
"..............................................................
............................";
```

are the spacer dots that appear before and after the message. This is not actually three lines of code but a single long line wrapped by the editor. *Warning:* Don't hit Enter when editing this line. Javascript will complain if it detects an end-of-line before the closing quotation mark.

These spacer dots create the illusion of a delay between each appearance of the message text and provide a little visual space between the end of one appearance of your message and the start of the next one. The length of this string, and not your message, determines the total length of your scrolling message when using the "all" scrolling method (which scrolls the phrase as a unit). A message of one character will take just as long to make a complete scrolling circuit as one of 60 characters. By contrast, word and character scrolling recycle after all the words or letters in your message have scrolled onto the screen, so shorter messages will repeat more rapidly in these modes.

Lines 4 and 5:

```
//    var spacer =
"                                                                    ":
```

create a blank space before and after the message. The variable `spacer` can have only one value, so this second option is commented out using the `"//"` characters. We describe how to select between options in the customization section later in this chapter.

The last line of the configuration block:

```
var speed = 100; // scrolling speed, smaller numbers are faster
```

defines the speed at which the message scrolls, and this value is theoretically the number of milliseconds, delay between each scrolling movement of the text. However, we've found that the actual scrolling speed varies quite a bit. You'll want to experiment with this number to determine the appropriate speed for your message.

The actual scrolling message text is set within your HTML page as part of the Javascript function call to the main `scroller()` routine of the script.

Hair Saver

You may have noticed that the first three lines of the configuration block, after the comments (where you set the spacer length and type), are actually one line that breaks because of the page width of the book. When you open the script file on the CD-ROM, you'll find that the line is continuous, and it should wrap only to the next line by itself. As mentioned in Chapter 4, "Giving Your Visitor a Hint (or Two) Using Javascript," you should not press Enter when modifying Javascript code. Although doing so generally will not cause a problem, avoiding this is a good habit to get into whenever you modify an existing program. (The Perl scripts later in the book are less picky about unexpected carriage returns.)

Step 2: Installation

Once you've configured the *scrolljs.txt* file to your satisfaction, copy it into your HTML page immediately following a `<HEAD>`, `</TITLE>`, or `</META>` tag, as instructed in Chapter 5.

Using the *scroller* Script in Your Pages

To use the scrolling status line on your page, add the `onLoad` event call to the `<BODY>` tag so that it looks like this:

```
<BODY onLoad="scroller('Your Message Here', 'all');">
```

As mentioned in Chapter 4, "Giving Your Visitor a Hint (or Two) Using Javascript," the Javascript `onLoad` event handler triggers the script to begin as soon as the browser loads the page. Replace the "Your Message Here" banner with your message. The `all` parameter causes the entire message to scroll as a unit. To make the message scroll word by word, replace `all` with `word`. To have the message appear one character at a time, replace `all` with `char`.

To use the scrolling form field on your page, add this code instead (after the script):

```
<BODY onLoad="scroller('Your Message Here', 'all',
document.formname.scrollfield);">
```

where `formname` is the name of the form specified with a `NAME="xxx"` parameter in the `<FORM>` tag, and `scrollfield` is the name of an `<INPUT TYPE="TEXT">` field within the form. As with the status line scroller, `all` may be replaced with `word` or `char`.

To add a stop scrolling button to your page, add this code after the script:

```
<FORM><INPUT TYPE="BUTTON" VALUE = "Stop Scrolling"
   onClick="scrolloff();"></FORM>
```

When the button is clicked, Javascript will execute the `scrolloff()` function, thereby stopping the message in its tracks. A non-Javascript browser will render an `<INPUT TYPE="BUTTON">` field as a normal text input field (since the browser doesn't understand the `TYPE="BUTTON"` parameter). To say the least, this will confuse your visitors. To avoid this confusion, you can use Javascript's ability to write HTML into the document to "create" the form by using a mini-script. Most non-Javascript browsers ignore the `<SCRIPT>` and `</SCRIPT>` tags, since they don't support them, but we have seen some browsers try to interpret the Javascript as HTML. Browsers that do support Javascript, on the other hand, will execute the mini-script as the page is loaded. The mini-script is given in Listing 6.2.

Listing 6.2   **Mini-script to create a stop scrolling button for the *scroller* script**

```
<SCRIPT LANGUAGE="JavaScript">
<!--
document.write("<FORM NAME=\"stop\"><INPUT TYPE=\"BUTTON\" VALUE=\"Scroll Off!\"
onClick=\"scrolloff();\"></FORM>");
//-->
</SCRIPT>
```

The `document.write` method (*method* is Javascript lingo for a function) writes the text contained in its single parameter into the HTML document at the point where the script appears. In this case, it creates a form with a single field consisting of a button that calls the `scrolloff()` function when clicked. Notice how we hide the Javascript code from non-Javascript browsers by putting it inside an HTML comment. This prevents those browsers from rendering the Javascript code as text in the browser window. What finally ends up in the HTML is

```
<FORM NAME="stop">
   <INPUT TYPE="BUTTON" VALUE="Scroll Off!" onClick="scrolloff();">
   </FORM>
```

You can also add a hyperlink that accomplishes the same thing using this bit of code:

```
<A NAME="here" HREF="#here" onClick="scrolloff();">Stop Scrolling!</A>
```

Unfortunately, *Internet Explorer* 3.01 doesn't support the `onClick=` event from a hypertext link. And while non-Javascript browsers will display this hyperlink, nothing will happen if the user clicks it, since it links to itself. To create a control that works on both *Internet Explorer* and *Netscape,* you should use the previous mini-script technique to create a hyperlink as follows:

```
SCRIPT LANGUAGE="JavaScript">
<!--
document.write("<A HREF=\"Javascript:scrolloff();\">Stop
Scrolling!</A>");
//-->
</SCRIPT>
```

This hyperlink won't appear at all on non-Javascript browsers, since it is generated by a Javascript program. It uses the `Javascript:` command in the `HREF=` parameter rather than linking to a location. This method works on all browsers. Its only downside is a slightly more complex page design.

Change the `Stop Scrolling!` text to suit your specific requirements. (Unfortunately, since we're using the Javascript `onLoad` event to start the scrolling, there is no way to prevent the *scroller* script from restarting if the user reloads or resizes the page.)

To change the interval between message repeats, simply add or delete an appropriate number of dots from the `spacer` variable. If you want to use blank spaces rather than dots to stagger the repeats, comment out the dot `var spacer` (add `//` at the front of the line) and uncomment the blank `var spacer` (remove the `//`). Add to the blank spaces using the spacebar, if desired. You can also use other characters, in the spacer such as brackets `<><><><>` or `_-^-_-^`. To use a different character string, just replace one of the two we've provided. (Another option is to create a third character string, following the format we've given, and comment out the other two using the `//` characters.)

To make the text scroll more slowly, increase the value of the `speed` variable. We've found that a value of 100 works well with most messages, but you should experiment based on the length and content of the message you want to convey.

This should get you up and running with the *scroller* script. The basic *hint* script has been appended to *scrolljs.htm* to show you how they work together. To use the full *hint* script, just copy it into the HTML along with the *scroller* script. Both can reside in the same page without problems. If necessary, refer to Chapter 4, "Giving Your Visitor a Hint (or Two) Using Javascript" to see how to call a *hint* from within your page.

What We Covered in Chapter 6

- How to use Javascript to present a scrolling text banner in the browser window status line or in a form input field
- A scrolling text function that offers character-by-character, word-by-word, or complete phrase scrolling options
- How to modify the configuration block to select the message spacer characters and to set the scrolling speed
- How to modify the HTML tags on your page to call one of the scroll functions

Chapter 7
Automating Graphics Changes on Your Web Site with Perl

Features of the *pid.cgi* Script

- Displays different images on a Web page using three different types of image selection rules: random, time-based, and random+time-based.
- All image URLs and selection rules are stored in a simple text control file. Almost no editing of the script is required.
- Multiple images, locations, and selection rules can be contained in one control file.
- Multiple control files are allowed.

What You Need to Use This Script

- Perl version 4 or 5 on your ISP or SA's Web server
- Authorization to execute CGI or SSI scripts from your Web directory *or* to have the script installed in a central script directory on your ISP or SA's Web server
- FTP and Telnet clients
- Text editor

Why You Would Want to Use This Script

Throughout your organization, change is a fact of life. New products or services are introduced, press releases are distributed, and marketing managers come up with the "killer" ad campaign (of the week). Naturally, the Web site has to feature the new data or sport the new look asap.

Adding to these pressures, the Internet itself is a dynamic environment. Denizens of the Web have a low tolerance for old news and a still lower tolerance for stale Web sites. (You hardly need reminding that a site is considered stale when it hasn't been updated in a month.) Keeping your site content up to date is the Webmaster's supreme challenge.

We can't offer a solution for handling this onslaught of new information, but we do have a little gem that can make it easier for you to change the graphics on your Web site—the *pid.cgi* script.

Wouldn't it be nice if you could automatically place new images on your pages, change the background of every page on the site, and cycle new icons onto the site and then return them to the standard graphical bullets? And all without forcing you to edit a bunch of HTML files. The *pid.cgi* script we present in this chapter does all that, and more.

Introduction to the *pid.cgi* Script

The HTML specification does more than allow scripts to generate forms, query databases, and return text or HTML code. It also allows CGI scripts to return images for display by the browser. By specifying a CGI script in the SRC= parameter of the <IMG> tag, you can cause a CGI script to execute and return to the browser an image instead of text. You can do this in two ways. We've already used the first—Server-Side Includes—in the *vcount.cgi* script presented in Chapter 5 "Counting Visitors to Your Web Site with Perl." SSI scripts can insert the HTML reference to an image into the page as the page is sent to the browser. The browser then requests the image from the server just as if you'd entered the tag in the HTML yourself.

The second way is to "print" the binary image data to the Web server from the script. Recall that in Chapter 2 you learned how the CGI script tells the browser what's coming next with the Content-Type: text/html or Content-Type: text/plain HTTP header. Instead of a content header that specifies plain or HTML text, you can send a header that specifies an image. Two of the most common headers that do this are image/gif and image/jpeg. After you send the HTTP header specifying that an image is coming, you simply read the data from a disk file and "print" it to the server. The Web server passes the image data directly to the browser for display.

Nerd Note

There are actually three ways to use CGI to send an image to the browser. Along with the two mentioned in the text—allowing a CGI script to specify an image file for display via SSI and send the binary data, it is possible to "point" the server to another URL to fetch the image. This is called *server redirection*. It uses a `Location: URL` HTTP header to specify the URL of the image to fetch. It can be used to redirect the server to any object that has a URL, not just to an image. We considered using this method with the *pid.cgi* script because it is very simple to implement and can specify images anywhere on the Internet. However, it won't work because browsers first attempt to retrieve images from their internal cache, rather than fetch data from the server. If we had used server redirection with *pid.cgi*, you would always see the same image because as long as the browser would retrieve it from the cache rather than let the script pick a different one.

The *pid.cgi* script lets you display different images on your Web pages without having to modify the HTML. It has three modes of operation:

1. You specify a list of image files, and the script will choose one at random from the list.

2. The script picks an image based on the current date and time.

3. The script combines the first two modes and randomly picks an image from a list of those that have valid times/dates.

These options allow great flexibility in programming the script to display various images based on your needs.

How *pid.cig* Works

The script reads a control file that contains one or more named lists of images called *groups*. Each group contains a list of images and the rule the script will use when choosing between the images. We designed the *pid.cgi* script so that you don't have to edit the script itself. All modification takes place in a control file you create with your text editor.

Here are the three picking rules for images:

1. `random`. The script chooses one image at random from the group.

2. `timed`. You specify a starting and ending time and date range for each image in the list. The script scans the list from top to bottom and displays the first image whose current day and time corresponds to the appropriate starting and ending day and times. An alternative to specifying a full date and time is to simply specify a starting and ending hour and minute. These time-only ranges apply to every day. Figure 7.1 shows our Dr. Download Web site with the Doc sporting head gear appropriate to the season (*http:// www.drdownload.com*). The image displayed on the site is determined by the *pid.cgi* script.

3. `randomtimed`. The script combines the `random` and `timed` rules to randomly pick an image from all the images that have valid time/dates or time-only ranges.

Through the magic of advanced computer science, the script automatically figures out whether you are doing an SSI or a CGI call and returns the proper output. What

Figure 7.1 *The commercial Dr. Download Web site showing the* pid.cgi *script in action*

is returned is either HTML code with an `<IMG SRC="picked-img.gif">` tag (for SSI) or an HTTP header for the image followed by the binary image data (for CGI).

Nerd Note

> Although it may look like magic, the script actually reads a special set of variables called **environment variables** that are set by the Web server. These are used to pass data items about the Web server and the browser to the CGI script, including the method used to invoke the script.

Configuring and Installing *pid.cgi*

Configuration of the *pid.cgi* script is simplicity itself. If your ISP/SA has already installed this script in a central location, then you are done! All you have to do is create the control file and modify your HTML pages to call the script. Otherwise, you will have to configure the script to work on your Web server.

Step 1: Configuration

To configure the *pid.cgi* script, which is in the */scripts/pid/* subdirectory on the CD-ROM, load it into your favorite text editor. Since *pid.cgi* is a Perl script, the first line of the script will look like this:

```
#!/usr/bin/perl
```

This code tells the server to run this script using the Perl interpreter found in the */usr/bin* directory. Change this line to match the location of the Perl interpreter on your server. Check your ISP/SA questionnaire if you haven't yet memorized its location (or tattooed it on your arm or other easily accessible body part). Save the edited script to a convenient location for upload to the Web server.

As we've mentioned, most of the customizing of *pid.cgi* takes place in the control file. To use the script, you need to create a control file that has at least one group. The name of the file is not critical, but you may want to call it something that makes sense, such as *pid.cnf*.

Listing 7.1 presents a sample control file.

Listing 7.1   **An example *pid.cgi* control file**

```
##############################################################
# sample control file for the pid.cgi script
# blank lines and everything following a # are ignored
# the first line in each list of images is a group identifier
group header # we can also have comments in lines with data
random # next is the rule for picking the image
# in this case one of the following images will be picked at random
/~joeuser/images/header1.gif
/~joeuser/images/header2.gif
/~joeuser/images/header3.gif

group seasons # might be for backgrounds
timed
/~joeuser/images/bkgnds/winter.gif 0000/11/22/95 2359/2/22/96
/~joeuser/images/bkgnds/spring.gif 0000/2/23/96 0000/5/22/96
/~joeuser/images/summer.gif 1800/5/23/96 2300/8/21/96
/~joeuser/images/bkgnds/autum.gif 0000/8/22/96 2350/11/21/96
# if none of the others matches this will
/~joeuser/alt/images/backgnds/default.gif 0000 2359 # every day
```

From the control file, you can see that the file contains three different types of lines (four if you count comments):

1. The group names

2. The image picking rule

3. The image file locations.

The first non-comment line must begin with the word "group" followed by a name. The names are case sensitive. We always use all lowercase for these types of names in our scripts, but you can use uppercase and lowercase, as your karma directs you.

The next line contains the image picking rule. The picking rule must be one of the three valid types: random, timed, or randomtimed. The rule type can be in uppercase or lowercase in the control file. The script will choose from the images listed in the following lines up to either the end of the file or the start of the next group. Enter the path and filename for each image in the list of choices for this group. You can enter as many images here as you like, one per line. Be sure the path to the image is an absolute path from the Web server document root (see the next Hot Tip). For example, say your home page URL is *http://www.isp.com/~juser/* and your images are stored in a subdirectory called *images*. In the *pid.cgi* control file, the path to your image files will be */~juser/images/xxx.gif* (note the leading /).

Hair Saver

Be sure to use the \ character to separate directories on Windows and Windows NT servers. Sometimes the Web server will translate / characters in URLs, so you may be able to get away with / in your HTML pages. CGI scripts are not as forgiving. Just another hardship you have to put up with in the rugged world of CGI programming.

Hot Tip

To find the absolute path to your Web page, subtract from the page's URL everything up to and including the name of the Web server. For example,

```
http://www.isp.com/~juser/news/new.html
```

becomes

```
/~juser/news/new.html
```

Use this method to figure out the absolute path to your image files. They might be something like

```
/~juser/images/header.gif
```

If you are using the `timed` or `randomtimed` rule, you also will need to enter a range of times, and possibly dates, when the image is valid. If you want the image to be valid every day, just include a start and end time in military format (e.g., 0400 and 1832). If you want the image to be valid between a specific set of dates, then append the starting and ending date to the time in standard dd/mm/yy format. Use numbers for the day and month. Use only two digits for the year, for example, 97.

Hair Saver

Don't put quotation marks around any part of the group name line. Just put the word *group* followed by one space and then the name. Uppercase and lowercase are ignored for the word *group* but are significant in the name. So "group Main" and "group main" are two different groups, but "group main" and "Group main" are the same. To be safe, just use lowercase. It'll save some hair. The script stops searching when it finds the first group name that matches the name specified in the HTML. So if you have duplicate group name lines, the script will never see the second one.

> If you aren't seeing the changes you're making to your control file in the final output, make sure you don't have duplicate group names.
>
> Also be sure you put the correct group rule in your file on a line directly following the group name. It must be exactly `random`, `timed`, or `randomtimed`. Versions such as `rand`, `randomized`, `time`, `randomtime`, or `rtimed` won't work. However, case is ignored for the picking rule, so `Random`, `RANDOM`, and `random` are all OK.

We usually create a group for each set of images we want to display. You might have a group for header or background images chosen randomly (`random`), a group for your vacation slides (to keep visitors coming back, you show only one each week) chosen by date (`timed`), and a group containing seasonal hometown pictures chosen randomly from those that match the appropriate season and hour (`randomtimed`). For testing purposes, you should have at least one `random` group with a few images on hand. Once you've created your control file, save it and prepare to upload!

Finally, you need at least one blank line between groups. You can have as many groups as you like in a control file, and you can create multiple control files. The *pid.cgi* script is very accommodating.

Step 2: Installation

Installation of the *pid.cgi* script is very straightforward. If you've already installed the scripts presented in previous chapters, then you know the drill. Those who like to skip chapters should read Chapter 3 before proceeding, if you haven't already done so.

Using your FTP client in ASCII mode, upload the edited version of the *pid.cgi* script file to the Web server and place the control file in the same directory. Then use your FTP or Telnet client to change the file permissions.

To run a quick test of the script, enter the following line in your Telnet client:

```
./pid.cgi pid.cnf groupname
```

where `pid.cnf` and `groupname` correspond, respectively, to the name of your control file and one of the groups it contains. Provided you didn't choose a `timed` group, in which no images are valid, you should see something like the following output from the script:

```
<IMG SRC= "/~juser/images/header1.gif">
```

This shows that the script is working. It read the control file correctly and picked an image.

If you chose a `random` group, you can execute the script repeatedly. You should get a random selection of the images from the group.

If you have a `timed` group, check to see that the correct image is being returned. If it's not, you probably made a mistake in the format of your dates and times for the files.

That's it. Installation is complete.

Using the *pid.cgi* Script in Your Pages

To illustrate some of the ways *pid.cgi* can be used, here are a couple of example applications. We're confident you will devise many other uses for a versatile script like this.

Example 1: Roll Them Bones

In this example, we create a simple HTML page to display the images of two dice. You'll get a different roll each time you load the page. Listing 7.2 shows the content of the control file.

Listing 7.2	*pid.cgi* control file for dice-rolling example

```
# Roll them bones
group dice
random
/~juser/images/dice/one.gif
/~juser/images/dice/two.gif
/~juser/images/dice/three.gif
/~juser/images/dice/four.gif
/~juser/images/dice/five.gif
/~juser/images/dice/six.gif
```

As you can see, the control file has only one group, which lists six images stored in the *dice* subdirectory under juser's main *images* directory. Listing 7.3 shows an HTML file called *dice.html,* which calls the *pid.cgi* script to display a random pair of dice images. Clicking the link below the images reloads the page and generates a new set of dice images.

Listing 7.3   **HTML for dice-rolling example**

```
<HTML>
<HEAD>
<META HTTP-EQUIV="Pragma" CONTENT="no-cache">
<TITLE>Roll them bones: an example of the pid.cgi script</TITLE>
</HEAD>
<BODY BGCOLOR="#FFFFFF">
<H1>Roll Em!</H1>
<!--#exec cmd="cgi/pid.cgi cgi/pid.cnf dice" -->
<!--#exec cmd="cgi/pid.cgi cgi/pid.cnf dice" -->
<P><A HREF=dice.html>Baby needs a new pair of shoes!</A>
</BODY></HTML>
```

Included in this example is an HTML command you might not have used before: the HTML *META* command. This command is used for various special purposes. In this case, `HTTP-EQUIV` tells the server to add a line to the HTTP header for this file. The command, `Pragma:no-cache` tells the browser not to cache this page. Without this line the browser would simply fetch the page from cache and you'd get the same results over and over. Not very exciting.

Figure 7.2 shows a screen capture of *dice.html* loaded in the browser. If you want to try this example for yourself, the control and HTML files are located on the CD-ROM in the */scripts/pid/examples/dice/* directory.

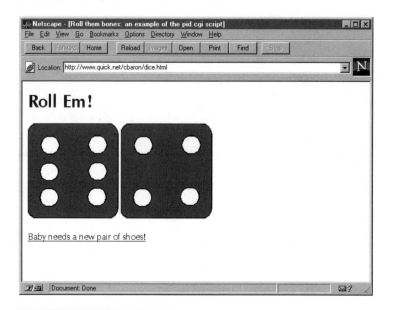

Figure 7.2 *Browser output of the dice-rolling example*

Example 2: A Timely Greeting

In the next example, we create a script that greets the visitor to a Web page with an appropriate message based on the time of day (local to the Web server). We also give a couple of special greetings for holidays. Listing 7.4 shows the *pid.cnf* file for the greeting example.

Listing 7.4	*pid.cnf* control file for the greeting example

```
# Greetings based on time of day and date
group holiday
timed
# a couple of holidays
/~juser/images/xmas.gif 0000/12/20/96 2359/12/25/96
/~juser/images/cinco.gif 0000/05/01/96 2359/05/05/96 # Cinco de Mayo
/~juser/images/nix.gif 0000 2359 # the default if nothing matches
group greet
timed
# these work every day
/~juser/images/morn.gif 0500 1200
/~juser/images/afternoo.gif 1201 1700
/~juser/images/evening.gif 1701 2200
/~juser/images/night.gif 2201 2359
# we have to add this because the script doesn't work across midnight
/~juser/images/night.gif 0000 0459
```

Looking at this control file, you can see a couple of differences from Example 1. This file has two groups, "holidays" and "greet". Both are of type `timed`, which means the script will scan the list of images and compare the time range beside each image entry against the local time on the Web server. When the script finds a time range that is acceptable and there is no date range specified, it stops searching and returns the image. If a date range is specified, it also is checked. The script continues until it either finds a valid date/time or reaches the end of the group. In "greet," we don't specify any date ranges, so the script knows these images are to be used on a daily basis. "holiday" entries are valid only for a range of days around a specific date. Since a full day/month/year date is required, you can't, for example, set the script to execute every Christmas; you need to add an entry for each specific year. (The would-be nerds among you will be so bothered by this that you'll learn to program Perl just to add this feature, thereby launching grand and glorious careers as master programmers. Just a little extra service we provide at no additional charge.)

Hot Tip

You can mix time-only specifications and date/time specifications in the same group. Additionally, you can ensure the script always returns an image by adding a line like this:

```
/~juser/images/default.gif 0000 2359 # always
```

This time specification will always be valid, so you'll never get the broken image icon if, for example, you forget to update your celebrity_birthdays group to the new year. Be sure to put this line last, unless you don't really want to see the other images.

Listing 7.5 shows the HTML file for the greeting example.

Listing 7.5	HTML for the greeting example

```
<HTML>
<HEAD>
<META HTTP-EQUIV="Pragma" CONTENT="no-cache">
<!-- refresh this page each hour -->
<META HTTP-EQUIV="Refresh" CONTENT=3600>
<TITLE>Greetings: An example of timed groups using pid.cgi</TITLE>
</HEAD>
<BODY BGCOLOR="#FFFFFF">
<CENTER><H1>GOOD</H1>
<IMG SRC="cgi/pid.cgi?cfile=/home/user/juser/public_html/cgi/
pid.cnf&group=greet">
</CENTER>
<P> You need to get out and buy presents for:<BR>
<IMG SRC="cgi/pid.cgi?cfile=/home/user/juser/public_html/cgi/
pid.cnf&group=holiday">
</BODY></HTML>
```

Those of you with sharp eyes will already have noticed a new <META> tag in this example. The Refresh header line causes the browser to automatically re-request the page from the server once every *x* number of seconds, as specified in the Content part of the tag, in our example, every 3,600 seconds, or once per hour. At the time of this writing, more than 90 percent of browsers support this feature, so we include it in the example. Figure 7.3 shows what the output might look like on any given day.

Figure 7.4 shows a more visually appleaing use of the script, determining the dialogue graphic to be used by time of day.

Figure 7.3 *Browser output of the timed greeting example*

Hair Saver

When testing and using this script, you may have problems with your browser caching the image even though we put `Pragma: no-cache` in the script and in the HTML. Microsoft *Internet Explorer* 3.01 is especially stubborn in this area. Alternatives to prevent this include using the SSI method, turning off image caching in the browser, setting the "verify document" setting to "every time" or "always," manually flushing your image cache, or quitting and restarting your browser. If the script runs correctly from the command line, it will almost certainly work when called by the Web server, if you can get the browser to cooperate. The SSI method of invocation doesn't suffer from this problem as much because reloading the page fetches the HTML again, thus causing the server to re-execute the SSI commands.

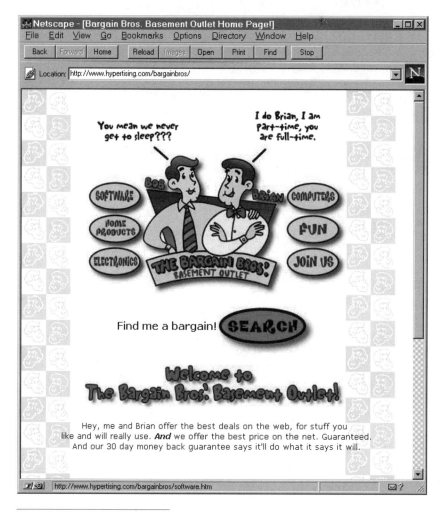

Figure 7.4 *Browser output of an after-hours character dialog image, using* pid.cgi

This completes the installation and configuration of the *pid.cgi* script. In the next chapter, we present some additional applications for this script.

What We Covered in Chapter 7

- An introduction to dynamic Web page creation
- Use of random, time-based, and random and time-based display criteria for updating images on Web pages
- How to choose an image to display
- Some functions of the <META> HTML tag

Chapter 8

Remote Controls for All Occasions Using Javascript

Features of the *remote* Script

- Opens a remote (separate) window above the browser window.
- The remote may be summoned when the page loads or when the visitor clicks a hyperlink.
- The remote may contain a combination of images and HTML text.
- The remote can include text, image, or button links to other pages.
- The remote can be configured to automatically catalogue all the internal links within a page "on the fly" and display them as text links.

What You Need to Use This Script

- HTML or text editor
- Netscape version 2.02 or greater or Microsoft Internet Explorer version 3.0 or greater (to test scripts locally)

This is the most complex and sophisticated Javascript script we've presented so far. The concepts on which it is based aren't any harder to understand; there's just a few more of them. As in the previous chapters, careful modification of the script configuration block and conscientious testing will ensure success.

Before proceeding, we recommend that you locate the *remote.htm* file, found in the */scripts/js/remote* directory on the CD-ROM, and view it in your browser to familiarize yourself with the range of functions we built into the *remote* script.

Why You Would Want to Use This Script

Remote windows look really cool, and they are still comparatively uncommon on the Internet. Creating remote windows can enhance your Web site, as you will see shortly.

On larger Web sites, it's easy to crowd out content with too many navigational options. On a recent project, we made extensive use of frames to provide the visitor with easy ways to move vertically and laterally through the Web site. It looked great, but in so doing we reduced the area available to the content by a good 35 percent. Giving the visitor the option to forgo the frames would have required us to create two versions of each page. From both a budgetary and maintenance standpoint, this was not an attractive option. On the other hand, it would be very easy to create a floating remote window that has navigation links. The visitor could then summon or dismiss this window at will.

Like hints and scrolling, remotes are something you want to use sparingly. Specifically, remotes can be used to do the following:

- Present the visitor with a graphic or hypertext-based map of your site.
- Display a number of internal hyperlinks for the current page (particularly to denote subheads in long pages that cannot be broken up into many smaller pages, such as legal documents or research papers).
- Offer your visitor graphic or text hyperlinks to areas of interest related to the page they are viewing, either on your site or elsewhere.
- Display commonly used links in a window at all times, such as a link to your home page, site map, or search engine.

You can probably come up with a dozen other applications for this little device. We've even seen remotes serve a purely decorative function. On one site, the remote contains a *.wav* file that plays continuously as the visitor peruses the pages. On another, an artist features a different thumbnail from her portfolio on individual remotes that load with every page. When the browser is closed, the litter of windows created by her site remains. The resulting on-screen "art gallery" makes quite an impression.

Introduction to the *remote* Script

One of the most useful things about Javascript is its ability to create new browser windows and specify the contents of those windows, either by loading an HTML file or by generating the HTML programmatically. This feature, as well as the HTML language extensions that allow a click on a hyperlink in one window to affect a document loaded into another window, gives you the tools to create useful remote control browser windows.

How the *remote* Script Works

The *remote* script offers a choice of three different remote styles suited to different uses within your Web site.

1. HTML-type

2. Button-bar

3. Anchor-type

The examples shown in this chapter are contained in a file called *remote.htm* located in the */scripts/remote/* directory on the CD-ROM. You can load this file into your browser and try out the different types of remotes as we describe them here.

The most common type of remote you'll see on the Internet consists of a mini-browser window with a client-side imagemap that permits control of the contents of the main browser window. We call this an **HTML-type remote.** Figure 8.1 shows an example in action on one of our client Web sites. This type of remote gives you maximum flexibility because you can put anything in the remote window that you can put in a regular HTML page. This includes text, imagemaps, video clips, sound files—just about anything.

The **button-bar remote** is simpler. It displays a vertical row of buttons with labels you define (see Figure 8.2). Clicking one of these buttons causes the main browser window to load a different page.

Nerd Note

You may have already figured out that we're using onClick= Javascript events with these buttons. We combine these with a location method (function) that allows a Javascript to set the URL of the browser window to create the desired effect.

Figure 8.1 *Browser view of the HTML-type remote on the Mission Hospital Web site*

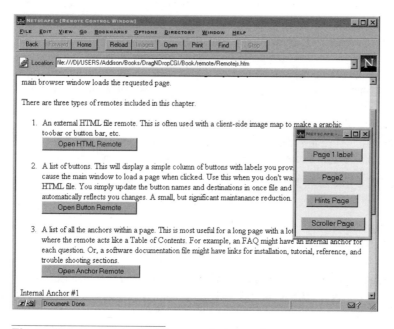

Figure 8.2 *Browser output showing the button-bar remote*

The button-bar remote doesn't require you to create and maintain a separate HTML document just for your remote. Instead, you specify a list of the button labels and URLs within your main HTML file. The *remote* script then takes care of creating the HTML for the remote window for you. The major drawback to the button-bar remote is its rather utilitarian appearance.

The third type of remote is the anchor type. It is most useful for long documents that have many internal hyperlink anchors. Examples of this type of document are software documentation files, HTML files automatically created from word-processor documents, and frequently-asked-question lists. The script automatically creates a remote with a textual list of all the internal anchors in your document (see Figure 8.3). Due to limitations in the Javascript language, you must use a fairly rigid naming convention for your internal anchors. Clicking a link in the remote causes the main browser window to jump to the specified internal anchor location. You can think of this type of remote as an automatic table-of-contents generator.

One limitation of our *remote* script (we prefer to call it a feature) is that only one remote window can be open at a time. If a user attempts to open a second remote, the new remote will replace the existing one. If you find this feature disappointing, check the book's Web site from time to time. We just may have had enough requests for multiple remote windows to add that function to the script. With some medium-level Javascript programming, you can modify the script yourself to open multiple remote windows.

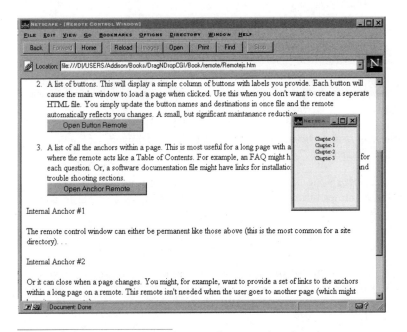

Figure 8.3 *Browser output showing the internal anchor-type remote*

Configuring and Installing the *remote* Script

Step 1: Configuration

To start the configuration process, fire up your HTML or text editor and load the
remote.txt file from the */scripts/remote/* directory on the CD-ROM. Like the other
Javascripts we've presented, the file contains only the script itself and not a complete
HTML file. The configuration block for the *remote* script is shown in Listing 8.1,
with some default values for the variables.

Listing 8.1	The *remote* script configuration block before editing

```
/*

   ***************************************************
   Configuration Block
   ***************************************************
*/
   remotebg = "#FFFF80";           // window bkgnd color, balloon help yellow
   rwintitle = "Remote";           // remote window title
   asize = "3";            // size of text for links on anchor-remote
   aprefix = "Chapter";            // each anchor must be of the
               // form aprefix-# where # is a number
               // starting from 0 for the first anchor
/*
   ***************************************************
   End of Configuration Block
   ***************************************************
*/
```

As with our other Javascripts, the configuration block is located near the top of the
script (following the copyright information). The definition and usage of each variable is fairly straightforward:

- remotebg. Controls the background color for the remote window. Use hex
  values or color names here just as you would in the BGCOLOR= parameter of
  an HTML <BODY> tag.

- rwintitle. Controls the value inserted by the script into the <TITLE> section of the remote window HTML.

- asize. Controls the size of the link text that appears in an anchor-style
  remote window. Specify this like you would in a <FONT> tag, since that's
  where it goes in the remote window HTML.

- `aprefix`. We cover this variable in detail later in the chapter, but for now, be aware that each internal anchor must follow a certain format. This variable forms the first part of the anchor name for each of the internal anchors in your document. The complete anchor name also includes a "-" and the anchor's ordinal number counting from the top of the file.

Step 2: Installation

Installing the *remote* script involves only setting these variables and pasting the modified script into your HTML file.

Using the *remote* Script in Your Pages

In this section, we cover how to create each type of remote and how to invoke the powers of the *remote* script to call them into being. Before you start, you should give some thought to what type of remote you want, what you want in it, when you want it to appear, and how long you want it to remain open. As with most enterprises, a little advance planning can make the journey a lot smoother.

The *remote* script's elegant simplicity means there are only two functions you call to access its features: `openRemote()` and `checkSticky()`. `openRemote()` creates each remote window according to the parameters you supply. `checkSticky()` is used to close the remote window if you want it to disappear when a different page is loaded in the main browser window. In the following discussion, you will probably find it helpful to load the *remote.htm* demonstration file so that you can see how we implement the different types of remote.

The calling format of the `openRemote()` function is as follows:

```
openRemote('type', sticky, 'window options' [,URL or button label,
button URL, ...]);
```

The parameters are as follows:

- `type`. The type of remote to open. Must be either `html`, `button`, or `anchor`. Be sure to use single quotation marks around the type as shown here. This parameter is case insensitive, so, for example, both `'html'` and `'HtMl'` will work.

- `sticky`. Set to 1 if the window should stay open after the page changes in the main window; set to 0 (zero) if the remote should close when the main window changes.

- `window options`. Contains the options you can specify for the appearance of the remote window. Remember, remotes are actually identical to a full browser window with most of the menus and buttons turned off. In some cases, you might want to have one or more of the usual browser window features available. Keep in mind that Javascript is very picky about the format of this option string. You must follow the format shown in the example file, or Javascript will ignore some or all of your settings. The parameters can appear in any order, but they must be separated by commas and the entire parameter string *cannot contain any spaces*.

  These are the available options:

  - width, height. The size in pixels of the new window
  - toolbar. Set to 1 (yes) to display the button bar; set to 0 (no) otherwise.
  - location. Set to 1 to show the location field; set to 0 otherwise.
  - directories. Set to 1 to show the directory buttons; set to 0 otherwise.
  - status. Set to 1 to show the status line at the bottom of the window; set to 0 otherwise.
  - menubar. Set to 1 to show the menus at the top of the window; set to 0 otherwise.
  - scrollbars. Set to 1 to put scroll bars on the window if needed; set to 0 otherwise.
  - resizable. Set to 1 to make this window resizable by dragging the window frame; set to 0 otherwise.

  The `window options` is the last parameter to appear when calling an anchor-type remote.

- `URL`. Present only for the HTML-type remote. It contains the URL of the external HTML file to load into the remote window. This file will probably be somewhere within your Web site, but it also can be a full external URL.

- `button` parameters. Used only for the button-bar remote. You add two additional parameters for each button: the button label, and the URL that the button will load into the main window. This URL can be relative within your Web site or a full URL for an external site. Use the same format you would for a text or graphic hyperlink on your main HTML page.

Hair Saver

Javascript is very particular about the format of the `window options parameter`. If your remote window doesn't look the way you wanted it to, double-check this parameter for spaces or missing equals signs. We lost a few hairs over this one, until we learned this rule.

As if that wasn't bad enough, some versions of *Netscape* require that you include *all* of these parameters and explicitly set them to 1 or 0. *Netscape* 3.x doesn't require this. Nor does *Internet Explorer* 3.0.

There is also a minimum size at which the window will be created. Different browsers have different minimum sizes, so if you need a very small remote you should test with a variety of browsers to see if the window will respond to your wishes. The window will always open; it just might be larger than you want.

Hot Tip

You can load any URL you like into your remote; for example, a sound file or video clip. Or you could load an FTP directory from which the user can select files to download.

Since there is nothing quite like seeing real-live code to understand how this all fits together, here is an example of the `openRemote()` function call in use:

```
<INPUT TYPE="BUTTON" VALUE="Open HTML Remote"
   onClick="openRemote('HTML', 1, 'width=120,height=150,scrollbars=0,resizable=0',
   'ctrl.html');">
```

In this example, we're opening an HTML-type remote with a plain window. The file *ctrl.html* is loaded into the window. The `sticky` parameter is set to 1, so the window will remain open until closed by the user. Listing 8.2 shows the HTML for the control file.

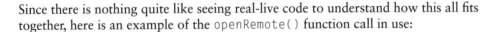

Listing 8.2	Example HTML file for the HTML-type remote

```
<HTML><HEAD>
   <TITLE>Control Window</TITLE>
</HEAD><BODY BGCOLOR="White">
<IMG SRC="buttonbar.gif" WIDTH=99 HEIGHT=112 BORDER=0 ALT="" USEMAP="#ButtonBar" ISMAP>
   <MAP NAME="ButtonBar" TARGET="opener">
```

```
    <AREA SHAPE=RECT COORDS="5,4,95,29" HREF=page1.html TARGET="creator">
    <AREA SHAPE=RECT COORDS="3,30,98,53" HREF=page2.html TARGET="creator">
    <AREA SHAPE=RECT COORDS="2,58,100,81" HREF=hints.html TARGET= "creator">
    <AREA SHAPE=RECT COORDS="2,84,103,109" HREF=scroller.html TARGET="creator">
</MAP>
</BODY></HTML>
```

As you can see, the file consists of a single image with a client-side image map. When you open a remote from a browser window, the *remote* script creates a special Javascript property for the new window called `creator`. This is a reference back to the window that created the remote. Specifying `TARGET="creator"` in a remote hyperlink causes the hyperlink to affect the parent window instead of the remote. You can use the `TARGET=` parameter on both graphical and text hyperlinks along with client-side image maps as we've done here:

```
<A NAME="here" HREF="#here" onClick="openRemote('HTML', 1,
'width=120,height=150,scrollbars=0,resizable=0', 'ctrl.html');">text link</A>
```

This example uses a text hyperlink to open the same HTML-type remote window. `NAME=` and `HREF=` refer to the same location because the `onClick` function doesn't prevent the browser from jumping to the hyperlink destination. In this case, the destination is the same as the hyperlink location, so the browser view doesn't change. Non-Javascript browsers will ignore the `onClick` parameter and hence won't have a problem with this method.

Unfortunately, the `onClick` function doesn't work with *Internet Explorer* 3.01 for text and graphics hyperlinks. An alternative workaround is to use the tag-hiding technique we showed you in Chapter 6, "Fun with Scrolling Text Using Javascript," to hide the stop scrolling button from non-Javascript browsers. Using this technique, our text hyperlink looks like this:

```
<SCRIPT LANGUAGE="JavaScript">
<!--
document.write("<A  HREF=\"Javascript:openRemote('HTML', 1,
'width=120,height=150,scrollbars=0,resizable=0', 'ctrl.html');\">this one does</A>");
//-->
</SCRIPT>
```

The hyperlink HTML text is written only to Javascript browsers. All others will ignore the `<SCRIPT>` and `</SCRIPT>` tags and the Javascript code within the HTML comment block. Notice that we changed from a normal `HREF` destination to a `"Javascript:openRemote(...)"` destination. Instead of loading a new page or moving to a new location in the current page, the `HREF"Javascript=` destination executes some Javascript code.

```
<INPUT TYPE="BUTTON" VALUE="Open Anchor Remote"
    onClick="openRemote('anchor', 0,
    'width=120,height=150,scrollbars=0,resizable=0,menubar=0');">
```

Here we open an anchor-type remote. This remote has the `sticky` parameter set to 0, so it will close when a different page loads in the main browser window. Observe the format of the internal anchors in the *remote.htm* file. The names are formed from the `aprefix` variable we specified in the configuration block, a dash - character, and a number starting from 0. These anchors aren't actually read by the script. Rather, the script "assumes" that the anchors will be in this format and creates a set of links to them in the remote window. If your anchor naming doesn't follow this exact format, the remote links won't work with your page. Unfortunately, we had to do it this way to work around a limitation in Javascript.

```
<INPUT TYPE="BUTTON" VALUE="Open Button Remote"
    onClick="openRemote('button', 1,
    'width=140,height=180,scrollbars=0,resizable=1,menubar=0',
    'Page 1 label', 'page1.html', '        Page2        ', 'page2.html',
    'Hints Page', 'hints-js.html', 'Scroller Page', 'scroller-js.html');">
```

This call opens a button-bar type remote with four buttons. One of the button labels is padded with spaces to make it larger. You can experiment with padding your labels to try to make them all the same size. The button appearance will vary depending on what browser you use. Figure 8.4 shows the same button-bar remote opened under *Netscape* 3.0 and Internet *Explorer* 3.0.

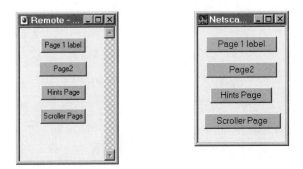

Figure 8.4 *Identical button-bar remotes as rendered by Internet* Explorer *and* Netscape

As with the HTML-type remote, you can use hyperlinks or a button to open button-bar and anchor-type remotes.

Finally, you might want to call up the remote when your page loads so that the visitor doesn't have to do anything to make the remote appear. To do this, add the `openRemote()` call to an `onLoad()` event handler in the `<BODY>` tag of your HTML file, like this:

```
<BODY onLoad=("openRemote('anchor', 0,
   'width=120,height=150,scrollbars=0,resizable=0,menubar=0');">
```

You can, of course, add the usual link color and background parameters to the `<BODY>` tag as well. Non-Javascript browsers will ignore the `onLoad()` parameter, so you can safely use it in your pages without fear of offending the non-Javascript-enabled browsers of the world.

To automatically close your remote when the browser loads a new page, place a call to the `checkSticky()` function in an `onUnload` event handler, placed in the `<BODY>` tag. This event triggers just as the page is about to unload in preparation for loading the new one. It allows your script a last chance to clean up before being sent to bit-heaven. There are no parameters to `checkSticky()`, so the call is simplicity itself:

```
<BODY onUnload=("checkSticky();")>
```

The `checkSticky()` call can be combined in the same `<BODY>` tag with a call to `openRemote()`. Using these events, you can fully automate the creation and closing of your remote control windows.

With a little practice, you'll soon be wowing the locals and the Internet at large with an awesome remote-controlled Web site. Study the example file and play around. The nice thing about Javascript is that you can test it all you want on your local machine and get immediate feedback. Much more pleasant than uploading a CGI script to the server after every change to the code.

What We Covered in Chapter 8

- **What remote windows are and why you might want to use one on your Web site**
- **How remote control windows work using Javascript**
- **The remote script and its modes of operation: HTML-type, button bar, and anchor type**
- **Tips on calling Javascript functions from various types of hyperlinks and for hiding them from non-Javascript browsers**

Chapter 9

Processing and Responding to Interactive Forms Using Perl

Features of the *formp.cgi* Script

- This single script can be used to process your HTML forms.
- Form data can be returned via e-mail, stored in a database, or both.
- Automatic checking of required fields is provided.
- For greater security, a configuration file may be used to hide details of the form processing.

What You Need to Use This Script

- Perl 4 or 5 on your Web server
- The capability to execute CGI scripts from your Web directory *or* to have the script installed in a central script directory on your ISP or SA's Web server
- The *cgi-lib.pl* form processing function library (included on the CD-ROM) either installed on your Web server or placed in your directory
- FTP client; Telnet client
- Text editor

This script makes use of public domain code written by an interesting guy calling himself "Selena Sol" on the Internet. His Web site (*http://www.eff.extropia.com/*) features many free CGI scripts along with links to other sites with free scripts. (Be prepared for some real Perl programming if you want to use them, however.)

Why You Would Want to Use This Script

Well, you've bitten the bullet and decided to use your Web site to collect information. Since the standard HTML `mailto:` function hardly qualifies as a data collection tool, you need to have real control over the information your visitors send you.

Not only do you need control over the type of information submitted (who knows what those marketing guys have in mind), you'll also want to decide the format of the data as it's collected. You're probably going to want some kind of simple input validation routine; for example, maybe a particular field cannot be left blank. You may even want the data stored in a particular database-ready format.

If you have created created a form in HTML, a CGI program is the only way to process and send the data you collect. This is where the form-processing power of a language such as Perl fills the bill perfectly. Until now, we've presented primarily the kinder, gentler side of Perl. In this chapter, we show you how to harness the beast in Perl to process even the most complex form and have it do your bidding.

Introduction to the *formp.cgi* Script

Fill-in forms are one of the truly great features of HTML and have contributed much to the explosive growth of the Web for commercial applications. Unless you are very new to HTML, you've already created a few forms for yourself. Most HTML books have sections on designing forms and describe how to lay out each of the different input elements. Where these books usually fall short is on the back end, that is, processing the form data. Generally, you're given a simple example and a reference to a couple of Perl CGI libraries. After that, you're on your own. Well, we won't leave you high and dry like that. You won't need to wrestle Perl into submission in order to develop CGI form-handling routines. We give you a single Perl script that can handle data from all your forms and dispatch it via e-mail and/or store it in a database on your server. Best of all, you don't have to change the script to handle different forms. All this along with the *Ginsu* steak knives! Now how much would you pay?

Security Concerns

Before we dive into the details, we take a minute to consider some important security aspects of this script. While the *formp.cgi* script is not insecure as such, it may reveal more about your system than you'd like, information about you and your system that normal CGI scripts do not. For example, depending on how you set up the script, users may be able to view the e-mail address to which you send form data. They may also be able to see the name of a file or files that anyone can write to, delete, or modify. This could put all your form data at risk. For serious business or personal applications, use the named data set option discussed later.

Another feature of the *formp.cgi* script is the ability to process forms from anywhere on the Internet. This is possible because complete control information is stored within the form. Anyone who knows the path to your *formp.cgi* script (by looking at any one of your forms) can send form data to your server for processing with the results sent via e-mail anywhere in the world. You probably wouldn't allow your personal mailbox to be used for anonymous transfers of unknown mail. A restricted access feature of the script can prevent form processing requests except from your own pages. We recommend that you leave this feature turned on for all your forms.

How the *formp.cgi* Script Works

The *formp.cgi* script works by responding to control information stored in HTML form fields of TYPE="HIDDEN." These fields cannot be modified by the user, but their data is read by a CGI script in the same way as other form fields. The script uses this feature to read embedded information in the HTML form that tells the script what to do with the form data. Global information about what commands are allowed for your forms is stored in a configuration file (commonly *formp.cnf*). Listing 9.1 shows a simple form with *formp.cgi* control fields.

Listing 9.1	An HTML form with *formp.cgi* control fields

```
<HTML><HEAD><TITLE>A Simple formp.cgi form</TITLE></HEAD>
<BODY>
<H2>Fill me in!</H2>
<FORM METHOD=POST ACTION="cgi/formp.cgi">
<!--formp.cgi control fields-->
   <INPUT TYPE="HIDDEN" NAME="config_file" VALUE="./formp.cnf">
   <INPUT TYPE="HIDDEN" NAME="mailto" VALUE="juser@someisp.com">
   <INPUT TYPE="HIDDEN" NAME="email_subject" VALUE="Color Survey Response">
   <INPUT TYPE="HIDDEN" NAME="variable_order" VALUE="name|color">
   <INPUT TYPE="HIDDEN" NAME="required_variables" VALUE="name">
   <INPUT TYPE="HIDDEN" NAME="html_response" VALUE="<h1>Thanks for the input</h1>">
<!--form input fields-->
```

```
<P>Your Name:<BR>
<INPUT TYPE="TEXT" NAME="name" VALUE="">
<P>Your Favorite Color:<BR>
Red <INPUT TYPE="RADIO" NAME="color" VALUE="red"><BR>
Blue <INPUT TYPE="RADIO" NAME="color" VALUE="blue"><BR>
Puce <INPUT TYPE="RADIO" NAME="color" VALUE="puce" CHECKED><BR>
<P><INPUT TYPE="SUBMIT" >
</FORM>
</BODY></HTML>
```

Figure 9.1 shows the form as it appears in the browser, and Figure 9.2 shows the Data Accepted page that is generated after successful data submission.

formp.cgi Control Fields

Near the top of the form definition, notice several hidden fields. These hold the control information for this form:

- The `config_file` field gives the path and filename of a file that contains global configuration information.
- The `mailto` field, big surprise, defines to whom the script will e-mail the data. The `email_subject` field contains the data that forms the subject line of the e-mail message.
- The `variable_order` field defines in what order the form data is stored for both e-mail and database output methods.

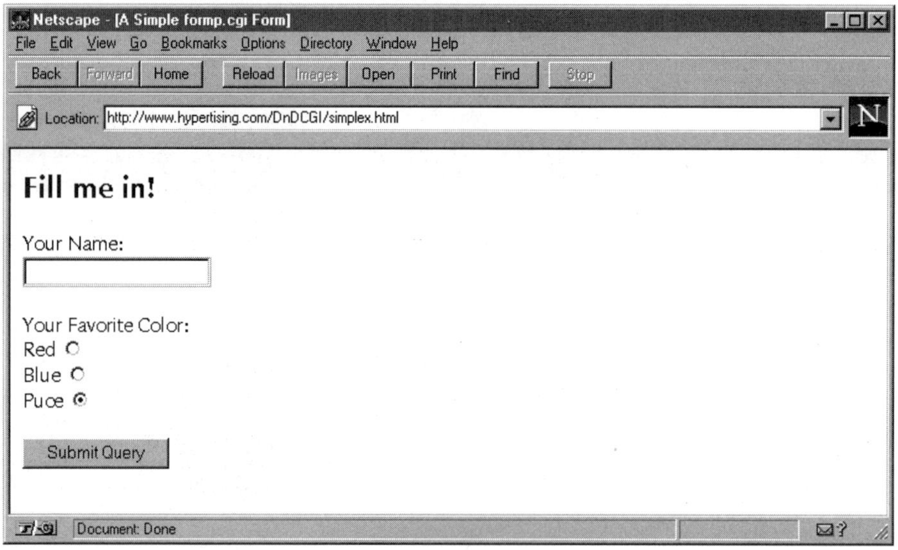

Figure 9.1 *Browser output of a simple* formp.cgi *example*

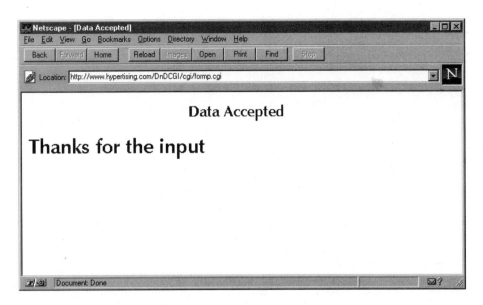

Figure 9.2 *Browser output of Data Accepted page from* formp.cgi

The form fields are listed in the `variable_order` value by the same string that appears in the `NAME=` parameter. The names are separated by the vertical bar, a.k.a. the pipe character `|`.

Nerd Note

The pipe character `|` is so-named because of a feature of the UNIX operating system called, believe it or not, **pipes.** A pipe allows the output from one command to be sent or "piped" to the input of another. For example, if you want to view the output of the directory listing command *ls* one screen-full at a time, you could type the following line at your terminal:

```
ls | more
```

This command line runs the *ls* command and passes the output (the listing of all the files in the current directory) to the *more* command, which shows a screen-full and then waits for you to hit a key to display more output. This is one of the most powerful and best-loved features of UNIX-type operating systems.

- The `required_variables` field, as you might expect, contains a list of those fields that must have a value input by the user when the form is submitted.

- The `html_response` field contains the text you wish to show the user after a successful submission.

This example should give you a feel for how things are done with *formp.cgi*. By creating the appropriate hidden fields in your forms, you can direct the script to handle your form data differently for each form without having to reprogram the script or create a similar but different script for each form. Maintenance is simplified because you can use your favorite HTML editor to change the behavior of the script rather than editing the Perl code.

The *formp.cgi* script supports quite a few control parameters. Here is the complete list:

- `config_file`. Specifies the path and filename of a file containing additional control information. The control file specifies global options and, optionally, specific data for individual forms. (See later in the chapter for a description of the configuration file format.) This field is required in order to use the `data_set` field (explained later). Otherwise it is optional.

- `mailto`. The e-mail address to which to send the form data. This should be in standard (*name@xyz.com*) format. This field is required for e-mail.

- `email_subject`. The text that will appear in the subject line of the e-mail. This is useful for easily identifying from which form the mail comes. Some mail clients will sort incoming mail based on the subject line. This field is optional.

- `include_blanks`. Indicates whether the e-mail output should include the fields with blank input. Sometimes you might want to receive only the fields for which the user input data and not the blank fields. The default is `Yes` if this parameter is not included. This field is optional.

- `database_name`. Path and filename of the database file to which data should be appended. This path should be relative to the location of the script, not of the Web page. This field is required for database output.

- `database_delimiter`. The character to print between the database fields. Common delimiters are ",", " "(space), "|", ":", and the tab character. Place the single character delimiter for the database fields in the `VALUE` parameter of the fields. The string "tab" will cause the program to use a tab character as the delimiter. This field is required for database output.

- `variable_order`. Lists all the fields in the form in the order you wish them to appear in the output. If you fail to list a field name in this parameter, data from the field won't be sent in e-mail or stored in the database. This field is required.

- `time_stamp`. Adds a date and time stamp to the database record. The default is `No` where no time/date stamp is appended. If the value is set to either `First` or `Last`, the time stamp, consisting of two fields, will be appended to the database record in the specified position. The time stamp has the format of HH:MM:SS, where HH are the hours, MM are the minutes, and SS arc thc scconds of the time the form was submitted. The separator character is a colon ":" by default, but you can change it in the configuration block of the script. Similarly, the date stamp has the form MM/DD/YY, where MM is the numeric month, DD is the day, and YY is the year. The default separator is the slash /. It can also be changed in the configuration block of the script. The date and time are separated by the database delimiter defined earlier in this list. This field is optional.

- `required_variables`. A list of field names that must have some input; otherwise, an error message will be returned to the user and the data will not be accepted. This field is optional.

- `echo_data`. Indicates whether the information input by the visitor will be displayed on the response page. You may not want to echo a large amount of data on the response page if all you want to do is say something like, "Thanks, Dude." This field is optional.

- `url_of_this_form`. The URL of the form HTML. This is used to add a link back to the form on the page in the event of an input error. *Note:* Using this link will cause the previous data to be lost. The `back` function of the browser retains the data input. This field is optional.

- `body`. This is the guts of the HTML `<BODY>` tag. Use this parameter to specify items such as background image/color, text color, and link color. This allows you to maintain a consistent look with the rest of your site. What you enter here will be placed verbatim in the `<BODY>` tag, following `BODY` but before the closing > character. This is used for both successful submission and for error messages. This field is optional.

- `response_title`. The title of the page generated following a successful form submission. This field is optional.

- `html_response`. The HTML code to put on the successful response page. This text is placed in the body section between the `<BODY> </BODY>` tag pair. This field is optional.

- `html_error`. The HTML code to put on the page generated by a nonfatal error. This version of *formp.cgi* uses this only when required data is missing. (Fatal errors, such as not being able to open the *send/mail* program, have their own messages.)

- `return_link_url`. A link back to your site that users should use once they have completed the form. This link will be placed on the successful submission page. The contents of this variable are inserted after the `HREF=` tag. This field is optional.

- `return_link_name`. The text of the hyperlink presented on the successful response page. This text goes between the `<A></A>` tags. This field is optional.

- `data_set`. Specifies the name of a set of data stored in the file specified by the `config_file` parameter. It allows you to hide data, such as e-mail addresses and database names, that would normally be visible to the user in the HTML source. This field is optional.

Hot Tip

Hidden fields don't have to be hidden. They can just as easily be visible. While in most cases you don't want the user modifying the fields, letting them do so can be useful in certain situations. For example, if you have a general information request form, you could use a radio button list or a `<SELECT>` menu to set the `email_subject` or even the `mailto` field. Since radio buttons and select lists aren't modifiable text, only one of the choices you give can be picked.

Hair Saver

The path to the background image file must be relative to the directory in which the script, not the form, resides. You may have to use some ../ path modifiers to get to the correct image directory.

An additional field, `client_email`, should not be hidden. Use it to provide a space for users to enter their e-mail addresses. Data from this field will be included on the script-generated e-mail messages in the `From:` field. This field is optional, but it makes it easy to reply to the user who submitted the form by simply using the `reply` function of your e-mail client.

One final note, hidden fields are not really hidden. They appear in the HTML source for the form, and you can see them by using the browser's *view source* command. Since you might not want users to know where the form data is going, we've included the option to place all or part of the control information in a configuration file. Using this option, you identify only the name of the configuration file and the name for the control information within each form so that users cannot view the form data handling information from the HTML source.

Configuring and Installing the *formp.cgi* Script

Configuration of the *formp.cgi* script is straightforward (ever notice how people who have already done something always think it's easy?). If your ISP or SA has already installed *formp.cgi* in a central directory, it really is easy. Just get out your trusty ISP/SA questionnaire to see where it's installed. Those of you who need to install it, or those who want a local copy, will want to read on. Those who can't run CGI scripts at all will need to get a new ISP and rejoin the rest of us later.

Step 1: Configuration

Load the *formp.cgi* script, located in the */scripts/formp/* directory on the CD-ROM, into your favorite text editor. As usual with Perl scripts, you'll need to edit the first line of the script to point to the Perl interpreter on your ISP or SA's server. Use your ISP/SA questionnaire to find the path to the Perl executable and modify the first line to match. You should have something like

```
#!/usr/bin/perl
```

Next, scan down the file past all the credits and copyright stuff to the configuration block. Listing 9.2 shows the configuration block as it appears in the CD-ROM file.

Listing 9.2   *formp.cgi* **configuration block**

```
###################################################################
#
# Configuration Block
#
###################################################################
#
# cgi-lib.pl contains form processing and support routines
# we need to indicate the path to the library
#
# examples:
#   require "/usr/local/lib/perl/cgi-lib.pl"; # global library
#   require "./cgi-lib.pl";:; # in same directory as the script
require "./cgi-lib.pl";
#
# the $mail_program is the command for the mail sending
# program.  The script will open an output pipe to the mail
# program and send the form data to it.
#
# example:
# $mail_program = "/usr/bin/sendmail -t -n";
$mail_program = "/usr/bin/sendmail -t -n";
#
```

```
# $flock_ok is a flag which tells the script if your
# Web server supports the Perl flock() command
# in general UNIX servers do and Windows servers do not
# the script will work with all servers if $flock_ok=0 but will
# perform more file I/O and hence be slower.
#
# examples:
# $flock_ok = 1; # for UNIX servers
# $flock_ok = 0; # for Windows servers
$flock_ok = 0;
#
# default values for items from the configuration file
# ISPs may want to set these if the script is to be run
# from a central CGI directory.
# Items the users set in a config_file will NOT override these
# values.  Use them to turn off e-mail or databases.
#
# $email_of_sender - appears in the From: field of the e-mail
#    ex: joeuser@myisp.com
# $restricted_use - verify server which form is submitted from
#    values: 'yes' or 'no'
# $your_server_name - requests allowed from this server only
#    values: 'yes' or 'no'
# $wrong_server_error_msg - output when a restricted use violation
# is detected.  Make this as scary as you like
#    ex: <h1>Security Violation!</h1>Valid only from myisp.com
# $should_i_mail - flag to allow e-mail response
#    values: 'yes' or 'no'
# $should_i_append_a_database - same for database files
#    values: 'yes' or 'no'
#
# comment these values out if you wish to control
# the script completely from a configuration file
# Note, use single quotes >'< around these strings
# $email_of_sender = 'me@myisp.com';
$restricted_use = 'no';
# $your_server_name = 'www.myisp.com';
# $wrong_server_error_msg = 'Security Violation!';
$should_i_mail = 'yes';
$should_i_append_a_database = 'yes';
# time separator character for time_stamp
$tsep = ':';
# date separator character for time_stamp
$dsep = '/';

###############################################################
#
# End of Configuration Block
#
###############################################################
```

The first line in the configuration block is a command to load a CGI form-processing library called *cgi-lib.pl*. This library was written by Steven Brenner and is a de facto standard within the CGI world. You will need to supply the path to the library. Check your ISP/SA questionnaire to see if the library is installed on your server. If it is, modify this line to match the path given by your ISP or SA. You should have something like the following when you are done:

```
require "/usr/lib/perl/cgi-lib.pl";
```

If your ISP or SA doesn't have *cgi-lib.pl* installed, you'll need to upload a copy of the file to your CGI directory. For your convenience, we've included the library on the CD-ROM in the */scripts/formp/* directory. However, you might want to check for a newer version at the *cgi-lib.pl* Web site *http://www.bio.cam.ac.uk/cgi-lib/*. If you're installing *cgi-lib.pl* in your personal directory, the *require* command will look something like this:

```
require "./cgi-lib.pl";
```

The string ./ tells the script to look for the library in the directory in which the script is running. We usually put the library and the script in the same directory, to keep things nice and tidy.

If your ISP or SA has installed the library in a central directory, check your ISP/SA questionnaire for the path to the file. It will look something like this:

```
/usr/local/lib/perl/cgi-lib.pl
```

You must have this library installed somewhere on your server for the script to run.

The next item is the $mail_program variable. This variable gives the path and name of the *sendmail* program on your server. Those of you with UNIX servers will almost certainly have this program installed on your server. (Windows NT users should check the *rsrcs.html* file on the CD-ROM for information on a *sendmail* clone for Windows.) Check your ISP/SA questionnaire for the path to *sendmail* and modify the line to match. You should end up with something like this:

```
$mail_program = '/usr/sbin/sendmail -t -n';
```

The next variable, $flock_ok, is a flag that tells the script whether the Perl flock() file locking command is available on your server. UNIX servers almost always have it; the current version of Perl for Windows does not. If you have UNIX, change this to 1. If you are running on Windows, use 0. If you're not sure or you have a strange version of UNIX, 0 should work on all systems.

The next six items are clones of the items in the configuration file described in Listing 9.2. The values in the script will override the values you place in the configuration file (and in the form). This is a security feature, since some ISPs don't allow CGI scripts to write files on their systems. To retain complete control in the configuration file, leave the values commented out (add the # character at the beginning of the line.) To set the items for all the forms processed by this script, remove the # and set the variable to the desired value. A typical setup might look like this:

```
# $email_of_sender = 'joeuser@myisp.com';
$restricted_use = 'yes';
$your_server_name = 'www.myisp.com';
# $wrong_server_error_msg = "<H1>Access Denied</H1>Only the www.myisp.com
#    server is    allowed to use this script";
# $should_i_mail = 'yes';
$should_i_append_a_database = 'no': # not allowed on MY server!
```

In this example, $email_of_sender, $wrong_server_error_msg, and $should_i_mail are commented out; the settings in the configuration file will control their values. The $restricted_use, $your_server_name, and $should_i_append_a_database variables are hard-coded into the script and can't be changed by the configuration file.

formp.cgi Configuration File Format

The configuration file (normally called *formp.cnf)* contains control information for your forms' server plus specific rules and global options for *formp.cgi.* The config_file field described in the previous subsection tells the script the file's path and name. This feature allows the script to be used by people who are unable to run the script from their personal directories. The script itself can be configured and installed in a central *cgi-bin* directory by the ISP, while the configuration file resides in the user's directory along with the HTML forms. The file format reflects the fact that this file is actually Perl code (don't panic) incorporated into the script at runtime. The configuration block of the script (Listing 9.3) may contain default values for these variables that will override the values in both the form and the configuration file. So even if you have a security-crazed ISP, you should be able to use the script. You'll just be limited to the options that the ISP sets in the script. By creating multiple configuration files, you can design different behavior for each form or for "families" of forms.

Here are the contents of the configuration file:

- $email_of_sender. This variable holds the return address placed in the From: field of each e-mail sent by the script. If you include the client_email field in your form, it will be used instead of the $email_of_sender value.

- $restricted_use. This is a security feature of the *formp.cgi* script. Set this variable to Yes if you want to restrict form submission to your server alone. If you omit this variable or set it to No, people on other Web servers will be able to use your script to process their forms. This feature is optional, but recommended.

- $your_server_name. This variable's value is checked if
  $restricted_use is set to Yes. An error message is output if this value and
  the HTTP_REFERRER environment variable set by the Web server don't
  match. The value of this variable will be the first part of your home page
  URL, that is, the part following the *http://* up through the upper-level
  domain (*.com*, *.org*, or *.edu*, etc., and the country identifier for those outside
  the United States).

- $wrong_server_error_message. This string will be sent to the user if the
  script detects an attempt to use the script from another server. It is used only
  if the $restricted_use variable is set to Yes.

- $should_i_mail. Set this variable to Yes if you want to be able to e-mail
  the results of the form. If this is omitted or set to No, mail will not be sent
  even if the mail_to field is set in the form or configuration file data set.

- $should_i_append_a_database. Set this variable to Yes if you want to
  allow the writing of form data to a database. If this variable is omitted or set
  to No, no data will be written to a database even if the database_name field
  is set in the form or configuration file.

As mentioned previously, you can put a named data set in your configuration file to
hide or change the control information for your forms. This is done by creating a Perl
data structure that is merged with the data from the form. Listing 9.3 gives a complete example configuration file.

Listing 9.3　　　　　　　　　　　　　*formp.cgi* **configuration file format**

```
# Example formp.cgi configuration file normally named
# formp.cnf and placed in the same directory as the script
# if you have a central installation of the script you
# place it in any convenient location
$email_of_sender = 'joeuser@myisp.com';
$restricted_use = 'yes';
$your_server_name = 'www.myisp.com';
$wrong_server_error_message = 'Sorry bud, no can do. You're not on my server';
$should_i_mail = 'yes';
$should_i_append_a_database = 'yes';

# this is how a control data set should look
# this is the name "form1" that you put in the data_set parameter
# in your form (case sensitive).
%form1 = {
    'mailto', 'joeuser@myisp.com',
    'email_subject', 'Eggplant Consumption Survey',
    'database_name', 'ep_surv.dat',
    'database_delimiter', ':',
```

```
          'variable_order', 'name|email|address|ep_consumption',
          'required_variables', 'name|email|address|ep_consumption',
          'echo_data', 'yes',
          'url_of_this_form', '../forms/ep_surv.html',
          'body', 'bkgnd="../images/eggplant.gif" TEXT="#000000" LINK="#0000FF"
              VLINK="#800080" ',
          'response_title', 'Eggplants forever!',
          'html_response', '<P>Thank you for your input. It will be used to improve
              eggplants for all mankind',
          'return_link_url', '../index.html',
          'return_link_name', 'Home Page',
          'echo_data', 'no',
          'html_error', '' # no comma on the last item
      }; # end of form1 data set
      # the next form data_set goes here
      # %form2 = {
      # ... etc.
```

Nerd Note

> The data sets are actually stored in Perl associative arrays, as is the form data returned by the CGI function library. The two arrays are merged to make a complete set of data, which the script interprets. Since the form data is read in first, putting the same parameter in the configuration file will overwrite the value from the form.

Since this file is Perl code, some parts of the format are critical if you want it to work. Here are a few points to be aware of to help you get it right:

- You must have a $ before the configuration variable names and a % before the data set names. These characters indicate the type of variable in the Perl language (see Appendix A).

- You must have a semicolon (;) at the end of each variable definition. This marks the end of a Perl statement.

- Be sure you use commas between all the elements of the data set definition. Listing 9.3 shows the name and value set up as a pair (name, value pair). You must put a comma between the "value" element and the next "name" element. Use single quotation marks around the elements. This tells Perl to store the string exactly as typed and not to try to interpret any special characters that Perl cares about.

Hair Saver

> Forgetting a comma or semicolon is very easy to do. After you create your configuration file, go back and double-check for the points mentioned in the list. If the script won't run, go back and check again. Your problem is probably in this file.

The bottom line on configuration of the script is this: Use the configuration file options if you can. If the ISP or SA hard codes certain options with the script in a common directory, you can still use the script, but you'll be limited in what you can do with it.

This completes the configuration of *formp.cgi*. It's not as simple as we would have liked. But form processing is such an important part of many CGI applications, we thought a little added flexibility was worth the trade-off in complexity.

Step 2: Installation

After configuration is complete, save your edited file in a convenient place for uploading to your server.

Following the directions presented in Chapter 3, upload the edited script file (*formp.cgi*) into the *cgi* or *cgi-bin* directory on your Web server. If you need to install the *cgi-lib.pl* library, upload it to the same directory. Finally, upload any configuration files you've created.

Remember to tell the server that the *formp.cgi* file is an executable script by setting the file permissions with either your FTP or Telnet client.

Next, you create a directory in which to store your database files. Since the directory with the database file must have write permission for all users, you should create a separate directory and not use the normal *cgi* or *html* directories. From your Telnet client, use the *mkdir* (make directory) command to create a directory like this:

```
mkdir Databases
```

Then change the file permissions using the *chmod* command:

```
chmod 777 Databases
```

You can also use your FTP client to do this. Finally, perform a simple test to see if the script will run. Enter the name of the script on the command line by itself, as in:

```
formp.cgi
```

If everything is working, the following lines should be returned:

```
Content-type: text/html
<HTML>
<HEAD>
<TITLE>Data Accepted</TITLE>
</HEAD><BODY>
<H2>
<CENTER>Data Accepted</CENTER>
</H2>
```

Here are some common Perl error messages and what they mean.

```
Can't locate ../cgi-lib.pl in @INC at .//formp.cgi line 50.
```

This means the path to the *cgi-lib.pl* file is incorrect in the script configuration block. If you think you have the location right, but your script still won't work, try the following commands from a Telnet session on your server:

```
locate cgi-lib.pl
which cgi-lib.pl
whereis cgi-lib.pl
```

These may not work on all systems, but they're worth a try. If they do work, you will get the path to the *cgi-lib.pl* file. Edit the configuration file to match, and your script should work.

You may also get an error like this:

```
syntax error in file formp.cgi at line 115, next 2 tokens "print "Content"
   (Might be a runaway multiline "" string starting on line 60)
Execution of formp.cgi aborted due to compilation errors.
```

In this case, your problem is almost certainly in the config block. *Note:* Perl is guessing that there is a missing string delimiter (which is correct), thereby causing the whole script to be included in the string. Go back and double-check that you have a string delimiter (' or ") at the start and end of each parameter, and make sure the string delimiters are the same. Also, make sure each statement ends with a semicolon. You will need to edit and save the script on your local machine and then FTP it again to the server. Repeat this until the script loads and runs.

Hot Tip

A lot of programming involves the ole "cut and try" method. That is, if you can't figure out why something isn't working, take your best guess, change something, and see if it works. If not, try something else. Even the best programmers do this; they just make better guesses than the beginners. Note, change only one thing at a time. In doing so, you won't accidentally cancel out a correct change with a later incorrect one. The clandestine programmers' cabal (CPC) will be after us for divulging this secret programmer's method, but we figure it's worth taking the risk, for you, our dear readers.

This completes the installation of the *formp.cgi* script. In the next section, we look at the various script options in a couple of examples.

Using the *formp.cgi* Script in Your Pages

The first example lets you play around with the different options available in the *formp.cgi* script. By creating a form with visible fields for those that are normally hidden, this becomes an interactive test bed for the script. Be very careful about doing this in your real-life forms. The *formp.cgi* control fields are not meant to be modified by the user. You have been warned.

Listing 9.4 shows the HTML for our test-bed form. The upper section has the *formp.cgi* control fields. A few sample data fields are placed in the lower section of the form. You can put as many fields in this section as you like to get a feel for how the script works.

Listing 9.4   **HTML for the *formp.cgi* test-bed example**

```
<HTML><HEAD>
<TITLE>Formp.cgi Test-Bed</TITLE></HEAD>
<BODY >
<H1>Formp.cgi Test Bed</H1>
<H3>Control Fields</H3>
<FORM METHOD=POST ACTION="cgi/formp.cgi">

<!--formp.cgi control fields-->
config_file<BR>
<INPUT TYPE="TEXT" SIZE=70 NAME="config_file" VALUE="./formp.cnf">
<P>mailto <BR>
<INPUT TYPE="TEXT" SIZE=70 NAME="mailto" VALUE="juser@someisp.com"><BR>
```

```
<P>email_subject<BR>
<INPUT TYPE="TEXT" SIZE=70 NAME="email_subject" VALUE="Color Survey Response"><BR>
<P>database_name<BR>
<INPUT TYPE="TEXT" SIZE=70 NAME="database_name" VALUE="./test-bed.txt">
<P>database_delimiter <BR>
<INPUT TYPE="TEXT" SIZE=70 NAME="database_delimiter" VALUE=",">
<P>variable_order: <BR>
<INPUT TYPE="TEXT" SIZE=70 NAME="variable_order" VALUE="name|color"><BR>
<P>required_variables:<BR>
<INPUT TYPE="TEXT" SIZE=70 NAME="required_variables" VALUE="name"><BR>
<P>echo_data <BR>
<INPUT TYPE="TEXT" SIZE=70 NAME="echo_data" VALUE="yes">
<P>url_of_this_form <BR>
<INPUT TYPE="TEXT" SIZE=70 NAME="url_of_this_form" VALUE="../test-bed.html">
<P>body <BR>
<INPUT TYPE="TEXT" SIZE=70 NAME="body" VALUE="bgcolor=000080 text=000000 link=ff0000">
<P>response_title<BR>
<INPUT TYPE="TEXT" SIZE=70 NAME="response_title" VALUE="Test Bed Response">
<P>html_response:<BR>
<INPUT TYPE="TEXT" SIZE=70 NAME="html_response" VALUE="<h1>Thanks for the input</h1>">
<P>return_link_url<BR>
<INPUT TYPE="TEXT" SIZE=70 NAME="return_link_url" VALUE="index.html">
<P>return_link_name<BR>
<INPUT TYPE="TEXT" SIZE=70 NAME="return_link_name" VALUE="My Home Page">
<P>data_set<BR>
<INPUT TYPE="TEXT" SIZE=70 NAME="data_set" VALUE="">
<P><HR><HR>
<H3>Form Input Fields</H3>
<!--form input fields-->
    <P>Your Name(name):<BR>
    <INPUT TYPE="TEXT" NAME="name" VALUE="">
    <P>Your Email (client_email):<BR>
    <INPUT TYPE="TEXT" NAME="client_email" VALUE="">
    <P>Your Favorite Color(color):<BR>
    Red <INPUT TYPE="RADIO" NAME="color" VALUE="red"><BR>
    Blue <INPUT TYPE="RADIO" NAME="color" VALUE="blue"><BR>
    Puce <INPUT TYPE="RADIO" NAME="color" VALUE="puce" CHECKED><BR>
    <P><INPUT TYPE="SUBMIT" >
</FORM>
</BODY></HTML>
```

If you don't feel like typing this rather long example yourself, you can find it on the CD-ROM as */scripts/formp/test-bed.html*. Customize the bottom section of the form to your liking and then upload it to your ISP or SA's server in your usual HTML directory. (Remember to modify the ACTION= parameter of the <FORM> tag to match the path to the script.) If the script is stored in a central *cgi-bin* directory, you will probably use an absolute path such as this:

```
ACTION="/usr/local/httpd/cgi-bin/formp.cgi"
```

If the script is in a local directory, you'll want to use a path relative to the HTML page. If the script is stored in a directory called *cgi* under your HTML directory, the path will look like this:

```
ACTION="cgi/formp.cgi"
```

For a full test of *formp.cgi* capabilities, you should create a configuration file to go with the form. Listing 9.5 shows a configuration file with the control parameters and one data set. You can either enter this by hand or copy it from the */scripts/formp/ test-bed.cnf* file on the CD-ROM.

Listing 9.5	Test-bed example configuration file

```
# Test Bed configuration file
#
# global options
# if you don't use client_email
$email_of_sender ='jojo@weewee.com';
$your_server_name = "www.myisp.com";
$restricted_use = "no";
$should_i_mail = "yes";
$should_i_append_a_database = "yes";
$wrong_server_error_message = "bummer dude wrong server";

# forms section

#

%test_bed = (
    'mailto', 'me@myisp.com',
    'html_response', 'Thanks for the form dude',
    'email_subject', 'Test-bed email',
    'variable_order', 'name|client_email|color',
    'required_variables', 'name|client_email|color',
    'echo_data', 'yes',
    'url_of_this_form', 'http://www.myisp.com/~me/test-bed.html',
    'body', 'text=000000 bgcolor="#ffffff" link="#ff0000" vlink="#0000ff"',
    'response_title', 'Test-Bed Response',
    'return_link_url', '../index.html',
    'return_link_name', 'Home Page',
    'database_name', './Databases/testbed_data.txt',
    'database_delimiter', ",", # must be a single character
                # or the string "tab"
#   'client_email', 'client@powpow.com'
    );
```

Remember, the settings from the config block in the script will be used, if they exist, even if you specify values for them in a configuration file. Just comment out the default parameters. To do so, place a # character at the beginning of the line in the configuration block. Be sure *not* to comment out the `require` line, `$mail_program`, or `$flock_ok`. Also, control parameters specified in a configuration file data set will override those from the form. Once you are satisfied with the HTML and your configuration file, upload them to your ISP's or SA's server. Put the form in the directory with your HTML files. Place the configuration file in the same directory as the *formp.cgi* script, if you can; if not, put it in with your HTML files. When you load the form into your browser, you should see a page that looks like that depicted in Figure 9.3.

Try different options in the control fields to make the form send you mail and store the data in a database file. Make sure you can read data from the configuration file and from a data set. Once you've worked through a few different options, you should have a solid understanding of how the script works. Once you gain some experience with this script, you'll be girded and ready for battle! The mention of HTML form processing with a CGI script will no longer send you screaming from the room.

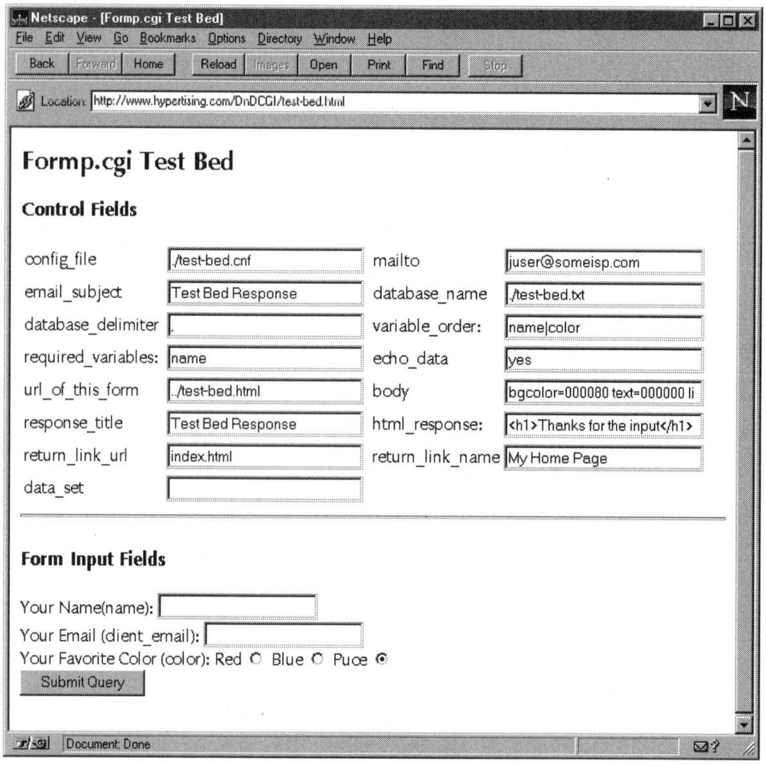

Figure 9.3 *Browser output of* formp.cgi *test-bed form*

What We Covered in Chapter 9

- Form processing using hidden control fields
- How *formp.cgi* works
- Customizing the script for your needs
- Installing and using the test-bed form to test the script

*C*hapter *10*

Example Form-Processing Applications Using Perl

Form Examples Included in This Chapter

- A request-for-information form
- A simple guest book
- An on-line test form

What You Need to Use These Examples

- The *formp.cgi* script installed and running on your Web server
- Server-Side Include script capability for the guest-book example
- An HTML or text editor
- FTP client or Telnet clients

Why You Would Want to Use This Script

As mentioned in Chapter 9, "Processing and Responding to Interactive Forms Using Perl," real-time form processing is one of the keys to creating interactive sites. We recently prototyped an Interactive Cardiac Health Assessment Questionnaire for Southern California Hospital. The form was developed jointly by the hospital Marketing Department and the Cardiac Center. A visitor to the site will answer a series of questions, press the submit button, and voilà, a cardiac health appraisal (complete with legal disclaimer) will be returned in a few moments.

Beyond its obvious value as a tool, the questionnaire will be seen as a public service to the community and the Internet world at large. It will help draw visitors to the site, who may incidentally explore the other Web pages. Since the hospital will be one of the first offering interactive forms on the Internet, this will be newsworthy. Being newsworthy often translates into free write-ups in the trade journals and local newspapers—the best kind of publicity.

On balance, the cost of implementing such a form is insignificant compared to the "good press" it can generate. After you've delved into the examples that follow, you'll likely want to find new and innovative ways to exploit these form-processing techniques on the Web sites you develop. So let's delve!

If you've completed the installation of *formp.cgi* that we covered in Chapter 9, you should have an idea of what the script can do and how it can simplify your HTML form-processing life.

In this chapter, we present three example forms and describe some interesting and useful elements of *formp.cgi*:

1. A simple request-for-information form that allows the visitor to request information from several departments within a company

2. A guest-book script that invites users to sign in. A listing of prior guests is displayed in response to a successful entry. (This example requires that your ISP's or SA's server support SSI.)

3. An on-line test that returns the results instantly.

Each example demonstrates a different aspect of the script and what the script can do when processing form data.

Before proceeding with the examples presented in this chapter, you should install the *formp.cgi* script described in Chapter 9, "Processing and Responding to Interactive Forms Using Perl."

A Request-for-Information Form

This example uses a couple of interesting features of the *formp.cgi* script to both control where the form data is sent and to format the e-mail output. Figure 10.1 shows how the form looks in the browser, and Listing 10.1 shows the HTML source.

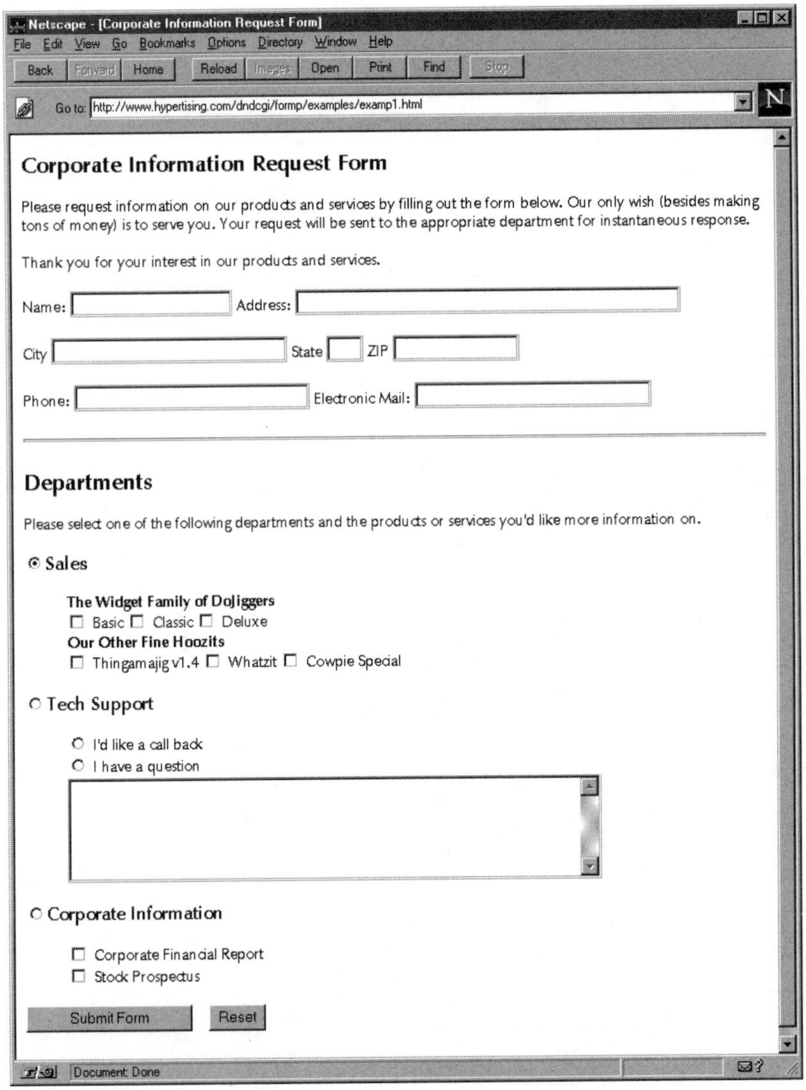

Figure 10.1 *Corporate request-for-information form—example browser output*

Listing 10.1   **Corporate request-for-information form—example HTML**

```html
<HTML><HEAD>
<TITLE>Corporate Information Request Form</TITLE></HEAD>
<BODY >

<H2>Corporate Information Request Form</H2>
<P>Please request information on our products and services by filling out the form
below.  Our only wish (besides making tons of money) is to serve you.  Your request
will be sent to the appropriate department for instantaneous response.

<P>Thank you for your interest in our products and services.
<P>
<FORM METHOD=POST ACTION="cgi-bin/formp.cgi">
<!--formp.cgi control fields-->
   <INPUT TYPE="HIDDEN" NAME="email_subject" VALUE="Web Site Information Request">
   <INPUT TYPE=hidden NAME="include_blanks" VALUE="no">
   <INPUT TYPE=hidden NAME="variable_order" VALUE="User Information|
|Name|Address|City|State|Zip|Phone|  |Information Requested for|  |Widget Basic|Widget
Classic|Widget Deluxe|Thingamajig|Whatzit|Cowpie|Request a|Have a|Question|Corporate
Report|Prospectus">
   <INPUT TYPE=hidden NAME="required_variables" VALUE="Name|Phone">
   <INPUT TYPE="HIDDEN" NAME="html_response" VALUE="Your request has been sent.  We
will be contacting you very shortly with a response.  Thank you for your interest." >

<!-- dummy fields for comments in e-mail -->
   <INPUT TYPE="HIDDEN" NAME="User Information" VALUE="  ">
   <INPUT TYPE="HIDDEN" NAME="  " VALUE="  ">
   <INPUT TYPE="HIDDEN" NAME="Information Requested for" VALUE="   ">

<!--form input fields-->
   <P>Name:
   <INPUT TYPE="TEXT" NAME="Name" VALUE="" size=20>
   Address:
   <INPUT TYPE="TEXT" NAME="Address" VALUE="" SIZE=50 MAXLENGTH=50>
   <P>City <INPUT TYPE="TEXT" NAME="City" VALUE="" SIZE=30 MAXLENGTH=0>
   State <INPUT TYPE="TEXT" NAME="State" VALUE="" SIZE=3 MAXLENGTH=0>
   ZIP <INPUT TYPE="TEXT" NAME="Zip" VALUE="" SIZE=15 MAXLENGTH=0>
   <P>Phone: <INPUT TYPE="TEXT" NAME="Phone" VALUE="" SIZE=20 MAXLENGTH=0>
   Electronic Mail: <INPUT TYPE="TEXT" NAME="client_email" VALUE="" SIZE=30
MAXLENGTH=0>

<P>
<hr>
<h2>Departments</h2>
<P>Please select one of the following departments and the products or services you'd
like more information on.

<h3><INPUT TYPE=radio CHECKED NAME="mailto" VALUE="chris@localhost">Sales</h3>
<DL><DD><B>The Widget Family of DoJiggers</B>
```

```
<DD>
   <INPUT TYPE=checkbox NAME="Widget Basic" VALUE="  "> Basic
   <INPUT TYPE=checkbox NAME="Widget Classic" VALUE="  "> Classic
   <INPUT TYPE=checkbox NAME="Widget Deluxe" VALUE="  "> Deluxe
<DD><B>Our Other Fine Hoozits</B>
<DD>
   <INPUT TYPE="CHECKBOX" NAME="Thingamajig" VALUE="  "> Thingamajig v1.4
   <INPUT TYPE="CHECKBOX" NAME="Whatzit" VALUE="  "> Whatzit
   <INPUT TYPE="CHECKBOX" NAME="Cowpie" VALUE="  "> Cowpie Special
</DL>

<h3><INPUT TYPE=radio NAME="mailto" VALUE="chris@localhost">Tech Support</h3>
<DL><DD>
   <INPUT TYPE=checkbox NAME="Request a" VALUE="Call Back"> I'd like a call back<BR>
   <INPUT TYPE=checkbox NAME="Have a" VALUE="Question"> I have a question<BR>
   <TEXTAREA NAME="Question" ROWS=5 COLS=60 WRAP=ON></TEXTAREA>
</DL>

<h3><INPUT TYPE=radio NAME="mailto" VALUE="chris@localhost">Corporate Information</h3>
<DL><DD>
   <INPUT TYPE="CHECKBOX" NAME="Corporate Report" VALUE="Yes">
      Corporate Financial Report<BR>
   <INPUT TYPE="CHECKBOX" NAME="Prospectus" VALUE="Yes"> Our Stock Prospectus
</DL>

   <P><INPUT TYPE="SUBMIT"  VALUE="    Submit Form     ">    
   <INPUT TYPE="RESET"  VALUE="Reset">

</FORM>

</BODY></HTML>
```

This form will send e-mail to the department selected by the user, along with a nicely formatted message. Fields for the products and services that the user doesn't click won't appear in the e-mail, and the message is fairly readable and looks customized for each department. We make use of several different features of the script to accomplish this. Read on to find out how.

How the Form Works

The first interesting feature of this form is that it will send e-mail to one of several addresses based on user input. The three departments we want to send mail to are sales, technical support, and corporate information. Normally, the destination address is contained in a hidden field and can't be changed by user input. But as we mentioned in Chapter 9, the control fields don't have to be hidden. We take advantage of this by creating a group of radio buttons with the name `mailto`. This just happens to be the name of the form field that controls the destination of the e-mail sent by the script. The VALUE of each radio button is the e-mail address in the department (*sales@bigcorp.com, support@bigcorp.com,* or *info@bigcorp.com).* To make sure at least one of these departments is chosen, we check the sales button by default. If we didn't do this, the user could submit a form without a department (and thus no e-mail address) selected. To force the user to pick a valid address, you could also use a <SELECT> menu. The key is to provide user selection while restricting the choice to only valid addresses.

Hot Tip

> Don't use an input field with TYPE=TEXT for the mailto field unless you want users to be sending e-mail all over the Internet from your server.

We set the include_blanks control field to VALUE='no' to prevent the names of fields that contain no data from appearing in the e-mail. Only non-blank responses appropriate to the destination department will be sent. There isn't anything to prevent the user from checking items outside the department they've chosen, so this system works best if users are cooperative and do what we want them to do (a good argument for clear instructions). But, even if they check a few extra items, the e-mail will still be comprehensible.

We're not trying to process this data in a database, so we can exploit case-sensitivity and the ability to include spaces in the field names to create a nicely formatted e-mail message. In Listing 10.1, you can see that we include a few fields just for the purpose of inserting them in the e-mail output (just after the hidden control fields). Although these fields are also hidden from the user, they will be faithfully echoed in the e-mail by the script. Listing 10.2 shows what a mail message to the sales department might look like.

Listing 10.2   E-mail output from the example request-for-information form

```
From chris@hypertising.com Wed Oct 16 16:28:03 1996
Return-Path: chris@hypertising.com
Received: (from nobody@hypertising.com) by mailhost (8.7.4/8.7.3) id QAA00964; Wed, 16
Oct 1996 16:28:02 -0700
Date: Wed, 16 Oct 1996 16:28:02 -0700
Message-Id: <199610162328.QAA00964@baron1>
To: sales@bigcorp.com
From: chris@hypertising.com
```

```
Subject: Web Site Information Request
X-Mozilla-Status: 0001

This data was submitted on: Wednesday, October 16, 1996 at 16:27:01

User Information:
  :
Name: Chris Baron
Address: One Jacob Way
City: Reading
State: MA
Zip: 01867
Phone: 213-555-1212
  :
Information Requested for:
  :
Widget Basic:
Widget Classic:
Widget Deluxe:
Thingamajig:
Whatzit:
Cowpie:
```

Nerd Note

If you look carefully at the message in Listing 10.2, you can see an interesting arti-fact of the UNIX operating system. It would appear, based on the value in the `Received` field (*nobody@hypertising.com*) that user "nobody" sent the message. But who is user "nobody"? Within the UNIX operating system, a user can be created for entities other than human users. Commonly, users are created to define a set of files and directories that they "own." This provides an additional level of security, since the UNIX permission system controls access to files based on who a user is and sometimes of which user-group a user is part. The punchline: This is of interest to you, dear reader, because in almost all cases the Web server daemon *httpd* runs as user "nobody." Webmasters wisely set up user "nobody" with very limited permis-sions and access to very restricted parts of the server's file system. Any Internet crackers breaking into the system by impersonating poor old user "nobody" won't be able to do much damage.

How can this affect you as a Webmaster? When you log onto your Web server via FTP and Telnet to test scripts, install files, and so on, you have a standard human user set of permissions and accesses. But when the Web server runs your CGI scripts, it will be running as user "nobody." Scripts and other programs that run fine on your terminal when you test them by hand may not run for Mr. "nobody" because he doesn't have permission. Read Appendix B for details on the UNIX file permission system and how to set permissions for files and directories.

You can see how the dummy fields we created appear in the message. Notice also that we inserted the blank field `NAME=' '` in the `variable_order` field multiple times. We use it in the e-mail to give us an (almost) blank line between the user information section and the information requested section. When *formp.cgi* creates the e-mail, it scans the value of the `variable_order` field to get each of the field values in turn. Putting the same field in multiple times is perfectly legal, although we probably wouldn't want to do this if we were storing the data in a database.

A Guest Book

In this example, we use *formp.cgi* to create an electronic guest book for visitors to your Web site to "sign." The guest book features

- a return `mailto:` hyperlink for e-mail,
- a favorite URL, complete with an active hyperlink, and
- a comment area.

How can we do all this, you ask? Read on, grasshopper, and all will be revealed.

Figure 10.2 shows how the guest book looks in the browser. You'll notice a couple of guests have already signed it.

Listing 10.3 gives the HTML source for the form. For those of you with carpal tunnel syndrome, the HTML is on the CD-ROM in the */scripts/formp/examples/ guestbk.html* file.

Listing 10.3	HTML source for the guest book form

```
<HTML><HEAD>
<TITLE>A Formp Guestbook</TITLE></HEAD>
<BODY >

<H2>Please Sign the Guestbook</H2>
<FORM METHOD=POST ACTION="cgi-bin/formp.cgi">
<!--formp.cgi control fields-->
   <INPUT TYPE="HIDDEN" NAME="response_title" VALUE="Thanks for Signing">
```

```
    <INPUT TYPE="HIDDEN" NAME="html_response" VALUE="Glad you stopped by.">
    <INPUT TYPE="HIDDEN" NAME="echo_data" VALUE="no">
    <INPUT TYPE="HIDDEN" NAME="return_link_url" VALUE="../guestbk.html">
    <INPUT TYPE="HIDDEN" NAME="return_link_name" VALUE="Back to the Guest Book">
    <INPUT TYPE=hidden NAME="database_name" VALUE="guests/guestbk.dat">
    <INPUT TYPE="HIDDEN" NAME="database_delimiter" VALUE=" ">
    <INPUT TYPE="HIDDEN" NAME="time_stamp" VALUE="last">
    <INPUT TYPE="HIDDEN" NAME="required_variables" VALUE="Name|City">
    <INPUT TYPE=hidden NAME="variable_order" VALUE="p|am2|E-mail|abr|Name|aend|aka|Nick
Name|from|City|br|url|ahr|Recommended URL|abr|Recommended URL|aend|br|cmt|Comment">

<!-- dummy formatting fields -->
    <INPUT TYPE="HIDDEN" NAME="aka" VALUE=" a.k.a. ">
    <INPUT TYPE=hidden NAME="am2" VALUE="&lt;A HREF=&quot;mailto:">
    <INPUT TYPE=hidden NAME="abr" VALUE="&quot;&gt;">
    <INPUT TYPE="HIDDEN" NAME="aend" VALUE="&lt;/A&gt;">
    <INPUT TYPE="HIDDEN" NAME="p" VALUE="&lt;P&gt;">
    <INPUT TYPE="HIDDEN" NAME="br" VALUE="&lt;BR&gt;">
    <INPUT TYPE="HIDDEN" NAME="url" VALUE="Recommended URL: ">
    <INPUT TYPE="HIDDEN" NAME="cmt" VALUE="Comment: ">
    <INPUT TYPE=hidden NAME="ahr" VALUE="&lt;A HREF=&quot;">
    <INPUT TYPE=hidden NAME="from" VALUE="from">

<!--form input fields-->
    <P>Your Name:<BR>
    <INPUT TYPE="TEXT" NAME="Name" VALUE="">
    <P>Your City:<BR>
    <INPUT TYPE="TEXT" NAME="City">
    <P>Your Nickname:<BR>
    <INPUT TYPE="TEXT" NAME="Nick Name" VALUE="">
    <P>Your E-mail<BR>
    <INPUT TYPE="TEXT" NAME="E-mail" VALUE="">
    <P>A Recommended URL:<BR>
    <INPUT TYPE="TEXT" NAME="Recommended URL" VALUE="" SIZE=40>
    <P>A comment we all need to read (HTML OK):<BR>
    <INPUT TYPE="TEXT" NAME="Comment" VALUE="" SIZE=40 MAXLENGTH=256>
    <P><INPUT TYPE="SUBMIT" VALUE="   Add Me!   ">

</FORM>
 <HR><HR>
<H2>Previous Guests</H2>

<!--#include file="cgi-bin/guests/guestbk.dat" -->

</BODY></HTML>
```

When the user fills in the form and submits it to the server, his data is added to the guest book database. Reloading the page will cause the new data to be displayed, along with that of previous visitors.

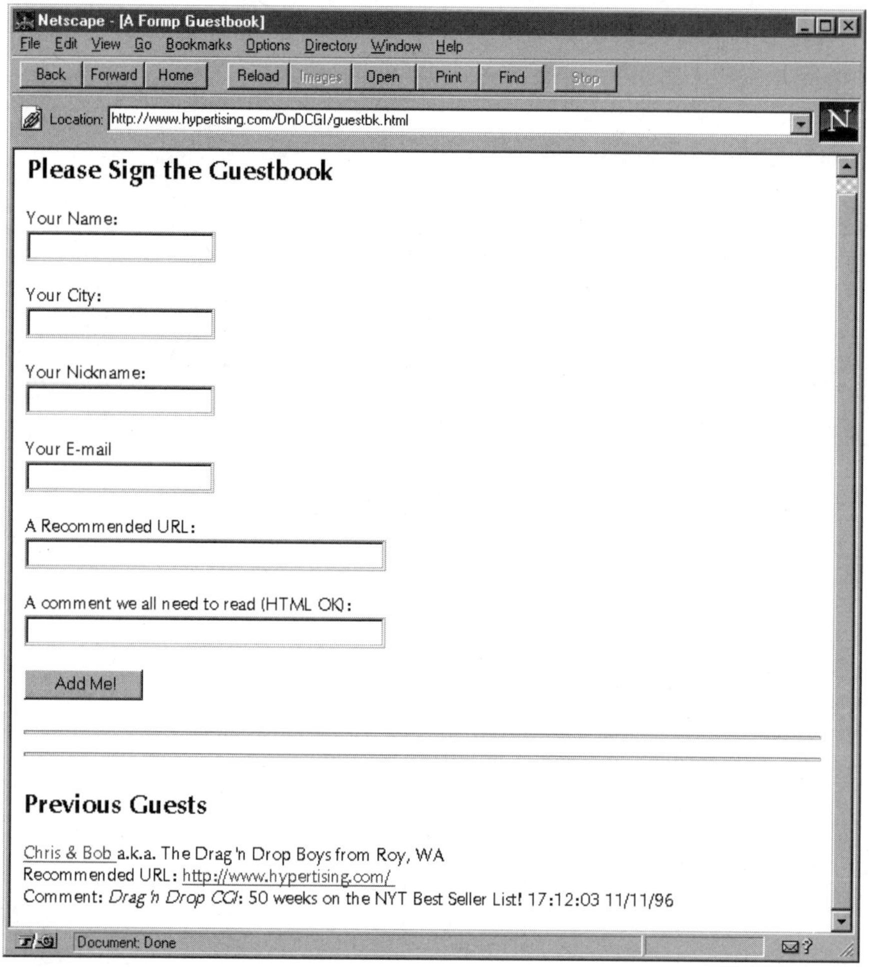

Figure 10.2 *Browser output of the guest book form*

How the Form Works

This example works by making *formp.cgi* store the data in a database file in a form that is legal HTML. By using an SSI command, we can insert the database file back into the page. Thus the database of previous guest book signers is displayed. We'll run through the HTML so that you can see how this works.

At the top of the file is a section for the *formp.cgi* control fields (using INPUT fields, with TYPE=HIDDEN). We are not going to echo the form data to the response page. Nor are we going to be sending the form data out by e-mail.

The `database_delimiter` is the space character (generally ignored by HTML browsers). This gives us the freedom to insert HTML code in other `HIDDEN` fields to control the formatting of the output data.

The `response_url` field provides a hyperlink back to the form page. If the user follows this link, the page will be reloaded and the new data displayed via SSI from the database file. We also use the `time_stamp` field to cause the script to write the time and date of the visit into the database.

The `variable_order` field is the real cornerstone of this script. Below the control field section are several `TYPE=HIDDEN` fields. These hold the fragments of HTML and text label strings that are combined with the user input data to format the database file as valid HTML. From the `variable_order` field, you can see how we take the user input and surround it with text from the hidden fields to create the HTML output we want.

If we were to set the `echo_data` parameter to `yes`, we would see ugly fragments and invalid hyperlinks on the response page. You can try this yourself to see what happens. Similarly, if we were to e-mail the form data, those fields would be included in the e-mail.

The final section of the form is the user input area. Nothing much to comment on here, except to note that to offset potential mischief, we've limited the field length to 256 characters. (This keeps errant souls from pasting an executable binary file, or something equally irrelevant, into the field.)

After the end of the form we see the SSI command that inserts the database file into the page following the form for display by the browser. If Your ISA's or SA's Web server doesn't have SSI turned on or your ISP or SA won't let you run SSI in your pages, you're pretty much out of luck using this script.

There is a potential security risk here since we don't check the comment field in any way. Because this field is included verbatim in the data file (and hence in the HTML page), a user could potentially put something in here that would cause problems with the page or with the Web server. If this happens, you'll have to go into the data file and edit out the offending record by hand. A more likely problem is that the database will just keep growing and growing until your guest book form page takes hours to load.

There are any number of possible applications for this particular script. For example, it could be used as an on-line BBS or discussion forum, with one form designated for each discussion topic or thread.

An On-line Test Form

In our third and final example using *formp.cgi*, we show you how to create an on-line test with automatic grading. There are only two grades, fail (0) and pass (100%), but that's sufficient for certain types of tests. When the user successfully completes the test, e-mail is sent to the instructor for recording.

Figure 10.3 shows the browser output of the on-line test form. Only multiple-choice questions are used because the current version of *formp.cgi* doesn't yet support the grading of essay questions.

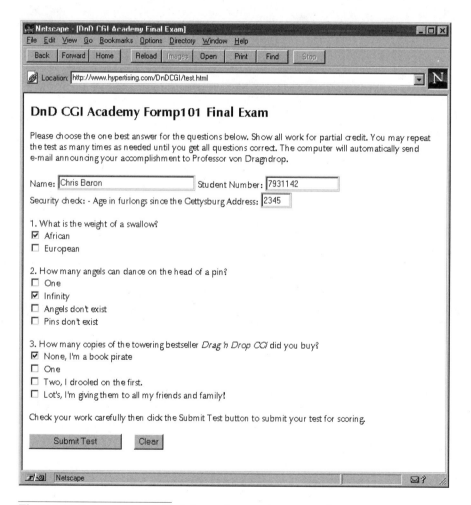

Figure 10.3 *Browser output of the on-line test form example*

Listing 10.4 presents the HTML for the form, which is located on the CD-ROM in the */scripts/formp/examples/test.html* file. You will also find the configuration file (*test.cnf,* shown in Listing 10.5) in the same directory.

Listing 10.4   **HTML source for the on-line test form**

```
<HTML><HEAD>
<TITLE>DnD CGI Academy Final Exam</TITLE></HEAD>
<BODY >
<H2>DnD CGI Academy Formp101 Final Exam</H2>
<P>Please choose the one best answer for the questions below.  Show all work
for partial credit.
You may repeat the test as many times as needed until you get all questions
correct.  The computer
will automatically send e-mail announcing your accomplishment to Professor
von Dragndrop.

<FORM METHOD=POST ACTION="cgi-bin/formp.cgi">
<!--formp.cgi control fields-->

<INPUT TYPE="HIDDEN" NAME="config_file" VALUE="../../test.cnf">
<INPUT TYPE="HIDDEN" NAME="data_set" VALUE="test">

<!--Test fields-->
<P>Name:
<INPUT TYPE="TEXT" NAME="name" VALUE="" SIZE=30 MAXLENGTH=60>
Student Number:
<INPUT TYPE="TEXT" NAME="stunum" VALUE="" SIZE=15 MAXLENGTH=30><BR>
Security check: - Age in furlongs since the Gettysburg Address:
<INPUT TYPE="TEXT" NAME="age" VALUE="" SIZE=5 MAXLENGTH=5>

    <P>1.  What is the weight of a swallow?<BR>
    <INPUT TYPE="CHECKBOX" NAME="Swallow-1" > African<BR>
    <INPUT TYPE="CHECKBOX" NAME="Swallow-2" > European
    <P>2.  How many angels can dance on the head of a pin?<BR>
    <INPUT TYPE="CHECKBOX" NAME="Angels-1" > One<BR>
    <INPUT TYPE="CHECKBOX" NAME="Angels-2" > Infinity<BR>
    <INPUT TYPE="CHECKBOX" NAME="Angels-3" > Angels don't exist<BR>
    <INPUT TYPE="CHECKBOX" NAME="Angels-4" > Pins don't exist
    <P>3.  How many copies of the towering bestseller <I>Drag 'n Drop CGI</I>
did you buy?<BR>
    <INPUT TYPE="CHECKBOX" NAME="Book-1" > None, I'll borrow someone
else's<BR>
    <INPUT TYPE="CHECKBOX" NAME="Book-2" > One<BR>
    <INPUT TYPE="CHECKBOX" NAME="Book-3" > Two, I usually loan books to the
other joker.<BR>
    <INPUT TYPE="CHECKBOX" NAME="Book-4" > Lots, I'm giving them to all my
friends and family!
```

```
<P> Check your work carefully then click the Submit Test button to submit
your test for scoring.

    <P><INPUT TYPE="SUBMIT"  VALUE="      Submit Test        ">    
    <INPUT TYPE="RESET"  VALUE="Clear">

</FORM>

</BODY></HTML>
```

Listing 10.5   **Configuration file for the on-line test form**

```
$email_of_sender = 'A Clueless Student';
$restricted_use = "no";
$should_i_mail = "yes";
$should_i_append_a_database = "no";

# forms section

# the form name is used as the name of the assoc array
# use the form
#
# %name = ( 'var', 'value'... );

%test = (
    'mailto', 'profdnd@dndacademy.edu',
    'html_response', 'Congratulations you scored 100%',
    'html_error', 'Sorry, you answered one or more questions incorrectly',
    'email_subject', 'Test Results',
    'variable_order', 'name|stunum|age|Swallow-1|Swallow-2|Angels-1|Angels-2|
Angels-3|Angels-4|Book-1|Book-2|Book-3|Book-4',
    'required_variables', 'name|stunum|age|Swallow-1|Angels-2|Book-4',
    'echo_data', 'yes',
    'include_blanks', 'no',
    'url_of_this_form', 'http://www.dndacademy.edu/test.html',
    'body', 'text=000000  link="#00ff00" vlink="#0000ff"',
    'response_title', 'Good Job!',
    'return_link_url', 'http://www.beer.com/',
    'return_link_name', "It's Time for a BREWSKI!",
    );
```

How the Form Works

Since it wouldn't do for smart students to list the source HTML for the form and get the correct answers to the test, we put most of the control information in a control file. Even smarter students could figure out how to make the browser list the contents of the control file, since all the files within the HTML directory tree have to be readable by the Web server. So we moved the control file outside the HTML document hierarchy by using the UNIX ../ idiom in the path to the configuration file. Thus our *formp.cgi* script resides in the */home/users/joeuser/public_html/cgi-bin/* directory. The location of our control file is specified as *../../test.cnf*. This results in a final path to the configuration file of */home/users/joeuser/*.

Nerd Note

> As a security feature, most Web servers will not read documents outside of the user's *public_html/* directory (also called, e.g., *www/*, *htdocs/*, or *html/*) and its subdirectories. CGI scripts, which need to access all kinds of system resources to act as a Common Gateway Interface, don't have any such restriction (which is partly why some ISPs don't allow them.)

A quick scan through the rest of the form shows no special tricks being used. A rudimentary security feature is included, since anyone could access the form and forge another student's name. Astute readers will have noticed the format of the test questions and said to themselves, "That's a dumb way to do it. I'd use a radio button group." To this, we reply, "We would have, too, except it won't work." To grade the test, we use the `required_variables` control field. With the correct answers in this field, the script will return the error page if all the correct answers are not present. Had we used a radio button group, we wouldn't have been able to distinguish correct answers from incorrect answers. Why? All that `required_variables` checks is that the form field contains a value. By using a separate check box field for each possible answer, we can check for all correct answers. Perceptive readers will say, "But the student can just check all the check boxes, and they'll always include the correct answer!" This would be true, but we defeat this strategy by using both the `variable_order` and `include_blanks` fields. By including all the possible answers in the `variable_order` field, we report all the fields that were checked. Nonchecked answers won't be included in the e-mail to the professor because setting `include_blanks` to `No` causes empty fields not to be sent.

Figures 10.4 and 10.5 show the browser response to successful and unsuccessful test attempts. We use the control field `html_error` to give the unsuccessful test error message. The default error message lists the required fields; this would give all the test answers to the students. Unfortunately, we'll get this same error if the student forgets to put in his or her name, student number, or age, since we have only one possible response to a missing required variable.

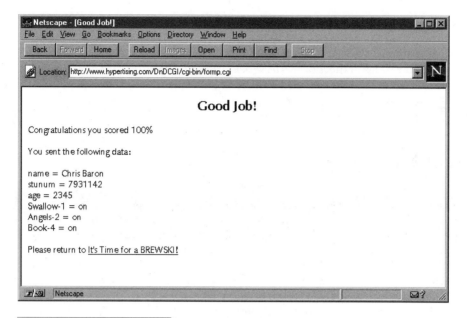

Figure 10.4 *Browser output of a successful test*

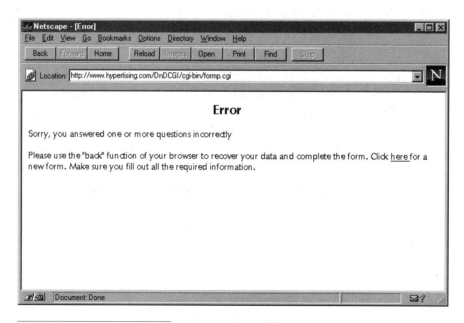

Figure 10.5 *Browser output of an unsuccessful test*

Listing 10.6 shows a typical e-mail output from the script.

Listing 10.6	E-mail response from on-line test form

```
Return-Path: <www@hypertising.com>
Date: Tue, 12 Nov 1996 18:13:16 -0800
To: profdnd@dndacademy.edu
From: A.Clueless.Student@dndacademy.edu
Subject: Test Results

This data was submitted on: Tuesday, November 12, 1996 at 18:13:16

name: Chris Baron
stunum: 7931142
age: 2345
Swallow-1: on
Angels-2: on
Book-4: on
```

While we don't recommend actually using *formp.cgi* as a testing script, you can see the usefulness of the `required_variables` field as a way to check content and the completeness of the form responses.

You may never use *formp.cgi* for anything beyond simply processing form data to e-mail data files gathering, but we hope these examples will help you to start thinking about more refined uses for this script.

Nerd Note

Coming up with unintended or unimagined uses for programs is the essence of computer hacking. If you follow these examples and proceed to develop unique applications of *formp.cgi*, you're well on the road to becoming a true *formp.cgi* hacker.

What We Covered in Chapter 10

- Sending form data to different e-mail locations, based on user input
- Writing extra formatting information into the form data using hidden form fields
- Including database files into HTML pages using SSI
- Checking for the content of the form data using the `required_variables` control field

Chapter 11

Client-side Form Validation with Javascript

Features of the *formv* Script

- Checks the contents of form fields to verify that data is in the proper format, without CGI access to the host
- Checks a single field or the entire form
- Checks either the value in a field or the presence of a value only
- Works with the *hint* and *scroller* scripts, presented in Chapter 4, "Giving Your Visitor a Hint (or Two) Using Javascript" and Chapter 6, "Fun with Scrolling Text Using Javascript"

What You Need to Use This Script

- A Javascript-capable browser such as Netscape Navigator version 2.02 or higher or Microsoft Internet Explorer version 3.0 or higher
- HTML or a text editor

Why You Would Want to Use This Script

Once you've made the decision to use forms on your Web site to collect data, the next question is, how do you *handle* that data? You can always have the data sent as e-mail, especially if the volume is expected to be small. You could even collect it in a single file and print it out from time to time. But why worry about an input error by a visitor, especially if this script won't tell you whether the address they typed in actually exists?

By giving people a uniform method of communicating with your organization, you've created a stream of potentially valuable, and usable, data. Information is not readily usable if it arrives in an e-mail message or on a printed sheet. Putting information in a database allows it to be added to over time, manipulated and analyzed, and bashed against supplementary data from other sources. For example, once you have a person's name, address, and phone number, you can often purchase demographic data to append to that record.

Properly implemented, forms can allow you to build a profile of visitors to your site, whether they are potential or actual users of your product or service. The possibilities are endless, as anyone in Marketing will chime in, once they see what you're up to with this form stuff.

Now that you're dealing with databases, you have standards you need to follow: field length, data type, and absence or presence of a value. Rather than trying to clean up data at the back end, it makes more sense for you to bring in the best data possible at the front end. The *formv* script allows you to get as finicky about the data as you need to. And it makes the responses you get from your forms that much easier to integrate into your other databases.

Introduction to the *formv* Script

In the last two chapters, we gave you a way to use the *formp.cgi* script to handle data sent to your ISP or SA's Web server from HTML forms. But *formp.cgi* is a general purpose script, and it isn't well-suited to checking the contents of the form. Error checking is limited to verifying that a set of fields is not left blank on the server side. Client-side validation of a field or form is the raison d'etre of the *formv* script, which can not only check for blank fields, but you can also determine if a correct value has been entered.

The fact that the script runs on the client rather than the server has several other benefits. It allows your visitor to move quickly and interactively through the form, validating input on the fly without making repeated calls to the server. In addition to saving a visitor's time, a client-side script such as *formv* provides a broad range of validation options to the site designer.

Unfortunately, this script can't prevent the submission of bad data that is in the proper format. But there really isn't much a script can do about that type of problem. You're on your own when it comes to enlightening visitors on the proper way to complete your forms. We'll just have to trust your persuasive skills and your visitors' good will.

Figure 11.1 shows *formv* in action on one of our commercial Web sites. The pop-up dialog notifies the user that a required field is empty.

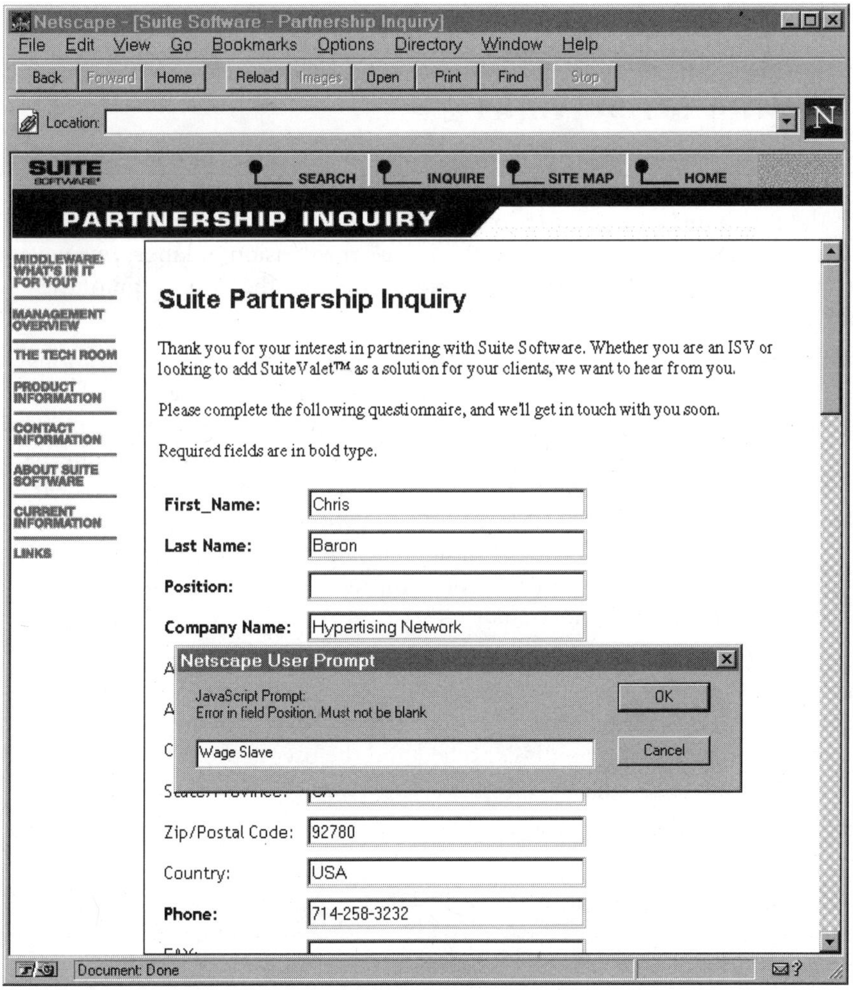

Figure 11.1 *The* formv *script in action at the Suite Software Web site at* http://www.suite.com

This script was extensively tested with Netscape *Navigator* 3.01 and Microsoft Internet *Explorer* 3.01 on Windows 95. Unfortunately, the implementation of Javascript is not always consistent across different operating systems, even within the same browser version number. So your mileage may vary on another OS. As we proceed through the chapter, we'll note functions we know about that don't work on various browsers. We've tried hard to prevent the script from crashing no matter what browser your users are running. For functions not supported by a particular browser, we've tried to design the script to simply ignore calls to that particular function.

Before proceeding, you may want to take a few minutes to review the sample file *formvtst.htm* in the *scripts/formv* directory on the CD-ROM. While checking out how the validation process works, be sure to view the document source to see what's going on under the hood.

How the *formv* Script Works

The *formv* script is a set of Javascript routines designed to check the contents of HTML form fields and notify the user of data format problems. It is designed to work with the Perl-based *formp.cgi* script described in Chapter 9 "Processing and Responding to Interactive Forms Using Perl." Here's the division of labor: *formv* validates the data on the user's browser, and *formp.cgi* handles the disposition of the data on the server.

To invoke the awesome power of *formv*, you first create a list of field specifications describing the fields to be checked, the type of data it should contain, and, in the case of numeric data, minimum and maximum values. These parameters are set using two *formv* functions called `required()` and `warn()`. These functions create an internal validation array containing the field specifications. To check the contents of a field, you need to add a call to the `check()` function from within the HTML form in response to an event, such as clicking a button (`onClick` or when the insertion point leaves a field (`onBlur`. (See Chapters 4, 6 and 8 for more information about Javascript events and event-handler functions.)

Alternatively, the `check_all()` routine is used to check all the fields in a form, one after another. This function is usually called by an `onSubmit` Javascript event when the user clicks the submit button on the form. If errors are encountered in any required fields, the form submission is cancelled and the user is prompted to correct the data. Errors in warning-only fields generate a message to the user but don't block form submission.

Configuring and Installing the *formv* Script

As with all Javascript scripts, configuring and installing *formv* does not require that any files be uploaded to the Web server. A nice aspect of working with Javascript that you've probably already noticed is that you can fully test the script on your local machine without its being connected to the network. So configuration and installation consist of pasting the *formv* script into your HTML page and setting the script variables to your liking.

Hair Saver

> Microsoft doesn't tell you this, but in their implementation of Javascript (JScript), several of the functions don't work unless *Internet Explorer* 3.0 is accessing a page on the network. The most notable of these is the `submit` function. The browser simply ignores any attempt to submit the form if the client machine isn't connected to a TCP/IP network. This prevents off-line testing of the `onSubmit()` event. (For our present task, it doesn't matter because the form data that *formv* needs to access isn't available to the `onSubmit()` event handler in JScript.) Fortunately, Netscape *Navigator does* work off-line. Bottom line: If your script won't run with Internet *Explorer* off-line, retry it after uploading the HTML page to your ISP's or SA's Web server.

Preparing *formv* for use in your pages consists of three steps:

1. Configure the text messages that the script displays in response to a form error.

2. Specify each field you want to have checked by calling either the `required()` or `warn()` functions from within your HTML page.

3. Activate the checking methods either by adding an `onBlur()` event for each field or creating a button or hyperlink to explicitly check a given field.

The `check_all()` function allows you to check all the fields one after the other and give the user a chance to correct the error or cancel the submission. (As of version 3.01, Microsoft *Internet Explorer* doesn't support this function. So be aware if the visitor is using *Explorer* or another non-Netscape browser, the script simply submits the form without checking the fields.)

Step 1: Configuration

To start the configuration process, either copy the *formv.txt* from the CD-ROM to your local hard disk for editing or paste the script into the <HEAD> section of your HTML file following the <TITLE> tag and any <META> tags you may have. The *formv* script is quite a bit larger than our other Javascript scripts, weighing in at a little over 350 lines of code. This will add about 11K to the size of your HTML file.

Listing 11.1 shows the configuration block for the *formv* script.

Listing 11.1	*formv* script configuration block

```
/*

    ****************************************************
    Configuration Block
    ****************************************************
    - The various xxx_Text variables make up the text for the
    messages sent to the user.  Customize these for your language
    and location.

    - Put each of the form fields that you would like validated into
    the following format and call the check() function in your code

    - If your page has multiple forms don't
    duplicate names unless you want them validated in exactly the same way.
    required(FieldName, any);
    required(FieldName, phone|zip|email);
    required(FieldName, Int|Float, min, max);
    or
    warn(FieldName...

    - The entire form can be validated with the checkall() function as
    follows
    add the following to the <FORM> tag
    onSubmit="return check_all(document.formname);"
*/
//   User messages are formed by req_Text + fieldname + type_Text
//   for example, "Error in field: FullName. Must not be blank"
     req_Text = "Error in field:";
     warn_Text = "Warning! field ";
     any_Text = ". Must not be blank";
     radio_Text = ". One must be selected";
     phone_Text = ". Must be a valid phone number";
     zip_Text = ". Must contain a valid ZIP code";
//   these are used to form the numeric range message
//   req_Text + fieldname + int_Text + minimum + and_Text + maximum
//   for example: Error in field Age.  Enter an integer between 0 and 100
     int_Text = ". Enter an integer between ";
```

```
        float_Text = ". must be between ";
        and_Text = " and ";

/*
        ********************************************************
        End of Configuration Block
        ********************************************************
*/
```

Recall that the /* */ pair indicates a multi-line comment section to Javascript and the "//" string indicates a one-line comment. Everything outside the comment section is Javascript code and needs to be in proper Javascript language format. Start configuring the script by customizing the text strings that go into making up an error message to the user. Figure 11.2 shows an error message generated by the script, with the variables used to create each part shown as call-outs.

These variable definitions start with the line

```
req_Text = "Error in field:";
```

Modify the variables by changing the text within the double quotation marks to match your language and the message you wish to present. As you might suspect, required variables will use the req_Text message, while those needing only a warning message will use the warn_Text message. Each type of field that can be checked has a unique text message, so you can provide a meaningful error message. As you customize these variables, be sure to surround the text with double quotation marks and end each line with a semicolon. Javascript is as picky as Perl in this regard and will give you nasty messages if you don't do things its way. (See Figure 11.3.)

You will probably have to tweak these messages to get the final combined error message to look right. For now, just take your best shot and finalize the text after you have seen how they look in action.

Next, you need to tell the script how you want each of your form fields validated. If you don't have an existing form, you should create one now in your usual manner.

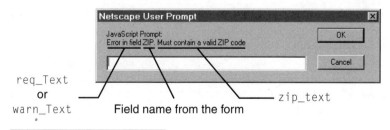

Figure 11.2 *formv error message showing variable locations*

Once you are happy with the look of your form, you can add the validation functions to it by creating a series of calls to the check and check_all functions.

The required and warn functions create an entry in a validation array that the script uses to determine whether the data in the form field is in the proper format. In the example HTML file *formvtst.htm*, located on the CD-ROM in the */scripts/formv/* directory, you'll find a block similar to Listing 11.2.

Listing 11.2	Javascript block specifying form validation criteria to the *formv* script

```
<SCRIPT LANGUAGE="JavaScript">
<!--
//Specify how each field in your forms should be checked
required("Full_Name", "any");
warn("Phone", "phone");
required("ZIP", "zip");
required("Age", "Int", 18, 35);
warn("BatAvg", "Float", 0.000, 0.999);
required("Favorite", "any");
//-->
</SCRIPT>
```

Since these are Javascript function calls, you need to surround them with the <SCRIPT> and </SCRIPT> tags. Both functions have the same format. The first parameter is the name of the form field as specified in the NAME="fieldname" part of the <INPUT> or <TEXTAREA> tags.

Hair Saver

The NAME parameter and the string you put in the call to required() or warn() must match exactly. Javascript, unlike HTML, is case sensitive. Use cut-and-paste to make sure the spelling and capitalization are the same.

Also avoid using spaces in the field name. Spaces are legal in HTML, and our *formp.cgi* examples use them to good effect. However, Javascript isn't quite so liberal about the characters it allows in field names. Here's a good coder's rule of thumb: Don't use spaces in your field names. If necessary, use the programmer's equivalent of a space, which is the underscore _ character (for example, my_house).

The second parameter is the type of data this field should contain. Following are the legal values:

- `any`. Requires the field not be empty; otherwise, it is considered OK.

- `phone`. Requires a U.S.-style phone number with either 7 or 10 digits. Parentheses and dash characters are ignored. All other characters cause an error.

- `zip`. Requires a U.S.-style ZIP code with either 5, 9, or 11 digits. Dash characters and spaces are ignored.

- `email`. Requires a string containing an @ character and at least one period ".". Note, there are many valid e-mail addresses that don't contain these characters. Use this validation type with caution, especially on internal networks.

- `int` (age, in the example file). Requires an integer number consisting only of digits, possibly with a minus sign –. The value must fall between the numbers given in the third and fourth parameters. The values are inclusive, and commas and spaces are not allowed in the number. *Note:* Don't put quotation marks around the numbers.

- `float` (batting average, in the example file). Requires a floating-point value consisting of digits, a period, and the exponential notation characters "E, e, +, and –" and spaces. As with `int`, the third and fourth parameters specify, respectively, the upper and lower bounds of acceptable values. Also, as with `int`, the values are inclusive, and commas are not allowed.

Create a `required()` or `warn()` entry for each field you want checked, making sure to include the minimum and maximum values for integer and floating-point numeric fields. Fields that don't have an entry in this block will be ignored by the script.

Hot Tip

The *formv* script can be used to check fields in multiple forms on your page. Just give all the fields different names and include them all in the calls to `required()` and `warn()`. If you have multiple fields that contain exactly the same data (such as a name or phone number), you can enable checking for all the fields with a single call to `required()` or `warn()`. Simply use the same `NAME=` parameter for the identical fields. *formv* can tell from which form the entry came and will validate the entry for that form.

Conversely, if you want different checking done on two different fields, don't use the same `NAME=` parameter. This is necessary because *formv* creates just a single entry in the validation array for a given field name, so only the last entry will be retained.

Step 2: Installation

Since *formv* is Javascript, there is no installation as such. However, before continuing, you should save your HTML page (which now includes the *formv* script) and preview it as a local file with your Web browser. If you've made an error in the variable definitions or in the calls to `required()` and `warn()`, you'll see an error message like that shown in Figure 11.3.

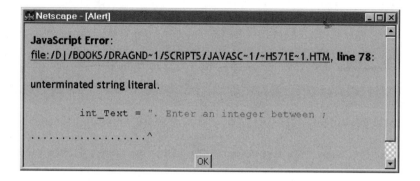

Figure 11.3 *Javascript error message for* formv

This error was caused by a missing quotation mark in one of the message text variable definitions. When Javascript encounters an error in a script, it attempts to locate the error by line and lets you know where it thinks the problem lies. The line number and the problem are only Javascript's best guess, so if you don't find the problem there be sure to look at other lines in the general vicinity.

Once you get the page to load without problems, you're ready to modify your HTML forms to call the field validation routines.

Using the *formv* Script in Your Pages

The *formv* script includes support for the two most common validation points: on field entry and on form submission. Single field validation occurs when the user moves the cursor out of a field by either clicking in another field or by using the tab key to it. If there is an error in the data entered in the field, *formv* will show the user a pop-up dialog requesting corrected data (see Figure 11.2). This gives users immediate feedback and helps them get the form right the first time. (Our own *formp.cgi* and other CGI-based form processors make users wait until they submit the entire form to see if there are any problems with it.)

The second validation point occurs when the user has finished filling out the form and attempts to submit it to the server. Use this if you want to avoid nagging users as they fill out the form. This method has the advantage of letting you prompt them for all the needed corrections in a single "whack" before allowing the form to be submitted.

You'll have to make the call (yes, it's a pun) whether one method or a combination of the two is best for your target user and your Web site.

Checking a Single Field

One method for checking a single field is to use the check() function to examine the contents of a single field. This function takes a single parameter containing the name of the field to be checked. You can use it either within an <INPUT> form tag, triggered by an onBlur Javascript event, or by explicitly calling the function from a button or hyperlink using an onClick event.

Since check boxes, selection lists, hidden fields, plain buttons, submit buttons, and reset buttons can't contain user-entered data, it isn't necessary to check them.

Radio button groups, on the other hand, may be checked using validation type any. This is necessary if a button group, created without a default selection, requires a user selection to be valid. Figure 11.4 shows the error pop-up dialog generated for an empty radio button group.

A run-of-the-mill text input field might look like this in your HTML page:

```
<INPUT TYPE="TEXT" NAME="Phone" SIZE="12" MAXLENGTH="15">
```

By adding a simple call to the *formv* check() routine, you can transform this field from a meek patsy that accepts any and all data into a demanding tyrant that will tolerate data only in exactly the correct format. The modified tag looks like this:

```
<INPUT TYPE="TEXT" NAME="Phone" SIZE="12" MAXLENGTH="15"
onBlur="check(Phone);">
```

Figure 11.4 formv *error pop-up dialog for radio buttons*

This additional text executes the Javascript code between the quotation marks when an `onBlur` event is detected for this field (the user either clicks elsewhere on the screen or tabs to the next field). In this case, the Javascript code consists of a call to the *formv* `check()` function with the name of the form field. *Note:* Don't put quotation marks around the field name in the `check()` call.

Nerd Note

We don't put quotation marks around the field name in this function call because the parameter we're passing to the function isn't a string containing the name of the field but rather a reference to the actual form field object. The field object encapsulates all the data items about this form element, including its type, name, current contents (value), and in which form it resides. The object also contains a method (function) to allow Javascript to change the contents of the field. We use all this information within the *formv* script to perform our magic. The nice thing for you, the page designer, is that you don't have to worry about passing around all this data. The elegance of having this provided in a nice package with the form object is one of the benefits of an object-oriented programming language such as Javascript.

If the field contains a valid phone number, the script allows the user to proceed. If the field is blank or contains invalid data, a pop-up window displays the current contents of the field so that the user can enter a correction. If the user exits the pop-up by hitting the Enter key or by clicking the ok button, the data in the form field is updated with the contents of the pop-up. If the user clicks `Cancel` or the close window button (top right corner in Windows 95), the original data is left in the field.

If you've specified that this is a required field (by your call to the `required` function), the updated data is checked and, if there is still an error, the pop-up window is displayed again. The user can break out of this loop by exiting the pop-up using the cancel button. Warning fields respect the user's wishes and move on to the next field without checking the updated data. This behavior follows what users expect from pop-up windows of this type.

A second method of checking a single field is to call the check function from a button or hyperlink. Adding the following form element to your HTML will allow your users to manually check the contents of a field:

```
<INPUT TYPE="BUTTON" NAME="chk_phone" VALUE="Check Phone Field"
onClick="check(Phone);">
```

This code creates a button labeled "Check Phone Field." Clicking the button executes the call to the `check` function. Again, don't put quotation marks around the name of the field. Similarly, you can use a textual or graphical hyperlink to do the same thing. One major drawback of this method is that non-Javascript browsers will still display this hyperlink. It won't do anything, but good user interface design dictates that you minimize useless controls.

An alternative way to call the check function is for you to generate the hyperlink programmatically using Javascript. Obviously a non-Javascript browser won't see this link, since it will exist only if the browser supports Javascript. This mini-script will generate a link on Javascript-supporting browsers that will work with both *Navigator* and *Internet Explorer*. Note the use of the backslash \, which allows quotation marks within the document.write parameter.

```
<SCRIPT LANGUAGE="JavaScript">
<!--
// note, put this all on a single line
document.write("<A  HREF=\"Javascript:check(Phone);\">Check Phone
Field</A>");
//-->
</SCRIPT>
```

Hair Saver

Browser Alert! This is a good time to remind you that no two browsers completely agree on a single HTML, Javascript, or Java implementation. As of this writing (May 1997), Netscape *Navigator* 3.01 supports all the functions we cover in this book. Most non-Netscape browsers, including Microsoft *Internet Explorer* 3.01, do not support several functions we use in the *formv* script. If you know your site will be accessed by non-Netscape users (and you care about them), use the check function for each form field, rather than the check_all function (which will simply cause the form to be submitted without validation). *Note:* Of course, this may have changed by the time you read this. With the next round of the browser bruisefest, *Internet Explorer* could leapfrog *Navigator*. Gotta love those browser wars; they sure make life interesting.

Radio button checks require that you use the following format:

```
<INPUT TYPE="BUTTON" NAME="chk_rad" VALUE="Check Radio Buttons"
onClick="check(Radios[0]);">
```

This is due to the way radio buttons are stored in Javascript.

Of the onClick and the onBlur methods of checking fields, the onBlur method is preferable. Non-Javascript browsers will ignore the onBlur= parameter in the field tag, and the form will operate normally for these browsers. Alternatively, if you hide the button or hyperlink from non-Javascript browsers, the onClick method gives better control over when the field is checked (at the expense of some added complexity in your HTML pages).

Hot Tip

> *Reality Check Time!* Even though you can create field check buttons or hyperlinks, your average Internet users are unlikely to actually use them. They are more likely to just fill in all the fields and hit the submit button. The `onBlur` call to the `check()` function will force a validation check on the fields.

Checking an Entire Form

The `check_all` function is used to check all the form fields with entries in the validation array, one after the other. This is most useful when the user is attempting to submit the form to the server. However, you can create a button or hyperlink to call the `check_all` function using the methods we described previously if you like. This function takes the name of the form to be checked as its single parameter. As with the parameter for the `check` function, don't put quotation marks around the name of the form. Again, we're passing a reference to the form object to the checking function rather than simply passing the name.

If an entry with a name matching the field's NAME= parameter exists in the validation array, the `check` function is called by `check_all` to validate the contents of the field. The `check_all` function will continue checking fields until either the last field is checked, or the user clicks Cancel to exit an error pop-up window. In the former case, `check_all` gives the go-ahead to submit the form. In the latter, it reports an error code that will prevent the form from being submitted.

Putting It All Together

Listing 11.3 shows part of the example HTML file *formvtst.htm* that demonstrates the features of *formv*. Figure 11.5 shows the browser output of this demonstration file.

Listing 11.3   *formvtst.htm* **demonstration HTML file**

```
<BODY>
<H2>Fun With Forms</H2>
<H3>Form #1</H3>
<FORM NAME="form1" onSubmit="return check_all(document.form1);">
<SCRIPT LANGUAGE="JavaScript">
```

```
<!--
//     Specify how each field in your forms should be checked
       required("Full_Name", "any");
       required("Email", "email");
       warn("Phone", "phone");
       required("ZIP", "zip");
       required("Age", "Int", 18, 35);
       warn("BatAvg", "Float", 0.000, 0.999);
       required("Favorite", "any");
//-->
</SCRIPT>
       Your Name: <INPUT TYPE="TEXT" NAME="Full_Name" onBlur="check(Full_Name);">
       <INPUT TYPE="BUTTON" Name="nm_chk" VALUE = "Check Name Field"
            onClick="check(Full_Name);"> or a hyperlink
       <SCRIPT LANGUAGE="JavaScript">
       <!--
       document.write("<A  HREF=\"Javascript:check(Full_Name);\">Check Name</A>");
       //-->
       </SCRIPT><BR>
       Your Email: <INPUT TYPE="TEXT" NAME="Email" onBlur="check(Email);"><BR>
       Your Phone: <INPUT TYPE="TEXT" NAME="Phone" onBlur="check(Phone);"><BR>
       Your ZIP Code: <INPUT TYPE="TEXT" NAME="ZIP" VALUE="" SIZE=12
       onBlur="check(ZIP);">
       <A HREF="#zip" NAME="zip" onClick="check(ZIP);">check ZIP</A> (Doesn't work with
MSIE)<BR>
       Your Age: <INPUT TYPE="TEXT" NAME="Age" VALUE="" SIZE=5 onBlur="check(Age);">
       (between 18 and 35)<BR>
       Your Batting Average: <INPUT TYPE="TEXT" NAME="BatAvg" VALUE="" SIZE=8
            onBlur="check(BatAvg);"> (between 0.00 and 1.00)<BR>
       Your IQ: (don't lie) <INPUT TYPE="TEXT" NAME="IQ" VALUE="" onBlur="check(IQ);">
            Not Checked
       <P>Favorite Color: (can't check until submit time unless you use a button/
link)<BR>
       <INPUT TYPE="RADIO" NAME="Favorite" VALUE="Red" onClick=0 > Red
       <INPUT TYPE="RADIO" NAME="Favorite" VALUE="Blue" onClick=0> Blue
       <INPUT TYPE="RADIO" NAME="Favorite" VALUE="Puce" onClick=0> Puce<BR>
       <A HREF="#here" NAME="here" onClick="check(Favorite[0]);">
<IMG SRC="check.gif" WIDTH=24 HEIGHT=24 BORDER=1 ALT="chk field" ALIGN="BOTTOM"></A>
       Check radio(Doesn't work with MSIE)
       <P><INPUT TYPE="SUBMIT" NAME="Submit" VALUE="Check All and Submit" >
</FORM>
<H3>Form #2</H3>
<FORM NAME="form2" onSubmit= "return check_all(form2);">
<P>These fields are duplicates of the fields above.
       <P>Your Name: <INPUT TYPE="TEXT" NAME="Full_Name" onBlur="check(Full_Name);">
<BR>
       Your Phone: <INPUT TYPE="TEXT" NAME="Phone" onBlur="check(Phone);">
       <P><INPUT TYPE="SUBMIT" NAME="Submit" VALUE="Check All and Submit Form #2" >
</FORM>
</BODY>
</HTML>
```

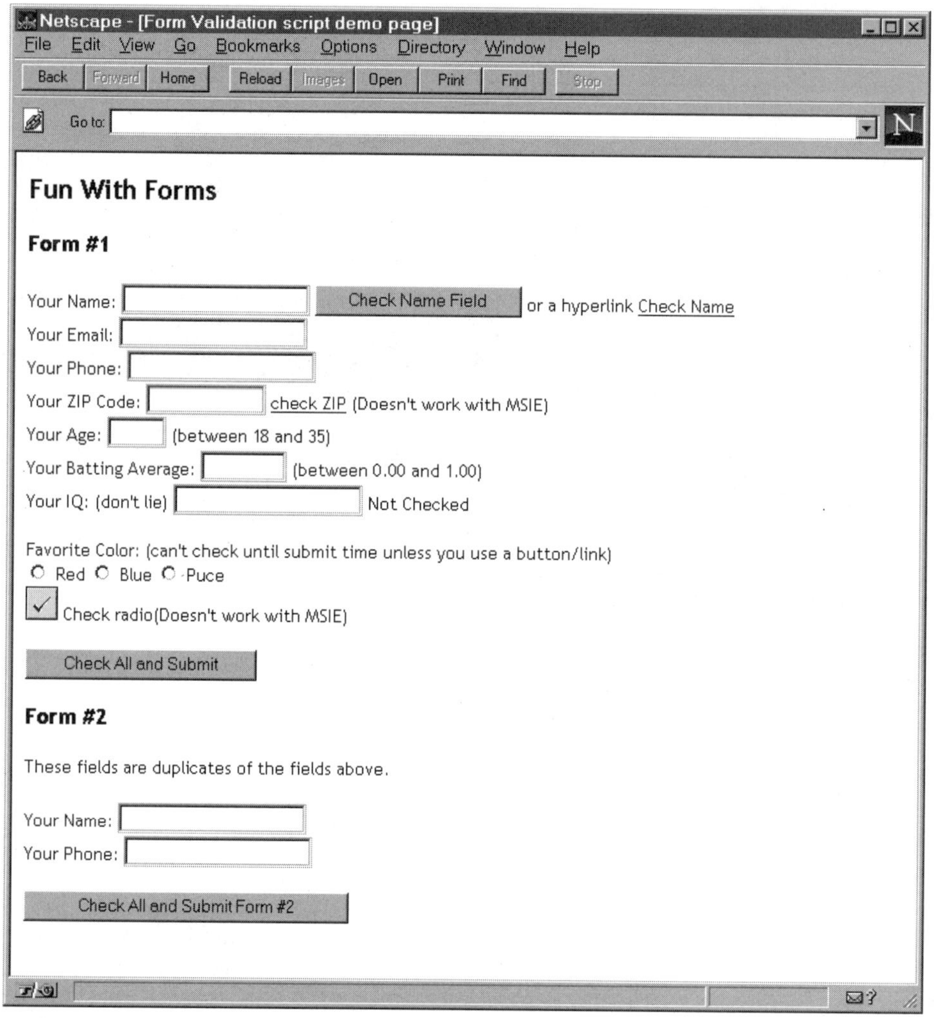

Figure 11.5 *Browser output of the* formvtst.htm *file*

Although it may not seem so at this point, the *formv* script will become an important part of your Webmaster's toolkit. Once you've mastered its use, you'll find yourself validating most forms, especially those destined for use in a database. The key with Javascript is to master the experiment-test-modify-retest cycle, and use it to refine scripts like *formv* until they work the way you want.

What We Covered in Chapter 11

- Client-side form validation versus server-side CGI form validation
- Configuring the *formv* text messages for different types of fields
- Creating a validation array of fields to be checked by the script
- Different ways to use *formv* to check a single field
- How to check an entire form using the `check_all` function

Chapter 12

A Perl-based Web Site Search Engine

Features of the *ice.pl* Script

- Returns links to pages matching search criteria
- Searches multiple directories
- Thesaurus feature for synonyms and abbreviations
- Allows "and" and "or" combinations of search words
- Very simple installation
- Runs on UNIX, Windows, and the Mac
- Very simple to generate search indexes
- Suitable for Web sites up of to a few thousand documents

What You Need to Use This Script

- Perl version 4 or 5
- Text editor
- FTP client
- Telnet client

Why You Would Want to Use This Script

We'll go on record as saying that any text-heavy site over ten full pages in length would benefit from a search engine. Before you run off and implement this script, though, take a moment to think about your objectives in building the site. Sites like the following probably do not require a search engine:

- A personal "vanity" page
- A graphics-heavy portfolio site for a sole proprietor, a small service provider, or a product provider
- A straightforward "storefront" site consisting mostly of graphics and some marketing copy (even if the site is 10 to 15 pages in length)
- The typical converted-brochure, four-page "gotta-have-a-Web-site-now" presence with which many small companies begin their Internet life

A logical layout complemented by a thoughtfully designed index and/or visual sitemap will probably do the job for sites like these.

On the other hand, Web sites seeking to deliver large amounts of information efficiently are naturals for search engines. For example:

- A site that offers extensive product or technical support content
- A site featuring dynamic content (e.g., catalogues that have products and descriptions that change frequently)
- Any database-driven site, particularly those used in corporate intranets
- A Web site of any size that visitors will need to search for particular words or concepts

To ensure good performance at runtime (regardless of Web site size), we selected a search engine that relies on a precompiled index. This has a couple of implications for creating and maintaining the site. First, graphics and "artistic text" (graphics that contain words) are not captured when indexing Web pages. And second, the index must be regenerated whenever new site content is added. In either case, the ease-of-use benefits to the site visitor outweigh the disadvantages.

The script presented in this chapter is called *ICE*. Written by Christian Neuss of Germany, *ICE* is copyrighted, but freely distributable. His Web site (*http://www.informatik.th-darmstadt.de/~neuss/ice/ice.html*) contains the latest release of the code. Here are the conditions for the use of his software, as set out on his Web site:

> This code is free, but copyrighted. No liability whatsoever is accepted for any loss or damage of any kind resulting from any defect or inaccuracy in this information or code.

Feel free to modify the forms' front-end according to your needs, but please leave the pointer to the ICE homepage in there, so that people can always find an up to date version of the software.

If you really like ICE, or if you want to inspire new features or enhancements, you may feel free to send me a token of appreciation. This could be a such as a sample of your favorite beer, music, or literature – or even a postcard from your home town.

If you use ICE on a professional server, or install it as a commercial service for your customer, I'd appreciate a small shareware fee.

We decided to use *ICE* instead of writing our own search script for several reasons. First, it was freely distributable, and Herr Neuss gave us permission to include it in this book. Second, it is written in Perl, while most other search engines use C. Third, and most important, it already exists and it has been real-world tested.

Nerd Note

One of the cardinal rules of the Internet and programming:

Never code yourself something you can snarf off the Net for free.

We enthusiastically subscribe to this idea, as you can see from the various scripts included in this book. To loosely paraphrase a famous dead guy: "If I reach great heights, it is only because I stand on the shoulders of giants" (Sir Isaac Newton, circa 1676).

Introduction to the *ICE* Scripts

Because of the free-form nature of the Web and the Internet in general, search engines are probably the most-used Internet utility. The basic idea behind search engines is simple enough. Each HTML document is broken down into individual words (HTML tags are ignored). All the words are stored in a database with pointers back to the original document. The search engine searches the database and returns a set of hyperlinks to the documents matching the user's query. It will also cross-reference a thesaurus, if one exists, for any predefined synonyms. Other features, such as "close" matching or phonetic (sounds-like) matching, require much more complicated search algorithms than *ICE* uses. Presumably, your Web site search needs are a little more modest than those of Internet-wide search engines. According to its author, *ICE* should perform well when indexing and searching Web sites that have up to a few thousand documents.

How the *ICE* Scripts Work

ICE is actually a system that consists of two scripts: *ice-idx.pl* and *ice-form.cgi*. *ice-idx.pl* is a command-line indexing script that searches through a directory tree of HTML documents and creates the Web site word index file. It is run either manually each time the Web pages change or by means of a scheduled "batch" utility such as the UNIX *cron* facility. The index produced by *ice-idx.pl* is a text file listing of each word that occurs in each document. Also included in the index is the title of the document, taken from the document's <TITLE> section. *ICE* also can cross-reference a thesaurus, thereby enabling users to use acronyms, abbreviations, and synonyms in the search. The thesaurus file must be created and maintained by hand. We show you an example of a thesaurus file later in the chapter.

The second part of the *ICE* system is *ice-form.cgi*. This script does the actual search of the word index and returns the list of matching documents based on the user's query. *Ice-form.cgi* will both generate the query form and format the output into a set of HTML hyperlinks. It is possible to customize both the query form and the output by editing this script. A custom input form can be used in place of the form generated by the script if desired, as long as you take care to use the same NAME= parameters for the form fields. We show examples of both methods. Unfortunately, customizing the output page is not as easy. We point out where in the script the output page is generated and then set you loose to customize it the best you can. It's not hard, but it does involve modifying the Perl code. Be sure to keep a (working) backup copy of the script before you have at it.

Figures 12.1a and 12.1b show what the pages look like in the browser, and Listing 12.1 shows the index generated by *ice-idx.pl*.

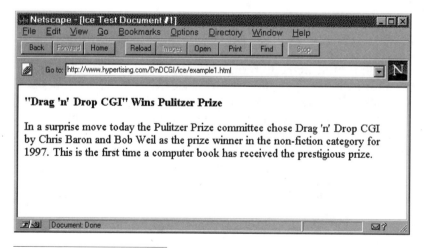

Figure 12.1a *Browser output of example HTML pages*

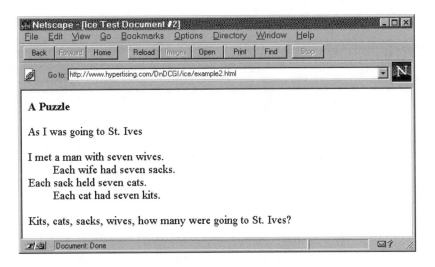

Figure 12.1b *Browser output of example HTML pages*

Listing 12.1   Index file generated by *ice-idx.pl*

```
@f /home/hypertising/www/DnDCGI/ice/        2 received
   exampl.html                              2 surprise
@t Ice Test Document 1                      10 the
@m 850407821                                1 this
2 CGI                                       2 time
2 and                                       2 today
1 baron                                     1 weil
1 bob                                       2 winner
2 book                                      1 wins
2 category                                  @f /home/hypertising/www/DnDCGI/ice/
2 cgi                                          examp2.html
2 chose                                     @t Ice Test Document 2
1 chris                                     @m 850407823
2 committee                                 2 cat
2 computer                                  4 cats
2 drag                                      3 each
2 drop                                      4 going
2 fiction                                   4 had
2 first                                     2 held
2 for                                       2 how
2 has                                       2 ives
2 move                                      3 kits
2 non                                       2 man
2 prestigious                               2 many
6 prize                                     2 met
2 pulitzer                                  1 puzzle
```

```
2 sack              2 were
4 sacks             2 wife
8 seven             2 with
2 was               4 wives
```

At the top of the file is the full path to each indexed file (the @f line), the title (@t) taken from the HTML `<TITLE>` tag, and the time the file was last modified (@m) in milliseconds since the epoch. Following the file information is the list of the words that occur within the document. A configuration option allows you to ignore words that have fewer than a certain number of letters. The number alongside the word is the number of times the word occurs in that particular document. This number is used in sorting the list of matches and in presenting the page with the highest number of matched words at the top. The rest of the index file follows this convention for every file included in the index. Unfortunately, no additional inclusion/exclusion rules are available in this version of the script.

Amazing Factoid

> An *epoch* is a specially defined instant in time. For UNIX systems, it is defined as 12:00:00.000 midnight January 1, 1970, Universal Time Coordinated (UTC). All UNIX system clocks are referenced to this point with millisecond resolution (i.e., to .001 seconds). This gives a continuous uniform time standard for all UNIX-based systems.

The user will interact with the *ice-form.cgi* script and the predefined index at runtime. As already mentioned, this script can present the search form, accept the query, and return the search results to the user. Figure 12.2 shows the search form as it appears in the *ice-form.cgi* script before any customizing has been done.

As you can see, *ICE* includes several interesting options. For example, the "Don't Show documents older than X days" field allows users to search only for documents that have changed within the specified number of days. A simple Boolean search capability is implemented that allows the use of *and* and *or* to qualify the search terms. The thesaurus option allows alternative words to match the search terms. Substring matching allows the user to match search terms on parts of words or on whole words only. The "Choose the Area to search" field allows the user to restrict the search to certain sections of your Web site. For example, the user might want to search only the product information directory, not the whole Web site. This function is based on file directories, so it is useful only if you have multiple directories of HTML documents within your Web site. The options that appear in this `<SELECT>` list are set manually during the configuration of the script.

![ICE Indexing Gateway Netscape window screenshot]

ICE Indexing Gateway

- Enter a keyword or several keywords connected with "and" and "or".
  Example: *"picture and binary"*.

  ```
  book or cat
  ```
- **Don't Show** documents older than [ ] days, leave this empty to get all documents available.
- ☐ Use **Thesaurus** to extend a search to all synonyms of a term.
  Example: the query *"mail"* will return *"mail"* and *"message"*
- ☑ Use **Substring Matching** to extend searches to words which contain the given term as a substring.
  Example: the query *"mail"* will return *"mail"* and *"email"*
- **Choose the Area** to search: [Search in all documents ▼]

- **Start search:** [Start] Reset: [Reset]

This searchable archive was implemented with the ICE search engine

Figure 12.2 *The default* ice-form.cgi *search form*

Hair Saver

> The index must be regenerated after each change to a file on your Web site in order for *ICE* to detect the change. If you don't rerun the *ice-idx.pl* script, *ICE* won't know about the modifications and may even return invalid links if you've deleted or renamed files. Bottom line: Remember to run *ice-idx.pl* after each change or set it to run periodically using *cron* or another scheduled execution utility.

Figure 12.3 shows the results of a search query. The results page that comes with the script is quite generic. You'll probably want to customize it to match the look of the rest of your Web site.

Each match from the script contains the title of the document and the last modification date, presented as a hyperlink to the document. Also presented is the URL of the

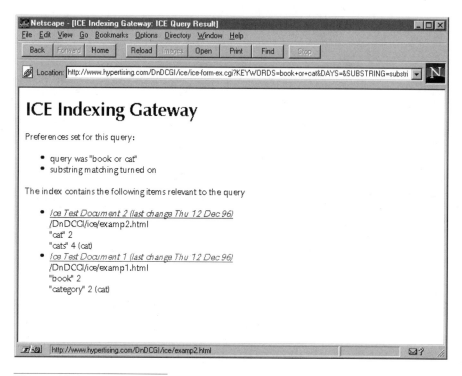

Figure 12.3 *Search results from* ice-form.cgi

document relative to the server root, the search terms that matched, and the number of matching occurrences within the document. Thesaurus matches are shown in the same way as substring matches—the matched word being followed by the search term in parentheses.

Now that you have an idea of how *ICE* works, let's move on to configuring the scripts for use on your Web site.

Configuring and Installing the *ICE* Scripts

Configuring *ICE* is largely a matter of setting the directory paths and Web server aliases in the configuration sections of the two script files. The script will work perfectly well without a thesaurus file (which we'll show you how to create later in this chapter). Don't feel pressured to come up with valid alternates for the words in your pages at this point (e.g., "physician" for "doctor"). Follow these steps to install and configure *ICE*.

Step 1: Configuration

We start our configuration party with the indexing script. Load the script, called */scripts/ice/ice-idx.pl*, from the CD-ROM into your editor. We'll point out the lines that need to be changed by line number in the original file, since *ICE* doesn't follow the configuration block format of the other scripts in the book. Be sure to turn line-wrapping off in your editor so that your line numbers will be the same as ours.

Hair Saver

Keep in mind that as you edit the script files—adding and deleting lines—that the lines below the added/deleted lines will change numbers. We configure the items in order from top to bottom, so just look down a few lines from the last item to find the next. In other words, the normal process of customizing your script will cause your line numbers to differ from those in the original file.

As always, you need to check the first line of the file (e.g., #!/usr/bin/perl) for the correct path to your Perl interpreter. Check your ISP/SA questionnaire and modify this line as needed.

Listing 12.2 shows a section of *ice-idx.pl* starting at line 19.

Listing 12.2	Configuration portion of *ice-idx.pl*

```
#--- start of configuration --- put your changes here ---
# NOTE: Depending on your Perl implementation, you may
# have to use different path separators in the following
# paths when you are on a Macintosh or PC system. In that
# case, a path may look like e.g. "usr:foo:bar" (Mac), or
# "\\usr\\foo\\bar" resp. '\usr\foo\bar' (PC).
# The physical directory/directories to scan for html-files.
# It's better to supply a tailing "/" for each directory,
# since otherwise automounting may not work.
# Example:
#  @SEARCHDIRS=('/usr/www/dir','/tmp/html','/usr/foo/html-dir');
@SEARCHDIRS=(
  '/tmp/',
);
# Location of the index file.
# Example:
#  $INDEXFILE='/usr/local/httpd/index.idx';
$INDEXFILE='/tmp/index.idx';
```

```
# The ICE indexer will support full international characters by
# converting them to their html equivalent if $ISO is set.
# This has a slightly negative impact on the indexing speed, so
# set it to "y" only if you index files with 8 bit international
# charcters. OTHERWISE DONT! iso2html seems to cause a memory
# leak, causing the indexer to run forever. I'm working on it.
$ISO="n";
# Type of system (for figuring out the path delimiting character)
# that ice-idx.pl runs on. Select one of "UNIX", "MAC", or "PC"
$TYPE="UNIX";
# Minimum length of word to be indexed
$MINLEN=3;
#--- end of configuration --- don't change anything below ---
```

Scan down through the file to line 31. You should see the Perl array variable @SEARCHDIRS. This variable defines an array of directories to search for HTML files. Files in subdirectories below these directories will also be indexed. Unless you are indexing multiple Web sites, you will probably have only one entry here. Enter the full path to your root HTML directory in line 32, which currently reads:

```
'/tmp/',
```

(Check your ISP/SA questionnaire if you don't have the path memorized.) The edited block should look something like this:

```
@SEARCHDIRS=(
'/home/users/joeuser/public_html',
);
```

Windows users will need to include the disk drive letter and use the backslash character, in this manner:

```
@SEARCHDIRS=(
'd:\httpd\htdocs\joeuser',
);
```

The author of *ICE* recommends putting the trailing slash on the directory name to force UNIX to mount a remote disk if needed. We don't recommend you do this, since it's unlikely you'll need to mount any disks on your Web server. Try running the script without the trailing slash. If *ice-idx.pl* complains about not being able to find the files, you can add it.

Normally, one directory and its subdirectories should be all you'll need to index. To include more directories, simply place each directory's full path on a line by itself. Each directory must be enclosed within single quotation marks and have a comma after the closing mark, as follows:

```
@SEARCHDIRS=(
'/home/users/joeuser/public_html',
'/home/companies/joescorp/public_html/prod_specs',
);
```

Next, you set the location of the index file. We normally put the index file in the *cgi-bin/* directory along with the scripts, but you can put it anywhere you like. You'll need to edit line 38 in the file to change the $INDEXFILE variable

```
$INDEXFILE='/tmp/index.idx';
```

to point to a convenient location such as

```
$INDEXFILE = '/home/users/joeuser/public_html/cgi-bin/index.idx';
```

Be sure to put single quotation marks around the file specification and end the line with a semicolon to keep Perl happy.

The next three variables are settings that, if acceptable, you can safely leave alone.

- Line 46 contains a variable called $ISO. This variable controls whether extended ISO-Latin characters (such as umlauts in German) are converted to their HTML equivalent. If your Web pages contain these characters, set this variable to y; otherwise, leave it as is.

- Line 50 contains the variable $TYPE. This variable defines the type of directory separators used in the file path. The three options are "UNIX", "MAC", and "PC". Change this variable to match your system if you aren't using UNIX.

- Line 53 contains the $MINLEN variable. This variable sets the length of the smallest word to be included in the index. Setting it to a larger value will produce slightly smaller indexes, since the short words, such as conjunctions, won't be included. We recommend you leave this value as is unless you have a compelling reason to change it.

When you've finished editing the script, save it to a convenient location for upload to your Web server.

Next, you configure the actual search script—*ice-form.cgi*—located on the CD-ROM as */scripts/ice/ice-form.pl*. After loading the script into your editor, check the first line of the file and set the correct path to your Perl interpreter.

Listing 12.3 shows the configuration section of the *ice-form.pl* file.

Listing 12.3   **Configuration section of *ice-form.pl***

```perl
#!/usr/local/bin/perl
#
# ice-form.pl -- cgi compliant ICE search interface // Jun 24 1996
#
# ICE Version 1.31
# (C) Christian Neuss (http://www.informatik.th-darmstadt.de/~neuss)
#--- start of configuration --- put your changes here ---
# Title or name of your server:
#    Example: local($title)="ICE Indexing Gateway";
local($title)="ICE Indexing Gateway";
# search directories to present in the search dialogue
#    Example:
# local(@directories)=(
#    "Image Communication Information Board (/icib)",
#    "WISE (/some/where/wise)"
# );
local(@directories)=(
    "Image Communication Information Board (/icib)",
    "WISE (/www/projects/wise)",
    "Multimedia Survey (/www/projects/mms)",
    "Department A2 (/www/igd-a2)",
    "Department A8 (/www/igd-a8)",
    "Department A9 (/www/igd-a9)",
    "DZSIM (/www/projects/dzsim)",
    "CSCW Laboratory (/www/projects/cscw-lab)",
    "Software Catalog (/www/projects/sw-catalog)",
    "WWW-Schulung (/www/igd-a3/schulung)",
    "DZSIM (/www/projects/dzsim)",
    "ZGDV User Interface GROUP (/www/zgdv-uig)"
);
# Location of the indexfile:
#    Note: under Windows or Windows NT, add the drive letter
#    Example: $indexfile='/usr/local/etc/httpd/index/index.idx';
$indexfile='/tmp/index.idx';
# Location of the thesaurus data file:
#    Example: $thesfile='/igd/a3/home1/neuss/Perl/thes.dat';
$thesfile='/igd/a3/home1/neuss/Perl/thes.dat';
# URL Mappings (a.k.a Aliases) that your server does
# map "/" to some path to reflect a "document root"
#    Example
#    %urltopath = (
#    '/projects',   '/usr/stud/proj',
#    '/people',     '/usr3/webstuff/staff',
#    '/',           '/usr3/webstuff/documents',
#    );
#
```

```
%urltopath = (
  '/',            '',
);
#--- end of configuration --- you don't have to change anything below ---
```

The first configuration item, after the location of Perl, is located at line 11 in the file:

```
local($title)="ICE Indexing Gateway";
```

The $title variable defines the title of the search form and the <H1> heading that appears on the search form and results pages. If you modify the title, make sure to keep double quotation marks in place before and after the string and to end the line with a semicolon.

The next item provides a way for the user to search only a portion of the Web site (by default, all directories are searched). The lines starting at line 20 look like this:

```
local(@directories)=(
    "Image Communication Information Board (/icib)",
    "WISE (/www/projects/wise)",
    "Multimedia Survey (/www/projects/mms)",
    "Department A2 (/www/igd-a2)",
    "Department A8 (/www/igd-a8)",
    "Department A9 (/www/igd-a9)",
    "DZSIM (/www/projects/dzsim)",
    "CSCW Laboratory (/www/projects/cscw-lab)",
    "Software Catalog (/www/projects/sw-catalog)",
    "WWW-Schulung (/www/igd-a3/schulung)",
    "DZSIM (/www/projects/dzsim)",
    "ZGDV User Interface GROUP (/www/zgdv-uig)"
);
```

First, you should delete all the lines between local (@directories) = and);
unless your server happens to have exactly the same directory setup (not very likely). More likely, you'll need to enter your own list of names and directories *relative to the server root*. For example, if the URL of your home page is

```
http://www.myco.com/
```

you may have several directories within your Web site to keep things organized, something like this:

```
http://www.myco.com/products/
http://www.myco.com/news/
http://www.myco.com/downloads/
```

```
http://www.myco.com/company_info/
http://www.myco.com/people/openings/
```

To offer users the option of selectively searching each of these directories, you would create the following list:

```
local (@directories) = (
'Product Information (/products)',
'MyCo in the News (/news)',
'Free Downloads! (/downloads)',
'All about MyCo (/company_info)',
'Help Wanted (/people/openings)',
);
```

You don't need to provide an entry for the whole site because that's included by default. Notice that only the part of the URL after the domain name is included. You must include that part of the line shown in parentheses. The script reads this information to create the links returned by the search engine. As always, be sure to enclose the text within single quotation marks and separate the entries with a comma. Also make sure you include both parentheses. Later, you will define the mapping between the URL and the actual file location on the server. If you have only a few files, or if they're all located in a single directory, you can comment out this variable. Just place a # in front of everything from the `local (@directories)=` line to the closing `);` line.

Next, you specify the location of the index file. Line 38 in the original file looks like this:

```
$indexfile='/tmp/index.idx';
```

You must make this variable match the entry you put in the *ice-idx.pl* script. If they don't match, you won't get much searching done.

Line 43 contains the location of the thesaurus file:

```
$thesfile='/igd/a3/home1/neuss/Perl/thes.dat';
```

As with the index file location, this variable gives the full path to the file. You can comment out this line if you don't have a thesaurus. We cover creating a thesaurus later in the chapter. For now, comment out the line so that you can run some tests.

Last, but certainly not least, is the most important configuration item: the mapping between your URLs and the actual directory paths on the Web server. If you make a mistake here, the search will probably appear to work, but all the returned links will be incorrect. This will frustrate your users and do nothing for your budding reputation as a Perl-meister.

Starting at line 46 we see the following lines in the script:

```
#     Example
#     %urltopath = (
#     '/projects',   '/usr/stud/proj',
#     '/people',   '/usr3/webstuff/staff',
#     '/',         '/usr3/webstuff/documents',
#     );
#
%urltopath = (
  '/',            '',
);
```

You must have at least one entry in the %urltopath variable; namely, the path to your root Web directory. A typical entry might look like this:

```
%urltopath = (
'/~joeuser', '/home/users/joeuser/public_html'
);
```

This would work if you have a typical "user" Web page with a URL that looks like this:

```
http://www.myisp.com/~joeuser/
```

In contrast, a virtual domain Web page with a URL like

```
http://www.myco.com/
```

might have an entry like

```
%urltopath = (
'/', '/home/corp/myco/public_html'
);
```

In this case, the Web server has an "alias" set up so that the root of *myco.com* ('/') is the file path above ('*/home/myco/public_html*'). If you have a dedicated Web server, your URL will look like the virtual domain example. However, you likely will have an entry more like this:

```
%urltopath = (
'/', '/usr/local/httpd/htdocs'
);
```

where the path is the directory where the Web server expects to find the root HTML files. This directory is set within the server configuration files.

You can create other entries in the `%urltopath` variable if your server has other aliases set up. For example, you might have an entry like this:

```
%urltopath = (
'/', '/usr/local/httpd/htdocs',
'/products', '/usr/marketing/prod/web_stuff'
);
```

Notice that the *'/products'* directory has a much different path on the server than does the home page. It might even be on a different machine, with the remote disk mounted via a network file system. Most people will probably be able to get away with just the root directory entry. But if you have parts of your Web site spread around your server, you can get *ICE* to recognize it by configuring the `%urltopath` variable.

Hair Saver

> Be sure to include all of the paths to the parts of your Web site in the *ice-idx.pl* `@SEARCHDIRS` variable. Otherwise, the documents in those directories won't be indexed and all your hard work editing `%urltopath` will be for nought.

When you are finished editing both *ice-idx.pl* and *ice-form.pl*, save them in a convenient location for upload to the Web server. Remember, you may have to rename *ice-form.pl* to *ice-form.cgi*, depending on the file extension requirements for your Web server. Check your ISP/SA questionnaire if in doubt.

That concludes the basic configuration of the two *ICE* scripts. We cover advanced configuration of the input and output of *ICE* along with creating a thesaurus file in the "Advanced ICE Configuration" section later in the chapter. For some quick gratification, move on to installing and testing the scripts in their current state.

Step 2: Installation

If you've installed scripts from earlier chapters in this book, you can probably install *ICE* with your eyes closed. For those who skipped the earlier chapters, we recommend that you read Chapter 3, "The Nonprogrammer's Toolbox," for the specifics.

Start your FTP client and upload the *ice-idx.pl* and *ice-form.pl* files to the *cgi-bin* directory (also called *cgi* or *htbin*). Be sure to use ASCII mode when transferring the Perl scripts.

Once the script files are safely aboard your Web server, you need to change the file permissions to tell the system that they are executable files.

Remember: You may need to rename your *ice-form* script to have a *.cgi* extension depending on the requirements of your Web server.

That's all there is to installing the scripts on your server. Creating the actual Web site index is the final step in the *ICE* installation. If you've edited everything correctly in the script files, entering the following command from your Telnet client will generate the index of your site:

```
./ice-idx.pl
```

The script doesn't produce any output to the screen, but you can check for the index file at the location you specified in the script's configuration block. If you told the script to put your file somewhere other than in the *cgi-bin/* directory, list the contents of that directory using *ls*. You don't actually have to change to the directory to list it. Just give the complete path to the directory you want to list and *ls* will oblige. The command

```
ls /home/users/joeuser/public_html/cgi-bin
```

will give you a list of the files in that directory from anywhere on the server (note the leading /, which makes the path absolute from the file system root). On Windows, the syntax is

```
dir d:\users\joeuser\htdocs\cgi-bin\
```

Once you've verified that the index file exists, you can conduct a little test of the search function by running the *ice-form.cgi* script by hand. Enter the following command:

```
./ice-form.cgi
```

You should get a short message about running in test mode, and the script will do a search on the word "the." The output of the search will be a bunch of HTML that will scroll off the screen before you can read it. If you get this output, your script is working. You can play around with the test function by adding a less common word after the name of the script on the command line, such as "kumquat":

```
ice-form.cgi kumquat
```

The script will produce HTML that lists all the pages with the word "kumquat" (or words containing "kumquat" such as "kumquats" or "kumquatish") in them. Once you've finished amusing yourself with the form script, you can test it with the browser. Using your browser's Open Location function, enter your home page URL followed by the *cgi* directory and the script name:

```
http://www.myisp.com/~joeuser/cgi/ice-form.cgi
```

or

```
http://www.myco.com/cgi-bin/ice-form.cgi
```

The browser should respond with a search form like that shown in Figure 12.2. Enter a search word and submit the form. You should get a listing, resembling Figure 12.3, of all your pages containing the word you've chosen. Check the file-to-URL mapping by clicking one of the links. The page should load correctly on your browser.

There are only a few things that can go wrong with the scripts. One is that if the @SEARCHDIRS variable is set incorrectly, you won't index some or all of the directories with HTML files. If you don't get any matches to your search with words you know are in your pages, you will need to recheck the configuration of the indexing script. Just switch to your text editor and edit the script file. Save your changes and re-upload the script over the current one on the server. The file permissions won't need to be set again. Repeat this edit-upload-test cycle until things are working correctly. If you are correcting the index script, you'll need to generate a new index by executing the script on the Telnet client each time you make a change.

A much more common problem is that the *ice-form.cgi* script has correctly generated the index, but it returns incorrect links. This usually indicates a problem with the %urltopath variable in the *ice-form.cgi* file. Observe the links the script is generating and modify %urltopath to produce the correct output. After the basic search is working, try limiting the search to a specific directory if you listed more than one in the @directories variable. (Remember, these are URL fragments within the parentheses, not file paths.) Observe the search script output and make adjustments until it is producing valid links.

Congratulations, your Web site search engine is now installed and working!

Using the *ICE* Scripts in Your Pages

By now you've done all the hard work. To use the script in your pages, you simply call the form script with a hyperlink like this:

```
<A HREF="cgi-bin/ice-form.cgi">Search this site</A>
```

The *ice-form.cgi* script generates both the search request form and the search results page. You can also use "canned" searches that don't present a search form. For example, to search for all recently changed documents, you could have a link such as

```
<A HREF="cgi-bin/ice-form.cgi?DAYS=7">What's new this week</A>
```

or

```
<A HREF="cgi-bin/ice-form.cgi?DAYS=30&KEYWORDS=Game+and+Review:">
This Month's Game Reviews</A>
```

Take a look at the default search form using the View Source function of your browser. You'll be able to see the form element names and use them in your preset queries.

Nerd Note

> The *ICE* script presents the request form if it is called with no form data. If either GET or POST style form data is passed to the script, it parses the fields and uses the values for a search, presenting the results on the results page. The script can't tell if the form data came from an actual form or from a "canned" CGI call, as described previously.

As an alternative, you can create the search form with your favorite HTML editor and call the script with the ACTION= parameter of the <FORM> tag. The best way to do this is to capture the search form HTML generated by the script. Save the default form HTML to a file using the Save As function of your browser. Then you can edit the form HTML to match the look of your Web site. You can remove features you don't use from the form, such as the thesaurus check box, the older-than-X-days field, or the area to search select list. You must return the input field for the search words, but that's about all. You can, of course, change the prompting text and re-arrange the locations of the fields to suit your artistic sensibilities.

One limitation of the *ICE* system is that it doesn't give any context for the search results. That is, it just links you to a page. Your search term could be anywhere in a potentially very long document. This is often irritating when substring matching is used (when parts of longer words the user wasn't searching for are matched). The user may look through the page for a long time, only to discover the match was within some completely unrelated word.

At the time of this writing, we have a prototype modification to *ICE* that highlights the search words in the returned document, thus making them easy to pick out. Unfortunately, we didn't have time to test the modifications sufficiently to include them in this book (a good reason to buy the second edition, we think). Check the book's Web site (*http://www.hypertising.com/DnDCGI/*) periodically to see if we've finished this modification, as well as other enhancements to *ICE*.

Those of you who are happy with the default results page and who don't need a thesaurus can safely stop here and move on to another script. Those who want to modify the output page or create a thesaurus file should continue reading.

Advanced *ICE* Configuration

In this section, we show you how to create a thesaurus file and how to customize the search request form.

Thesaurus File Configuration

The thesaurus file is simply a text file that defines relationships between words. The *ICE* thesaurus supports three relationships:

1. Word1 EQ word2: Word1 is **EQ**ual to word2.
2. Word1 AB word2: Word1 is an **AB**breviation of word2.
3. Word1 UF word2: Word1 is Used For word2.

The format of the thesaurus file is very simple. A word is placed on a line by itself. On the next line, one or more spaces or tabs are followed by the relation and the alternative word separated by one or more spaces or tabs. Listing 12.4 shows a simple thesaurus file.

Listing 12.4   **A sample *ICE* thesaurus file**

```
doctor
   EQ physician
physician
   EQ doctor
doc
   AB doctor
doctor
   UF doc
```

ICE is a simple script, so these relationships are not very sophisticated. You must explicitly put in the EQ relations for both eventualities; that is, `doctor EQ physician` and `physician EQ doctor`. Also, the relations don't "chain." For example, searching for "doc" in Listing 12.4 with substring matching off will match *doctor* because of the `doc AB doctor` relation. But it will *not* match *physician* by following a chain of `doc AB doctor` and `doctor EQ physician`. Nevertheless, the thesaurus function adds a nice bit of help to users searching your Web site. It's not hard to create, and your users will appreciate it. Once you've created and uploaded the file, be sure to edit the *ice-form.cgi* file to point to its location. We suggest putting the thesaurus file in the same directory as the index file.

Search Request Form Configuration

There are two ways to customize the search request form to better match the requirement of your Web site. We've already discussed the first: creating a custom HTML form and using it to collect the search parameters rather than letting the script generate the form. We prefer this method because editing HTML files is simpler and easier than editing HTML generating code embedded within a script. However, for those of you who want your script to generate your input forms, we'll show you where the form is generated within the *ice-form.cgi* script.

Listing 12.5 shows the Perl **subroutines**—short pieces of code that perform a specific function—starting at line 80, that generate the request form (see Appendix A for more on Perl subroutines.)

Hair Saver

Because configuration of the form generated by the script involves modifying the Perl code, the discussion necessarily uses programming terminology. We don't have space in this chapter to fully define each instance of programmerese. If you find yourself baffled by the instructions we give, here are a couple of things you can do.

1. Read Appendix A: "Some Notes on Perl for Nonprogrammers." This appendix explains the different elements of a Perl program.

2. Use deduction. The syntax of the Perl code we discuss in this chapter is quite a bit like English. The structure of the lines of code (indention and blank lines) can also give you clues to where the specific blocks of code start and end.

3. Ask for help. If you have any programmer friends they should easily be able to figure out what we are trying to convey.

4. Get a book about Perl. You may want to invest in an introductory Perl text appropriate to your level of programming knowledge.

Listing 12.5	Search request form subroutines

```perl
# print the CGI script header
sub send_header {
    local($title)=@_;
    print "Content-type: text/html\n\n";
    print "<HEAD><TITLE>";
    print $title;
    print "</TITLE></HEAD>\n";
```

```
}
# display the Forms interface
sub send_index {
    local($scriptname) = $ENV{"SCRIPT_NAME"};
    print '<BODY>';
    print "<H1>$title</H1>";
    print "<FORM ACTION=\"$scriptname\">\n";
    print <<'END';
<UL>
<LI>Enter a keyword or several keywords
 connected with "and" and "or".<BR>
 Example: <I>"picture and binary".</I><P>
 <INPUT NAME="KEYWORDS"  SIZE=50><BR>
<LI><B>Don't Show</B> documents older than
 <INPUT NAME="DAYS" VALUE="" SIZE=2>  days,
 leave this empty to get all documents available.
<LI><inPUT TYPE="checkbox"
 NAME="THESAURUS" VALUE="thesaurus">   Use <B>Thesaurus</B>
 to extend a search to all synonyms of a term.<BR>
 Example: the query <I>"mail"</I> will return
 <I>"mail"</I> and <I>"message"</I>
<LI><inPUT TYPE="checkbox" NAME="SUBSTRING"
 VALUE="substring" checked> Use <B>Substring Matching</B>
 to extend searches to words which contain the given
 term as a substring.<BR>
 Example: the query <I>"mail"</I> will return
 <I>"mail"</I> and <I>"email"</I>
<LI><B>Choose the Area</B> to search:
 <SELECT name="CONTEXT">
 <OPTION> Search in all documents
END
    foreach $dir (@directories){
      print "<OPTION> $dir\n";
    }
    print <<'END';
</SELECT>
<P>
<LI><B>Start search</B>: <INPUT TYPE="submit" VALUE="Start">
  Reset: <inPUT TYPE="reset" VALUE="Reset"></FORM></OL>
<P><HR>
<!-- Please don't delete this message: -->
<I>This searchable archive was implemented with the
<A HREF="http://www.informatik.th-darmstadt.de/~neuss/ice/ice.html">
ICE search engine </A></I>
</BODY>
END
}
```

The `send_header` subroutine sends the required MIME type identifier to the Web browser along with the `<HEAD>` and `<TITLE>` tags. You can modify the Perl `print` statements to include other tags within the `<HEAD>` section of the HTML. The `send_index` subroutine generates the main section of the request form. The first few lines should look familiar.

The `print` statement is used to generate standard HTML code. You can customize this as you like. To insert a background image, for example, modify the line

```
print '<BODY>';
```

to read

```
print '<BODY BACKGROUND="../images/bkgnd.gif">';
```

Note the use of single quotation marks around the string and the file path idiom `../` that directs the script to move up a directory (from *cgi-bin/*) before searching the *images/* directory for the image file.

Hair Saver

We've said this before and we'll say it again. Use single quotation marks around text strings unless you want Perl to insert the value of a variable, as in

```
print "<H1>$title</H1>";
```

Some characters (\, $, @, %, ') have special meanings in Perl and will cause errors or unintended actions if you use them within a double-quoted string. If you need to use one of these in your HTML, use the backslash \ to tell Perl to ignore the special meaning of the following character within a double-quoted string. Perl doesn't try to interpret these characters in a single-quoted string; that's why we tell you to use them.

The next line of interest is

```
print <<'END';
```

This is a Perl statement that says "print everything up to the string END." The single quotation marks around `'END'` tell Perl to treat the lines that follow as if they, too, are surrounded by single quotation marks, that is, not to interpret special characters. If double quotation marks were placed around the `'END'` string, Perl would interpret the special characters.

As you can see, the text between the markers is standard HTML. You can put any-thing you like between the <<'END' and the END markers that would be legal in a normal HTML file. Don't modify the line that has 'END' on it; the script won't be able to find the end of the block and won't run.

Note that there is nothing special about the word *END* here; we could have used any combination of words. We usually insert a longer string to make it easy to spot in the source file, something like print<<'END_OF_FORM'; with a matching END_OF_FORM at the end of the block.

It's always a good practice to save a copy of your last working script before embark-ing on modifications. That way, if you go astray you can always start over with a working script.

Search Results Configuration

Customizing the HTML output of the search is a little trickier than customizing the request form. This is because the output is not located in a nice block. Rather, it's embedded within the Perl code and the output is generated in several locations within the code.

Hot Tip

> A good way to customize the output of this script is to capture the HTML output from the default script using the Save As function of your browser. Edit this using your HTML editor until the page looks the way you like. Be sure to allow for a vari-able number of returned links in your layout. Finally, as you work through the remaining paragraphs, you can compare the original HTML from the script with your edited HTML and easily see what changes to make in the Perl code to produce the HTML you want.

The top of the HTML document is generated starting at line 176. The main subrou-tine, starting at line 166, calls the send_header subroutine with the title of the page. You can modify the title string by changing the line

```
&send_header("$title: ICE Query Result");
```

Notice the double quotation marks that tell Perl to insert the value of the $title variable before the send_header subroutine is called to send the top portion of the HTML document to the browser. If you don't want to include the title from the search form, you can remove the $title variable. To specify the title explicitly, you could do this:

```
&send_header('My Corp Search Results');
```

Starting at line 211 is the code that responds to an error in the search. Modify the `print` statements to produce the HTML you need for the body section. If you are using tables to format your page, you might change the original code from

```
if($err){
    print "Query was: $query<BR>\n";
    print "Problem: $err\n";
    print "</BODY>";
    return undef;
  }
```

to

```
if($err){
    print "<TR><TD>Query was:</TD><TD>$query</TD></TR>\n";
    print "<TR><TD>Problem:</TD><TD>$err</TD></TR>\n";
    print "</TABLE></BODY>";
    return undef;
  }
```

Directly below this section is a series of `print` statements (lines 217–234) that produce a report of the preferences selected for the query using an HTML `<UL>` list. You can delete this section if you don't want to print the preferences, or you can change the style by editing the HTML code produced. For example, those of you who like to use those little colored balls for list bullets could do this:

```
print "Preferences set for this query:\n";
    print "<P>\n";
        if ($query) {
          print "<IMG SRC=\"../images/bluball.gif\"> query was
    \"$query\"\n";
          }
    if($context){
          print "<IMG SRC=\"../images/bluball.gif\"> context was
    set to $context.\n";
      ...
```

Notice the backslash \ before the double quotation marks within the line. They tell Perl to ignore the meaning of the special character that follows.

At line 235 is the code that produces the main listing of the returned links:

```
if($page){
    print "<P>The index contains the following\n";
    print "items relevant to the query\n";
    print "$page\n";
  }else{
```

```
    print "<P> Nothing found.\n";
  }
  print "</BODY>\n";
```

The if statement will print either the top section (before the word else) if the
search found some pages (stored in the $page variable) or the bottom section (print
"<P> Nothing found. \n";) if nothing was found. If you change the formatting
here, be sure to change both sections. The last line will always be printed, since it is
outside the if statement (see Appendix A regarding the if statement). You can add
things that should always appear on the page, such as navigation links just before the
</BODY> tag is printed.

The final section to configure produces the code for each document matched in the
search. The following code is found beginning at line 276:

```
foreach $w (@tmplist){
    local($freq,$file,$title,@hits)=split(/\n/,$w);
    $hitcount++;
    ###print "$freq,$title\n";
    unless($title) { $title="(NO TITLE)"; }
    $page .= "<LI> <A HREF=\"$file\"><I>$title</I></A><BR>\n";
    $page .= "$file<BR>\n";
    foreach $line (@hits){
      $page .= "$line<BR>\n";
    }
  }
```

To modify the HTML produced when the search document has no title, change the
$title variable as follows:

```
unless($title) { $title="(NO TITLE)"; }
```

Note: This $title variable holds the title of the document matched in the search
and is a different $title variable than that used for the page title.

The HTML produced for each matched document is contained in these lines:

```
$page .= "<LI> <A HREF=\"$file\"><I>$title</I></A><BR>\n";
$page .= "$file<BR>\n";
```

The $file variable holds the URL (relative to the server root) of the matched docu-
ment. The $title variable as described previously holds either the <TITLE> of the
HTML document or the (NO TITLE) string. The second line just prints the URL of
the file below the hyperlinked title. You can delete this line if you don't want your
filenames hanging out there for people to see. Displaying the actual URL of the file is
useful, however, when the results page is printed.

Once you've finished your modifications, save the script and upload it to your ISP or SA's server. We generally use a different name for scripts that contain major changes (e.g., *ice-form2.cgi*, *ice-form3.cgi*, and so on). If you do this, be sure to modify the search form to call the new script. Once the script is on the server, change the file permissions in the usual way with your FTP or Telnet client, and test it by entering the script name from the command line:

```
./ice-form2.cgi
```

If you made any mistakes modifying the code, you will see detailed error messages at this point. The most common will be missing quotation marks in strings or a missing backslash \ for a Perl special character within a double-quoted string. Once the script is happy running from the command line, it should work from the Web browser. If you changed the form script name (i.e., *ice-form2.cgi*), remember to change the ACTION= parameter on your custom search form. The script will use the new name automatically if you're using the script-generated search form.

Hot Tip

> When modifying scripts like this, we usually have the text editor, HTML editor, FTP client, Telnet client, and Web browser all running at the same time. When we change the code, we save the file, send it to the server with the FTP client, and test it with the Web browser or Telnet client. With practice, you'll soon be able to test scripts on the Web server almost as fast as you can save files to your local machine.

Whew! If you've stayed with us through that final section, you've come perilously close to becoming a Perl programmer. You are also very close to being able to look at any Perl script, locate the HTML-producing code, and mold it according to your mighty will. If you made a few mistakes in the process, you've also experienced both the frustration of the programmer and the exultation of finding and fixing an error. Be careful—it's addictive!

What We Covered in Chapter 12

- How Web site search engines work
- The two parts of the *ICE* search engine: the index and the search form scripts
- Customizing both the search request and results HTML output
- Creating a thesaurus file
- A bit more of the Perl language

Chapter 13

A Perl-based On-line Store System—Part 1: Installation

Features of the *PerlShop* On-line Store System

- Shopping cart–style user interface
- Secure commerce server support
- On-line credit card payments via SecureOrder or FirstVirtual
- Unlimited catalog size
- No database required; catalog is stored within HTML pages
- Flexible sales tax and shipping charge calculations
- Discounts based on quantity or price of orders
- Optional "cookie" feature allows users to leave store and return later with orders intact
- Support for optional item parameters such as Color, Size, and Style
- Orders stored on server in comma-delimited format for easy import to databases or spreadsheets
- Confirmation e-mail sent to customer and store owner for each transaction
- Built-in catalog search engine
- Works on UNIX and Windows systems
- Free!

What You Need to Install This Script

- Perl version 5
- FTP client
- Telnet client
- Text editor

PerlShop is far larger and more complicated than any other script presented in this book. To help you take things in manageable chunks, we've broken its installation into three chapters. The following overview shows what's included in each action-packed episode:

Chapter 13—Installation

- Configuring your ISP or SA's Web server for *PerlShop*
- Configuring *PerlShop* for your server
- Adding your business information
- Configuring payment options
- Configuring shipping and sales tax information
- Installing the script on your ISP or SA's server
- Setting up the secure HTTP server

Chapter 14—Setting Up the Store

- Entering the store
- Creating catalog pages
- Navigating the store
- Managing the contents of the shopping cart

Chapter 15—Processing Orders and Store Security

- The checkout process
- Credit card processing
- The back-end: order and customer files
- Using *cgiwrap* to increase Web server security
- Retrieving order data from the server
- Encryption with Pretty Good Privacy (PGP)

As on-line commerce moves from a novelty to a necessity, the ability to conduct business on-line in a secure and efficient manner is becoming a standard requirement of many businesses. *PerlShop* is a flexible and capable on-line shopping system for small- to medium-sized electronic stores. It is written in Perl and runs on both UNIX and Windows servers with Perl version 5.000 or higher installed. The script's many advanced features let you create sophisticated on-line stores and, as always, gives you what you need to do so without programming.

PerlShop was written by Edward Taussig and is published by ARPAnet Corp. (no relation to the original U.S. government ARPAnet project). It is distributed free and may be freely modified under a concept ARPAnet calls Adverware™. The only requirement for using *PerlShop* for personal or commercial purposes is that each page generated by *PerlShop* must include the "Powered by PerlShop" logo image, with a link back to the ARPAnet home page.

We thank Mr. Taussig for graciously allowing us to include his script in our book and for the help he provided during the preparation of these chapters. ARPAnet also offers customizing and installation services for *PerlShop*. If you find the script useful but need an additional feature or two, please consider ARPAnet. Contact information is available on the resources page (*/rsrcs.html*) on the CD-ROM.

Introduction to On-line Store Systems

If you've spent much time at all on the Web, you've probably encountered on-line stores. Typically, you browse through a catalog of products and place items you wish to purchase in an electronic "shopping cart" as you go. Once you are ready to buy, the system walks you through a "check out" procedure to complete the purchase. The shopping-cart motif is familiar to all of us and offers a pleasant experience similar to shopping in a real store. Figures 13.1 and 13.2 show the product order pages for several commercial Web sites that use *PerlShop*.

Implementing a shopping-cart type system requires that the programmers do some extra work to overcome the limitations (or, as programmers are fond of saying, features) of the HTTP protocol used on the Web. Recall from Chapter 2 that we described how HTTP is a "stateless" protocol that sends each request for an HTML page or graphic as a stand-alone call from the browser to the server. This works great for static objects like HTML pages and graphics. The server just handles the requests as quickly as possible; it doesn't care where they are going or in what order they arrive. Unfortunately for shopping-cart system designers, this protocol doesn't support the "memory" needed to maintain a set of items in the "cart." Several methods have been devised to sidestep this shortcoming. The most common approach, used by our new friend *PerlShop*, is to use a data file on the Web server to hold the contents of the visitor's shopping cart. The details of how this works aren't really critical, so we'll cut right to the mechanics of getting your store up and running.

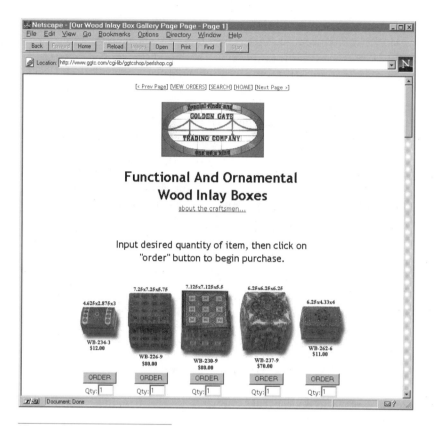

Figure 13.1 PerlShop *in use on the Golden Gate Trading Company Web site*

Nerd Note

For those of you who *do* care how *PerlShop* works, here is a brief summary. On entering the "store," the visitor is assigned a session identification number that keys all his or her actions to a record in the shopping-cart database. When the visitor fetches a page from the catalog, *PerlShop* either creates or modifies all the HTML links within the page to pass every request through the *PerlShop* CGI program.

These modified links include the requested page and the session ID of the user. Each time the visitor clicks a hyperlink within the catalog, the session ID is passed along. This allows the catalog system to keep track of the contents of the visitor's cart, in spite of the stateless HTTP protocol. Pretty slick.

Normally, each time a visitor enters the catalog "front-door" he or she is assigned a session number. However, if he or she jumps to another Web site and then returns to the catalog, he or she gets a new session ID card and the contents of his or her shopping cart are lost. *PerlShop*, however, avoids this situation by using a mechanism called a "cookie." A cookie allows the Web server to store a small data record on the user's machine. *PerlShop* uses the cookie to store the user session ID number so that when the user returns from his or her little jaunt to another Web site, he or she can resume shopping where he or she left off.

For on-line stores with a small number of products, the *PerlShop* approach of storing the product catalog information within HTML pages is more efficient than incurring the overhead of installing and maintaining a database management system (DBMS). This method also works for adding on-line shopping to existing on-line catalogs, since only small changes need to be made to the existing catalog pages. This is the method *PerlShop* uses.

Figure 13.2 PerlShop *in use on the Toad Suck Web site*

In stores with hundreds or thousands of products, it's not practical for each product to have its own HTML page. Keeping all those pages in sync would be a maintenance nightmare. Instead, each HTML product page is generated on the fly from a database that holds the price, the descriptive copy, a pointer to one or more images, and sometimes additional information such as optional items, accessories, or color and size availability. The catalog designer creates the overall layout of the page in a template, including the necessary placeholders for the catalog system to fill in with data from the database. In this way, a thousand-item catalog can be updated or given a new look very easily. If your on-line store needs are of this magnitude, *PerlShop* won't fill the bill. Check the CD-ROM links page for a list of large-scale catalog systems. However, before you jump into a really large on-line sales venture, it might be a good idea to "get your feet wet" with a small-scale on-line store using *PerlShop*.

The last and most important part of the ordering process is the routine that handles the completion of the order. The shopping system needs to be able to collect the visitor's payment information, address, and shipping costs and to calculate sales. Simpler systems merely collect the order information and e-mail it to the sales department for manual processing. However, more and more on-line store systems are linked to credit card processing companies to provide on-line validation and submission of credit card charges. To protect the buyer's credit card and other sensitive information, encryption is used. The Secure-Socket Layer (SSL) method, made popular by the Netscape Communications *Commerce Server* Web server, encrypts all sensitive data transmitted between the browser and the server. Additional encryption must be used to protect the credit card numbers and other personal data once they are stored on the server. When you're dealing with people's credit card number and other personal information, it's *very* important that your system be constructed securely. We discuss these issues in more detail in Chapter 15.

So-called back-end systems are used to process the order data after the order is completed. These systems kick off manufacturing, inventory management, or other production-related processes. In our examples, we show you enough to get quite a significant catalog on-line, with a full-featured shopping-cart interface. But we don't cover more advanced applications or interfacing with back-end systems. If you need anything fancier than e-mail notification and/or text file storage for your orders, you'll have to educate yourself quite a bit or hire people who know how to do this stuff.

Overview of the *PerlShop* System

In this and the following sections, we often talk about the Web server and its role in the *PerlShop* system. Just to be clear, *Web server* refers to the Web server software (the *httpd* daemon), and sometimes to the computer on which the *httpd* process is running. We assume *httpd* and *PerlShop* are both running on the same machine.

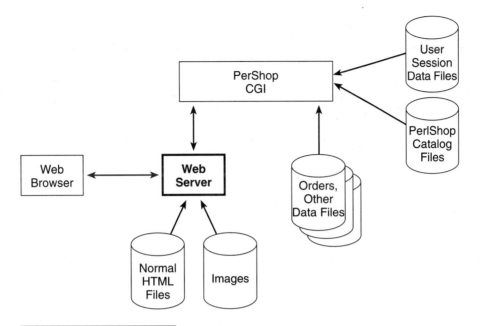

Figure 13.3 *Diagram of the* PerlShop *system*

Figure 13.3 shows a diagram of the *PerlShop* components and their relationship to the Web server software. A normal Web server configuration is shown in the bottom left and includes the browser, *httpd* server, HTML pages, images, and possibly sound or video files. Other CGI programs and sound and video files are not shown. *PerlShop* adds three items to this happy family:

1. *PerlShop* CGI script. Unlike some other systems, the *PerlShop* system consists of only a single Perl CGI script. This script receives the requests for pages and user form submissions from the Web server. Based on the specific request, *PerlShop* may generate a catalog page, modify the contents of a visitor's shopping cart, or transmit a credit card validation request to one of the supported credit card processing systems. Shipping charges, taxes, and discount information are stored within the script in configuration variables.

2. *PerlShop* catalog files. Data about products is stored in the product catalog HTML pages. This data is passed to the script in TYPE=HIDDEN HTML form tags. Storing the product specifics in an HTML page makes it easy to create and maintain your catalog using a regular HTML editor. This frees you from having to learn, install, and maintain a DBMS. *PerlShop* HTML pages are built using regular HTML. However, they may contain special

PerlShop specific tags that are interpolated by the script when the page is requested. These special tags are used to insert the visitor's session information into each form as it is sent to the browser. When the form is later submitted by the visitor, it will include the session ID number, which allows *PerlShop* to apply the requested changes to the correct shopping cart. Other tags create a navigation menu and allow server independence by inserting the correct URL into the HTML for hyperlinks, form SUBMIT buttons, and image tags. This is useful if you start your catalog on a user site with a URL like

```
http://www.myisp.net/~joeuser/Store.html
```

and then move to a dedicated server or virtual domain with a URL like

```
http://www.mystore.com/
```

You can update all your catalog pages to work with this new URL by simply changing a variable definition in the script.

3. Data files. *PerlShop* uses a special set of data files to store the session ID and the contents of the visitor's shopping cart on the Web server. Unless the cookie option is turned on, the shopping cart's contents will be lost if a visitor leaves the site without completing a purchase. The cookie feature lets the Web server store a copy of the session ID on the visitor's local computer in a special file. Cookies allow visitors to leave the store and then return later to resume their shopping without losing the contents of their shopping carts (see Nerd Note on page 226).

Hot Tip

Don't depend on cookie support for the proper operation of your store. While most browsers, including *Netscape* and *Internet Explorer,* support cookies, not all do. Also, some users will disable cookies on their browser. So make sure that once the visitor enters the store, he or she isn't offered links to outside pages and that all the information he or she needs is included in the store pages.

If this all sounds complicated, it's really not. *PerlShop* is a fairly complex script with a full set of features. However, once you get the initial configuration out of the way, adding on-line ordering to your new or existing pages is quite straightforward.

Configuring and Installing *PerlShop*

Configuring and installing *PerlShop* is a bit time-consuming, but it's still just this side of difficult. As the *PerlShop* author says on his home page:

> Simply copy the script to your *cgi-bin* directory and mark it as executable, create a few directories and change their permissions, and then just modify the script to customize it for your server address and business procedures.

We couldn't have put it better ourselves. Onward!

Step 1: Directory Configuration

Normally, we would have you modify the configuration variables in the script before doing any work with the Web server. However, the author of *PerlShop* recommends that you create the directory structure for your on-line store before configuring the script. Creating the directory structure first allows you to refer to an existing set of directories and should clarify how all the parts of *PerlShop* fit together. Figure 13.4 shows the default directory structure of a Web site with the *PerlShop* directories added. New directories are shown in bold type.

All *PerlShop* files are stored in a subdirectory tree under the main *cgi-bin* (might also be *cgi* or *htbin* or other) directory. The name of this directory (*MyStore* in the figure) can be anything you like. We recommend that you name it something related to your on-line store or even just "Store." Under the basic subdirectory, *PerlShop* expects to find a number of other directories in which to store its data files.

First, you may want to create directories for the images you use in your store (*storeimg/* in the example) and the base store HTML pages (*mystore/* in the example). These directories are optional. You can store your catalog images with your other images without problem. The *mystore/* HTML directory is intended only to hold the

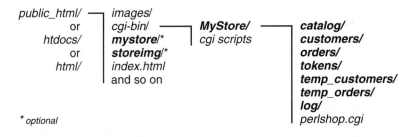

Figure 13.4 *The* PerlShop *directory structure*

introduction page to your store. All the pages manipulated by *PerlShop* need to be in the *catalog/* subdirectory below the *cgi-bin/* directory.

After you've got your base HTML directory in good shape, enter the *cgi-bin/* directory and create the *PerlShop* base directory (*MyStore/* in Figure 13.4.) Then, verify that the permissions are set to 755 (set them if needed).

Next, enter the directory you just created and create the seven subdirectories shown in the figure: *catalog/, customers/, orders/, tokens/, temp_customers/, temp_orders/,* and *log/.* Change the permissions on all these directories to 777 (read, write, and execute for all classes of users).

Review the directories as shown in Figure 13.4 and double-check that your server structure is the same. In the instructions that follow, we assume that you've created the directories as indicated. If you've made any changes, carefully make note of them so you can adapt our instructions to your server's setup. After you're satisfied with your directory structure, you can proceed to configure the script to match. You can disconnect from the network at this point, since we have quite a bit of configuration work to do before uploading the script to the server.

If you aren't comfortable enough with the operation of your FTP or Telnet client to create directories on the Web server, see Chapter 3 for detailed instructions. We're assuming you've successfully installed at least one of the other scripts in the book, so our instructions in this chapter are brief.

Step 2: Script Configuration

Load the *perlshop.cgi* script from the CD-ROM into your favorite text editor. It's located in the */scripts/perlshop/* directory. As always, change the first line

```
#!/usr/bin/perl
```

to match the location of Perl on your ISP/SA server. Check your ISP/SA questionnaire if you don't have it memorized by now.

Script Operation Section

Skip past all the copyright, disclaimer, and history information to about line 111 of the script. You will see the following:

```
require 5.000;        ## This script requires perl version 5.000 or higher
$|=1;                 ## Don't buffer output
$testing = 'no';      ## yes, no
```

The first line tells the Perl interpreter that it needs to be version 5.000 or higher. Check your ISP/SA questionnaire to see if your server is running Perl 5. (This script will not work with anything less than Perl 5.) If Perl 5 is not installed, you should contact your ISP or SA about upgrading. Perl 5 has been available for well over a year at the time of this writing, and there really is no good reason for it not to be installed on your ISP's or SA's Web server.

The next line ($| = 1;) tells Perl not to buffer the output of the script, but to send it to the server as it is printed. Finally, the variable $testing should be left set to 'no' for normal operation of the script.

Nerd Note

Normally, Perl uses a memory buffer to handle input and output requests until enough have accumulated to either fill (output) or empty (input) the buffer. Only then does it actually read or write the data to disk. It is more efficient to perform this single large input/output operation than many small read/write operations, especially for multitasking systems such as Web servers.

A feature (or limitation) of HTTP causes the browser time-out—to abandon a request after a certain length of time if there is no response from the server. Similarly, the server will kill a CGI script that has run too long without any output. In the case of static HTML pages, graphics, and simple CGI scripts, this is an efficient way to keep the browser from waiting around forever on a piece of data that isn't coming. However, when generating the HTML or graphics from a complex script, the runtime will sometimes exceed the server or browser time-out, even if nothing is wrong. To prevent this, we turn off Perl's output buffering by setting the $| variable to a nonzero value. Then, every time we write out a line of HTML from the script it is sent directly to the browser, thereby keeping both the Web server and the browser from cancelling the script.

The next series of lines control how the script works with your ISP/SA's server:

```
$use_cgiwrap = 'yes';## yes, no
$use_secure_server = 'yes';## yes, no
$add_navigation = 'yes';## yes, no (if yes, first line of script will
have prev,next page info)
$use_cookies = 'yes';## yes, no
$cookie_expire_days = 30;
$allow_ssi_cgi = 'no';## Do NOT set this to 'yes' unless you are
sure, it can create a big security hole.
$cardno_on_email = 'no';## Do NOT set this to 'yes' unless you are
sure, it can create a big security hole.
$allow_fractional_qty = 'no';
```

The $use_cgiwrap variable tells the script whether you are using a security program called *cgiwrap* for CGI scripts run on UNIX Web servers (Windows users don't need *cgiwrap).* This small program enhances CGI security by "wrapping" CGI scripts and causing them to run as your user ID rather than the normal Web server user ID of "nobody". Running CGI scripts under your user ID allows you to remove read and write permissions on your data files for all users except the owner (you). This greatly enhances the security of your data because only you will have access to the data files created by the Web server. Normally, Web server–created files must have read and write access for all classes of users. (We discuss *cgiwrap* in more detail in Chapter 15.) Set this variable to 'no' for now. You can change it later if you decide to use *cgiwrap*, once your store is up and running.

The `$use_secure_server` variable tells the script to generate URLs with the secure `https://` protocol rather than the normal `http://` for pages on which sensitive information will be collected. Using a URL starting with `https://` activates the SSL communications between the server and browser. Data sent under this protocol is encrypted against interception by evil people trying to steal credit card numbers. Contact your ISP or SA if you're not sure whether their Web server supports SSL. Often this is a premium service with an additional fee above and beyond your basic Web account fee. Set this variable to 'no' if your server doesn't support HTTPS or if you're not sure. You can turn on this capability later if needed. We discuss how to set up your store to use secure HTTP at the end of this chapter.

The `$add_navigation` variable controls whether *PerlShop* adds a set of navigation links to the top and bottom of each page in your catalog. These links allow users to move through the catalog pages in the order you specify. If you want *PerlShop* to add these links, set this value to 'yes'. If you want to design your own navigation links, set it to 'no'.

We've already mentioned the cookie capability of *PerlShop* to maintain the items in the visitor's "cart" if she leaves the store and then returns later. (The actual contents of the shopping cart are maintained on the server in a data file.) The `$use_cookies` variable controls whether the script sends a cookie containing the visitor's session ID to the browser. Set this variable to yes if you want to allow visitors to leave and return later; set it to no otherwise. Leave cookies turned on unless you have a compelling reason to turn it off. The script will still work correctly for visitors with browsers that don't support cookies if they have disabled cookies in their browser.

A related variable is `$cookie_expire_days`. This variable sets the number of days in the future when the cookie will expire. After the expiration date, the browser will automatically delete the cookie, and the visitor won't be able to recover the contents of her cart. Set this variable to a value smaller than the interval between significant changes in your catalog.

Hair Saver

The data files containing the visitor's cart data aren't updated to reflect any changes you make to your catalog pages. Thus, you can receive incorrect orders for items that are no longer available or whose prices have changed. Expiring the cookies after a couple of days will probably cover most of your users' needs and minimize your headaches.

Several scripts in the book use SSI commands. Usually, SSI commands won't work on script-generated pages. The author *PerlShop*, in response to users' pleas, has added functions to simulate several common SSI commands within the script. As of version 3.1, you can simply insert SSI commands into your files as usual. *perlshop.cgi* will duplicate the processing normally done by the Web server.

The `$allow_ssi_cgi` variable controls whether the script will execute other CGI programs when it encounters the SSI *exec* command in your catalog pages. You should leave this set to `'no'` unless you need to execute a CGI program using SSI.

The `$cardno_on_email` variable controls whether the visitor's credit card number is included on the order confirmation e-mail sent upon completion of an order. It is very risky to send un-encrypted credit card numbers through e-mail. We strongly recommend that you *not* enable this variable (set it to `'no'`) unless you have modified the script to send encrypted e-mail.

The `$allow_fractional_qty` variable is used when noninteger quantities of an item can be purchased. By default, the script expects quantities to be integer numbers of items. Sometimes, however, a fractional quantity makes more sense—for example, buying items by the pound. If this variable is set to `'no'`, the script will reject non-integer quantities. Set the value to `'yes'` to allow the customer to specify a fractional quantity.

Server Configuration

This section describes the server configuration for the script. Be sure to refer to Figure 13.4 if you aren't sure of the directory structure. Setting these variables incorrectly can be a major source of frustration (and early hair loss) among *PerlShop* beginners.

Skip down to about line 153 in the script, where you will find the following lines:

```
###############################################################################
##################### Server Customization Variables ##########################
###############################################################################
$server_address       = 'www.arpanet.com';
$secure_server_address = "http://$server_address";   ## "https://
```

```
ssl.pair.com/taussig"
$cgiwrap_directory   = '/cgi-sys/cgiwrap/taussig/PolishBooks';
$cgi_directory       = '/cgi-bin/PolishBooks';    ###must be actual
cgi directory name
(not 'cgi-bin' if aliased)
$mail_via       = 'sockets'; ### Either 'sockets' or 'sendmail' or 'blat'
$blat_loc       = 'c:\\winnt35\\system32\\blat';
$sendmail_loc    = '/usr/sbin/sendmail';
$smtp_addr      = '207.86.128.11'; ### must use ip address on Win95, not host-
name (hostname ok on NT)
$catalog_home    = '/PolishBooks';    ### This is a Subdirectory of
Public_Html, NOT cgi-bin!!!
$home_page     = 'demo.html';
$image_directory    = '/PolishBooks/images'; ### This is a Subdirectory
of Public_Html, NOT cgi-bin!!!
$secure_image_directory = '/taussig/PolishBooks/images';
$image_location    = "http://$server_address$image_directory";
$home_icon     = 'home.gif';        ### must reside in $image_directory
if it exists.
$create_page_log   = 'yes';    ### ("yes" or "no")
$create_search_log  = 'yes';
```

The $server_address variable should be set to the name of your ISP/SA's Web server (such as www.myisp.com). Just put the Web server domain name here without any path information. The paths are specified in other variables. You can also use an IP address (such as 192.168.0.2) if the Web server doesn't have a domain name. (Check with your ISP or SA for the IP address of their Web server if you need this information.) Most people will use a text name for the server. However, an IP address will be useful for people on intranets or for testing on an Internet-connected machine that doesn't have an officially registered name. Using the server-independence features discussed in Chapter 14, you can relocate your Web site to a new server by simply copying the files to the new location and changing this one variable.

The $secure_server_address variable contains the Web server URL that will be used for the check-out pages on which payment information is collected. Here's how to set this variable:

If you don't have access to a secure server, leave the variable set to the default:

```
$secure_server = "http://$server_address";
```

If you can run secure communications from the Web server, substitute https: for http: in the variable:

```
$secure_server = "https://$server_address";
```

The $cgiwrap_directory variable defines how the *cgiwrap* program is called, if you are using it. We discuss setting up *cgiwrap* more in Chapter 15. For now, set this variable to a null value (' ').

```
$cgiwrap_directory = '';
```

Once you get your store up and running, you can activate *cgiwrap* if you like.

The `$cgi_directory` variable contains the path, from the server root, to the *PerlShop* script. If you are running a user Web account and your home page URL looks like this:

```
http://www.myisp.com/~joeuser/
```

then you should set `$cgi_directory` as follows:

```
$cgi_directory = '/~joeuser/cgi-bin/MyStore';
```

If you have a dedicated Web server or a virtual domain with a URL like

```
http://www.mycompany.com/
```

set `$cgi_directory` to

```
$cgi_directory = '/cgi-bin/MyStore';
```

Hot Tip

Some Web servers allow the *cgi-bin* subdirectory to be located outside the normal Web directory tree. The server redirects accesses to the *cgi-bin* subdirectory to the real one. This is done for security and other administrative reasons. Check your ISP/SA questionnaire to see if your server is set up this way.

If your ISP or SA's Web server does this, you need to set `$cgi_directory` to the name of the actual directory in which the CGI scripts are stored rather than to the alias.

When a visitor completes an order, a confirmation e-mail message is sent to him as well as to the catalog administrator. The `$mail_via` variable controls the method the script uses to send these messages. Three methods are supported:

1. `$mail_via = 'sendmail';`. The most common setting for UNIX-based Web servers. If you have access to the standard *sendmail* command, you should use this setting. Check your ISP/SA questionnaire if you're not sure.

2. `$mail_via = 'blat';`. A *sendmail*-like program for Windows computers. If your server runs Windows, you probably have this available. Check your ISP/SA questionnaire to see if your ISP recommends using *blat*.

3. `$mail_via = 'sockets';`. Tells the script to send the mail messages directly to the SMTP mail server. Usually *sendmail* and *blat* will take care of this, but some ISPs don't provide access to *sendmail/blat*. This method should work on all Web servers.

The `$blat_loc` variable defines the path to the *blat* executable file. Check your ISP/SA questionnaire and set the variable to match if you are using *blat*. Note the format given in the example for the path separators used in Windows Perl. If you are not using *blat*, ignore this value.

`$sendmail_loc` gives the location of the *sendmail* executable. Your ISP/SA questionnaire should have this location.

`$smtp_addr` defines the IP address of your SMTP e-mail server. Check with your ISP or SA for this IP address. You can ignore this if you aren't using the socket method.

Nerd Note

> One quick way to check for the SMTP address yourself is to use the *ping* utility described in Appendix B. The standard name for the mail server machine is *mail*. So doing a *ping mail.myisp.com* will often give you the IP address of the mail server computer. You can use the *ping* utility that comes with your TCP/IP package on your desktop computer. For Windows 95, simply open an MS-DOS window while connected to the network or the Internet and enter
>
> `ping mail.myisp.com`

The `$catalog_home` variable points to the location, relative to the server root, of the page you'd like users to return to when they press the home button from within the store. This should be the page that contains the entry link into the store. If you created a special subdirectory to hold your store home page, add that subdirectory to the variable. Thus, if your catalog entry point is in your root HTML directory, you should set the value to

`$catalog_home = '/';`

and if you have a subdirectory as in the example above, set the value to:

`$catalog_home = '/mystore';`

The `$home_page` variable is the name of the actual store home page HTML file located within the directory stored in `$catalog_home`. Don't add any path information to the filename. A typical value might be

`$home_page = 'entry.html';`

The `$image_directory` variable defines the location of the images referenced within the catalog pages. You can either use your normal images directory:

```
$image_directory = '/images';
```

or the special catalog images directory (if you created one):

```
$image_directory = '/storeimg';
```

A related variable is `$secure_image_directory`. This variable is used for images appearing on the secure checkout pages. A different image directory variable is needed for these pages because of the way the secure server accesses the directories. We discuss setting this variable in the "Secure Server Setup" section at the end of the chapter.

The `$image_location` variable combines the `$server_address` location with the `$image_directory` to form the completed URL (minus the filename) for your catalog images. Take a look at the values you put in these two variables. If you combine them, do they make the proper URL to get to your images? If not, adjust their values until a proper URL is formed by appending them together.

The two variables, `$create_page_log` and `$create_search_log`, are optional. If you set `$create_page_log` to `yes`, *PerlShop* will create a log file and add an entry for each catalog page requested. If you set `$create_search_log` to `yes`, *PerlShop* will record all the search words that visitors input into the catalog search page. Both of these logs can be used to analyze how visitors are navigating your site and what they are looking for in your catalog. Setting the variables to `yes` does not adversely affect performance. If in doubt, leave them set to `yes`.

The seven variables starting at line 177 define the locations of the subdirectories that *PerlShop* needs. If you created your directory structure following the example given earlier in the chapter, the default settings will work fine and you can skip this section. If you set up a different directory structure, here is where you let *PerlShop* know about it. You must set either the `$current_dir` variable to the base directory for all the seven (if you moved them all together) or each variable individually to point to the correct location. These entries should be the full file path, *not* the URL path. The easy way to get the full file path is to log on to your ISP or SA's server and navigate to the directory in question. Using your Telnet client, enter either

```
pwd
```

or, for Windows,

```
cd
```

and observe the response. This is the path to your subdirectory. If you are using an FTP client, the directory name is at the top of the remote directory panel or window. This will contain the path to the current directory. To change all the directories at once, add a line above the `$customers_directory` to redefine the `$current_dir` variable. For Windows you might add something like

```
$current_dir = 'd:\\users\\joe\\mydirs\\';
```

or, for UNIX,

```
$current_dir = '/home/joeuser/mydirs/';
```

If you've moved the directories to different locations, specify each directory fully.

This covers the server configuration portion of the script. In the next section, we show you how to customize the appearance of the catalog pages and configure the script to match your business practices. Now might be a good time to save your work to make sure an errant lightning bolt or foot on the power cord doesn't destroy your work. Hang in there—we're halfway home!

Company Configuration

Skip down a few lines in the script to about line 208, where you'll find the following section, which consists of two sets of variables:

```
########################################################################
###################### Company Customization Variables #################
########################################################################
#==== To Include an Image on your pages =============#
$banner         = 'arpanet.gif';        ### arpanet.gif
$hspace         = '5';
$vspace         = '5';
$border         = '0';
$height         = '111';
$width          = '111';
$align          = 'center';
#===================================================#
#==== To Add background image or change color =======#
$background      = 'good1.jpg';         ### good1.jpg
$text_color      = "";
$background_color = "";     ### white=#FFFFFF
$link_color      = "";
$vlink_color     = "";
$alink_color     = "";
#===================================================#
```

These two sets of variables allow you to define how pages generated by *PerlShop*—the catalog pages and all checkout pages—will look. The first chunk of lines allows you to add a banner image to the top of each page. The seven variables are combined to create an `<IMG>` tag placed at the top of each *PerlShop*-generated page. The names of the variables correspond exactly with the parameters of the image tag. You should be able to figure out what to put in each.

If you don't want a banner image on your pages, set the `$banner` variable to an empty string:

```
$banner = '';
```

Note, the `$align` variable sets the `align=` parameter in the image tag. Not all browsers support this tag, especially for centering. As always, be sure to test your catalog with the current crop of browsers.

The next group of lines starting with

```
#===== To Add background image or change color =======#
```

defines the parts of the `<BODY>` tag that *PerlShop* will put on your pages. As with the image parameter variables, the variable names associated with the background correspond with the parameters of the `<BODY>` tag. Fill out these variables just like you would in an HTML tag.

Hot Tip

> Some pages in your store will be partially created by you (the catalog pages) and others entirely by *PerlShop*. To achieve a consistent look and feel for all the store pages, let *PerlShop* create the banner image and `<BODY>` tags for your catalog pages. In Chapter 14, we'll show you where in the script code the pages are generated so that you can modify the default layout to match the rest of your site.

The next three variables are used to create a footer for each *PerlShop*-generated page:

```
$company_name      = 'ARPAnet Corp.';
$company_address   = '182 5th Ave., # 1R<br>Brooklyn NY
11217<br>(718)399-0460 (9:00am-5:00pm est.)';
$company_email     = 'sales@arpanet.com';
```

The contents of these variables are printed into the page as it is being sent to the browser. You may include HTML tags within the variables, as you can see from the example `$company_address` value. You can also include images or `<FONT>` tags to change the appearance of the footer. The value of the `$company_name` variable is the text of a hyperlink `mailto:` tag pointing to the address in the `$company_email` variable. This allows visitors to click the company name and send e-mail to you.

Following the company information is the e-mail destination for the order notifications that are sent out with each successful transaction:

```
$mail_order_to      = 'orders@arpanet.com';
$line_length    = 80;
```

The `$line_length` variable controls the length of the lines in the e-mail notification. If your e-mail program wraps lines longer than a certain length, you should reduce this value to get a nicer looking e-mail note. The value also controls the confirmation e-mail sent to the user.

Hair Saver

Be sure to use single quotation marks around the variable values in this section to prevent Perl from trying to interpret any of Perl's reserved characters. In particular, the @ in e-mail addresses will cause Perl problems if used in a double-quoted variable definition. In general, it's best to use single quotation marks, unless you want Perl to insert the value of a variable into the value you are defining. See Appendix A for more information on single versus double quotation marks and Perl's special characters.

Payment Configuration

Following the company and contact section comes the part that should keenly interest you: the payment information. In this section, you define what forms of payment you will accept and which, if any, of the on-line credit card payment systems you are using.

First, define what forms of payment you'll accept in the `@accept_payment_by` variable:

```
@accept_payment_by = ('Credit', 'Check', 'COD', 'First Virtual');
```

The default includes all the currently supported forms of payment, so just erase any you don't want to accept and keep the rest. This variable is a Perl array (you can tell by the @ character in the name). Be sure to surround each entry with single quotation marks and separate the entries with commas. Note, this version of *PerlShop* (3.1) doesn't support CyberCash payments. Check the *PerlShop* Web site to see if the author has since added that capability.

If you accept credit cards, list the different card types in the @valid_credit_cards variable:

```
@valid_credit_cards = ('Visa', 'MasterCard');
```

Version 3.1 of *PerlShop* supports MasterCard, Visa, American Express, Optima, Carte Blanche, Diners Club, Discover, and JCB cards. Each item in the list must be surrounded by single quotation marks and separated by commas. Capitalize the names of the cards as shown.

The next lines configure the on-line credit payment and validation options supported by *PerlShop*. For now, leave them as is. We discuss these systems in detail in Chapter 15.

Payment Options

Skip down to line 253. This is where you set up the payment options for your store.

```
$cod_charge      = 3.00;   #### amount to add to order (0.00 if none)

@Handling_table = (       #### amount to add to order (0.00 if none)
['US', 2.75],
['CA', 5.00],
['OTHER', 10.00],
);

$Pay_checks_to  = 'ARPAnet Corp.';
```

If you accept COD orders, set the value of $cod_charge to the amount that you add to each order for COD delivery. Use a decimal format as shown in the default.

If you don't add anything for COD charges, set the value to 0.00.

The @Handling_table variable defines an array of handling charges added for shipping to the listed countries. Duplicate the format shown for each country for which you have a distinct handling charge. (Countries not explicitly listed will be charged the OTHER amount.) Be sure to use the correct ISO country code. *PerlShop* comes with an HTML file listing the current country codes. Check the file */scripts/perlshop/ country.htm* file on the CD-ROM if you need to get the country code for Kyrgyzstan or Vanuatu (for the curious, their codes are KG and VU).

The $Pay_checks_to variable is used to print payment information when the user selects the Check method of payment. Set this variable to the name you'd like to see on those stacks of order checks.

The $return_policy variable is printed on the final confirmation page just before the order is confirmed to alert the user to your return policy. This message also appears on the final invoice sent to the user via e-mail.

```
$return_policy        = 'All Sales are final. We will be glad to
exchange defective items only within 30 days from date of ';
$return_policy       .= 'sale. Any items returned must be sent back
prepaid in the same condition as when originally shipped. ';
$return_policy       .= 'Shipping and handling charges are not
refundable.';
```

In the example, these three lines are appended to the `$return _policy` variable by using the Perl `.=` operator. This operator appends the value to the right of the equals sign to the current value of the variable. You can duplicate this format, or you can enter your return policy in one long line. This format is simply a little easier to read and edit than a single line.

Formatting and Units

The next ten lines set up the units you will be using for currency and weight in describing your products. The local date and time formats are also set in this section.

```
$catalog_country    = 'US';      ### Must be all capital letters, 2
letter country code.
$accept_any_country  = 'yes';    ### ('yes' or 'no') #Allow orders
from countries not specifically listed in shipping rates table?
$local_currency      = 'USD';
$currency_decimal    = '.';  ### Decimal separator for currency format
$currency_separator  = ',';  ### Thousands separator for currency
format
$currency_symbol    = '$';  ### Symbol for currency
$local_weight       = 'lbs.';  ### Unit of measure for WEIGHT field if
used.
$local_time        = 'est';  ### The time zone your <<SERVER>> is
located in (eg: est, pst)
$date_format        = 'mmddyy';### Options are: mmddyy, ddmmyy,
mmddyyyy, ddmmyyyy
$date_separator      = '/';
```

You should be able to figure out the values to insert into these variables without our giving detailed instructions. Just make sure the variables are in proper Perl format with open and closing quotation marks and semicolons on the end of each line.

Control Buttons

The next group of lines allow you to specify the images used in creating the shopping-cart control buttons that appear on *PerlShop*-generated pages. These buttons activate *PerlShop* functions such as viewing the cart contents, starting the checkout process, or searching the catalog. This feature allows you to create an attractive catalog without using the default (and decidedly plain) form submit buttons that are used if you don't specify an image. The `%button_image` variable associates the name of the function and the name of the image file to use for that function. The format of these lines is a little different than a normal variable:

```
$button_image{'UPDATE'} = 'update_button.gif';
```

To instruct *PerlShop* to use an image for a particular function, insert the name of the image file between the quotation marks following the equals sign. Don't add any path information. The images are assumed to reside in the directory you specified in the `$image_directory` variable. Don't change the function name (`{'UPDATE'}`). If you do, you may want to leave these entries alone until you get your catalog working and then add images later to beautify it. If you specify images now, they must reside in the proper directory when you run the script.

Product Options

The next four lines are likely to be quite important to the operation of your catalog. These specify optional attributes the user can request for your products, such as color, size, or style.

```
$weight_caption   = 'Weight';   # e.g. 'Weight'
$option1_caption  = 'Color';    # e.g. 'Color'
$option2_caption  = 'Size';     # e.g. 'Size'
$option3_caption  = '';
```

The value of `$weight_caption` is used to label the column of weights listed on the order form. If you don't specify a weight for any of the items in your catalog pages, this label will be ignored. Use an appropriate word that means weight in your language rather than the unit of weight. You set the unit in the `$local_weight` variable.

The three `$optionX_caption` values are used to label the corresponding column on the shopping cart summary list and the order form. For example, you might allow your visitors to pick from one of several colors of a given product in your catalog pages. In the catalog, you identify the color the visitor picks as being the value of option #1 for that item. When all the products in the shopping cart are listed or the final order form is displayed, the column for each option's values will be labeled with the string you define here.

Hot Tip

> The program doesn't check that the value you specify in your catalog for option #1, option #2, or option #3 on a particular item matches the other items. So you can assign anything you like for each of the three options for any item in your catalog. However, only one label is provided for the column corresponding to each option on the summary listing pages. To use several different types of options with the same option number, choose a generic label for the `$optionX_caption`, such as "extras," "accessories," or "specs."

Shipping Charge Calculation

The next section of code lets you define the way in which shipping charges are calculated for items in your catalog.

```
$shipping_type = 'quantity';    ### shipping_type is either 'price'
or 'quantity' or 'weight' or 'included'
###  price or quantity means the minimum/maximum refers to total
prices or total quantities respectively.
### '+' means add the Amount specified to the order total
### '*' means multiply the Amount times the Number of items ordered.
### '%' means take the given percentage of the total Amount ordered.
### Country, Ship via, Minimum, Maximum, Add or Multiply or
Percentage, Amount ###
@Shipping_Rates = (
[$catalog_country, 'UPS Ground', 0, 2, '+', 5.00],    ### Index must
start at 0 in case $shipping_type='weight'
[$catalog_country, 'UPS Ground', 3, 5, '+', 10.00],   ### Min. should
be .01 more that prev max. if based on price
[$catalog_country, 'UPS Ground', 6, 99999999,'*', 2.00],
[$catalog_country, 'UPS Blue', 0, 2, '+', 10.00],
[$catalog_country, 'UPS Blue', 3, 5, '+', 15.00],
[$catalog_country, 'UPS Blue', 6, 99999999, '*', 3.00],
[$catalog_country, 'FedEx', 0, 99999999, '+', 10],
['ALL', 'Airborne Express',0, 2, '+', 7.00],### 'ALL' applies to any
country (but is overriden by $accept_any_country = 'no')
['ALL', 'Airborne Express',3, 99999999, '*', 5.00],### 'ALL'
applies to any country
['OTHER','DHL', 0, 3, '*', 5.00],         ### Default for any country
not specfically listed above.
['OTHER','DHL', 4, 99999999, '*', 4.00],  ### Default for any country
not specfically listed above.
);
```

The $shipping_type variable controls which method is used to calculate the shipping cost. $shipping_type may be any one of the following: quantity, price, or weight. A fourth option, called included, assumes the shipping cost has been added to the price of each individual item and no additional shipping charge will be calculated.

PerlShop Version 3.0 supports only one method of calculating the shipping charges. If you use different methods of calculating the shipping costs for each item, you should precalculate the cost and add it to the price of each item and specify the included value for $shipping_type.

The @Shipping_Rates array defines the actual formula used to calculate the shipping charges for each shipping carrier (i.e., United Parcel Service, Federal Express, or U.S. mail), each country (based on a two-letter code), and the different ranges of value for the amount of $shipping_type in the total order. If you are already shipping products, you will probably have well-established practices in place for calculating shipping charges. We won't attempt to tell you how to determine this for your business, but we will try to explain how to get *PerlShop* to duplicate the way you do your shipping calculations.

Each entry in the @Shipping_Rates array is itself an array of values. Surround each entry with square brackets "[]" and separate them with commas as shown in the example:

```
[$catalog_country, 'UPS Ground', 0, 2, '+', 5.00],
```

The values that make up each entry are, in order, country, shipper name, starting value, ending value, operator, and operand:

- country. Should be a valid two-letter ISO country code for the country to which the order is being shipped. In the previous example, the value of the $catalog_country variable is used for the country entry. You can optionally use this variable as is for shipping products to your country, or just put in the actual value (e.g. 'US').

- shipper name. A descriptive name for the shipping company and service type. For example, 'UPS Ground', 'UPS Blue', 'UPS Priority Overnight', and 'Federal Express Two-Day' should each have different entries if the cost is different. This allows the customer to pick the shipping method from those you support.

- minimum value. The lower bound of this range of values. For example, the shipping rate may be $5.00 per pound for orders between 0 and 2 pounds. At most, you will have a different @Shipping_Rates entry for each value range the shipper recognizes. (You can, of course, consolidate ranges to reduce the number of entries.) The first entry for each shipper should have a minimum value of zero. Each succeeding entry should have a minimum value at least 0.01 higher than the preceding maximum value.

- ■ maximum value. The corresponding upper limit to this range of values. It must be greater or equal to the minimum value. Put a value of 99999999 (a number much larger than the largest value you will get in an order) for the last upper value.

- ■ operator. For each entry, operator may be one of +, *, or %. + means add the amount of operand (see the next item in this list) to the order total for this range. This is a flat-rate charge for a given range of the value of $shipping_type. * means multiply the $shipping_type parameter value by operand. This allows a per pound or per item charge. % causes *PerlShop* to take the operand percentage of the $shipping_type parameter and add the result to the total.

- ■ operand. Either a value in currency (such as 5.00 dollars for the + and * operators) or a percentage (as in 10.00 for the % operator).

Following are some example entries with an explanation of the calculation:

```
[$catalog_country, 'UPS Ground', 0, 2, '+', 5.00],
```

When shipping an order to an in-country address using UPS Ground, add $5.00 to the order total if between zero and two items (or pounds, or dollars) are ordered.

```
['VU', 'DHL', 0, 9999999, '*', 15.00]
```

When shipping an order to the country of Vanuatu using the DHL carrier, the shipping cost is $15.00 per pound (or per item or per dollar) of the total order.

```
['OTHER', 'MAIL', 25.01, 50, '%', 1.00]
```

When shipping to any country not covered by another entry, use normal mail service. For orders between 25.01 and 50 pounds (or items or dollars), the shipping cost is 1.00% of the weight (or dollar value or number of items).

These examples should be enough to get you started. Just write down the current options you have for shipping and the way you currently calculate the shipping costs. You should be able to duplicate those calculations in *PerlShop* fairly easily. If not, you'll need to precalculate the shipping costs or go to a simplified or flat-rate model for your on-line store.

Discounts

PerlShop allows you to give different discounts based on ranges of either quantity or price for each order. The type of discount you offer is set with the $discount_type variable. Set the value of $discount_type to either quantity, price, or none.

The @Discount_Rates array is similar in format to that of the @Shipping_Rates variable. The values in each entry are minimum value, maximum value, and discount percentage. Create an entry for each range of order value or quantity where you offer a discount. As in the example, your first range should be a 0.00% discount range. Here is the default example in the script:

```
$discount_type = 'quantity'; ### $discount_type is either 'quantity'
or 'price' or 'none'.
@Discount_Rates = ( ### For no discount use: $discount_type = 'none';
[1, 3, 0.00],
[4, 99999999, 10.00],
);
```

This example applies discounts based on the quantity of items purchased. From one to three items in an order receive no discount. Four or more items receive a discount of 10.00% of the total dollar amount of the order.

PerlShop is very picky about the format of the @Discount_Rates variable. You must not have any gaps in the ranges. For quantity discounts, the maximum of one range must be exactly one less than the minimum of the next range. For price discounts, the difference must be 0.01. Finally, the maximum value of the ending range must be 99999999 (eight nines).

Sales Tax

PerlShop supports sales tax calculations based on the state to which the order will be shipped. It does not support different tax rates based on ZIP or postal code within a state. The @Tax_States array contains entries for each two-letter state abbreviation. If you don't specify a state in this section, sales to that state will not be charged sales tax. Each entry consists of the state abbreviation followed by one space and the tax rate. The example given in the script shows this process in operation:

```
@Tax_States = ("NY 8.25", "TX 7.00");   ### List of: States to Apply
Tax to, and Tax Rate (NOT percentage!) separated by a singe space
e.g. @Tax_States = ("NY 8.25", "CA 4.5");
```

Miscellaneous

Just a couple more housekeeping items, and we'll be done with our little configuration party. All good things must come to an end.

With the default configuration, *PerlShop* creates a special page to show the contents of the visitor's shopping cart. This page is displayed whenever the visitor selects an item for purchase or explicitly requests to look at the cart's contents. Some catalogs would benefit from showing the cart's contents on the same page as the catalog. To answer this need, the author of *PerlShop* provides an option to display the cart's current contents on the bottom of the current catalog page when the visitor selects an item for purchase. This is useful if you have an all-in-one, single-page catalog or if you just want the visitor to have access to the cart's contents and the order total from the product pages. The `$stay_on_page` variable controls this behavior. Set the variable to `yes` if you want the cart's contents appended to the bottom of each catalog page as it is displayed. *Note:* The cart appears only after at least one item is added. You can override this setting for an individual catalog page if you want the cart to appear only on certain pages.

Last but not least, the `${SO}` and `${SE}` variables hold the HTML tags that *PerlShop* places around the search keywords matched in the catalog pages returned by the search engine. You can modify these to add any HTML you like to highlight the keywords. An example that turns the keywords red as well as bold is

```
${SO} = '<B><FONT COLOR=RED>';
${SE} = '</FONT></B>';
```

Whew!

That completes the initial configuration of the *PerlShop* script. We skipped a number of configuration items that we'll complete in Chapters 14 and 15 before you can take your store on-line.

Now is an excellent time to save your newly modified script to a safe place on your hard drive. Go back through all the configuration variables and double-check for missing quotation marks and semicolons. Be sure all the array variables (they start with @) have parentheses around their elements. After you've done that, you can move on to installing the script.

Step 3: Installation

After that rather grueling configuration session, you'll be pleased to know that almost every aspect of the on-line store system is stored within the script itself, so you're well over halfway to getting your on-line store up and running.

To install the *PerlShop* script, upload the script file to the subdirectory below your *cgi-bin/* directory (`mystore/` in our example) with your FTP client. Figure 13.4 shows the recommended location of the *perlshop.cgi* script file. Review Chapter 3 for FTP and Telnet procedures, if necessary.

Next, change the file permissions to mark the script as an executable program.

Verify that all the directories have the `drwxrwxrwx` (777) permissions set. The *perlshop.cgi* script file should have a permission set of `-rwxr-xr-x` (755). To manually set the permissions on a directory, use the *chmod* command with your Telnet client or follow the procedure for your FTP client.

The final installation step is to run a quick check on the *perlshop.cgi* file to make sure there are no syntax errors (such as missing quotation marks). Enter

```
./perlshop.cgi
```

If the computer responds with

```
perlshop version 3.1 copyright (c) 1996 by ARPAnet Corp.
```

celebrate! Your script has been successfully installed. If, on the other hand, you get errors from Perl, you have made a mistake editing the script. Observe the error message carefully and try to locate the offending line. Search the configuration section of the script for missing or mismatched quotation marks or any of the common editing problems. Once you've found and corrected the problem, re-upload the script (you won't need to change permissions again) and retest. Repeat this process until Perl is happy with the script.

This completes the basic installation of the *PerlShop* script.

Secure Server Setup

If you have access to a secure server, you can offer your customers the added (and more and more expected) feature of secure transmission of their credit card data from the Web browser to the server. *PerlShop* fully supports secure server checkout. Note, these directions are really only general guidelines for UNIX servers, since secure server configuration varies quite a bit from server to server.

Before you start this section, verify with your ISP or SA that you are authorized to use the secure server. Also find out what the root directory is for pages served by the secure server. Many secure servers require that the pages sent securely be stored in a separate directory from your usual HTML pages. With this data in hand, you can set up *PerlShop* to use the secure server.

When a secure server is used, most of the pages visitors see are sent by the normal server. Only the pages containing sensitive information will be sent via the secure server. In particular, the checkout page (where payment information is collected) and the final confirmation page will be served securely.

To enable the secure server, set the $use_secure_server variable to 'yes'. Next, enter in the $secure_server_address variable the part of the secure URL up through the domain name. An example might look like this:

```
https://ssl.myisp.com
```

Note the use of the `https:` protocol identifier. The URL must start with `https:` otherwise the secure server won't respond to the request. Note also the machine name (ssl) that differs from the usual `www`.

Servers and ISPs will differ in the location requirements for each part of the *PerlShop* system. Try to get as much information (and examples if possible) from your ISP or SA concerning the requirements for using their secure server. A common requirement is to place the pages served by the secure server in a separate directory from the other pages. If this is the case, you'll need to place a copy of the *perlshop.cgi* script in that directory. You should duplicate the directory structure under your secure directory up to the directory that the *perlshop.cgi* script resides in (*cgi-bin/MyStore/* in the previous example). For example, if secure server pages must go in the directory,

```
/home/users/joeuser/public_ssl/
```

instead of

```
/home/users/joeuser/public_html
```

you will need to create the subdirectories *public_ssl/images* and *public_ssl/cgi-bin/MyStore*, at the very least, in order to get *PerlShop* to run. Place a copy of the *PerlShop.cgi* script into the mirror directory under your secure root (i.e., *public_ssl/cgi-bin/MyStore*). Copy all images that appear on the checkout pages to the mirror directory *images/*. You will need to set the `$secure_image_directory` variable to point to your secure images directory. Try setting this equal to the `$images_directory` variable to start with. If the script can't find your secure-side images, you'll need to adjust the variable until it does. Unfortunately, we can't give specific instructions than this, since secure server configurations vary.

You may have noticed that we didn't duplicate the *orders/, customers/,* and other directories. *PerlShop* needs to access the files stored in these directories from the secure directory, so you can't just create duplicate directories. The script writes the data files only to the main directory. So that the script can access the files, you need to create a UNIX link within the secure directory structure that points to the directory in the normal directories. (A file link is analogous to a shortcut in Windows and Mac operating systems.) These linked directories will act like they are located within the secure directory tree but will actually point to the regular directory located under the normal HTTP server's directories. To do this, enter the secure directory with your Telnet client and enter the following command for each directory (all on a single line):

```
ln -s /home/users/joeuser/public-html/cgi-bin/MyStore/orders /home/
users/joeuser/public_ssl/cgi-bin/MyStore/orders
```

Repeat this for each of the seven directories you created in Step 1. This command creates a link to the basic directories. Files in the basic directory may now be accessed from either "parent" directory. Some Web servers have a configuration option called `FollowSymLinks` that can be turned on or off. It controls whether the Web server accesses files in directories that are symbolic links. If you have problems accessing the data files from the secure server, ask your ISP or SA to enable this option for you.

Hair Saver

Now that you have two copies of the *perlshop.cgi* script, you've complicated your life a bit. Henceforth, you must be sure to make all configuration changes to *both* scripts. You must also ensure that the two image directories are kept in sync. As if your life wasn't hard enough already.

To test your secure setup, put some sample HTML files in your secure server root and try to access them using a secure `https:` URL. If they appear as you expect, chances are your secure server is set up correctly. Be careful about too much testing, however. Many ISPs charge for each page fetched by the secure server. You will have to wait until you have a catalog up and running to really test your server. But these instructions, along with a little perseverance on your part, should get you pretty close.

Up Next

In Chapter 14, we cover creating the catalog pages, navigating your store, and customizing the look of the shopping cart summary page and the order pages.

Chapter 15 gives details about processing the orders that will be pouring in to your *PerlShop* on-line store. To complete your store security, we give you a few pointers on how to encrypt your customers' sensitive data to protect it from hackers. The encryption software we use is the popular *Pretty Good Privacy* (PGP) data encryption software. PGP is free for personal and nonprofit use. A licensed version is available for commercial applications.

What We Covered in Chapter 13

- How on-line store systems such as *PerlShop* work
- Creating subdirectories on the Web server to hold *PerlShop*, its data files, and your product catalog
- Configuring *PerlShop* to run in your server environment
- Adding your business information to the script
- Configuring payment, shipping, and tax information
- Installing and testing the script for proper syntax
- Configuring the script to work with a secure HTTP server

Chapter 14

A Perl-based On-line Store System—Part 2: Setting Up the Store

What We Cover in This Chapter

- How *PerlShop* processes pages
- Entering the store
- Creating the catalog pages
- Navigating the store
- The built-in search engine
- Viewing the shopping cart
- Modifying the look of the *PerlShop*-generated pages

Where We Are Now

In Chapter 13, you coded much of the information about your business and your on-line store into the *perlshop.cgi* configuration variables. In this chapter, you'll finish setting up a basic store. We show you how to create the HTML forms *PerlShop* uses to hold your product information. We also show you how to create navigational links between your pages and how to use the built-in search engine so that your visitors can navigate through your store. Finally, we discuss how to customize the shopping cart contents page to match the look of the rest of your Web site.

The store setup presented in this chapter may well be sufficient for simple stores or those that don't need to accept credit card information. However, we realize most stores will require credit card processing capabilities and more security before they can go "live" on the Internet. To take you to this final phase, Chapter 15 shows you how to use the credit card processing systems that *PerlShop* supports and how to increase the security of the data you collect from your customers.

How *PerlShop* Processes Pages

In Chapter 2, we discussed how the HTTP protocol is used to communicate between the Web browser and the Web server. The HTTP protocol doesn't have a built-in means of distinguishing one data request from another, so shopping-cart systems need to add this user data into the HTTP data stream. *PerlShop* uses a couple of techniques to overcome this limitation in HTTP.

Recall from Chapter 13 that *PerlShop* generates a unique number for each store visitor called a session ID. *PerlShop* uses the session ID to associate each action the visitor takes with a set of data files stored on the server. These files contain the shopping-cart contents and other data pertinent to that particular visitor. As long as the session ID numbers are unique, any number of visitors can roam your electronic store without feeling crowded.

The cookie mechanism mentioned in Chapter 13 is the other means of keeping track of visitors. The *PerlShop* cookie data is stored on the visitor's computer (along with cookies from other servers) in a special "cookie jar" file. The cookie is sent to the *PerlShop* server whenever the browser requests a page. The session ID stored in the cookie stays with the user until it expires and is automatically deleted by the user's computer. Cookies are not quite as sweet as they seem, however. Not all browsers support them, and some users (concerned with Web servers writing data onto their machines) turn cookies off. As we mentioned in Chapter 13, you shouldn't depend on cookies to maintain session IDs.

PerlShop uses a combination of these two methods to track a visitor's actions. First, it makes sure the session ID is passed from the browser to the server for every link within the store. It does this by modifying the HTML of each catalog page as it is requested by a user. Each page presented to the visitor is actually the output of the *perlshop.cgi* script. The visitor's session ID is encoded into every hyperlink URL on the page when it is sent from the server. Thus, whenever a link is clicked or a form is submitted, *PerlShop* knows exactly which visitor is making the request.

Nerd Note

We wrote an article for the September 1996 issue of the magazine, *Dr. Dobb's Journal,* entitled "Implementing a Web Shopping Cart" that describes the methods of maintaining user state in a Web-based shopping-cart system. If you are interested in the details of how shopping carts work, the article provides more detail on the subject than we give here. It is a good place to start. Be warned, however, *Dr. Dobb's* is a serious nerd-programmer magazine. Read it only if you're willing to take the risk of developing a programmer's mind-set.

"How does *PerlShop* do that?" you may be asking. Patience, grasshopper, and all will be revealed.

For each hyperlink and form action, *PerlShop* creates each link to point back to itself with a URL that includes the session ID and other data (such as the page the user is requesting). Here's a typical *PerlShop*-generated URL:

```
http://www.hypertising.com/DnDCGI/PerlShop/cgi-bin/PaperStore/
perlshop.cgi?action=thispage&thispage=visua.html&ORDER_ID=179823241
```

This part

```
http://www.hypertising.com/DnDCGI/PerlShop/cgi-bin/PaperStore/perlshop.cgi
```

calls the *perlshop.cgi* script located in a subdirectory below the main *DnDCGI* Web site.

The rest of the line

```
action=thispage&thispage=visua.html&ORDER_ID=179823241
```

consists of arguments to the script.

You can see there is an action for the script to take (load `thispage`), the page name (*visua.html*), and the session ID (`ORDER_ID=179823241`). In the background, a set of data files are created on the Web server with filenames that include the session ID number. By including the session ID in all the URLs it generates, *PerlShop* can keep track of multiple visitors to the site at the same time and manipulate the proper data files. HTML forms within your site will pass the same kind of data to the script stored in TYPE=HIDDEN fields.

This method works for all browsers. The only drawback is that visitors can't leave the store and then return without losing the contents of their carts. This happens because they are given a new session ID when they re-enter the store. As we learned in Chapter 13, *PerlShop* gets around this limitation to a certain degree by storing a session ID cookie on browsers that allow it.

We've gone through this in so much detail in order to emphasize why *PerlShop* requires the catalog pages to be formatted the way they are. Appropriately enlightened, let's move on to actually creating some catalog pages.

Server-Independence Tags

PerlShop has two tags that simplify the creation of catalog pages (and thus make your life easier). The examples we give in the following sections use these tags, so we cover them first.

In the previous section, we described how *PerlShop* scans each requested page and inserts session-specific data to track a particular visitor's actions. *PerlShop* also scans the pages for special meta-tags and inserts address information specific to your ISP or SA's Web server when it encounters them. The two server-independence tags are !MYURL! and !MYWWW!.

The !MYURL! tag is a shortcut to call the *perlshop.cgi* script in <FORM> and hyperlink anchor (<A>) tags. When the *PerlShop* script scans a page and encounters the !MYURL! tag, it replaces it with the correct URL to call itself. This feature allows you to create your pages on one machine for development and testing and then move them to your production server, without having to modify every page to match the new server. Also, you have less chance of making a typo when entering the code for your pages. A typical use of !MYURL! is

```
<FORM ACTION="!MYURL!" METHOD=POST>
```

which *PerlShop* might expand to

```
<FORM ACTION="http://www.hypertising.com/DnDCGI/PerlShop/cgi-bin/
PaperStore/perlshop.cgi" METHOD=POST>
```

You can see how this saves time and reduces the chance for typing errors.

`!MYWWW!` is similar, but it is used for non-CGI references such as images and other multimedia files. For example, an image link might look like this:

```
<IMG SRC="!MYWWW!/images/product1.gif">
```

which *PerlShop* would expand to

```
<IMG SRC="http://www.hypertising.com/DnDCGI/perlshop/images/product1.gif">
```

You don't have to use these shortcuts if you don't want to, but the author of *PerlShop* recommends them—and we second that.

Entering the Store

Figure 14.1 shows the home page for a fictional high-quality paper maker called Allegretti Papers. Allegretti has just opened an on-line store using *PerlShop*, and they're very proud of it.

To generate the session ID, *PerlShop* requires that you call the script from an **entry link**. Figure 14.2 shows the *papers.html* page. This page previously contained an overview of the Allegretti product line. Near the bottom of the page, the Webmasters at Allegretti added the entry links to the on-line store. The entry link can be either an HTML form or a text/image hyperlink.

For example purposes, both types of entry link are included on this page. As a rule, you'll use one, but not both. Note, you can place the entry link on any or all of the other pages on your Web sites.

The text hyperlink is in the following format:

```
<A HREF="cgi-bin/PaperStore/perlshop.cgi?ACTION=ENTER&THISPAGE=
cathome.html&ORDER_ID=!ORDERID!">on-line store</A>.
```

The required elements of the link are as follows:

- `ACTION=ENTER`. The value `ENTER` in the `ACTION` parameter tells the script a new user is entering the store and to generate a new session ID for use by this user.

- `THISPAGE=cathome.html`. The `THISPAGE` parameter tells *PerlShop* which page to load and display next. These pages are all located in the directory specified by the `$catalog_directory` configuration variable. Usually, this directory is a subdirectory located below the directory in which the *perlshop.cgi* script resides. Refer to Figure 13.4 for the recommended directory structure.

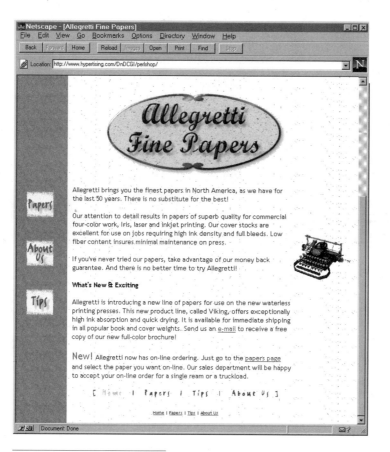

Figure 14.1 *The fictional Allegretti Papers home page*

- ORDER_ID=!ORDERID!. This parameter is a placeholder for the real session ID. For pages within the store, *PerlShop* will replace the !ORDERID! string with the actual session ID number.

A form-based entry link passes the same information to the script. The parameters are stored in TYPE=HIDDEN fields. Here is the HTML for our entry link form:

```
<FORM ACTION="http://www.hypertising.com/DnDCGI/PerlShop/cgi-bin/
PaperStore/perlshop.cgi" METHOD=POST>
<INPUT TYPE=submit NAME="ACTION" VALUE="ENTER SHOP">
<INPUT TYPE=hidden NAME="THISPAGE" VALUE="cathome.html">
<INPUT TYPE=hidden NAME="ORDER_ID" VALUE="!ORDERID!">
</FORM>
```

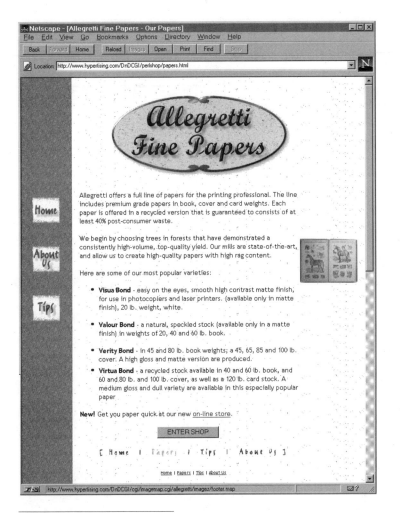

Figure 14.2 *Page showing* PerlShop *text and button entry links*

Hot Tip

We've called our catalog home page *cathome.html*. But there is nothing special about this particular name. *PerlShop* doesn't care which page it displays first from an entry link. In fact, you can create multiple entry links to any or all of your individual catalog pages.

You should create your catalog such that a visitor can't inadvertently leave the catalog. You also should provide a warning for any external links you do include, since, lacking a cookie, such a jump may cause visitors to lose the contents of their carts.

You can see the same parameters we used in the hypertext link coded into the hidden form fields. The notable difference is the label for the link. In the hypertext link, any text or image can be used for the visitor to click. When using a FORM, the VALUE of the SUBMIT field determines the label for the button that appears on the page. To give you some flexibility, *PerlShop* will accept ACTION values starting with any one of the following: "ENTER", "GO TO", "->", or "[".

Here are some example valid submit buttons:

```
<INPUT TYPE=SUBMIT NAME=ACTION VALUE="ENTER SHOP">
<INPUT TYPE=SUBMIT NAME=ACTION VALUE="ENTER The Dungeon!">
<INPUT TYPE=SUBMIT NAME=ACTION VALUE="GO TO STORE">
<INPUT TYPE=SUBMIT NAME=ACTION VALUE="-> Click HERE to Begin">
<INPUT TYPE=SUBMIT NAME=ACTION VALUE="[Why Wait?]">
```

If the look of the default form button insults your artistic sensibilities, you can replace it with an image. To do this, make the ACTION field a hidden field and add an image field to the form for the submit button.

```
<INPUT TYPE=HIDDEN NAME=ACTION VALUE="ENTER SHOP">
<INPUT NAME=dummy TYPE=IMAGE SRC="!MYWWW!/images/entercat.gif">
```

Hot Tip

> You may want to put different text on your button than that listed here. To do so, you can use the same method as for an image button and put any text on your entry button. Just make a dummy SUBMIT field with the value set to your text and make the ACTION field hidden.
>
> ```
> <INPUT TYPE=HIDDEN NAME=ACTION VALUE="ENTER SHOP">
> <INPUT NAME=dummy TYPE=SUBMIT VALUE="Oog say 'BUY!!'">
> ```

Creating the Catalog Pages

All the data about the products in your store are stored in the catalog HTML pages. This allows you to create your catalog pages using only an HTML editor, and frees you from the overhead of managing a DBMS. This simplicity comes at a price, however. You'll have to update your catalog pages by hand or develop your own system to create the pages from your off-line product database. *PerlShop* may not be the right choice for large stores, those with many product changes, or those with a complex structure. Read through this section and try to estimate how much work it will take to keep the store up to date. The initial effort of creating your store will soon be overshadowed by the ongoing maintenance effort.

PerlShop catalog pages are simply HTML files with a few *PerlShop* tags added for simplicity and portability. The catalog pages are not complete HTML files. As it scans the pages, *PerlShop* creates the initial <HTML> tag for the file. It also creates the <BODY> tag using the body tag–related configuration variables, such as $background and $text_color. Setting these variables in the script ensures a consistent look and feel between your catalog pages and the *PerlShop*-generated pages. If you defined a banner image (in the $banner configuration variable) for the top of the page, *PerlShop* will add that to each page as well.

The pages are stored in the directory defined in the $catalog_directory configuration variable. To keep the store organized, you can have as many subdirectories below this base directory as you like. For example, a home electronics store might create subdirectories below the main catalog/directory for VCRs, Televisions, Camcorders, and Stereos. You might create directories for special sales or "Web-only" special pricing on certain products.

Catalog items are placed in the shopping cart by submitting an HTML form to the *perlshop.cgi* script. The form contains all the information about the product. Forms can be submitted for a single product (single-item selection forms) or multiple items (multi-item selection forms). You can put as many forms on a page as you like. You can also mix single-item and multi-item forms on the same page.

Single-item Selection Form

Figure 14.3 shows a catalog page for one of the products in the Allegretti store.

Most of the page is coded using standard HTML. Note that the "Powered by *PerlShop*" logo at the bottom of the page is required by the *PerlShop* license agreement. The script will put this on the page for you, so you don't have to worry about it. The product information used by *PerlShop* is contained in Listing 14.1.

Listing 14.1	A *PerlShop* single-item selection form

```
<FORM ACTION="!MYURL!" METHOD=POST>
<INPUT TYPE=hidden NAME=ITEM_ID VALUE="P02">
<INPUT TYPE=hidden NAME=ITEM_NAME VALUE="Verity Bond">
<INPUT TYPE=hidden NAME=ITEM_OPTION2 VALUE="Matte">
<INPUT TYPE=hidden NAME=ITEM_WEIGHT VALUE="60">
Qty: <INPUT TYPE=TEXT SIZE=3 MaxLength=3 NAME=QTY VALUE="0"> <BR>
Stock: <SELECT NAME=ITEM_OPTION1>
  <OPTION>20 lb.
  <OPTION>40 lb.
  <OPTION>60 lb.
```

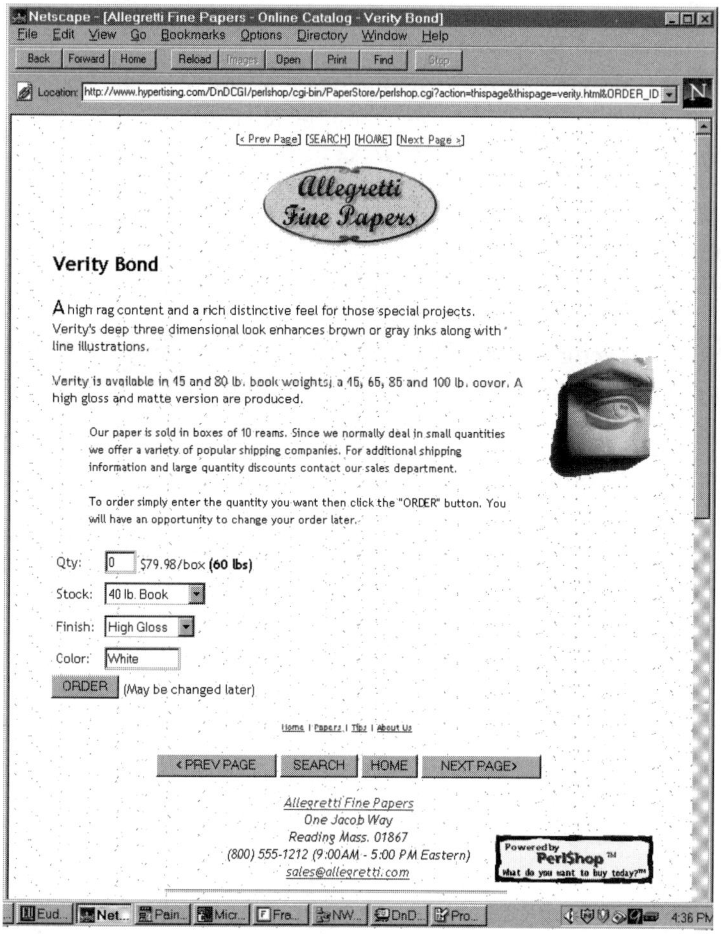

Figure 14.3 *A single-item catalog page*

```
</SELECT> <BR>
Color: <INPUT TYPE=text NAME=ITEM_OPTION3 VALUE="White" SIZE=10
MAXLENGTH=30>
<BR>$79.98/box   <strong>(60 lbs)</strong><br>
(matte finish only)<br>
<INPUT TYPE=submit NAME=ACTION VALUE="ORDER"> (May be changed later)
<INPUT TYPE=hidden NAME=THISPAGE VALUE="verity.html">
<INPUT TYPE=hidden NAME=ITEM_PRICE VALUE="79.98">
<INPUT TYPE=hidden NAME=ORDER_ID VALUE="!ORDERID!">
<INPUT TYPE=hidden NAME=ITEM_CODE VALUE="!ITEMCODE!">
</FORM>
```

We'll go through this form line-by-line so that by the time we're done, you'll know just about everything there is to know about creating catalog pages with *PerlShop*.

Hair Saver

> Don't put quotation marks around the `NAME=` parameters in the fields. *PerlShop* doesn't like them. Many HTML editors will put them in for you. If yours is one that does, you'll have to remove them by hand if you can. Microsoft *FrontPage* and other WYSIWYG editors are especially guilty of this because you don't normally get a chance to edit the HTML produced.
>
> We've asked the author of *PerlShop* to allow quotation marks in a future version. Check the book's Web site to see if a version of *PerlShop* has been released that doesn't have this "feature."

```
<FORM ACTION="!MYURL!" METHOD=POST>
```

The form uses the `!MYURL!` tag to call the *perlshop.cgi* script.

```
<INPUT TYPE=hidden NAME=ITEM_ID VALUE="P02">
```

Here is the first of the hidden tags that hold the information about this product. `ITEM_ID` can be thought of as a part number or stock-keeping-unit (SKU) for this product. Note, *PerlShop* doesn't keep or cross-reference a list of "real" `ITEM_ID` values, so you will need to ensure this number corresponds to an actual product. This value appears in the shopping-cart contents list and on the final order form.

```
<INPUT TYPE=hidden NAME=ITEM_NAME VALUE="Valour Bond">
```

`ITEM_NAME` refers to the product name. Again, no consistency is enforced between the `ITEM_ID` and the `ITEM_NAME`. You select the name that corresponds with the `ITEM_ID`.

```
<INPUT TYPE=hidden NAME=ITEM_OPTION2 VALUE="Matte">
```

Here we have one of the optional parameters for this item. We defined the title for this option category in the configuration variable `$option2_caption`. *PerlShop* allows you to define up to three different fields to hold additional information about the product, such as size, color, and style. In this case, we're setting the paper finish to `"Matte"` using a hidden tag. It is also acceptable to leave out an `ITEM_OPTIONx` tag altogether if it doesn't apply to a particular product.

```
<INPUT TYPE=hidden NAME=ITEM_WEIGHT VALUE="40">
```

This line sets the item weight and is used in the total weight calculations for shipping costs. If you are using price or quantity as your basis for calculating shipping charges, you can omit this tag without problems.

```
Qty: <INPUT TYPE=TEXT SIZE=3 MaxLength=3 NAME=QTY VALUE="0"> <BR>
```

Here we give the visitor a text field to enter the desired quantity. The QTY tag is the only quantity tag recognized by *PerlShop*, so don't try to use QUANTITY or ITEM_QTY in its place. You can either set this, as shown, with an input field or use radio buttons or a selection list. *PerlShop* will do some minimal checking to make sure a numeric value is entered here and that the field isn't equal to zero. Usually, *PerlShop* accepts only an integer number for the quantity. However, if you set $allow_fractional_qty = 'yes'$, *PerlShop* will accept noninteger values as well. If you want to set a minimum or maximum value for the quantity ordered, use the *formv* package from Chapter 11 to supplement *PerlShop*'s field checking.

Hot Tip

To sell items by the pound, set the ITEM_WEIGHT VALUE="1" and set the appropriate ITEM_PRICE for a single pound. The QTY value then orders the desired number of pounds (or ounces or kilograms). Voilà—pricing by the pound!

```
Stock: <SELECT NAME=ITEM_OPTION1>
  <OPTION>20 lb.
  <OPTION>40 lb.
  <OPTION>60 lb.
</SELECT> <BR>
```

These lines allow the visitor to set the value of another optional parameter using a selection list to choose a value for the weight of the paper stock. You might use something similar to restrict the choice of color or size for your products. For a small set of possible attribute values, it's best to use a selection list or group of radio buttons to force the visitor to pick from the available values.

```
Color: <INPUT TYPE=text NAME=ITEM_OPTION3 VALUE="White" SIZE=10 MAXLENGTH=30>
```

This is the final optional parameter. We're giving the visitor an input box to specify the color of paper they want. Note, if the visitor enters a color of, for example, "White" and later orders the same product with a color of "white", *PerlShop* will consider them two different items. This is an issue only with text input fields, which are case sensitive. It is also another argument for using selection lists or radio buttons, where you have complete control of the possible responses.

```
<BR>$79.98/box   <strong>(60 lbs)</strong><br>
(matte finish only)<br>
```

This HTML displays explanatory text for the visitors. There is no checking between what you display here for the price, weight, and so on, and what is sent to the script in the form fields. As usual with price tags, to avoid unhappy customers you need to ensure consistency between what you charge the customer and what they see displayed as the product's price.

```
<INPUT TYPE=submit NAME=ACTION VALUE="ORDER"> (May be changed later)
```

The form must include a field with the NAME=ACTION and a VALUE="ORDER" in order for *PerlShop* to recognize this form and add the contents to the shopping cart. Usually, the order field will be in a SUBMIT button, but it doesn't have to be. The SUBMIT field can appear anywhere in the form definition except as the last item (see later in the chapter for more on the required order of the fields). You can use an image for your order button by following the same technique we showed you for the entry link. Simply make the ACTION field hidden and create a dummy TYPE=IMAGE button to submit the form.

Hot Tip

Visitors to your site may be unsure when the order is actually placed. We've added the message "(May be changed later)" to inform them that they will have a chance to modify their order before it is actually placed.

```
<INPUT TYPE=hidden NAME=THISPAGE VALUE="verity.html">
```

The THISPAGE parameter tells *PerlShop* from which page the order was generated. *PerlShop* gives the user an option to "Continue Shopping" after displaying the contents of the shopping cart. THISPAGE can be used to return a visitor to a page or to redirect the visitor to a different catalog page, such as an index page. It is generally used to return to the same page after the visitor has seen that his or her item has been added to the shopping cart.

```
<INPUT TYPE=hidden NAME=ITEM_PRICE VALUE="79.98">
```

As you might guess, `ITEM_PRICE` sets the numeric price for a single unit of this product. Don't place any currency symbols in this field. *PerlShop* doesn't check that the price you enter on this page for this product is the same as the price you enter for the same product on a different page or in descriptive text. Enforcing consistency is up to you.

```
<INPUT TYPE=hidden NAME=ORDER_ID VALUE="!ORDERID!">
```

The `ORDER_ID` field is a placeholder for the session ID number *PerlShop* creates for each user. When *PerlShop* sends this page to the visitor's, browser, the `!ORDERID!` string is replaced with a numeric session ID. When the form is submitted, *PerlShop* reads the `ORDER_ID` value to identify which user is making the request.

```
<INPUT TYPE=hidden NAME=ITEM_CODE VALUE="!ITEMCODE!">
</FORM>
```

The `ITEM_CODE` field is also a placeholder. *PerlShop* incorporates several security features to ensure that the form submitted actually came from the *perlshop.cgi* script and that it wasn't altered by a devious user. When *PerlShop* generates the form, it calculates a special number (called a *hash-code*) based on the characters in the form.

Nerd Note

The hash-code is calculated using something called the **secure-hash-algorithm** (SHA). This algorithm uses encryption techniques to make the hash code easy to calculate but *very* difficult to forge. For all practical purposes, it's impossible to alter the form and have it produce the same hash-code as the original. *Note:* SHA doesn't encrypt the form, so it doesn't protect you from someone viewing the form. It simply ensures that the SHA codes on disk and in the submitted form are identical; that is, the form hasn't been modified, before it allows the form to be processed.

The hash-code is inserted in place of the `!ITEMCODE!` string in the page sent to the browser. *PerlShop* stores a copy of the number on disk to compare with the hash-code of the submitted form. If the two numbers don't match, *PerlShop* rejects the request. The `ITEM_CODE` field *must* be the last field in the form before the closing `</FORM>` tag.

A product option not shown here is called `TAXTYPE`. This tag is used to mark an item as nontaxable. It overrides the setting of the `@Tax_States` configuration variable for this item only. To mark an item nontaxable, insert a hidden field as follows:

```
<INPUT TYPE=HIDDEN NAME=ITEM_TAXTYPE VALUE="none">
```

TAXTYPE should be placed with the other optional tags (see later in the chapter for tag ordering rules). Unfortunately, there is no easy way to set this for some tax locations but not others. For example, food may not be taxed in New York but is taxed in New Jersey. You would have to give your customers separate New York and New Jersey order links (or buttons) to properly handle this situation. If this is a serious problem for your store, you'll have to modify the script yourself or contact the author of *PerlShop* for a customized version.

Usually when a visitor clicks an order button or hyperlink, *PerlShop* displays the updated contents of the user's shopping cart on a new page. If you set the configuration variable $stay_on_page='yes', you tell the *PerlShop* to show the shopping-cart contents at the bottom of the current page rather than on a new page. To override the behavior set by the $stay_on_page variable, add a hidden form field like this:

```
<INPUT TYPE=HIDDEN NAME=StayOnPage VALUE="yes">
```

If you want to offer the visitor the option of changing this, create a check box for the order form with the name of StayOnPage and a VALUE of "YES".

You can place several single-item forms on each HTML page. However, if you have multiple single-item forms on a page, only the data from a single form is passed to the script when the user presses the order button. To order the other products, the visitor must return to the page and select the order button for each. It's best to use multiple single-item forms when the visitor isn't likely to select several items from the page at one time.

Hot Tip

> If your item doesn't have any specifiable options and is available only in fixed quantities, you can URL-encode these form fields as we did with the entry link. This allows visitors to order an item by simply clicking a text or image hyperlink. One application for this might be to create a compact listing of one-of-a-kind items. Since everything about the item is fixed, a form isn't needed.

Multi-item Selection Form

Figure 14.4 shows the Allegretti catalog home page. This page is designed to let experienced buyers complete their orders in one step. Using the multi-item form on this page, the visitor can order as many boxes of each of the papers as needed. For those who want additional info on a particular product, a link to individual product pages is provided. We used one of these product pages in the single-item form example.

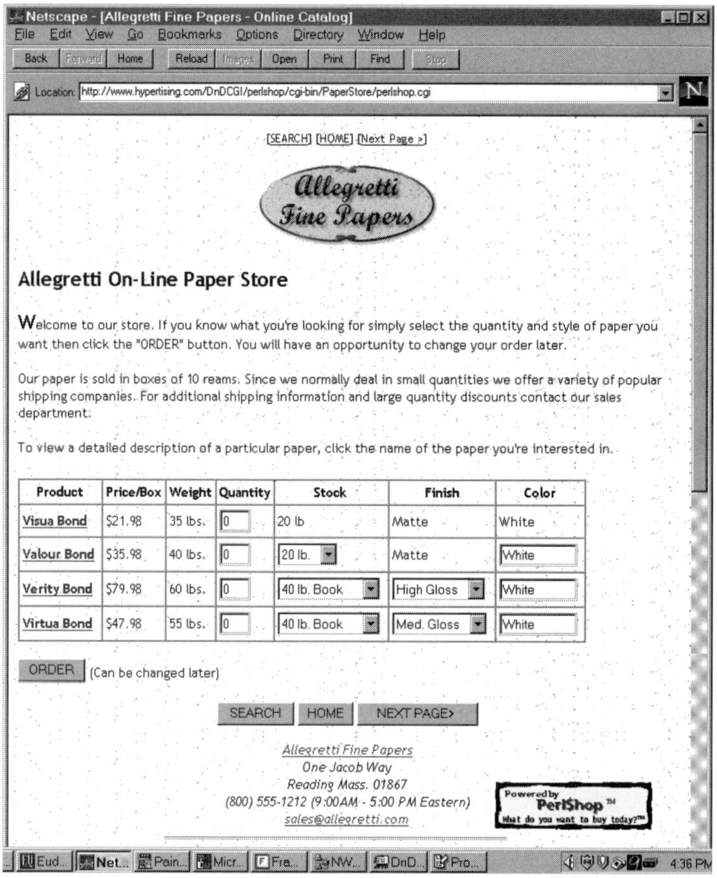

Figure 14.4 *A multi-item catalog page*

The multi-item form is constructed very similarly to several single-item forms. You enter the hidden data about each product and provide input fields for quantity and the optional parameters. Since all your products are listed on a single form, you need only one <FORM> tag. You also need only one each of the ORDER_ID and ITEM_CODE fields. You can have multiple submit buttons if you like. Simply set the name of each submit button to ACTION and the value to ORDER. You can also use an image as an order button with a hidden ACTION field. Listing 14.2 shows the multi-item selection form used to create Figure 14.4.

Listing 14.2   **HTML for the multi-item selection form**

```
<FORM ACTION="!MYURL!" METHOD=POST>
<TABLE border=1 CELLPADDING="3" CELLSPACING="0">
<TR><TD ROWSPAN=7><P></TD></tr>
<TR>
  <TH>Product</TH><TH>Price/Box</TH><TH>Weight</TH><TH>Quantity</TH>
  <TH>Stock</TH><TH>Finish</TH><TH>Color</TH>
</TR>
<!-- Visua Bond -->
<tr>
<td>
<INPUT TYPE=hidden NAME=ITEM_ID VALUE="P01">
<INPUT TYPE=hidden NAME=ITEM_NAME VALUE="Visua Bond">
<INPUT TYPE=hidden NAME=ITEM_OPTION1 VALUE="20 lb.">
<INPUT TYPE=hidden NAME=ITEM_OPTION2 VALUE="Matte">
<INPUT TYPE=hidden NAME=ITEM_OPTION3 VALUE="White">
<INPUT TYPE=hidden NAME=ITEM_WEIGHT VALUE="35">
<INPUT TYPE=hidden NAME=ITEM_PRICE VALUE="21.98">
<a HREF="!MYURL!?action=thispage&thispage=visua.html&ORDER_ID=!ORDERID!">
<B>Visua Bond</B></a>
</TD>
<TD>$21.98</TD>
<td>35 lbs.</TD>
<TD><INPUT TYPE=TEXT SIZE=3 MaxLength=3 NAME=QTY VALUE="0"></TD>
<TD>20 lb</TD>
<TD>Matte</TD>
<TD>White</TD>
</TR>
<!-- Valour Bond -->
<tr>
<td>
<INPUT TYPE=hidden NAME=ITEM_ID VALUE="P02">
<INPUT TYPE=hidden NAME=ITEM_NAME VALUE="Valour Bond">
<INPUT TYPE=hidden NAME=ITEM_WEIGHT VALUE="40">
<a href="!MYURL!?action=thispage&thispage=valour.html&ORDER_ID=!ORDERID!">
<b>Valour Bond</b></a>
</TD>
<TD>$35.98</TD><td>40 lbs.</TD>
<TD><INPUT TYPE=TEXT SIZE=3 MaxLength=3 NAME=QTY VALUE="0"></TD>
<TD><SELECT NAME=ITEM_OPTION1>
  <OPTION>20 lb.
  <OPTION>40 lb.
  <OPTION>60 lb.
</SELECT> </TD>
<TD>Matte<INPUT TYPE=hidden NAME=ITEM_OPTION2 VALUE="Matte"></TD>
<TD><INPUT TYPE=text NAME=ITEM_OPTION3 VALUE="White" SIZE=10 MAXLENGTH=30>
<INPUT TYPE=hidden NAME=ITEM_PRICE VALUE="35.98">
</TD>
</TR>
<!-- Verity Bond -->
```

```
<tr>
<td>
<INPUT TYPE=hidden NAME=ITEM_ID VALUE="P03">
<INPUT TYPE=hidden NAME=ITEM_NAME VALUE="Verity Bond">
<INPUT TYPE=hidden NAME=ITEM_WEIGHT VALUE="60">
<A
HREF="perlshop.cgi?action=thispage&thispage=verity.html&ORDER_ID=!ORDERID!">
<B>Verity Bond</B></A>
</TD>
<TD>$79.98</TD><td>60 lbs.</TD>
<TD><INPUT TYPE=TEXT SIZE=3 MaxLength=3 NAME=QTY VALUE="0"></TD>
<TD><SELECT NAME=ITEM_OPTION1>
<OPTION>40 lb. Book
<OPTION>80 lb. Book
<OPTION>65 lb. Cover
<OPTION>85 lb. Cover
<OPTION>100 lb. Cover
</SELECT> </TD>
<TD><SELECT NAME=ITEM_OPTION2>
<OPTION>High Gloss
<OPTION>Matte
</SELECT> </TD>
<TD><INPUT TYPE=text NAME=ITEM_OPTION3 VALUE="White" SIZE=10 MAXLENGTH=30>
<INPUT TYPE=hidden NAME=ITEM_PRICE VALUE="79.98">
</TD>
</TR>
<!-- Virtua Bond -->
<tr>
<td>
<INPUT TYPE=hidden NAME=ITEM_ID VALUE="P04">
<INPUT TYPE=hidden NAME=ITEM_NAME VALUE="Virtua Bond">
<INPUT TYPE=hidden NAME=ITEM_WEIGHT VALUE="55">
<A HREF=!MYURL!?action=thispage&thispage=virtua.html&ORDER_ID=!ORDERID!>
<B>Virtua Bond</B></A>
</TD>
<TD>$47.98</TD><td>55 lbs.</TD>
<TD><INPUT TYPE=TEXT SIZE=3 MaxLength=3 NAME=QTY VALUE="0"></TD>
<TD><SELECT NAME=ITEM_OPTION1>
<OPTION>40 lb. Book
<OPTION>60 lb. Book
<OPTION>60 lb. Cover
<OPTION>80 lb. Cover
<OPTION>100 lb. Cover
<OPTION>120 lb. Card
</SELECT> </TD>
<TD><SELECT NAME=ITEM_OPTION2>
<OPTION>Med. Gloss
<OPTION>Matte
<OPTION>Dull
</SELECT> </TD>
<TD><INPUT TYPE=text NAME=ITEM_OPTION3 VALUE="White" SIZE=10 MAXLENGTH=30>
<INPUT TYPE=hidden NAME=ITEM_PRICE VALUE="47.98"></TD>
```

```
</TR>
</table>
<INPUT TYPE=HIDDEN NAME=thispage value=cathome.html>
<P>
<INPUT TYPE=submit NAME=action VALUE="ORDER">  (Can be changed later) <BR>
<INPUT TYPE=HIDDEN NAME=ORDER_ID VALUE="!ORDERID!">
<INPUT TYPE=HIDDEN NAME=ITEM_CODE value="!ITEMCODE!">
</FORM>
```

Constructing the multi-item form is quite straightforward. Simply group the hidden fields for each product and provide input fields for the options. Notice the hyperlinks we created to the individual product pages.

```
<a HREF="!MYURL!?action=thispage&thispage=visua.html&ORDER_ID=!ORDERID!">
<B>Visua Bond</B></a>

<a HREF="!MYURL!?action=thispage&thispage=valour.html&ORDER_ID=!ORDERID!">
<b>Valour Bond</b></a>

<A HREF="perlshop.cgi?action=thispage&thispage=verity.html&ORDER_ID=!
ORDERID!">
<B>Verity Bond</B></A>

<A HREF=!MYURL!?action=thispage&thispage=virtua.html&ORDER_ID=!ORDERID!>
<B>Virtua Bond</B></A>
```

On the Verity Bond hyperlink, we didn't use the !MYURL! shortcut. Not doing so works fine, but it is slightly less portable than using the shortcut to fill in the script name for you.

A couple of reminders:

- Prices and other data about the products don't automatically match what you enter for the same product on another page. You must manually synchronize all the data for a particular product on all the pages on which the product appears.

- You need to ensure consistency between a product's descriptive text and the product's actual attributes as included in the script.

Selection Form Tag Order

PerlShop has a few rules about the order and format of the hidden form tags:

1. Tags with one of the *PerlShop* shortcuts (!MYWWW!, !MYURL!, !ORDERID!, and !ITEM_CODE!) should appear on a line by themselves.

2. Don't use quotation marks around the NAME= parameter of the fields.

3. Any optional product tags (ITEM_WEIGHT, ITEM_OPTIONx, or ITEM_TAXTYPE) must appear *before* both the ITEM_ID and ITEM_PRICE fields.

4. The ITEM_CODE field *must* be the last field in the form before the closing </FORM> tag.

Navigating the Store

Once you've created your product forms, you might like to give your visitors a way to get around in your store. You can't use normal hyperlinks because *PerlShop* scans and modifies each catalog page before it sends the page to the browser. Luckily, *PerlShop* provides two methods for interpage linking within your catalog.

The first method we've already explained. You create a hyperlink to the *perlshop.cgi* script with an ACTION parameter of THISPAGE and a THISPAGE parameter with a value set to the name of the page you want to display, as follows:

```
<A HREF="!MYURL!?ACTION=THISPAGE&THISPAGE=productx.html&ORDERID=!ORDERID!">
All about Product X</A>
```

You can use a form to accomplish the same thing:

```
<FORM ACTION="!MYURL!" METHOD=POST>
<INPUT TYPE=SUBMIT NAME=ACTION VALUE="THISPAGE">
<INPUT TYPE=HIDDEN NAME=THISPAGE VALUE="productx.html">
<INPUT TYPE=HIDDEN NAME=ORDER_ID VALUE="!ORDERID!">
</FORM>
```

In addition to the explicit links you create, placing a special *PerlShop* tag as the first line of a catalog file inserts a "next page" and a "previous page" navigational link at the top of the page. With the second method, *PerlShop* does all the work for you. This gives you an easy way to provide links for visitors to walk through your catalog pages one after another in the order you choose. Look at the upper portions of Figures 14.3 and 14.4 to see these links. The format of the navigational tag is

```
<PSTAG prevpage=page1.html nextpage=page3.html>
```

where page1.html and page3.html are the names of HTML files in your catalog directory.

If the current page is the first page in the catalog, set prevpage to the current filename; *PerlShop* won't generate a "previous page" link. Similarly, if the current page is the last page in the catalog, set `nextpage` to the current filename; *PerlShop* will omit the "next page" link. These links can point to any of your catalog pages; you don't need a linear structure to your catalog. For example, you could set the `prevpage` parameter to point back to the catalog home page rather than to a different product page.

If the `<PSTAG>` tag is used, *PerlShop* will also add navigational form buttons to the control buttons at the bottom of each catalog page. Both Figures 14.3 and 14.4 show these buttons at the bottom of the page. You can disable this feature by setting the `$add_navigation` configuration variable to `'no'`. Do this if you want to design your own interpage navigational links.

Hot Tip

> Unfortunately, the `<PSTAG>` tag is not legal HTML. If your HTML editor enforces correct HTML syntax, you may have trouble getting it to insert this tag. At our request, the author of *PerlShop* changed his script to allow `<PSTAG>` to reside in an HTML comment. So an alternative form of the tag is
>
> `<!--PSTAG prevpage=pageX.html nextpage=pageY.html -->`
>
> This should keep even the pickiest HTML editor happy.

The Built-in Search Engine

PerlShop includes a simple search engine that will search your catalog pages for keywords and return a list of pages on which they occur. Search engines such as *ICE* (introduced in Chapter 12) won't work on a *PerlShop* catalog because *PerlShop* needs to process each catalog page before it is presented to the visitor. The links returned by the search engine need to be in the form shown previously for hypertext navigational links. Figure 14.5 shows the search page generated by the script. Note, this page is generated entirely by the script. You don't need to create an HTML file for use as a template. The background color/image and the other `<BODY>` tag options are taken from configuration variables.

The search engine doesn't offer complex "and" or "or" combinations of the search terms. It reports a match if a catalog page contains any of the search terms. The check boxes allow visitors to modify the search criteria slightly. The regular expression option allows visitors familiar with Perl regular expressions to use the powerful pattern matching functions available to Perl programmers. This option is likely to be confusing for most visitors. You may want to modify the script code (see page 280)

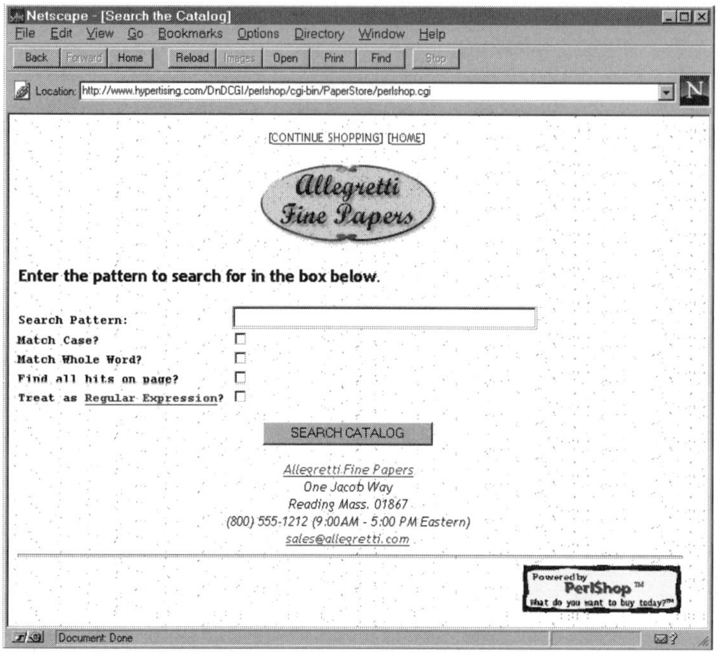

Figure 14.5 *The* PerlShop *search engine interface*

to eliminate this option from the form. The *perlre.htm* file that comes with the *PerlShop* distribution explains Perl regular expressions somewhat.

For those of you planning a complex store structure, the search engine will search all subdirectories under your main *catalog/* directory. Figure 14.6 shows the output of the search engine.

Clicking a catalog page name will bring up that page for the visitor.

"Driving" the Shopping Cart

When a visitor clicks the order button or hyperlink as you've defined it, *PerlShop* attempts to add the requested items to the visitor's shopping cart. If the quantity ordered is zero or the item is already in the cart, an error message is returned and no change is made to the cart. If everything is correct with the request, the item is added to the cart, the data files on the server are updated, and the shopping-cart contents page is displayed (see Figure 14.7). As with the search page, the cart's contents page is generated entirely by the *perlshop.cgi* script. You don't need to create a page to hold the shopping-cart contents.

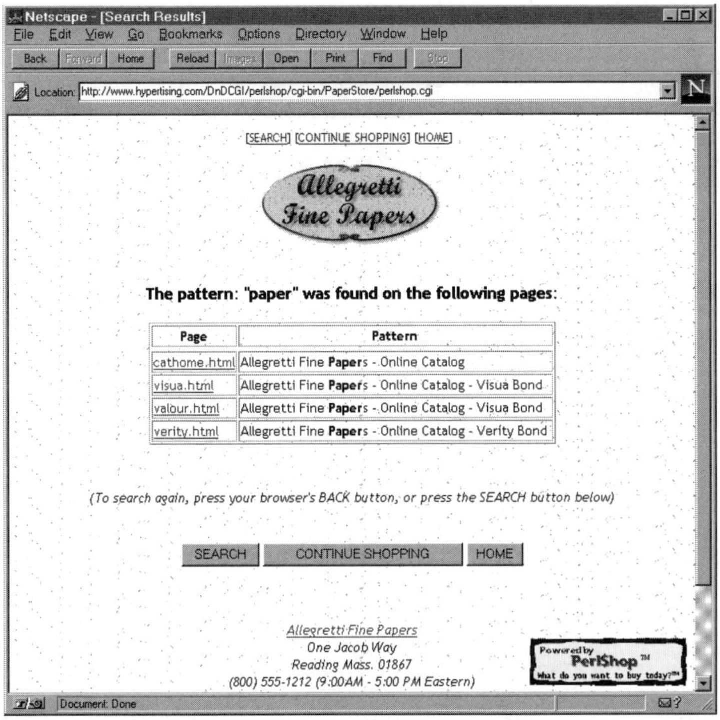

Figure 14.6 PerlShop *search engine sample results page*

This page serves as a kind of hub for the visitor once he or she decides to put something in the cart. Quantities may be changed, items may be removed, and the final ordering process is started from this page. Every time a new item is added to the cart, this page is displayed so that the visitor always knows the current state of his or her order. Here are the controls available on the cart's contents page:

- UPDATE. Updates the shopping cart with the current state of the "Qty" input boxes for the items in the cart. *PerlShop* recalculates the total and updates the cart files on disk. Setting a quantity to zero removes that item from the cart. This is the only way the quantity of an item may be changed once the item is in the cart.

- CHECKOUT. Begins the final checkout process. We cover this in detail in Chapter 15.

- CONTINUE SHOPPING. Takes the user to the page specified in the THIS-PAGE field of the form that caused this page to appear. You can set this to return the visitor either to the same page or to another page, such as the catalog home page.

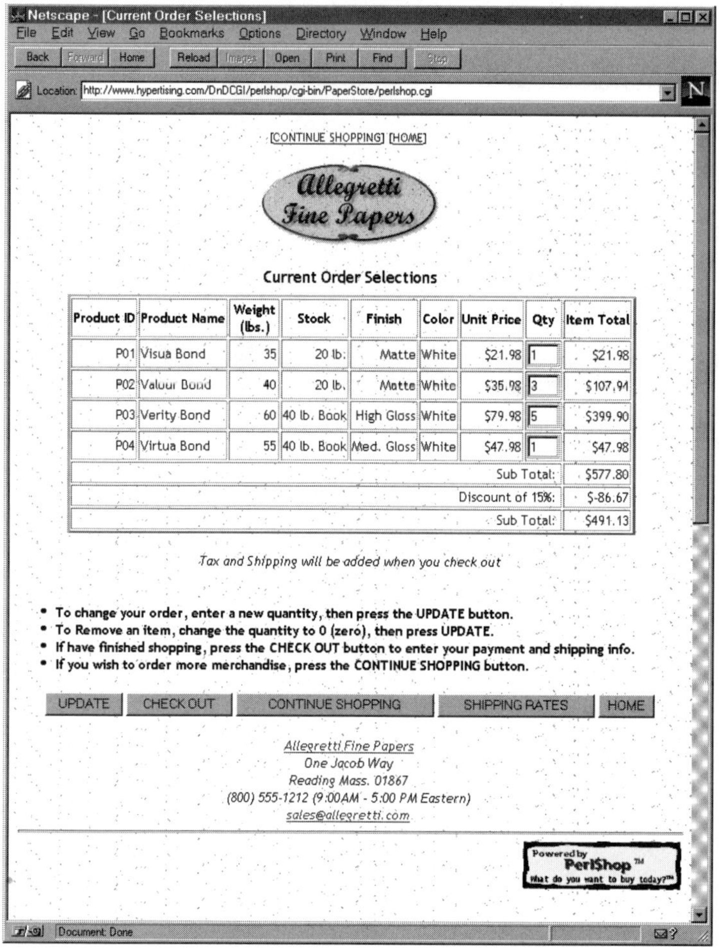

Figure 14.7 PerlShop *shopping cart contents page*

- **SHIPPING RATES.** Displays a summary page with the rates for the different shipping companies; see Figure 14.8. This information is stored in the `@Shipping_Rates` configuration variable.

- **HOME.** This takes the user to the page contained in the `$home_page` variable. **Warning:** This button will take your visitor to an HTML page outside your catalog—and thus can cause your visitor to lose the contents of his or her cart and become very unhappy with you. We advise you to place a warning message somewhere in your pages regarding this.

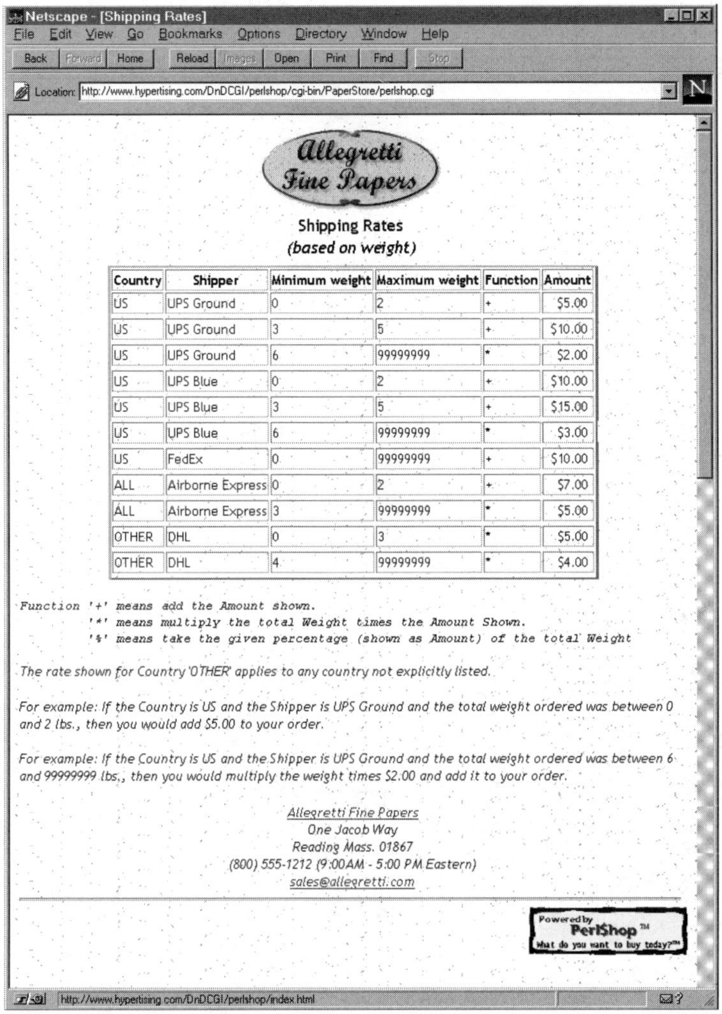

Netscape - [Shipping Rates]

File Edit View Go Bookmarks Options Directory Window Help

Location: http://www.hypertising.com/DnDCGI/perlshop/cgi-bin/PaperStore/perlshop.cgi

Allegretti Fine Papers

Shipping Rates

(based on weight)

Country	Shipper	Minimum weight	Maximum weight	Function	Amount
US	UPS Ground	0	2	+	$5.00
US	UPS Ground	3	5	+	$10.00
US	UPS Ground	6	99999999	*	$2.00
US	UPS Blue	0	2	+	$10.00
US	UPS Blue	3	5	+	$15.00
US	UPS Blue	6	99999999	*	$3.00
US	FedEx	0	99999999	+	$10.00
ALL	Airborne Express	0	2	+	$7.00
ALL	Airborne Express	3	99999999	*	$5.00
OTHER	DHL	0	3	*	$5.00
OTHER	DHL	4	99999999	*	$4.00

Function '+' means add the Amount shown.
'' means multiply the total Weight times the Amount Shown.*
'%' means take the given percentage (shown as Amount) of the total Weight

The rate shown for Country 'OTHER' applies to any country not explicitly listed.

For example: If the Country is US and the Shipper is UPS Ground and the total weight ordered was between 0 and 2 lbs., then you would add $5.00 to your order.

For example: If the Country is US and the Shipper is UPS Ground and the total weight ordered was between 6 and 99999999 lbs., then you would multiply the weight times $2.00 and add it to your order.

Allegretti Fine Papers
One Jacob Way
Reading Mass. 01867
(800) 555-1212 (9:00AM - 5:00 PM Eastern)
sales@allegretti.com

Powered by PerlShop™ What do you want to buy today?™

http://www.hypertising.com/DnDCGI/perlshop/index.html

Figure 14.8 *The* PerlShop *shipping rate table*

That covers the basic operation of the *PerlShop* system, except for the final checkout process. We'll discuss that in Chapter 15. The next section shows how to modify the PerlShop script to customize the look of the script-generated pages.

Customizing the Script

The default *PerlShop* pages are OK, but they won't win any design awards. We've requested that the author of *PerlShop* create a mechanism to allow the shopping-cart contents and other *PerlShop* HTML to appear on user-designed pages. Until he makes the change, however, you are stuck with modifying the look of the pages the old-fashioned way: hacking up the script as we've done here. If you've worked through the other scripts in this book, the idea of modifying the script code shouldn't bother you. You already have almost complete control over the look of the catalog pages, except for the text links at the top and the buttons at the bottom. The parameters of the `<BODY>` tag are set by the configuration variables, and you can specify the banner image used on the pages.

Following are the locations within the script that generate the HTML for the various pages in the system. Try to confine your changes to `print` statements where you can clearly see what code the script is generating.

Hair Saver

Before you start modifying the script, here are a couple of tips that may let you hang on to a few more of your hairs for a while.

- Always keep the original distribution script somewhere safe to use as a reference or ultimate fall-back.

- When you make a change that works, save the file and make a copy of it to modify further. That way you can always revert to a working version.

- Make small changes and test often. This will involve lots of uploading and testing with your Web server, but that's the price you pay for going the extra mile for a killer Web site.

The *PerlShop* Logo

All pages generated by the script are required to display the "Powered by *PerlShop*" logo. You can choose between two different logo images. Unfortunately, a configuration variable is not provided to select which to use. To use the alternate logo, you should modify the `add_company_footer` subroutine starting around line 1,658 in the script. This is the line that specifies the logo image:

```
print "<hr width=\"100%\"><div align=right><a href=\"http://
www.arpanet.com/PerlShop/PerlShop.html\"><img src=\"$image_location/
perllogo.gif\" border=0 height=51 width=171></a></div>";
```

Simply change *perllogo.gif* to the alternate filename (*perlloyo.jpy*) and change the image dimensions.

Page Header

Starting at line 1,669, the `add_company_header` subroutine generates the `<BODY>` tag and the banner image. You can either modify this code or replace the lines

```
print "<body $body >";
print $banner;
```

with the code you want for your page. You can also add any page layout tags such as `<TABLE>` in this section. Simply use the `print` statement to insert it into the HTML generated for each page. You will probably have to do lots of experimentation to get it right, but that's all part of the fun of being a script hacker. You can use the `add_company_footer` subroutine to close out any tables or other formatting elements you start in this subroutine.

Shopping-Cart Contents

Your visitors will spend a lot of time looking at the shopping-cart summary page. If you are going to modify any of the *PerlShop*-generated pages to improve their look, this is probably the one you should concentrate on the most. The `view_cart` subroutine starts on line 1,252. The shopping-cart page is laid out as a table within a `<FORM>`. Look carefully through the page to see where each of the elements that appears on the page is generated. Finding the `<TD>` and `<TH>` tags will help you locate the lines that produce HTML. You are probably better off not trying to modify the main table. Instead, concentrate on laying out the page on which it appears.

Order Form

The `display_order_form` subroutine, starting at line 1,698, generates the HTML for this form. This is a fairly complex subroutine, but you should be able to see which lines of code generate the HTML for the page. Modify it carefully testing each step, and you should be fine.

Confirmation Message

The `send_confirmation` subroutine located at line 1,998 is even more complex. It prints out a variety of different messages depending on the options you set. Fortunately, the author of *PerlShop* has used variable names that make it easy to figure out what the script is doing. We recommend that you confine your customization to creating an attractive page layout rather than getting into the code that produces the order summary text.

Shipping Rates Page

The `show_shipping_rates` subroutine generates the table of shipping rates from the `@Shipping_Rates` variable. This subroutine starts at line 2,973. Again, it's pretty simple to locate the lines that generate the HTML code and modify them to match your page layout.

Button and Menu Bar

The `add_button_bar` (line 3,033) and `add_menu_bar` (line 3,075) subroutines generate the button bar at the bottom of the page and the menu links bar at the top of the page. These are fairly short subroutines that don't do a lot of heavy processing, so you should be able to modify them without too much trouble.

Search Page

The `add_search_screen` subroutine creates the search page. If you've modified the other pages already, this one will be a piece of cake. It starts on line 1,228.

Up Next

In Chapter 15, we'll cover credit card processing and ways to enhance store security as part of the final steps necessary to take your store on-line. We introduce PGP (Pretty Good Privacy) as a means of encrypting your customers' credit card information. You're on the home stretch!

What We Covered in Chapter 14

- How *PerlShop* processes your catalog files
- Creating single- and multi-item catalog pages
- Catalog navigational tags and options
- *PerlShop* functions, including a built-in search engine and shopping-cart review page
- How to customize the look of the pages to match your Web site

Chapter 15

A Perl-based On-line Store System—Part 3: Processing Orders and Security

What We Cover in This Chapter

- The *PerlShop* checkout process
- Credit card processing
- Output from the ordering process
- Ways to increase your store's security
- Some tips on using Pretty Good Privacy (PGP) to encrypt sensitive information

Where We Are Now

In this final *PerlShop* chapter, we cover the back-end of the script: the final checkout process. We also show you how to retrieve the order files stored on the server. We conclude with a discussion of ways to increase the security of your on-line store.

Processing credit card charges on-line is becoming more and more common. *PerlShop* includes support for the FirstVirtual™ on-line payment system (which doesn't use credit card numbers) and the SecureOrder™ on-line credit card validation service. We'll show you how to enable support for these services in *PerlShop*.

These services require you to open an account—called a **merchant account**—with the payment system company before you can process orders using its services. FirstVirtual also requires the visitor to open an account, and they make it very easy to do so. The CD-ROM includes links to the home pages of FirstVirtual and Secure Order. Other systems such as Cybercash™ and E-Cash™ are not supported in this version (3.1) of *PerlShop*. If you need a feature or function not included in the script, check the *PerlShop* home page for a later version (*http://www.arpanet.com*). You can also contract with the author of *PerlShop* for a customized version.

The Payment and Shipping Process

The *PerlShop* checkout process is initiated when the visitor presses the CHECK OUT or SECURE CHECK OUT button on the shopping-cart summary page. In response, the script will display the shipping and payment form shown in Figure 15.1.

The top section of the form collects information about the purchaser, including address and phone number. All the fields are required except Street2, Nighttime Phone, and Fax. The contents of the numeric fields are checked for correct format similar to how our *formv* Javascript script validates fields. The fields are checked to see that the proper number of digits and special characters are present, but no real validation is done.

Like the shopping-cart review page, this form is generated entirely by the script. It's a standard form and except for a couple of things, not much needs to be said about it. For U.S. addresses, the State/Province field is verified to be a valid two-letter state code. Similarly, the ZIP code and phone number fields must contain the correct number of digits. For international addresses, *PerlShop* distributes a supplementary page called *country.html* that lists all current two-letter country codes. Clicking the hyperlink on the form displays the *country.html* file to help users fill out the Country field correctly. You can customize the *country.html* file to add text or graphics as you see fit.

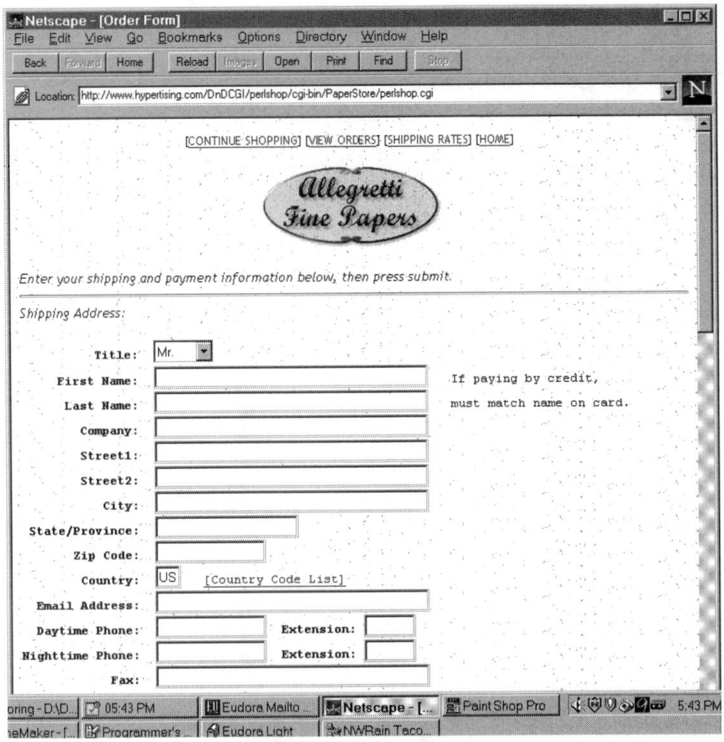

Figure 15.1 PerlShop *shipping and payment form—purchaser information*

The bottom section of the form accepts the payment and shipping methods the visitor desires. The valid selections for each field or check box are determined by the values of the @accept_payment_by, @valid_credit_cards, $online_credit_verify, $accept_first_virtual, and @Shipping_Rates configuration variables. You should have already set these to match your business requirements. Enable the FirstVirtual and SecureOrder options only after you've opened a merchant account with the appropriate service provider. Figure 15.2 shows the shipping and payment section of the form.

If you are running on a secure HTTP server, set $use_secure_server = 'yes' and set the $secure_server_address variable to the first part of your secure server's URL (through the domain name). The form will display on the browser in secure mode. Browsers indicate secure mode in different ways. For example, in Netscape the top window border and the key icon at the bottom of the window turn blue. Regardless of how secure mode is displayed, the visitor will have a clear indication that it's safe to enter a credit card number.

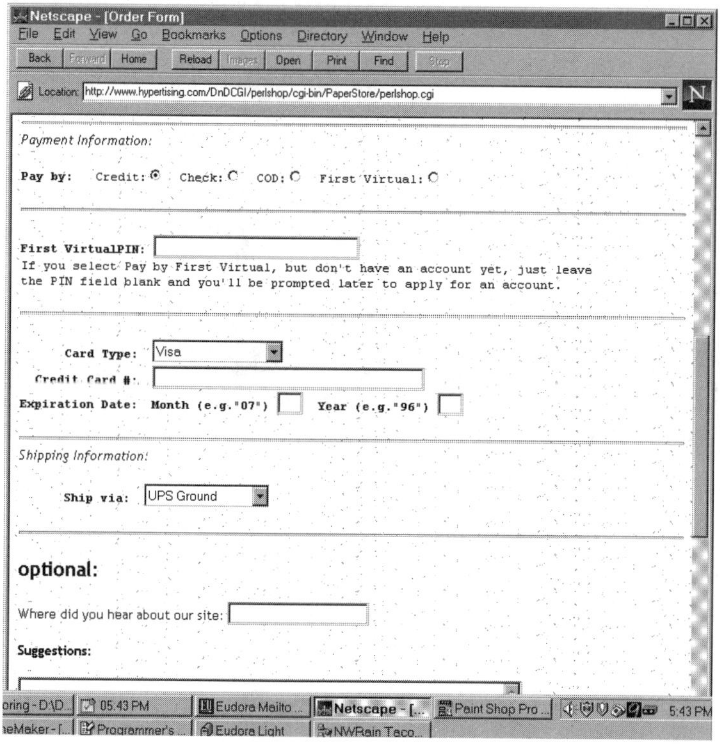

Figure 15.2 PerlShop *shipping and payment form—shipping and payment info*

Hot Tip

Many visitors connecting to the Internet through a "firewall" won't be able to use a secure HTTP server. *PerlShop* always offers a nonsecure order option even if you are using a secure server. However, the insecure server exposes the visitor's credit card number to interception. You should always offer your customers a fax or phone option.

If you don't have access to a secure server, you should be very careful about asking visitors to enter their credit card numbers. Some visitors refuse to enter credit card data on an insecure server (or on a secure one for that matter), so don't make on-line credit validation your only payment option.

A visitor can use the FirstVirtual payment system by checking the first virtual radio button and entering his PIN number. This system does not transmit the visitor's credit card information over the Internet. It also provides the benefit of direct deposit of the payment into your bank account. As we said, you must have previously established a merchant account with FirstVirtual in order to offer this payment option. A visitor establishes an account by leaving the `first virtual PIN` field blank. Doing this takes the visitor to the account sign-up page at FirstVirtual. Once the visitor's FirstVirtual account is activated, he or she can complete the purchase.

To enable FirstVirtual support in *PerlShop*, you must add `'First Virtual'` to your list of accepted credit cards in the `@accept_payment_by` configuration variable. This variable is located at about line 237 in the *perlshop.cgi* script. At line 243, set the `$accept_first_virtual` variable to `'yes'` and configure the `$fv_seller_pin` and `$fv_ips` variables with the information you received from FirstVirtual when you opened your account. When a visitor selects the FirstVirtual payment option, the script handles all the transactions with the FirstVirtual server that are necessary to process the payment. All you do is ship the order.

The SecureOrder system provides credit card validation similar to that used by real-world stores that have a credit-approval terminal. Under this system, the script communicates the visitor's credit card number, expiration date, and other information to the SecureOrder service provider over a secure channel. If the credit charge is accepted, the checkout process proceeds. Otherwise, the script displays the error message returned by the SecureOrder server. As with FirstVirtual, you must have an active merchant account with a SecureOrder provider before you can offer this service. Unlike FirstVirtual, however, the visitor does not have to set up an account with the SecureOrder provider.

To configure SecureOrder support, set the `$online_credit_verify` configuration variable located around line 241 to `yes`. Edit the SecureOrder configuration variables (`$SecureOrder_check_url` and `$SecureOrder_credit_url`), beginning at line 256, with the credit-check and credit-charge URLs you received from your Secure-Order provider. Make sure these are the production `https:` URLs (not the test URLs); otherwise, the visitor's credit card won't actually be charged and you won't get any money.

The final item in this part of the form lets the visitor select the desired shipping company. The available options are set in the `@Shipping_Rates` variable located at line 323. The customer may view the formulas used to calculate the shipping charges by clicking the shipping rates button at the bottom of the page.

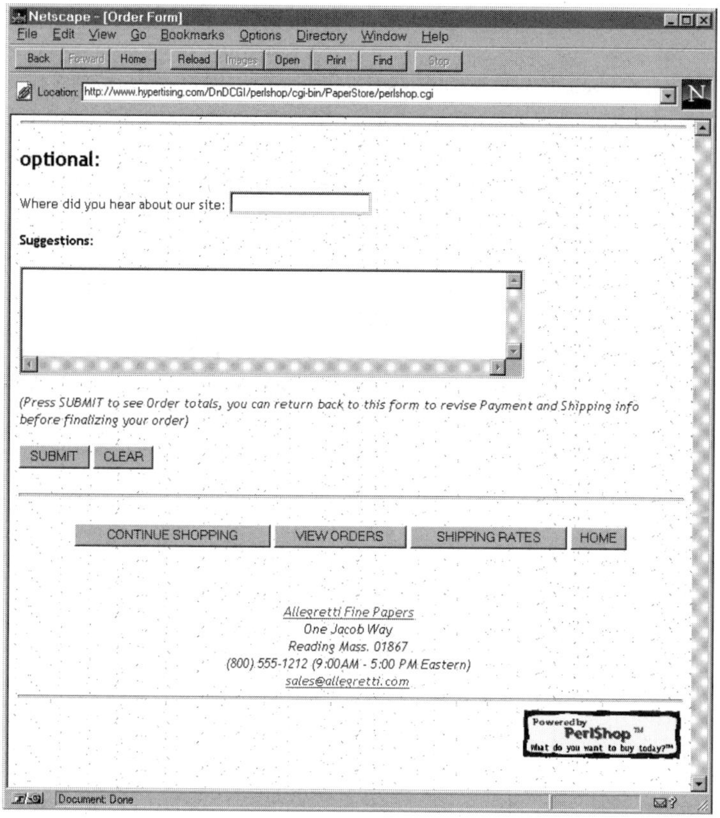

Figure 15.3 PerlShop *shipping and payment form—user feedback section*

Hair Saver

PerlShop checks the country the visitor entered in the top section of the form against the @Shipping_Rates array to ensure that the chosen shipping company can deliver to that country. If a shipper delivers to certain countries but not all, you will need to create an entry in the array for each country that the shipper supports. If no specific country entries exist for a given shipper, the country code of ALL must be used. Be sure to add entries for all supported countries for each shipper (unless they cover them all) to avoid frustrating your visitors.

The final section of the shipping and payment form is shown in Figure 15.3. The optional fields in this part of the form are not required by the order process, but they can generate useful demographic data to help you improve your service. For example, the `Where did you hear about our site` field might give you some valuable insight into the effectiveness of that expensive Web banner ad you just bought. Suggestions from visitors fresh from shopping, especially those who have decided to buy something, are always valuable. The nice thing about this method of feedback is that visitors will often tell you candidly if they don't like something about your store.

To launch this valuable packet of data on its way to your server, the visitor presses the submit button. (The clear button, as you might guess, returns the form to its initial state). When a secure server is used, the submit button will say secure submit.

The bottom four buttons have the same function as the corresponding buttons on other *PerlShop* pages. Continue shopping returns the visitor to the last catalog page he or she visited. To control to which page the visitor returns, you can set the `THISPAGE` parameter in the product form, as discussed in Chapter 14. View orders takes the visitor back to the shopping-cart summary page, where he or she can manipulate the contents of his or her cart.

We've already discussed the shipping rates button. The home button takes the visitor to the HTML page defined in the `$home_page` variable, thus causing him to leave the store. See Chapter 14 for issues associated with leaving the store.

Recall also from Chapter 14 that any button that takes the visitor back to the catalog or the shopping-cart summary page will cause the visitor's shipping and payment information to be lost; *PerlShop* doesn't save this information. It would be a nice gesture to warn your visitors of this.

When the visitor clicks the submit or secure submit button, the form fields are checked to ensure that they are not blank and are in the proper format. The credit card number is checked to ensure that it contains the correct number of digits for that type of card. A check digit is calculated from the digits in the card number to ensure that the user hasn't made a typographical error. (The actual validation of the charge isn't made until the next step.) If any of these checks fail, the visitor is given an error message and directed to use the Back button on the browser to return to the form. This process continues until all the initial checks on the form contents pass. The visitor is given a final chance to review his order and to make any last minute changes before the order is submitted and his credit card is charged.

Figure 15.4 shows the final confirmation page. The only new item on this page is the place order button. This button causes the script to complete the final processing of the order. If SecureOrder or FirstVirtual is being used, the script attempts to process the charge through the appropriate server. If the attempt fails for some reason, an error message from the credit system is passed on to the visitor. If the charge goes through, the charges are applied to the visitor's credit card immediately. When no credit processing is required, nothing more is done with the customer's payment

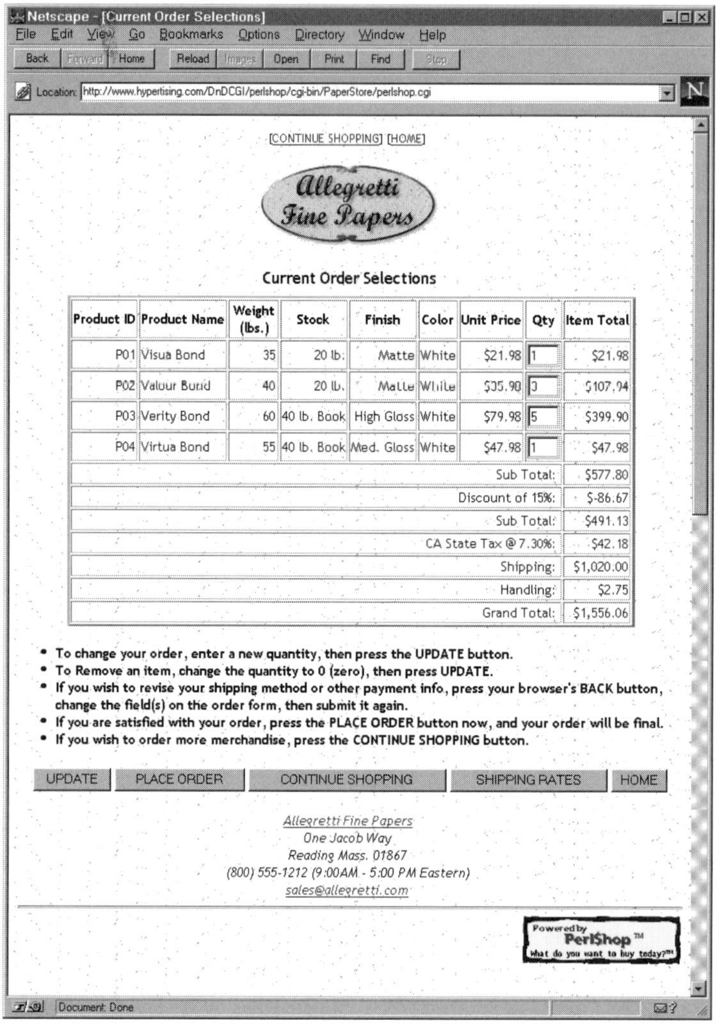

Figure 15.4 PerlShop *final order confirmation page*

information. Upon the completion of the credit card processing, if any, the order is considered complete.

PerlShop generates two types of output to record this joyous event. First, the order is written to two files on the server. Second, an invoice is displayed for the visitor, and e-mail copies are sent to the visitor and the order department at your company. We review these outputs in detail in the next section.

Ordering Process Outputs

To ease processing of the order data by databases and spreadsheets, *PerlShop* writes data files in a standard format called **comma-separated-variable** (CSV). CSV is an ASCII text format, with each data field surrounded by double quotation marks and separated by commas. The fields may be of any length and may contain spaces and any other characters (except double quotation marks). CSV is a very common platform-independent format used by databases and spreadsheet applications to exchange information.

Here is an example CSV record:

```
"field 1","this is field two it is long","field 3","","field 5 - field 4 is blank"
```

PerlShop creates two CSV data files: a customer file and an order file for each order. Both have as a filename the invoice number generated by *PerlShop*.

The Customer File

The customer file contains the address and payment information for the order, including the credit card number (if used). Also included in the customer file are the shipping, handling, tax, and the total cost for the order. By default, the customer file is located in the *customers/* directory below the directory in which the *perlshop.cgi* script resides. The location of this file is controlled by the $customer_directory configuration variable.

The fields in the customer file are as follows:

- Invoice number
- Customer IP address
- Date
- Time
- Customer title
- First name
- Last name
- Company
- Street address line 1
- Street address line 2
- City
- State
- ZIP
- Country
- E-mail
- Day phone
- Day extension
- Nighttime phone
- Nighttime extension
- Fax number
- Shipping company
- Payment type
- Credit card type
- Credit card number
- Expiration month
- Expiration year

- "How did you find us" comment
- Suggestions comment
- Order subtotal
- Tax
- Shipping
- Grand total
- Discount amount
- COD charge
- Handling charge

All fields appear in each record. Fields with no data appear as blank fields (""). Each customer file consists of a single CSV record. The CSV record for our example Allegretti order is given next (note that each record is one continuous line, broken here to fit on the page):

```
"165267202","205.134.204.201","3/27/97","13:13:59","Mr.","Chris",
"Baron","The Hypertising Network","1395 Warner Ave.
","","Tustin","CA","92780","US","chris@hypertising.com","1(714)258-
3232","","","","1(714)555-1313","Airborne
Express","Credit","MasterCard","1234567812345678","11","98","Alta
Vista","Great site.  You need a highly absorbent paper for ink jet
printers.","","559.78","40.86","2825.00","3344.42","-
83.97","0","2.75"
```

The Order File

An order file is created for each completed order. The order file contains multiple CSV records—one record for each item ordered. The record includes all the optional parameters such as weight, tax type, and the three optional attributes for the item. The fields in each record of the order file are as follows:

- Invoice number
- Item ID number
- Item name
- Price
- Quantity
- Weight
- Tax type
- Option 1
- Option 2
- Option 3

All fields appear in each record. As in the customer file, a parameter with no value appears as blank. The order file for our example looks like this:

```
"165267202","P01","Visua Bond","21.98","2","35","","20 lb.","Matte","White"
"165267202","P02","Valour Bond","35.98","1","40","","40 lb.","Matte","White"
"165267202","P03","Verity Bond","79.98","3","60","","85 lb. Cover","High
Gloss","green"
"165267202","P04","Virtua Bond","47.98","5","55","","120 lb. Card","Med.
Gloss","pale blue"
```

Note that the invoice number is listed first in both the customer and order files. This permits easy sorting and correlation between the customer data and the order data. A relational database such as Microsoft *Access* can easily merge this data, using the invoice number as a key.

The Invoice

Once the data files are safely stored on disk, the visitor is presented with a printable invoice of the transaction on the Web browser. An e-mail copy of this invoice is sent to the visitor as a permanent record of the order. Another copy of the invoice is sent to the address set in the $mail_orders_to configuration variable.

Listing 15.1 shows the e-mail generated from the Allegretti order we've been using as an example. You can control the width of the lines in the e-mail with the $line_length configuration variable.

Listing 15.1	*PerlShop*-generated invoice

```
Return-Path: <www@hypertising.com>
Date: Thu, 27 Mar 1997 13:14:13 -0800 (PST)
To: chris@hypertising.com
From: sales@allegretti.com
Subject: Order
                    Allegretti Fine Papers
One Jacob Way<BR>Reading Mass. 01867<BR>(800) 555-1212 (9:00AM - 5:00 PM
Eastern)
                      SALES INVOICE
Invoice #: 165267202            Invoice Date: 3/27/97    Time: 1:13pm pst
Sold To:  Mr. Chris Baron
          The Hypertising Network
          1395 Warner Ave.
          Tustin, CA   92780
          Daytime Phone: 1(714)258-3232
          Fax:  1(714)555-1313
          Email:  chris@hypertising.com
Paid by:  CHECK      Ship via: Airborne Express
```

```
-------------------------------------------------------------
Product ID    Product Name         Unit Price    Qty    Item Total
-------------------------------------------------------------
    P01    Visua Bond                 $21.98       2        $43.96
           Weight (lbs.): 35
           Stock: 20 lb.
           Finish: Matte
           Color: White
    P02    Valour Bond                $35.98       1        $35.98
           Weight (lbs.): 40
           Stock: 40 lb.
           Finish: Matte
           Color: White
    P03    Verity Bond                $79.98       3       $239.94
           Weight (lbs.): 60
           Stock: 85 lb. Cover
           Finish: High Gloss
           Color: green
    P04    Virtua Bond                $47.98       5       $239.90
           Weight (lbs.): 55
           Stock: 120 lb. Card
           Finish: Med. Gloss
           Color: pale blue
--------------------------------------------------------------
                              Sub Total:          $559.78
                    Discount of     15%:          $-83.97
                    ------------------------------------------
                              Sub Total:          $475.81
                CA State Tax  @  7.30%:            $40.86
                               Shipping:        $2,825.00
                               Handling:            $2.75
                    ------------------------------------------
                            Grand Total:        $3,344.42
                        RETURN POLICY
All Sales are final. We will be glad to exchange defective items only within
30 days from date of sale. Any items returned must be sent back prepaid in
the same condition as when originally shipped. Shipping and handling charges
are not refundable.
```

To retrieve these data files from your Web server, use your FTP client. Be sure to use the ASCII transfer mode when downloading. Be sure you include a space in your database for all the fields in the record, including those that are usually blank, such as the tax type.

Hair Saver

> Unfortunately, the customer files and order files for each order have the same file-name. If you download them into the same directory, the second file you download will overwrite the first. Be sure to put the files in different directories or download them with different names. You can also enable the "Do you really want to wipe out this file?" notification in your FTP client to warn you before you overwrite a file.

As soon as the files are downloaded to your local computer, delete them from the Web server. Obviously, the customer files with their credit card numbers are a tempting target for thieves. As long as those files are on an Internet-connected server, they pose a security risk both to you and to your customers. Ideally, you should check your e-mail several times a day for order invoices and immediately download and then delete the files from the server. The default *PerlShop* configuration is very insecure for such important data. We talk about some things you can do to tighten up store security later in the chapter.

So far, we've described the basic operation of the *PerlShop* system. Using what you've learned in Chapters 13 and 14 and to this point in the current one, you can create a fully functional on-line store with on-line credit card processing. The rest of the chapter covers security precautions that you can take to increase the security of your store. We strongly advise that you read this section and implement as many of these security measures as you can.

Increasing Store Security

An inescapable law of the universe regarding computer security is "increased security reduces ease of use." Every time you add a security measure to a system, you increase the amount of effort and time it takes for authorized users to perform their functions. The simplest example of this is log-on passwords. Most UNIX systems require users to log on with a password even for single-user systems, while most PC operating systems such as Windows and the MacOS don't. Any person with physical access to the PC can access any data on the system. To do this on a UNIX system, a person must steal a password or bypass the log-on procedure. The increase in security is significant. The UNIX computer requires a determined attack to break into the system, while the PC requires only physical access.

Amazing Factoid

We are perfectly aware that later versions of both Windows and MacOS include security features, including log-on passwords. Our point is partly historical and partly about practical security differences between the systems. UNIX has always been a multiuser system and has many security features as a basic part of the operating system. PCs were designed as, and are still largely used as, single-user systems with no need for such features. For any randomly selected PC, chances are you can simply walk up to it and access its data. Randomly select any UNIX machine, and you'll need to know a password to get access to even part of the data.

The cost of this increased security is the additional workload on the users to remember their passwords and correctly perform the log-on procedure each time they want to access their data. The effort to administer the system is also increased, since initial passwords must be assigned and new ones created for users who forget their passwords. For most professional users, the increase in security far outweighs the increased effort. For most home users, however, the added protection isn't worth the added effort.

Web server security is in some ways analogous to protecting your automobile from theft. Making either your Web server or your automobile totally secure is prohibitive in both cost and the effort required. What you want is just enough security to make the thief (or hacker) go somewhere else, while requiring minimal additional work on your part. With that in mind, we give you several measures here that you can take to increase your store security, starting from the simplest and easiest and progressing to the more difficult and elaborate.

Amazing Factoid

Contrary to what is often presented on the movie screen, many highly classified military computer systems don't use retinal scanners, thumbprint matching, or data encryption to protect their data. They rely on one simple, very effective security measure—physical isolation. By not allowing even a single outside connection, the system is 100 percent protected from outside electronic attacks. The physical security of the individual computers and network components is highly guarded as well. These measures allow the military to use normal commercial operating systems and software to process classified data with good security.

The main area of the *PerlShop* system that needs protection is the customer files with their precious credit card numbers. The transmission of a credit card number between the browser and the server is transient and hard to intercept. In any case, using a secure HTTP server will prevent these transmissions from being intercepted. Sometimes, however, a secure server can give store owners a false sense of security. While it's true that the credit card number can't be intercepted during its transmission between the browser and the server, the numbers are decrypted before they are passed to the CGI script. What happens with the data after the Web server passes it over to the CGI script is the Web site owner's responsibility. The customer files (unlike browser/server transmissions) may sit on the server for hours or even days. This gives the hacker a stationary target to go after. So good security on your Web server is very important.

Add *index.html* Files

The default *PerlShop* configuration allows anyone with a Web browser to access and download your customer files by manually entering the URL of the customer directory, such as

```
http://www.company.com/cgi-bin/MyStore/customers/
```

Entering this URL on your browser will probably bring up a listing of the files in the *customers/* directory. Downloading the files is as simple as clicking the mouse. There are a couple of things you can do to prevent this. First and simplest is to add an *index.html* (or whatever the proper default HTML file is for your server) file to each of the directories. If your Web server finds this file when the directory is accessed, it will display the HTML file instead of a directory listing. These *index.html* files won't interfere with the normal operation of *PerlShop*. You can make them blank or give the user a message and a pointer back to your home page.

A related measure is to disable the directory index display by your Web server. Most Web servers have a configuration setting either to display the directory listing or to return an error if the *index.html* file is missing from a directory. Your ISP/SA may already have directory listings disabled. If so, you won't need to add the *index.html* files to your directories. If not, you may want to request that this setting be applied to your Web directory. It's never a good idea to allow strangers to browse around your directories, even if you aren't running an on-line store.

Relocate the Store Directories

The default *PerlShop* configuration has all the *PerlShop*-related directories as a sub-directory below the root HTML directory. By relocating these directories outside the HTML directory tree, you prevent any access to these files by a Web browser.

PerlShop will still be able to access the directories, since CGI programs are able to find files anywhere on the server (given proper permission, of course). Figure 15.5 shows a modification of the default *PerlShop* directory structure presented in Figure 13.4.

The main advantage of this directory structure, as mentioned, is that it places the sensitive *PerlShop* files outside the HTML directory tree. You may have noticed that we moved the *catalog/* directory from a *cgi-bin/* subdirectory to a subdirectory off the main HTML directory. While this is not necessary for security, it allows the catalog pages to be indexed by Internet search engines. These search engines normally don't index files within *cgi/* or *cgi-bin/* directories. To make *PerlShop* work with this structure, you will need to modify the subdirectory configuration variables located around line 177 in the script. To do this, you can either modify the $curr_dir variable or set the path manually. Here is an example that matches the directory structure shown in Figure 15.5:

```
$token_directory       = $curr_dir . 'tokens';
$log_directory         = $curr_dir . 'log';
$curr_dir = '/home/users/mycompany/MyStore/';
$customers_directory= $curr_dir . 'customers';
$orders_directory      = $curr_dir . 'orders';
$temp_customers_directory    = $curr_dir . 'temp_customers';
$temp_orders_directory       = $curr_dir . 'temp_orders';
$catalog_directory       = '/home/users/mycompany/public_html/
catalog';
```

We reordered these lines from the original *perlshop.cgi* file to make as few changes as possible to the definitions. You can, if you like, specify all the paths explicitly, as we've done with the $catalog_directory variable.

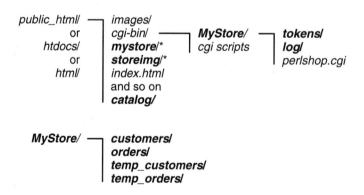

Figure 15.5 *A more secure* PerlShop *directory structure*

Using *cgiwrap*

The previous security measures protect your data only against people who might be casually poking around your site to see what they can find. The files all still have read and write permission set for all users and are still insecure. What we've done so far is simply make them a little harder to find.

The *cgiwrap* program (located on the CD-ROM in the */scripts/PerlShop/cgiwrap* directory and written by Nathan Neulinger) is a "wrapper" for CGI scripts running on UNIX-based Web servers. When *cgiwrap* is used, the Web server doesn't execute the CGI script directly. Instead, it calls *cgiwrap*, which in turn executes the script. The really important thing to remember about *cgiwrap* is that the script runs *under your user ID* rather than under the Web server's user ID. This is a very crucial point because it means that the files accessed by your CGI script can be set to allow absolutely no access by any user other than yourself. Your files are protected by the full might of the UNIX security system. To gain access to your files when *cgiwrap* is used, the hacker would have to gain system administrator (highest level) access to the entire Web server. And if that happened, nothing on the server would be safe, including encryption systems (they can be modified). Fortunately, your ISP/SA is probably very concerned about preventing hackers from gaining system administrator access to his or her system as well.

Using *cgiwrap* has a downside, however. Unless you are the ISP/SA, you can't install it yourself. It requires a user with system administrator access to complete the installation. This is because the program needs to have system administrator privileges in order to run a CGI script that is started by one user (the Web server) but is to be run as another user (you).

You will need to persuade or pay your ISP/SA to install *cgiwrap*. The source code distribution is available on the CD-ROM, and a link to the *cgiwrap* author's Web site is given on the resources page.

cgiwrap Configuration

The following configuration instructions assume you have *cgiwrap* installed. You will also need to get the details on how to call a CGI script using *cgiwrap* according to how your ISP/SA has installed it.

cgiwrap is called using a modified URL for your CGI script. The normal CGI URL is something like this for an individual user:

```
http://www.myisp.com/~joeuser/cgi-bin/MyStore/perlshop.cgi
```

and like this for a user with a dedicated server or virtual Web server account:

```
http://www.mycompany.com/cgi-bin/MyStore/perlshop.cgi
```

The *cgiwrap* modified form of these URLs would look like this:

```
http://www.myisp.com/cgi-bin/cgiwrap/joeuser/MyStore/perlshop.cgi
http://www.mycompany.com/cgi-bin/cgiwrap/youruserid/MyStore/perlshop.cgi
```

On its creation, *cgiwrap* is given the default location within a user's directory space to find the CGI scripts. This location typically will be *~/public_html/cgi-bin* (~ stands for the user's home UNIX directory). The *cgiwrap* URL is formed from the path to the *cgiwrap* script (*/cgi-bin/cgiwrap*), the user ID (*joeuser*), and the path to the CGI script (*/MyStore/perlshop.cgi*) from the starting point—all appended together. Look carefully at the previous example URLs, and you can see how the URLs are modified when using *cgiwrap*.

We're going through this in such excruciating detail so that you'll be able to set the *PerlShop* configuration variables correctly for use on your ISP or SA's server. After you have *cgiwrap* installed, you need to set two configuration variables to tell *perlshop.cgi* to use it. The first is $use_cgiwrap. This variable is located at around line 114 in the script and should be set to yes. The second is $cgiwrap_directory, located at line 155. This variable should be set to that part of the full *cgiwrap* URL following the server name, but not including the actual script. For example, with a *cgiwrap* URL of

```
http://www.mycompany.com/cgi-bin/cgiwrap/cbaron/MyStore/perlshop.cgi
```

the proper setting of $cgiwrap_directory would be

```
$cgiwrap_directory = '/cgi-bin/cgiwrap/cbaron/MyStore';
```

If you created your catalog using the !MYURL! shortcut, you won't need to change your catalog files to use *cgiwrap*. *PerlShop* will automatically generate the correct *cgiwrap* URLs. However, you will need to change the entry link in order to use the full *cgiwrap* URL.

If you can't get the links in your store to function, check the URLs that the script is generating by viewing the HTML source generated by the script. Observe the hyperlinks it generates in the browser status line, and adjust the value of the $cgiwrap_directory until the proper URLs are formed.

Hot Tip

> Once *cgiwrap* is working, there is no reason not to use it for all your CGI scripts. Because of security concerns, we purposely limited the scripts in this book that wrote data files to the Web server. But some need to write data to the server. In particular, the *formp.cgi* script presented in Chapters 9 and 10 would benefit from increased security on the database files it stores on the server.

Once *cgiwrap* is working with *PerlShop*, you should modify the file permissions on all your *PerlShop*-related files and directories. To do this, you can use either your FTP client or your Telnet client. Set the permissions to rwx for the owner and - - - for group and world. This translates to a file mode of 700. The following Telnet command will do the job on the *orders* directory.

```
chmod 700 orders/
```

Repeat this procedure for all the *PerlShop* directories and for the *perlshop.cgi* script itself.

If you implement all the security measures we've discussed in this section and use a secure HTTP server, you will have good security for your on-line store. In fact, your security will be as good as for the operating system itself. You won't be able to do any better without using encryption. You will never be 100 percent secure from the theft of your data, just as you are never 100 percent secure from physical theft. However, as long as you are diligent about removing the customer files from the server in a timely fashion, there is no reason why you should be concerned about selling your products over the Internet. In fact, many on-line stores are currently operating with far less security than we've described here.

In the next section we'll talk about encrypting your data so that even if a hacker gets access to your files he will have to crack a very tough code to get at the data.

Encryption

PerlShop unfortunately does not support encryption of the order data or e-mail transmissions in the current version. We feel that encryption is a very important security measure that needs to be widely implemented before Internet commerce can become as safe as buying something in a real-world store. Check the *PerlShop* home page to see if the author may have added this feature to a version later than that presented here (version 3.1).

Before you start hacking code, you should understand what encryption is. In this section, we give a brief overview of encryption methods, along with a few ideas about how an enterprising person (perhaps you) can add support for the popular PGP encryption system to *PerlShop*.

Encryption is the process of taking a piece of information and rendering it unreadable using a mathematical algorithm. To transform the unencrypted data (clear-text) into the encrypted data (cipher-text), the algorithm requires a special number called a **key.** This key, in combination with the algorithm, defines how characters in the clear-text are transformed into the cipher-text. Encryption algorithms are designed to make it *extremely* difficult to decode the message without the key. The "brute-force" method of simply trying all possible keys can theoretically take millions of years, even using today's fast computers. However, methods of cracking the code that exploit weaknesses in the encryption algorithm are possible. All widely used encryption algorithms have been rigorously tested by a special breed of nerd who lives to crack a well-known encryption algorithm. Those that stand the test of time (survival of the fittest) are secure enough for any conceivable civilian application.

Conventional encryption techniques use the same key to both encrypt and decrypt the data. This is called **secret-key encryption** because the encrypted data is secure only if the key is kept secret. If a hacker gets the encryption key, every message encrypted with it is no more secure than is clear-text. Secret-key encryption really isn't practical for systems such as *PerlShop* because the encryption key must be stored on the Web server somewhere for use by the script. All a hacker has to do is find the key.

Much better for our use is a relatively recent development in encryption technology called **public-key encryption.** Unlike secret-key encryption, this method uses two different keys. One key is used to encrypt the message, and a second, different, key is required to decrypt it. The encryption key is called the **public-key.** This key can be used only to encrypt messages, so it can be freely given to anyone. The decryption key (called the **private-key**) must be kept secret. This system works great for an application such as *PerlShop*. The script encrypts the visitor's sensitive data using the public-key, and only you can decrypt it, using the private-key that you keep secure on your desktop machine. If a hacker were to break into the server and steal the encrypted data, the public-key wouldn't help him a bit.

Pretty Good Privacy (PGP)

The most popular public-key encryption system is called *Pretty Good Privacy* (PGP). PGP was written by Phil Zimmerman as a strong, general-purpose encryption system for "the masses." It is available in a free version for noncommercial use from MIT in the United States. An international version, also free, is available from many places in Europe and elsewhere. A commercial version is available from Mr. Zimmerman's company, PGP Inc. Check the CD-ROM resources file for links to several PGP-related pages. The free and commercial versions use the same commands, so you can use a free version to develop and test your system and then purchase a license for the commercial version when you start using it to make money.

PGP is written in the C programming language and works on both UNIX and Windows machines. It is distributed as source code for UNIX systems; you will need access to a C compiler to install the free version of PGP on your UNIX system. It is distributed as source and a precompiled binary for MS-DOS. Versions have also been produced for the Mac and many other operating systems. Unlike *cgiwrap*, PGP is designed to be installed either by a single user or as a systemwide application. Check with your ISP or SA to see if PGP is already installed on their server. If it isn't, you'll need to install it yourself.

PGP can be used to encrypt both disk files and a stream of data produced by a program. Thus it can be used to encrypt *PerlShop*'s customer and order files and to encrypt the e-mail invoice that the program sends. We can't give you detailed instructions on how to modify the *perlshop.cgi* script to use PGP. However, we do give you some hints on how to start modifying the script yourself.

Modifying *PerlShop* to Use PGP

Your best approach is to figure out the manual PGP command you would enter to encrypt the customer file. It might look like this:

```
/usr/bin/pgp -eatw customers/1234567 your-user-id
```

This command encrypts a customer file with your public-key, writes the encrypted data to an ASCII text file for easy transport over FTP, and then wipes the original file from the disk. The `your-user-id` parameter is your user ID as stored in the PGP public-key file. You can do the same for the order file. Once you determine the correct manual command line, insert it into the script. Line 902 of the *perlshop.cgi* script (`close out_file;`) closes the customer file after writing it to disk. You should place your encryption command as the next line. Since you're running the command from within the script, you can use in the PGP command the variables that create the plain-text customer file. After inserting the appropriate variables, your command would look like this:

```
`/usr/bin/pgp -eatw $customer_directory/$unique_id your-user-id`;
```

You can use a similar command to encrypt the order file.

The invoice e-mail normally doesn't need to be encrypted, since it doesn't contain any credit card information. However, version 3.1 of *PerlShop* includes the `$creditno_on_email` configuration variable. If this variable is set to `'yes'`, the user's credit card number will be included in the invoice. If this information is sent in unencrypted form, it poses a very large security risk. To encrypt this message as it is created, you need to modify the Perl command that opens an output stream to the mail server. The most common method of sending mail from a CGI script on UNIX machines is by using the *sendmail* command. The script writes the data to this program at line 2,306 with this section of code:

```
if (lc $mail_via eq 'sendmail')
{
open (MAIL, "|$sendmail_loc -t -oi") || &err_trap("Can't open
$sendmail_loc!\n");
print MAIL "To: $to\n";
...
```

This code opens a UNIX pipe to the *sendmail* utility using various command options. You can insert PGP into this stream by modifying the open line as follows:

```
if (lc $mail_via eq 'sendmail')
{
open (MAIL, "| /usr/bin/pgp -eatf your-user-id | $sendmail_loc -oi
$to") || &err_trap("Can't open PGP or $sendmail_loc!\n");
#print MAIL "To: $to\n"; # commented out for use with PGP
```

This new open statement sends all the e-mail data through PGP for encryption before sending it to the *sendmail* utility. Note that this code is only a starting point. You will probably have to adjust it to get satisfactory results.

Several add-on programs exist for e-mail applications, such as *Eudora,* to help you handle PGP encrypted e-mail. These programs let you encrypt your e-mail before you send it and help you decrypt e-mail that you receive. Once you have a system like this installed, you can send secret messages to all your friends as well as read the encrypted orders from your store.

That's all the encryption coverage we have time and space for. We'll leave the final integration of PGP and *PerlShop* up to you. You can do it. Whether or not you realize it, if you've worked through most of the scripts in this book you are now pretty close to being a CGI programmer.

If *PerlShop* is useful to you, be sure to let its author know. And tell him that the Drag 'n' Drop CGI boys sent you.

What We Covered in Chapter 15

- The final *PerlShop* checkout process
- The format of the data files produced by the script
- The contents of the invoice e-mail
- Some simple security measures you can take to increase security for your store
- The basics of encryption technology
- A few pointers on adding PGP encryption support to *PerlShop* yourself

Chapter 16
What's Next

What (We Think) We've Given You

The techniques and scripts presented in this book should give you a good starting point on the road to enhancing your Web site. Many of them can be modified to suit new requirements. For example, the *pid.cgi* script described in Chapter 7 can be reworked to allow you to change out blocks of HTML text, as well as images. By altering some of the Javascript for the remotes covered in Chapter 8, you can create full-fledged Netscape windows that include script-generated HTML content, rather than hyperlinks.

To do some of this, you'll need to continue your research and learning, either through other books or by using on-line resources. Later in this chapter, we point you to some of those resources. You may end up writing some code, but we think that is the next logical step, and it shouldn't be difficult if you've managed to get this far. Even the artistic types among you are probably fairly impressed with what you've been able to accomplish.

Becoming a Script Hacker: Is It for You?

If you've worked through a few of the script chapters, installed and run the scripts, and enhanced your Web pages, you've done a lot. You should be proud of yourself. You're on a first-name basis with a couple of programming languages, you've learned a bit about the UNIX operating system, and you know quite a bit (perhaps more than you wanted) about how Web servers and CGI programs work.

In selecting these scripts, we tried to balance functionality and simplicity. It was sometimes hard to choose the best compromise between making the scripts easy to install and use and including a particular feature set. In some cases, we may have simplified too much and, in others, given in to the programmer's desire to include just one more cool feature. You'll have to let us know how well we succeeded. Please send us e-mail at this address and tell us what you think: *dndcgi@hypertising.com*. We'll try to post "improved" versions of scripts on the book's Web site from time to time, based on your feedback.

Where you go next with CGI and client-side scripting depends partly on your experience with the scripts in this book and partly on where you want/need to go with your Web site. Assuming you weren't completely turned off, or that your present and future needs weren't 100 percent satisfied by this book, you'll need to decide on one of two paths to adding more enhancements to your Web site.

> *Path one:* You abandon trying to do CGI scripts yourself and either purchase pre-packaged "solutions" to meet your needs or hire someone (full-time or on a consulting basis) to develop your scripts for you.

Buying functionality "off-the-shelf" allows you to take advantage of the lower cost of commercial software and, in some cases, gain the benefit of technical support. However, a principle we like to call WYGIWYG (pronounced wiggy-wig) applies to off-the-shelf solutions. It stands for "What You Get Is What You Get." It means that you are at the mercy of what the market chooses to provide. It is difficult to gain a technology advantage over your competition using this approach. And if the marketplace doesn't offer what you need, you're simply out of luck.

Hiring someone allows you to concentrate on your primary job. Professional programmers can usually get a given job done more quickly and efficiently than you would be able to, if you can afford them. If you aren't already accustomed to the process of programming, we think that this book will help you deal with these strange and arcane individuals. You now know, in general terms, what's possible with CGI and what it takes to modify an existing script and get it running on the server. You'll be able to talk to the programmer in his or her native language and won't be "snowed" by a lot of buzzwords. If you know something well enough to at least be terrible at it, then you know it well enough to hire someone else to do it for you.

> *Path two:* You decide to learn either to create the scripts you need from scratch or to find something with similar features on the Internet and modify it to meet your needs.

To do this, you will need to understand much more about scripting languages and the logic of computer programming. To modify a program, you must understand in detail what it is doing. This means you will have to acquire additional programming skills. (Becoming a nerd is optional.)

This path is not for everyone. Some people just don't mesh with computers—the way they function and the principles on which they operate. For these people, programming is not fun and figuring out what to tell the computer to make it do what they want will always be a mystery, no matter how often it is explained. Don't feel bad if you fall into this group. As long as you can hire people who do mesh with the computer, you can get the job done.

For those who liked working with the scripts in this book, and for whom all this stuff makes sense, you can go as far as you like in programming. Learning to program a computer language involves learning both to think in a logical step-by-step fashion and to express yourself in a new mode of communication. Like mastering a human language, it takes study and practice. Working in your favor is the fact that, unlike human languages, the vocabulary of computer languages is very limited, and the syntax is fully defined. If your primary goal is to become a CGI programmer, you have many resources available. The books listed at the end of the chapter are a good place to start. You should purchase a beginning CGI book (or several) that will teach you programming along with teaching you CGI scripting. CGI programming is a very restricted area of programming, so you should be up to speed within just a few months. For those of you to whom this is an exciting prospect, we say "Go for it!" At worst, you'll find out that it's not for you. At best, you might just find a new vocation.

Where to Now?

We're going to pull a fast one on you here. We've spent the last 12 chapters giving you specific techniques for use on your Web sites. We've encouraged you to put them to work, and given you some ideas for possible applications. Along the way, you've undoubtedly come up with a bunch of ideas of your own.

Now we're going to tell you not to use these techniques. That is, not to use them *until* you review the objectives of your Web site one last time. Even if you are certain you know what your objectives are, pause a moment to recall your audience and purpose. As you do so, we are going to suggest a few techniques (that don't involve any code) for enhancing your site's chances of success. This discussion is not aimed only at the techies in the audience, but at anyone on the team responsible for putting the Web site in place. Although much of what we say will seem to be common sense, we've seen too many technically brilliant sites that "just don't get it."

Once we get the sermonizing out of our system, we'll quickly list some of the books that we think you'll find helpful. We suggest in particular some of the better Javascript and Perl self-training and reference books that are on the market as we write this. We also add several marketing and design books you might find useful.

Making Sure Your Web Site Makes Sense

We've all seen elegant solutions to a problem. They're generally called "elegant" because they seem so simple at first glance that we often ask ourselves, "Why didn't I think of that?" Although the inspiration for that simple solution may have occurred to its creator in a flash, you can be certain that, before that flash, that person completely understood the problem to be solved. Elegant solutions typically succeed not just because they do the job, but because the creator succeeded in making "form follow function."

Good software is no different than any other well-designed product. It either fulfills expectations, or it doesn't. But really good software goes one even further. It solves the problem in a straightforward way that just seems to make sense and is easy to use. Even software that simply "does the job" fails to earn our praise. We often call it clunky or kludgey precisely for its inelegant solution to the problem.

So why are we carrying on about software elegance and usability here? As most of us realize, Web sites *are* software. Yet rarely do they undergo rigorous evaluation or usability testing. And unlike most software, a Web site doesn't come with a manual. It is something a visitor has to comprehend and navigate without any instructions or specialized training.

In his book *The Design of Everyday Things,* Donald Norman describes how to succeed in creating a really terrible user interface. He's talking about software, but the points he makes apply to Web sites as well. It's worth a few laughs, but we've all seen these problems. Some of us can admit that we've been guilty of a few of them ourselves. Here are some examples:

Make things invisible. Widen the Gulf of Execution: give no hints to the operation expected. Establish a Gulf of Evaluation: give no feedback, no visible results of the action taken. Exploit the tyranny of the blank screen.

Be arbitrary. Use nonobvious command names or actions. Use arbitrary mappings between the intended action and what actually must be done.

Be inconsistent: change the rules. Let something be done one way in one mode and another way in another mode.

Make operations unintelligible. Use idiosyncratic language or abbreviations. Use uninformative error messages.

Be impolite. Treat erroneous actions by the user as breaches of contract. Snarl. Insult. Mumble unintelligible verbiage.

Make operations dangerous. Allow a single erroneous action to destroy valuable work.

(Norman, Donald A., *The Design of Everyday Things* [New York: Doubleday/Currency, 1989], p. 179.)

We've all been to sites where you attempt to submit a form and get back an error message. The error message either fails to give you a clear understanding of the nature of the problem or doesn't give you the opportunity to easily return to the registration form to correct it. (Most of the Internet cognoscente know to press the browser Back button, but what about the rest of us?)

Inscrutable navigational icons certainly fall into the category of "arbitrary mappings" mentioned in the second item.

But the look, feel, and navigability may not be the only problem dogging a site. Still worse is a site that sends the wrong message.

Targeting Your Audience

As you well know, Web sites are more than software. The best of them are an interactive multimedia experience that provides something of real value to the visitor while conveying some critical message and accepting input. The message can be either clear or muddled, targeted or diffuse. It can even miss its target audience entirely, while showing strong appeal to a group who will never buy the company's product.

A successful Web site needs more than a picture of corporate headquarters and a talking-head video from the CEO. You knew that before you opened this book. You also know that it isn't your boss, the marketing manager, or even the CEO who will decide whether the corporate Web site, intranet, or extranet is a success. It's your visitors who will make that call—the internal and external customers, potential clients, vendors, partners, and so on.

Knowing all this, you may wonder why those interested parties aren't involved more often in the Web site development process. Good point. Writing in *Strategic Internet Marketing,* Tom Vassos notes the following:

> Research conducted by the Gartner Group in 1996 suggests that 90 percent of business Web sites are not delivering content and services that meet their customers' requirements. As a result, Gartner predicts that 75 percent of Web sites will need to be rewritten or rearchitected within the first 12 months of operation.
>
> The Gartner study suggests that users . . . want useful applications such as advanced interactive technical support and the ability to query databases to get answers to their questions. They want to be able to access product information that specifically meets the needs they define.

(Vassos, Tom, *Strategic Internet Marketing* [Indianapolis: Que Business Computer Library, 1996], p. 83.)

This unfortunate cycle can be avoided by involving all stakeholders in the Web site development process from the start.

A Solution: Focus Groups and Usability Testing

To get a jump on market expectations, many companies conduct focus groups to evaluate a new product or service before and after its launch. This process involves bringing together some anticipated customers for a product and systematically evaluating their responses to it.

Recently, a computer peripheral manufacturer hired a firm to conduct focus groups to review a product it had on the drawing board. They wanted to get an idea of how the product would be received by customers and potential customers. The focus groups included casual computer users, business-only users, power users, and MIS-types in various age ranges. (Other focus groups included distributors of the company's other products.) The company wanted help in choosing a name that best suited the product, and they wanted to try to anticipate the questions or concerns customers would have so that answers could be included on the packaging and in the literature. They also wanted to find out what competing products the groups already saw on the market and how the new product might compare with those products. Useful conclusions about the product's perceived value and the way it should be presented were to be developed from these sessions.

Once the product was ready to test, focus groups were again used to see whether it lived up to expectations and to see how it was received compared to other market leaders. Among other questions, the groups were asked how they might be persuaded to buy the product.

Using similar techniques, we have conducted Web site usability testing, both prior to and after launch. In one case we're aware of, the launch of a Web site was delayed to incorporate the feedback gathered from potential visitors to the site. We believe the revised site will be much more effective in attracting visitors than the site originally planned would have been.

Although we recommend using outside resources to conduct focus groups, there's no reason why you can't do all or some of this analysis in-house, provided you have the following resources available to you:

- Facilities to seat six to eight people
- A way for management representatives to view the proceedings unobtrusively (if possible)
- A means to record the proceedings (videotape or audiotape) without intruding on the process
- Real-time access to your test Web site for each participant in each session
- A disinterested third party to conduct the evaluation
- A neutral introduction to the site for the participants that includes an explanation of the objectives of the site and that is presented by a nonstakeholder

- A time period (say 20 minutes) for the group members to evaluate the site on their own and make notes
- An incisive series of questions to be asked of the group after the site review (these should reflect a clear understanding of the site's objectives and ideally should be written by a disinterested third party who is familiar with the objectives and methods of focus groups)
- A disinterested group to evaluate the answers and suggest any site plan course corrections that may be necessary

As you can see, this is a pretty tall order. You really need all of the above for the greatest chance of success. Finding a disinterested third party within your organization may be the hardest thing to do. This person has to be prepared to ask some difficult questions and possibly listen to answers no one wants to hear from participants. That person also should have sufficient technical knowledge to understand how the Internet works and must be a good communicator and moderator.

You will want to conduct similar (although not identical) surveys of existing and prospective customers, distributors, and internal customers. Internal customers might include your internal marketing group, the Human Resources department, and salespeople who will use the site as a resource in their sales efforts.

We are reminded of a paper distributed by the Doblin Group at Siggraph 1993. In "What to Do with a Human Factor—A manifesto of sorts," Rick E. Robinson writes: "Bad research only tells you that your product is too blue or your brochure too complex. Great research enables you to see the realms of possibility, and make the things that people will use to realize them." *If you have any doubt that you can marshal the resources you need, locate experienced Web site research professionals to assist you.*

Visit Our Drag 'n' Drop Web Site

We hope you've found this book to be a good resource in your pursuit of the perfect Web site. We will continue to "enhance" the book from time to time on our own Web site at: *http://www.hypertising.com/DnDCGI/.*

We invite you to visit us and send us your comments about this book. We'll do our best to respond quickly. (There are just two of us and a lot of you.) You can send us e-mail at *dndcgi@hypertising.com.*

Some Great Books to Look For

In the course of our work and while writing this book, we have looked at, read, and loved or hated many books. The result is the following short list of books that may be of real value to you as you develop your Web site. Keep in mind that which book you choose will have a lot to do with how you like to learn and other personal preferences. Your mileage may vary.

Javascript Books

Lemay, Laura, and Michael Moncur. *Laura Lemay's Web Workshop Javascript.* Indianapolis: Sams Net, 1996.

> Good all-around tutorial. It covers the language and guides you through creating scripts. Lots of goodies on its CD-ROM.

Reynolds, Mark C. and Andrew Woolridge. *Using Javascript.* Indianapolis: Que Corporation, 1996.

> A very detailed (and big) reference.

Vander Veer, Emily A. *Javascript for Dummies.* Foster City, Calif.: IDG Books Worldwide, 1996.

> Decent, accessible (and short) introductory reference. The non-nerd co-author (can you guess which one?) found it helpful.

Perl Books

Wall, Larry, Tom Christiansen, and Randal L. Schwartz. *Programming Perl. 2d ed,* Sebastopol, Calif.: O'Reilly & Associates, 1996.

> *The* definitive Perl reference. Everyone involved with Perl should have this one.

Perl CGI Books

Gundarvaram, Shishir. *CGI Programming on the World Wide Web.* Sebastopol, Calif.: O'Reilly & Associates, 1996.

> A very complete CGI book (not for nonprogrammers). Covers more-advanced topics.

Johnson, Eric F. *Cross-Platform Perl,* Cambridge, Mass.: MIT Press, 1996.

> Covers Perl for UNIX and Windows, CGI, and other goodies; well-written and accurate.

Tittle, Ed, et al. *Foundations of World-Wide Web Programming with HTML & CGI.* Foster City, Calif.: IDG Books Worldwide, 1995.

> Covers a wide range of CGI programming topics, lots of examples, and applications to real-life problems.

Books on Web Site Design

Kristof, Ray and Amy Satran. *Interactivity by Design.* Mountain View, Calif.: Adobe Press, 1995.

> An excellent application of Donald Norman's usability concepts, and those of others, to the new media.

Lopuck, Lisa. *Designing Multimedia.* Berkeley, Calif.: Peachpit Press, 1995.

> A good visual guide to the look, feel, and architecture of multimedia and the audience.

McCoy, John. *Mastering Web Design,* San Francisco: Sybex, 1996.

> Somewhat misnamed, this book contains an excellent series of portraits of some major Web site design houses, including Red Sky Interactive and CKS Interactive.

Mok, Clement. *Designing Business.* Mountain View, Calif.: Adobe Press, 1996.

> This excellent book describes in some depth the multimedia design process used by Studio Archetype. Contains a number of Web site design projects.

Norman, Donald A. *The Design of Everyday Things.* New York: Doubleday/Currency, 1989.

> A great cult classic that adds the importance of smart design to the concepts of quality and service for gaining a competitive edge. No mention of the Internet here, but some great examples of good design and bad design.

Books on Internet Marketing

Komenar, Margo. *Electronic Marketing.* New York: John Wiley & Sons, Inc., 1997.

> This book offers extensive case histories from AT&T, The Gartner Group, VISA International, 1-800-Flowers, among others, about how they've used the Internet and intranets to grow market share.

Vassos, Tom. *Strategic Internet Marketing.* Indianapolis: Que Business Computer Library, 1996.

> One of the first books to attempt to cover all the bases in Internet marketing. It includes specific techniques to accomplish on-line marketing goals. Although a

bit populist in style, it makes a great introduction before you move on to the Komenar book.

A Short List of Web Resources

Here are a few Web sites that we find useful:

Perl language home page

> *http://www.perl.com/*

Perl reference, CGI on-line tutorials, and general Perl stuff

> *http://www.panix.com/~clay/perl/*

CGI debugging help

> *http://support.pair.com/howto/cgidebug.html*
> *http://www.perl.com/perl/faq/idiots-guide.html*

Netscape Javascript home page

> *http://home.netscape.com/eng/mozilla/3.0/handbook/javascript/index.html*

Javascript link index

> *http://www.cob.ohio-state.edu/~lindeman/javascript/andrew.html*

Javascript example scripts

> *http://www.webreference.com*

Links to additional Internet resources are provided on the CD-ROM that accompanies this book.

Appendix A
Some Notes on Perl for Nonprogrammers

What You'll Find in This Appendix

- A basic summary of the most common Perl language elements
- How to recognize HTML-generating Perl code
- How to figure out, more or less, what the code is doing

What You Won't Find in This Appendix

- A course on how to write computer programs
- A course on how to write Perl programs
- A complete reference to the Perl language

Do I Need to Read This If I Don't Want to Be a Perl Programmer?

You may be asking yourself why nonprogrammers would want any kind of reference to a programming language. And why would a book that bills itself as "how to enhance your Web site *without* programming" include one? We've done so because of the type of reader we expect will buy this book.

Some people can't stand the sight of computer code, get shaky when asked to format a floppy disk, and just about max out doing word processing with Microsoft *Word*. These are *not* the people for whom we wrote this book. Those of you who have penetrated this far will probably be willing now to try a few new things in order to conquer bold new worlds. We think that many of you will find this book a resource for making these and other scripts more comprehensible.

A Bit about Perl Programs

If you've worked through any of the scripts in this book, you already know that Perl programs or scripts are simply plain ASCII text files consisting of Perl language statements and commands. Unlike C, C++, Java, or Pascal programs (which are compiled into machine instructions), Perl programs are executed by an interpreter program that reads (interprets) the Perl code each time the program is run, that is, at runtime. This runtime interpretation process slows down the execution speed of the program quite a bit. For most CGI scripts, and all those included in this book, this speed penalty is not a problem. Since Perl omits an external compile step, development is significantly quicker for small programs written in Perl. An added bonus of the Perl development cycle is immediate feedback on whether the program is working.

On UNIX-based systems, a special comment line can cause the operating system to load the Perl language interpreter and pass to it the contents of a file for execution. This line likely will be very familiar to you by now:

```
#!\usr\bin\perl
```

The "sharp" character # (a.k.a. the pound sign) is a comment in most script languages and in the C language. The "bang" character ! tells the command shell that this is a special text file that contains command instructions for the program specified in the rest of the line. The command shell (see Appendix B) starts the Perl interpreter and tells it which script file called it to life. The interpreter reads the program code and executes the instructions. After the program finishes, the interpreter shuts down until called by another script.

This starting and shutting down of the Perl interpreter (which is a rather large program) also introduces some slowness in the execution of Perl scripts. Unlike compiled languages, which include only the code they actually use, the Perl interpreter contains the code for the entire language and all its commands. This large program is loaded for even the smallest Perl program. Fortunately, the overhead of starting and stopping the Perl interpreter for each CGI script invocation doesn't put a serious load on the Web server hardware in most cases.

The ease of development of Perl programs, coupled with the modest performance requirements of CGI scripts and today's speedy computers make Perl the king of CGI languages. Nevertheless, for systems on which extreme performance is needed or with very complex programs, Perl will probably not be suitable. In these situations, a compiled language such as C should be used.

Perl Data

Perl contains only a few **types** of data. A data type is a distinct kind of data, such as numbers or characters, that a given language recognizes. These are generally interchangeable without too much fuss within the program. Computer science types (nerds) will decry such a lack of discipline, but Perl programmers love the easy way Perl has of getting the job done. Perl can handle three major data types: numeric, string, and array. More complex data structures can be built as needed from these types. Following are the types of data.

Numeric

The **numeric type** is a number such as 1234, 5.234, 6.23E+24, 0xFFEE34 (base 16 or hexadecimal), and 0475 (base 8 or octal). Numbers are generally interchangeable with *strings* (see the next subsection). For example, the number 3 not only can be added, subtracted, multiplied, or divided. It also can be appended to a string to make a different string. For example, a number can be appended to the string 'blind mice' to make another string, '3 blind mice'. Perl doesn't require an explicit **type conversion** to do this. Some languages require you to call a special function to convert an item of one type to another. Perl makes these conversions without such a fuss.

String

A **string** is a collection of characters that can be handled as a unit. They are delimited (they have the start and end marked off) by any of three different characters: the single quotation mark ', the double quotation mark ", and the backtic `. Single-quoted strings are treated literally by Perl, meaning that whatever is between the single quotation marks is handled without modification. Double quotation marks are used when interpretation of variables or other special characters is desired. A backtic string is passed by Perl to the command shell as a command, just as if you had typed it by hand. The output of the command is the value of the string. Here's what these strings might look like in a Perl script:

`'<BODY><H1>Page Title</H1>'`   Single quotation marks; string is treated literally by Perl

`"<BODY><H1>$title</H1>"`   Double quotation marks; inserts the value of $title into the string

`` `date` ``   Backtic; returns the time and date from the operating system

You can also use a "q" or "qq" followed by a different delimiter. For example,

```
q/a single quoted string's characters/
qq(a double quoted "string" $variable)
```

Perl allows these in case you need to use the normal delimiters within the string. You can also use the backslash \ to disable special character processing for one character:

```
"I just want to say \"Hi can I borrow \$5\" dollars"
```

Within a double-quoted string, several shortcuts are available for inserting various text-formatting characters, such as a carriage return and a tab. These are the most common:

`\n = newline`   Causes a new line to be started at the left margin

`\t = tab`   Inserts a tab character into the string

One nice thing about Perl strings is their dynamic nature; that is, you don't have to declare beforehand how large a string is. Perl just expands the size of the string to fit the data.

Array

An **array** is a list of numbers or strings. Arrays are useful for manipulating several related items at once. Many Perl commands act differently depending on whether they are operating on a single value or on an array. Arrays look like this in Perl:

```
('abc', 'def', 1234, 0.3333, $title)
```

A single array can hold almost any number (limited by system memory) of numeric or string items. Items within an array are accessed by their position in this list using square brackets [ ] and the position number. One thing to remember is that Perl always makes the first element in the array [0]. This is called **zero-based indexing.** Here are some examples of array indexes:

[5]   Returns the sixth element in the array

[3,4,5]   Returns a smaller array of elements 4, 5, and 6

[1..10]   Returns all elements between 2 and 11 inclusive

Arrays are most useful when assigned to variables. We cover that soon.

Hash or Associative Array

An **associative array** is one of the most powerful features of Perl. Also known as a **hash array,** an associative array stores data in pairs like this:

```
(key1, value1, key2, value2, key3, value3)
('name', 'Chris', 'book', "Drag 'n' Drop CGI", 'num_sold', 1E+06)
```

Nerd Note

> The term **hash** refers to a computer science method of accessing data. Let's say you have a million data items in a large array and you want to find a given item. If the one you're looking for is the last item in the array (ever notice how when you're looking for something, it's always in the last place you look?), you might have to check all one million items. That's not very efficient. A better way would be to sort the data and create a table that would let you start looking "close" to your destination. This type of table is called a **hash table.**
>
> If you think of using a dictionary, it's easy to visualize a hash table. Take your one million words and sort them into alphabetical order. Then create a hash table containing the starting position of the words beginning with each letter. To find a given word, you look at the table to find the starting point for words beginning with the same letter as your word and start looking from that point. We all know how much time is saved when working with an alphabetized list. To get back to hash arrays: Perl uses a hash table to access data stored in associative arrays. This makes them fast, even for large sets of data.

The values are accessed by their keys, which are strings. Associative arrays are very common in the processing of CGI form data. The <FORM> field names are the keys, and the field values are stored in the associated hash values. To access the value of a field, you need to know only the name of the field. Accessing hash values is done with the curly brackets or braces { } because, as the author of Perl says, "you're doing something fancy." Here are a couple of examples:

| `{mailto}` | Returns the contents of the value associated with the key "mailto" |
| `{$var}` | Returns the value associated with the contents of the variable `$var` |

Perl Code

Perl, like all computer languages, provides the elements you need to construct a program.

■ *Variables* are named spaces in the computer's memory used to store data. Different types of Perl variables can store either single or multiple values.

■ *Operators* allow you to do calculations, such as mathematical functions, with the values of the variables.

■ *Conditionals* give you a way to compare the values of variables and data, such as whether two values are "equal" or one is "greater than" the other.

■ *Statements* control the flow of the program. They allow your program to decide what to do next based on the value of a variable or a conditional. Statements also allow your program to repeat a series of steps several times and to interact with other resources in the computer such as disk files and the Web server.

■ *Subroutines* allow you to break your program into pieces where each subroutine performs a specific function.

■ *Regular expressions* are a powerful Perl mechanism for matching patterns of text in variables or in data from files.

■ Perl's built-in *functions* can perform a variety of useful calculations on your data.

■ Perl provides several functions to *manipulate files* on the Web server to read or store data.

■ Perl automatically provides values for a set of *special variables* containing information about the Web server system.

The following sections will describe the most commonly used features of the Perl language in each of these areas.

Variables

Perl, like most programming languages, allows you to store data in named locations called variables. Perl variables are easy to spot because they all start with one of these special characters:

$ Scalar or single value variable

@   Array

%   Hash (associative array)

FILEHANDLE (no special character)

A filehandle is basically an input or output channel. Filehandles can be uppercase or lowercase or mixed, but Perl convention says to put them in all uppercase letters to make them easy to spot. Here are some examples of Perl variables:

```
$count = 100;                    #   A single value
@prices = (1, 2, 3, 4, 5); #   An array
%form_data = ('mailto', 'chris@hypertising.com', 'book', 'DnDCGI'); #
                                 A hash array
STDOUT                           #   A standard filehandle provided by Perl
```

One tricky thing about Perl variables is that the leading character changes depending on what you want to get out of the variable; for example:

```
@my_array = (1,2,3,'four','five'); #   Assigns the array to the variable
print $my_array[2];                #   Prints the number 3 (remember, zero-
                                        based indexing)
@his_array = @my_array;            #   Assigns an array to another variable
print $form_data{'mailto'};        #   Prints the value associated with the
                                        key "mailto"
```

When you're reading Perl code, look not only for the leading character, but also to see if an array index ({} or [ ]) is being used. These will tell you both the type of variable and the type of data being accessed.

Operators

Perl allows quite a number of operations on variables and data. These operators often do things with a single command that require many lines of code in other languages. This efficiency of expression is another reason for the popularity of Perl.

The assignment operator = stores whatever value is on the right-hand side into whatever is on the left-hand side. Here are the other common operators:

+   -   *   /   Add, subtract, multiply, divide

%		Modulo division (returns the remainder)
&&	||	Logical "and" and "or" functions
.		Concatenate two strings

and some examples:

```
$count = 5 * $number;
```
       # Sets variable `$count` equal to five times the value of variable `$number`

```
$output = $month[2].'/'.$date.'/'.$year;
```
       # `$output` could equal, for example, "March/5/1996"

These operators also allow a shortcut form of assignment like this:

```
$var += 5;       #  Short for $var = $var + 5;
```

In situations in which an operator symbol appears before the equals sign, then the operation is applied to the variable on the left-hand side using the argument on the right-hand side.

Conditionals

The following operators return either a logical true value or a false value depending on the values of their operators. For example,

```
$var == 5
```

returns a true value if `$var` is equal to 5 and a "false" otherwise. Conditionals are used in the `if` and looping statements, described in the next section, to control the flow of the program. Following are the most common conditionals you'll encounter in CGI programs. All compare the value on the left-hand side with the value on the right-hand side. These values can be a computed value (e.g., `$var * 3`), or a constant (e.g., 5 or `'test'`).

==	!=	Numerical equality, inequality
eq	ne	String equality, inequality
>	<	Numeric greater than, less than
>=	<=	Numeric greater than or equal to; less than or equal to

Statements

Perl statements control the flow of the program, allowing it, for example, to test some condition (via a conditional) in order to, among other things,

- decide what to do next,
- repeat a section of code several times, or
- step through each value of an array.

if

The `if` statement is probably the most common statement in all computer programming. It works like this in Perl:

```
if (expr) { true_stuff; } else { false_stuff; }
```

If the conditional `expr` is "true" (see the previous section), then Perl will execute the code between the `true_stuff` curly braces (it may be many lines of code). If `expr` is not "true," then Perl will execute everything between the braces after `else`. For example:

```
if ($var > 10) { print "High\n"; } else { print "Low\n";}
```

This statement says, in English, if the value of the variable named `$var` is greater than 10, then print "High" followed by a carriage return; otherwise (else) when the value is less than or equal to 10, print "low" followed by a carriage return. The `else` part is optional. If no `else` block is present, and the condition is "false," Perl jumps to the first line of code following the closing brace and resumes execution there.

There is an extended form of `if` that looks like this:

```
if (expr) { true_stuff;} elsif (expr2) { 1st_false_2nd_true; } else
{ false_stuff;}
```

The `elseif` section can be repeated as many times as needed. This form allows multiple tests to be made until one is "true." If none of the tests is "true," the code following `else` is executed.

for

`for` is a looping statement used to repeat a section of code a number of times until a condition is true. Here's how it's written:

```
for (expr1; expr2; expr3) { stuff; }
```

When the program first encounters the `for` statement, it sets the variable in `expr1`. Then it does the test in `expr2`. If the `expr` evaluates to "true," the program runs the code between the curly braces. After it executes the last statement in the curly brace block, it executes `expr3` to change the value of the variable in `expr1`. Then it checks to see if `expr2` is "false" yet. If not, the code between the braces is executed again. If `expr2` is "false", execution resumes following the closing brace. Here's a simple example:

```
for ($count=0; $count<10; $count += 1;) { print $count; }
print "all done.";
```

This example will print the numbers from 0 to 9 and then print "all done." Sometimes you'll see a `for` loop that looks like this:

```
for(;;) {
stuff;
if (something) {last;}
more_stuff;
}
```

"But wait," you're thinking, "there are no expressions!" The second expression (nothing, in this case) will never be "false" and the program will loop forever, right? The trick is a little Perl command called *last;*. This command immediately jumps out of a code block. If you run into a `for` loop like this in a CGI program, it will have the `last;` or `exit;` (which exits the program) statement somewhere within it. Some Perl programs might want to run forever (monitoring something in the system), but CGI programs almost never will.

while and until

Other looping statements are `while` and `until`. These work much the same as the `for` statement, except that they don't have a changing variable (called an *index*). They simply have a test and a block of code to execute. For example

```
$count = 0;
while ( $count < 10) {
print $count;
$count += 1; } # does the same thing as the for loop above
```

or

```
$count = 0;
unless ($count < 10) {
print $count;
$count++; }
```

These both do the same thing as the `for` example in the previous subsection. The difference is that the `while` loop does the block first and then checks the condition. Thus it will always execute at least once. The `unless` loop checks first and runs later. If you've been following closely, you've likely noticed that we've used another Perl shortcut. The ++ operator adds one to (increments) the variable and is equivalent to `$count += 1;` or `$count = $count + 1;`. There is also a `--` operator, as you might expect.

foreach

The final statement we'll look at is the `foreach` statement. This is very commonly used in CGI programs. It is used to execute a block of code "for each" element of an array or each key in a hash array. You don't have to know beforehand how many elements are in the array. Perl handles that at runtime. An example might be

```
foreach $field (@field_names) { print "$field is $form_data{'$field'}\n"; }
```

If you had all the names of your form fields stored in the `@field_names` array, you could use this code to access the form data returned by your CGI library in the hash array called `%form_data`. Many CGI scripts that send data from an HTML form to e-mail scripts (including *formp.cgi* in Chapter 9) use this exact code to print the contents of the form into a mail message.

Subroutines and Libraries

Perl allows you to create subroutines within your main program to perform a specific function. For example, to take the square root of a number you could write a subroutine and then call the subroutine, passing it the number whose root you wanted to take. This frees you from putting all the code for the root function (which might be quite large) at each location in your program where you wanted to compute a square root. Subroutines are also a good way to organize your program by isolating the various functions in a specific location for ease of debugging. Perl subroutines are declared as follows:

```
sub subroutine_name {
block of code
}
```

In your main program, you cause the subroutine to execute by calling it:

```
&subroutine_name();
```

Using our square root example, you would send data to the subroutine in this way:

```
sub sqrt {
($num) = @_; # special Perl variable for sending data to subroutines
$rt = square root code here;
return $rt;
}
# somewhere in the main program
$root = &sqrt(34.53);
```

This allows different numbers to be passed to a generic subroutine, which can return the results to the main program. The data passed to a subroutine are called the **arguments** of the subroutine.

Often Perl programs use subroutines from *function libraries*. For example, *cgi-lib.pl* is a very common CGI function library. In Perl version 4, these libraries are loaded into the program when it is started up. The *require* command actually adds the library code into the current Perl program to form a single large program:

```
require cgi-lib.pl;
```

To access the functions in a Perl 5 module, you include the *use* command to access the appropriate module:

```
use CGI.pm; # a CGI function library for Perl 5
```

Regular Expressions

Perl includes many very powerful text-processing functions built around the concept of **regular expressions**. A regular expression is an expression that defines the searching and replacing of text strings, based on matching patterns of text, in a very flexible way. Mastering this area of Perl can take months or years. We don't attempt to cover the theory here. Instead, we give you an idea of how to figure out what a regular expression is doing.

Regular expressions come in three flavors: matching, substitution, and translation. **Matching expressions** are used as conditionals in statements and in creating lists or for extracting information from strings and storing to a variable. The format is

```
/expr/
```

An expression like this will search the Perl built-in string variable $_ for expr. It will return "true" if it finds a match. It can also be used to return all the matches it finds into a variable or array.

Substitution expressions are the second type of regex (as they're called by Perl cognoscente). This form finds a match for an expression and replaces the matched substring with another string. The format looks like this:

```
s/pig/hog/;
```

In this example, the string "pig" is replaced with "hog".

Options allow you to replace the first match or all matches.

Translation expressions translate from one set of characters to another set. They are commonly used to translate uppercase to lowercase letters (or vice versa). The format looks like this:

```
tr/A..Z/a..z/
```

This tells Perl to translate all characters between *A* and *Z* inclusive to the corresponding characters between *a* and *z*.

If you want to decode these expressions in the CGI scripts you find in this book or out on the Web, you'll want to get yourself a Perl reference book. To help you out, both Chapter 16 and the CD-ROM list recommended sources.

Functions

Perl includes a large number of built-in functions to interact with the operating system and perform calculations on the program's data. The power of these functions is another reason programmers like Perl. It allows them to quickly, perhaps with a single function call, add a feature that in other languages would take many lines of code. We introduce here a small subset of the most common functions found in CGI programs.

File Manipulation Functions

Perl reads and writes to disk files through a special variable type called a filehandle. Filehandle variables have no identifying first character like scalar and array variables. They may be in upper- or lowercase, but the Perl convention is for them to be in all uppercase letters (i.e., FILEHANDLE.) Following are the major Perl functions dealing with files and filehandles.

- `<FILEHANDLE>`. Reads a single line from the file associated with the handle or, if assigned to an array, returns the whole file in one whack. Repeated calls to `<>` will return each line of the file in turn.

- `open FILEHANDLE, "<filename";`. Opens a disk file named *filename* and assigns its filehandle to the variable `FILEHANDLE`. Once open, the program can read or write to `FILEHANDLE` depending on how it was opened. A character before the filename tells Perl to open the file for reading (<), writing (>), appending (>>), or read and write (+>).

  A UNIX pipe to another program can be opened with this command using a | character in the `open` call. A common CGI pipe is to the *sendmail* program used to send e-mail:

  ```
  open MAIL, "|sendmail -t -n";
  ```

- `close FILEHANDLE;`. Closes the file and deletes the filehandle.

- `dbmopen, dbmclose`. Provides Perl 4 access to a DBM-type database file. Perl accesses this file as a hash array, and data can be read and written as with a normal hash array. The data is stored to disk when the file is closed.

- `tie, untie`. Provides Perl 5 access to DBM files.

- `stat('file');`. Gets the statistics on a file, such as size and date last modified.

- `print "string"; print FILEHANDLE "string";`. Prints to the terminal console or to a previously opened filehandle. Most CGI programs are concerned with printing HTML code. The Web server receives the output of the script by using the normal *print* command. Scanning the Perl code for `print` statements allows you to identify the areas that produce HTML. You can often modify the code to produce the HTML you want, even if you don't understand the inner workings of the program.

Miscellaneous Functions

Perl has several functions that don't fit easily into any of the other categories. The functions in this section fall into this category. Nevertheless they are commonly seen in CGI scripts so we've included them.

- `eval("text")`. Evaluates the text as Perl code.

- `local(variable)`. Creates a variable that can be used only in the current block of code. It is common in subroutines to protect the data in the main program from unintended corruption by a subroutine.

- `undef(variable)`. Destroys or "undefines" a variable and frees up its storage.

Special Variables

Perl has many variables that are automatically created for each Perl program by the interpreter when it starts the program. These include the following:

- `@ARGV`. An array containing the command line arguments with which the program was called. Common CGI usage is in SSI `#exec cmd="file arg1 arg2"` commands.

- `%ENV`. A hash array with all the current environment variables keyed by name. %ENV is a very important variable because CGI scripts receive almost all their data from the Web server through environment variables. Usually, the CGI library will take care of reading this special variable. But you may still run into a reference to `$ENV{'variable'};` from time to time.

This is as much of the Perl language as we can go into here. While in some computer languages everything is uniform and done in exactly the same manner, Perl has a wide variety of functions, interfaces, and formats. The Perl motto is "There's more than one way to do it." For more sources of information on Perl, see the end of Chapter 16 and the Perl Resources section of the CD-ROM.

What We Covered in Appendix A

- The basic elements of the Perl language
- How these elements are likely to be used in CGI scripts

Appendix B
A UNIX Command Reference for Non-nerds

What You'll Find in This Appendix

- A brief summary of the most useful UNIX commands for CGI installers
- How to use these commands to navigate the file system and to manipulate files
- An introduction to the UNIX file permission system
- A few UNIX odds and ends that might come in handy

What You Won't Find in This Appendix

- A complete reference to UNIX commands
- Instructions on programming, compilers, or the gory details of how UNIX works

Introduction to UNIX

Many people are intimidated by the thought of working in the UNIX environment. They are afraid they'll have to wear unfashionable clothes, use pocket protectors, and enjoy talking in acronyms about things like RAM and MIPS and TCP/IP. Well, we're here to tell you not to worry. You can work with UNIX computers and still be a normal person. All it takes is a little practice—and this book, of course.

Amazing Factoid

The UNIX operating system was invented by two researchers at Bell Labs in 1969 using a discarded PDP-7 computer. Eventually, the operating system was rewritten in the C programming language and made available, along with its source code, to universities and other institutions at comparatively low cost (for the time). Many universities began to use UNIX as a teaching tool, since the source code was available, unlike commercial operating systems from IBM, DEC, and others. They also developed many utilities and extensions to the operating system as part of their research. As a result, legions of programmers graduated from the booming computer science departments of the 1970s and 1980s fully trained in UNIX. It was natural for these nerd-types to continue using the operating system they loved best and for companies to adopt the operating system in which their people were already trained.

In 1982, a little corporation in Palo Alto, California, was founded. It produced the Stanford University Network computer, the SUN-1. From the beginning, Sun Microsystems and other UNIX workstation vendors produced low-cost/high-performance workstations running the UNIX operating system. The rest is history. The price-performance ratio of the UNIX workstation (compared to mainframes and minicomputers), combined with university support, created a coalition of forces destined to change the face of computing.

As the Internet expanded, it was natural for existing system administrators (power-nerds for the most part) to use UNIX-based systems as Internet servers. UNIX still dominates the Internet server world. With the exception of Windows NT, UNIX has no serious challengers today.

Just as UNIX was becoming bogged down by large corporations protecting their products, another freely available UNIX operating system, called Linux, was released to the world in 1991. Linux was originally developed by a Finnish graduate student named Linus Torvalds (*Linux* = Linus + UNIX). It is written in C, is freely available to the masses, and includes all the source code, just like the first UNIX. Linux runs on low-cost IBM PC compatible hardware (and others) and gives everyone the opportunity to own a multiuser UNIX workstation. Linux and other free UNIX systems are likely to continue UNIX as a focus of university research and operating system development well into the next century.

Deep within the UNIX operating system dwells a core program called the **kernel.** The kernel controls the entire machine. It starts and stops the execution of various programs, allocates system resources to them, and gives each, in turn, a chance to run according to a priority scheme. Some of these programs are system related and control various parts of the hardware. Some are user programs, while still others are involved in network and other communications with the outside world. Special programs called **command shells** are designed to translate the operating system's binary language to and from textual commands and responses. This allows the user to manually enter commands to manipulate files, run programs, and generally communicate with the operating system interactively.

The most common method of using a shell these days is to use a terminal emulation program on a PC. This program allows communication with the host computer by means of the Telnet protocol. Telnet is specifically designed to allow terminal-style communications over a TCP/IP network such as the Internet. The terminal emulator, as the name suggests, emulates the commands and display of one or more real-life terminal devices. The most common of these terminals was the VT-100 made by Digital Equipment Corporation; its descendent is still being manufactured today. Virtually all (we would say *all,* but you never know with UNIX) UNIX computers understand the VT-100 command set.

In recent years, graphical shells and operating environments such as MS-Windows, MacOS, and the X Windows system have allowed people to interact with their computers by manipulating graphical images. These graphical user interfaces (GUIs), as they are called, are very user-friendly and offer a more intuitive interaction with the computer. The problem with using them for CGI development is the amount of communication bandwidth they require. Sending the command to copy a file from a Telnet client to a host might require 50 bytes of data, but manipulating a graphical icon to drag a file to a folder icon takes many thousands of bytes. On your desktop computer, the bandwidth doesn't matter because the data stays within the same machine. But if you had to transmit that data over a 28.8K modem, you would quickly realize that using a GUI isn't practical over such a link. On top of the bandwidth problem, there is the lack of compatibility between different GUIs. The X Windows system is really the only attempt at a network GUI. Perhaps someday, Java or some other system will change this, but for now interacting directly with remote UNIX hosts is best done via good old Telnet.

Common Shell Commands

Using the shell commands given in this section, you'll be able to do everything required to install and test CGI programs. Many of the basic file manipulation functions can be performed with an FTP client as well. The best way to get familiar with these commands, as with most things, is by using them. Log on to your ISP/SA's Web server with your Telnet client and try them out.

Path Name Conventions

The UNIX system, like all operating systems in use today, allows you to place your files in directories. Directories can contain files and other directories, thus allowing you to organize your disk files. This should be familiar to anyone who uses a PC.

UNIX uses the forward slash / to separate directory names. A file may be specified by using its name alone. This indicates a file located in the current directory; for example:

```
logo.gif
```

Adding a directory name followed by a / before the filename indicates that the file is located in a subdirectory:

```
images/logo.gif
```

Appending a ../ string to the front of the filename indicates that the file is located in the directory one level higher in the directory tree:

```
../logo.gif # (from within a subdirectory)
```

This syntax should be familiar to HTML programmers as the convention for relative HTML addressing (ever wonder where that convention came from?). To point to files in the current directory, use the string "./". Why would you want to do this? Some shells are picky about how a program is invoked from the command line. For various obscure security reasons, you may need to enter ./*filename* if you want to run a program in the current directory from the command shell. So if you try to run a program in the current directory and you get a "file not found" error, don't just scream at the computer, "It's right there, you idiot machine!" Try putting "./" in front of the filename. Fortunately, CGI programs executed by the Web server won't have this problem.

Command Format Conventions

Most UNIX commands follow a consistent format. A command entered alone either operates on the current directory or assumes you are providing the command data from the keyboard. Putting a filename after the command causes the command to process that file. Adding a wild card character * to the filename results in all matching files being processed.

Most commands have various parameters to control how they behave. These options are indicated by a dash -, followed by one or more letters. For example, a sort command might have an -r option to indicate that the input should be sorted in reverse order. The general syntax for commands is

```
command -option_letters file(s)
```

The option letters represent shorthand for the desired option:

```
ls -al ../public_html/*.html
```

This example means "execute the *ls* command using options—*a* and—*l* on all HTML files within the directory *public_html* located one directory level above the current directory." (These options are defined in the "Directory and File Commands" section that follows.)

Some commands allow you to enter -h or --help after the name and receive a short message about how to use the command. More on getting help with commands later in this appendix.

Directory and File Commands

Directory and file commands allow you to navigate the UNIX file system and to manipulate files and directories.

ls

ls (list) is probably the most-used command in the UNIX universe. Entered with no arguments, it lists the filenames and subdirectory names in the current directory. To list files in a different directory, use the file path or include a path modifier (../ and ./). The most useful options are -a and -l. Normally, files starting with a period "." are not listed by *ls*. The -a option causes *ls* to list "all" files, even those with a period. The -l option causes the files to be listed in "long" format, that is, showing the size, file permissions, and modification date. (The -l format is very similar to the MS-DOS *dir* command.) Use ls -l to check the file permissions on your CGI scripts to make sure they have the execute permission set.

cd

cd stands for "change directory." It is probably the second most used UNIX command. Entered alone, it does nothing. You should follow the command with the directory to which you wish to change. The path shortcut ../ is especially useful here to move upward in the directory tree one level:

```
cd ../
```

or just

```
cd ..
```

You can also use *cd* with an absolute file path from the root of the file system and change directly to a given directory; for example:

```
cd /home/user/joe_user/public_html/cgi/pid/config_files/
```

Without the leading forward slash, the path is assumed to be relative to the current directory.

pwd

pwd stands for "print working directory." It prints your current directory to the screen from the file system root; for example:

```
pwd
/home/users/juser/public_html
```

Sometimes after a long series of *cd* commands you may be confused about exactly where you are. Typing "pwd" will show you.

cp

cp stands for "copy." As you might expect, it creates a copy of the file you specify. You need to give it a source filename (with optional wild cards) and a destination name.

mv

mv stands for "move." It is used to rename files or change their location; for example:

```
mv *.gif images
```

Here, all GIF files in the current directory will be moved to the subdirectory *images*.

rm

rm stands for "remove." It deletes the file(s) specified. *rm* is a dangerous command as there is no undo. A useful but *very* dangerous option is *-r*, which not only removes files from the current directory, but also from subdirectories; for example:

```
rm -r images
```

In this example, all files and subdirectories will be removed from the directory *images*. Then *images* itself will be removed.

mkdir

mkdir stands for "make directory." It creates a subdirectory in the current directory.

rmdir

rmdir stands for "remove directory." It is a safer command than *rm* in that it doesn't delete a directory unless it is empty.

more

more is known as a file "pager." It lists text files one "page" at a time and waits for you to hit a key to get more pages; for example:

```
more index.html
```

Entering a ? will get you help on the available *more* commands. As usual, you can use relative or absolute path modifiers to access files in different directories.

UNIX Permissions

The UNIX file permission system doesn't have an analog in PC operating systems such as MS-Windows or MacOS, which are designed for only a single user. From the start, UNIX was designed as a multiuser operating system. As such, there were certain files or programs to which only certain users or classes of users were to have access. The UNIX permission system classifies a user trying to access a file as one of three types:

- ■ "Owner." The user who created the file or who is later designated as the owner.
- ■ "Group." A group is a set of users that have access to the file. For example, all the programmers on a project might be members of the "programmer" group.
- ■ "Other." Refers to users who are neither the owner of the file nor a member of the file's group. This is sometimes called "world" access, since everyone in the "world" has this permission to access the file.

UNIX allows you to set the ability to read, write, and execute each file you own for the owner (yourself), users in your group, and the world at large. The -1 option of the *ls* command shows you the current file permissions. Entering ls -1 will give you a listing similar to this:

```
~/www/cgi> ls -l
total 8
drwxr-xr-x  2 cbaron  staff   512 Dec 20 13:49 data
-rwxr-xr-x  1 cbaron  staff  3877 Aug 12 13:46 pid.cgi
-rw-r--r--  1 cbaron  staff  2059 Oct 30 12:07 pid.cnf
~/www/cgi>
```

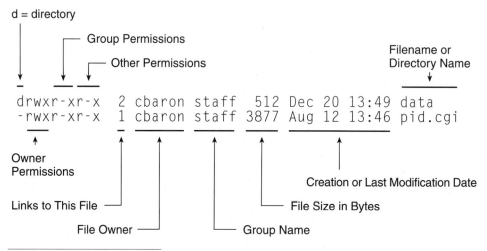

Figure B.1 *UNIX file listing structure*

Figure B.1 explains each field in this listing. From left to right are the

- file permissions,
- number of links to the file,
- owner,
- group,
- size in bytes,
- modification date, and
- file name.

The *d* in the file permission string shows that *data* is a directory, not a file. The file permissions are coded as r for read, w for write or delete, and x for execute. If a permission is allowed, the letter is present; if not, a short dash is printed. The *chmod* command is used to change the file permissions. The format is

```
chmod XXX filename
```

Where XXX is a numeric string, with each X representing the permissions for a class of user (owner, group, and other). The individual values are determined using a binary bit format. Table B.1 will make the format of the permission bits clear (we hope).

Table B.1 *UNIX file permission format*

Bits	Decimal Value	Permissions
000	0	- - - (no access allowed)
100	4	r - - (read only)
101	5	r - x (read, execute)
110	6	rw - (read, write)
111	7	rwx (read, write, execute)

Thus the common operation of setting the CGI script permissions to 755 with the command

```
chmod 755 script.cgi
```

results in the owner's having read, write, and execute permission, while the group and other users have only read and execute permission. Whenever a file is created, UNIX gives it a default set of permissions (usually rwx r - - r - -). Web servers qualify as other-type users.

How to Find Things and Get Help

To get more information about a particular command, you can use the on-line help facility called *man,* which UNIX has had from its very early days. For example, to view the documentation on the *ls* command, enter

```
man ls
```

The *man* page will be displayed on your terminal using the *more* program discussed above. There are also various HTML versions of the standard UNIX *man* pages available on the Web.

If you don't know exactly what command you need, you can use the - k option of *man* to search for commands with a particular keyword in their descriptions; for example:

```
man -k status
```

Here, you'll receive a list of commands (and programming library calls) with the word *status* in their description. This example command generates the following output on our Web server.

```
~> man -k status
clearerr, feof, ferror, fileno (3) - check and reset stream status
faxstat (1) - display HylaFAX status
faxstat (1) - display facsimile server status
fstat (1) - file status
netstat (1) - show network status
ps (1) - process status
rstat (1) - remote status display
ruptime (1) - show host status of local machines
rwhod (8) - system status server
stat, lstat, fstat (2) - get file status
status (5F) - server status database
strmode (3) - convert inode status information into a symbolic string
sync (2) - synchronize disk block in-core status with that on disk
uusnap (8) - show status of UUCP neighbor systems
~>
```

The number within the parentheses indicates the section of the manual in which the command may be found. User commands you are likely to be interested in reside in Section 1. System administration commands are in Section 8. Sections 2–7 have various programming calls and file formats that probably won't interest you at this stage.

Sometimes you may want to know the location of a system utility or program. For CGI programmers, knowing the location of the Perl interpreter is critical. The *which* command will show you the location of particular files located in your command path:

```
which perl
```

returns

```
/usr/bin/perl
```

on our system.

Another command your ISP/SA may have installed is the *whereis* command. This command searches an index of files for the location of a particular program. Depending on how your ISP/SA has configured the system, the *whereis* command can find all kinds of files all over the system.

Try both *which* and *where is* when you're looking for something.

Miscellaneous Commands

Here are a few miscellaneous commands you may need from time to time. Since you know how to use the *man* pages, we won't go into much detail on these commands. You can read about them yourself.

- *gzip* or *zip*. Creates a ZIP archive of a file. The file is replaced with the archive. Windows and Mac ZIP programs can read these archives.

- *gzip -d* or *gunzip* or *unzip*. UnZIPs a ZIP archive. The archive file is replaced with a file of the same name minus the extension. File extensions for ZIP archives are usually *.zip* or *.gz*.

- *tar*. Stands for "tape archive." *tar* is one of the most ancient and venerable UNIX commands. It stores and extracts files from a tar format archive. *tar* is often used in conjunction with a ZIP compression program because *tar* doesn't compress its archives. The normal tar extension is *.tar*. Sometimes you'll see file extensions such as *.tgz* or *.tz,* which are ZIP compressed tar archives.

Hair Saver

> There's one Really Big Difference between how UNIX handles archive files and how Windows or the Mac handle archive files. That is, when zipping files, UNIX replaces (i.e., deletes) the file it is zipping and leaves only the archive. When unzipping a file, it also deletes the archive as it creates the unzipped file(s). This should normally not be a problem. However, if you simply must have a copy of the file or archive, make the copy before zipping or unzipping your archive. Also, UNIX ZIP files may contain only one file, unlike Windows and Mac ZIP archives. The usual way around this is to create a *tar* archive of all the files first and then compress the *tar* archive with *zip* or *gzip.* That is why UNIX archives often have *.tz* or *.tgz* file extensions.

Some Useful Programs

UNIX includes a wide variety of standard programs, available on most systems. Here are several particularly useful ones:

- *pico*. You may want to do a quick edit of a file on the UNIX machine rather than editing the file on your local desktop machine and then sending it to the

UNIX box via FTP. You can do this with *pico*, a very simple editor used by the *Pine* e-mail program; however, it can be used alone as well. Other editors such as *vi* and *emacs* are also usually available, but they are more complicated to use.

■ *lynx*. This is a text-only Web client (that's right— no graphics!). It runs on a character terminal such as in a Telnet session. You can use it to test your pages for look and feel. A surprisingly large number of people still use *lynx*. We use it from time to time to check pages and to download Web files directly to the Web server rather than to our PC.

■ *ping*. This little program is the SA's best friend. It sends a test message to a given computer or IP address and times the response. Normal users can use it to check whether various Internet hosts are up and operating. For example, if you can't get a response from a Web page you can "ping" the server, as in this example:

```
ping www.netscape.com
```

An active server will respond to *ping*'s message, and *ping* will print the response time. By default, about ten *ping* messages are sent. Thus *ping* also gives you a crude indication of the reliability of the connection. A broken network or inactive server won't return a response, and *ping* will tell you this.

Amazing Factoid

The term *ping* has crept into popular usage. Even nontechnical types can be heard saying things like, "I think I'll ping Marketing and see where that product announcement is." When they say this, just smile condescendingly, because you know what *ping* really stands for, and even how to use it.

Conclusion

Using these commands and utilities, you should be able to manage your files on almost any UNIX-based Web server. Those of you with Windows- or Mac-based servers will probably already know how to get around and manipulate files. Be careful, you're close to becoming a computer nerd and UNIX hacker.

What We Covered in Appendix B

- Basic UNIX commands for manipulating files and directories
- More than you wanted to know about the UNIX file permission system
- How to use man to read the UNIX on-line manual to get help with commands
- How to find the locations of certain programs in the file system
- A few other useful commands that will come in handy sooner or later

Appendix C
What's on the CD-ROM

What You'll Find in This Appendix

- A guide to the directories on the CD-ROM included with this book
- A brief description of the various tools on the CD-ROM

What You Won't Find in This Appendix

- A user's guide or other documentation for the tools
- An explanation of The Meaning of Life

The CD-ROM Directories

Figure C.1 shows the directory structure of the CD-ROM included with this book. The following sections describe generally the contents of each directory. The sub-directories below these were still in flux as we went to press, so open *index.html* in the root for the latest information about the software included and where on the CD it can be found.

The Root Directory

In the root directory, you'll find the *index.html* and the *rsrcs.html* files. The *index.html* file gives you a set of hypertext links to the directories and files on the CD-ROM. The *rsrcs.html* file is an extensive list of Internet resources. Included in this file are links to the home pages of all the scripts and tools we use in the book along with links to many other CGI-related Web sites.

The */questionnaire* Directory

This directory contains the ISP/SA questionnaire in both Microsoft *Word*, RTF, and plain text formats.

The */scripts* Directory

This directory contains the scripts we present in the book along with their associated configuration files. The examples for each script are located in a subdirectory below its script directory. For example, scripts and associated files for the *hint* script presented in Chapter 4 are located in the */scripts/hint/* subdirectory on the CD-ROM.

The */tools* Directory

This directory contains the Telnet and FTP tools discussed in Chapter 3, "The Non-programmer's Toolbox." Each application is located in a subdirectory and is ready

```
/ ┬─── index.html
  │    rsrcs.html
  │    questionnaire/
  │    scripts/
  │    tools/
  │    nettools/
  │    commercial/
```

Figure C.1 *CD-ROM first-level directory map*

for installation. A link to the home page for each application is provided in the *rsrcs.html* file. After you install the version we provide on the CD-ROM, you may want to check the application's home page to see if a newer version is available.

The */nettools* Directory

This directory contains a selection of tools we've found useful in the creation of both this book and in our commercial Web business. Some of these applications are freeware, and some are shareware. Please read and follow the license agreement for each application. You are responsible for paying any shareware fees associated with a particular application. Here is a list of the tools we've included:

- *Append-It.* *Append-It* is one of those one-trick ponies that does one thing and one thing only—but it does it really well. This freeware utility allows you to replace file extensions in batch mode as needed. UNIX is case sensitive, and filenames created on other operating systems often arrive in a mixed bag of uppercase and lowercase. This can cause complications in your HTML code if you're running on a UNIX server. This tool can help you avoid these problems (and maybe save you some hair). *Append-It* can be found in the *append/* subdirectory and can be copied to any directory on your hard disk.

- *ColorHexer.* *ColorHexer* is a great freeware utility that allows you to interactively adjust text and background colors on your Web pages. Visited and unvisited hyperlink colors may be viewed against an adjustable color background. Hex values for each of these settings are stored in a window and can be copied and pasted directly into your HTML document. *ColorHexer* gives you the easiest way we've found to get exactly the color combinations you're looking for. This program is found in the *colorhex/* subdirectory and may be copied to an available directory on your hard disk.

- *ThumbsPlus.* This shareware version of *ThumbsPlus* allows you to conveniently catalog all of the graphics associated with the Web sites you're building. And since these graphics can change over time, the program even assists you in the version control process. *ThumbsPlus* is located in the *thumbs/* subdirectory. Simply run the setup program to install *ThumbsPlus* on your hard disk.

- *WingFlyer.* *WingFlyer* is an incredibly useful shareware product that lets you download entire Web sites for viewing on your local machine. Unlike many of the commercially available products, this program allows you to control most aspects of the site download process. This program is found in the *wingfly/* subdirectory and can be copied to a directory for immediate use. *WingFlyer* runs under Windows 95 and NT only.

The */commercial* Directory

This directory contains a trial version of the powerful Web site creation application NetObjects Fusion 2.0. NetObjects Fusion brings the power of desktop publishing to

Web page design and Web site construction. It gives you pixel-perfect positioning for graphics and text. It also offers strong support for databases, Java, and ActiveX. The CD-ROM contains a full-function, 30-day trial demonstration copy of Fusion that allows you to create complete Web sites with no limitation beyond the expiration date of the demo. If you decide to purchase NetObjects Fusion, all your projects can be opened by the commercial version of the product.

The program may be installed from the *fusion20/* subdirectory. Install Fusion by running *Setup.exe*. Fusion requires Windows 95 or Windows NT 4.0. A Macintosh version will be available by the time you read this book, and a trial copy can be downloaded from the NetObjects Web site at http://www.netobjects.com.

CD Warranty

Addison Wesley Longman warrants the enclosed disc to be free of defects in materials and faulty workmanship under normal use for a period of ninety days after purchase. If a defect is discovered in the disc during this warranty period, a replacement disc can be obtained at no charge by sending the defective disc, postage prepaid, with proof of purchase to:

Addison-Wesley Developers Press
Editorial Department
One Jacob Way
Reading, MA 01867

After the ninety-day period, a replacement will be sent upon receipt of the defective disc and a check or money order for $10.00, payable to Addison Wesley Longman, Inc.

Addison Wesley Longman makes no warranty or representation, either express or implied, with respect to this software, its quality, performance, merchantability, or fitness for a particular purpose. In no event will Addison Wesley Longman, its distributors, or dealers be liable for direct, indirect, special, incidental, or consequential damages arising out of the use or inability to use the software. The exclusion of implied warranties is not permitted in some states. Therefore, the above exclusion may not apply to you. This warranty provides you with specific legal rights. There may be other rights that you may have that vary from state to state.

Purchasers of this book may copy the code on the disc for use in developing their own applications. If the code is used in a commercial application, an acknowledgment must be included in the source code listing in the following form: "Segments of the code © 1997 Bob Weil and Chris Baron [or applicable copyright year and holder as noted on the copyright page of the CD-ROM]." Reproduction of the contents of the disc or redistribution of the code is otherwise prohibited without the express permission of Addison Wesley Longman.

More information and updates are available at
http://www.awl.com/devpress/titles/41966.html

Index

< (angle brackets), 54, 83, 107, 329

* (asterisk), 73, 183

@ (at sign), 87, 185, 217, 242, 250

\ (backslash), 189, 217, 219, 221

! (bang character), 318

^ (caret), 107

: (colon), 142

, (comma), 132, 142, 150, 151, 204, 208, 243, 292–293

{} (curly braces), 321–322, 323, 325

$ (dollar sign), 87, 150, 217

. (dots), 103, 104, 107

" (double quotes), 53, 62, 73, 75, 76, 87, 104, 115, 183, 188, 219

/ (forward slash), 72, 73, 104, 115, 183

– (minus sign), 185

() (parentheses), 72, 76, 250

% (percent sign), 87, 150, 217

. (period), 73

| (pipe character), 141, 142

(pound character), 148, 155, 318

; (semicolon), 54–55, 62, 73, 76, 87, 150, 151, 152, 183

' (single quote), 53, 204, 217, 242, 243, 320

[] (square brackets), 83, 323

_ (underline character), 107, 184

$add_navigation variable, 234, 275

$align variable, 241

$allow_ssi_cgi variable, 235

$background variable, 263

$banner variable, 241, 263

$button_image variable, 245

$catalog_country variable, 247

$catalog_directory variable, 259, 263, 300

$catalog_home variable, 238

$cgi_directory variable, 237

$cgiwrap_directory variable, 236–237, 302

$company_name variable, 242

$cookie_expires_days variable, 234

$create_page_log variable, 239

$create_search_long variable, 239

$current_dir variable, 239, 240

$digit_dir variable, 88

$discount_type variable, 248

$email_of_sender variable, 148

$file variable, 220

$flock_ok variable, 147, 155

$home_page variable, 238, 278

$image_directory variable, 239, 245

$image_location variable, 239

$length parameter, 90–91

$length variable, 89

$line_length variable, 242, 295

$mail_orders_to variable, 295

$mail_program variable, 147, 155

$option2_caption variable, 265

$Pay_checks_to variable, 243

$post_image variable, 94

$pre_image variable, 94

$restricted_use variable, 148

$return_policy variable, 243–244

$secure_image_directory variable, 239, 252

$secure_server_address variable, 236

$sendmail_loc variable, 238

$server_address variable, 236

$shipping_type variable, 247

$should_i_append_a_database variable, 149

$should_i_mail variable, 149

$smtp_addr variable, 238

$stay_on_page variable, 250

$testing variable, 233

$text_color variable, 263

$title variable, 207, 218, 220

$type variable, 205

$use_cgiwrap variable, 233–234, 301
$use_cookies variable, 234
$use_secure_server variable, 234, 251
$wrong_server_error_message variable, 149
$your_server_name variable, 149
%ENV variable, 330
%urltopath variable, 209–210, 212
@accept_first_virtual variable, 289
@accept_payment_by variable, 289
@ARGV variable, 330
@directories variable, 212
@Discount_Rates variable, 249
@Handling_table variable, 243
@SEARCHDIRS variable, 204, 210, 212
@Shipping_Rates variable, 278, 282, 289
@Tax_States variable, 268

A

<A> tag, 144, 257
Absolute paths, finding, 115
@accept_first_virtual variable, 289
@accept_payment_by variable, 289
Access (Microsoft), 294
ACTION field, 262, 270
ACTION parameter, 154, 155, 213, 221,
    259, 274
ActiveX technology, 350
add_button_bar subroutine, 282
add_company_footer subroutine, 280, 281
add_menu_bar subroutine, 282
add_navigation variable, 234, 275
add_search_screen subroutine, 282
Advertising, internet-based, 19
Adverware, 225
Algorithms, 268, 303
align parameter, 241
$align variable, 241
allow_fractional_qty variable, 235
$allow_ssi_cgi variable, 235
all parameter, 105
Amiga, 22
Anarchie, 39–45, 57–58
Anchor-type remotes, 127, 129–131, 135
angle brackets (<>), 54, 83, 107, 329
Animation, 16
Append-It, 349

Applets, basic description of, 21
aprefix variable, 131
@ARGV variable, 330
ARPA (Advanced Research Projects Admin-
    istration), 13
ARPAnet Corporation, 225
Array(s). *See also* Array variables
    associative, 150, 321, 323
    basic description of, 320–322, 323
Array variables
    @accept_first_virtual variable, 289
    @accept_payment_by variable, 289
    @ARGV variable, 330
    @directories variable, 212
    @Discount_Rates variable, 249
    @Handling_table variable, 243
    @SEARCHDIRS variable, 204, 210, 212
    @Shipping_Rates variable, 278, 282, 289
    @Tax_States variable, 268
art galleries, 126
ASCII (American Standard Code for Infor-
    mation Interchange), 33, 210, 296, 318
    CSV (comma-separated-variable) and,
    292–293
    FTP and, 37, 38, 304
    pid.cgi script and, 116
asize variable, 130
Associative arrays, 150, 321, 323
Asterisk (*), 73, 183
At sign (@), 87, 185, 217, 242, 250
Atari-ST, 22
Audiences, targeting, 311. *See also* Market-
    ing
Auto checkbox, 37

B

Background color, 72, 130, 241, 275
background variable, 263
Backslash (\), 189, 217, 219, 221
Bang character (!), 318
Banner images, 241, 263, 281
$banner variable, 241, 263
BBSs (bulletin-board services), 169
BGCOLOR attribute, 130
Binary transfers, 37, 38, 43
<BLINK> tag, 88

body parameter, 143
<BODY> tag, 74, 76, 82, 130, 135–136, 143, 217, 220, 241, 263, 275, 280–281
Bookmarks, saving, 43
Books, recommended, 314–316
Boolean searches, 200
Brackets ([]), 83, 323
Browsers. *See also* Internet Explorer browser; Netscape
Navigator browser (Netscape)
    basic description of, 12
    competition between, 69, 74, 189
    image caching settings for, 121–122
    non-Javascript, 105
    operating systems and, 22
    Save As functions for, 218
    sending images to, 111
Button(s)
    bars, 127–129, 132, 135, 282
    control, 244–245
    parameters, 76, 105, 132
$button_image variable, 245

C

C programming, 20, 22, 318, 319, 334
C++ programming, 20, 318
Caret (^), 107
Case-sensitivity, 89, 114, 164, 184, 243
Catalog(s), 224, 249–250
    creating pages for, 262–274
    entering, 269–272
    files, 229
    information, storing, 227–228
    multi-item selection forms in, 269–274
    single-item selection forms in, 263–269
$catalog_country variable, 247
$catalog_directory variable, 259, 263, 300
$catalog_home variable, 238
cathome.html, 261
cd command, 60, 337–338
CD-ROM (*Drag 'n' Drop CGI*), 6, 8, 28, 347–350
cgi-bin directory, 57, 58, 89, 148, 151, 154, 205, 210, 211, 231, 232, 237, 252, 300
cgi directory, 88–90, 151, 155, 231, 301
$cgi_directory variable, 237

cgi-lib.pl, 31, 147, 151, 152, 328
CGI scripts (listed by name). *See also* Scripts
    firstcgi.cgi script, 52–63
    formp.cgi script, 137–176
    formv script, 177–193, 286
    hint script, 65–77, 98, 102, 103, 107, 348
    ICE scripts, 197–222
    PerlShop script, 223–306
    pid.cgi script, 109–124, 307
    remote script, 125–136
    scroller script, 97–107
    vcount.cgi script, 79–95
cgiwrap, 224, 233–234, 236–237, 301–304, 349
$cgiwrap_directory variable, 236–237, 302
check_all() function, 179, 181, 184, 189, 190
check() function, 179, 184, 187–190
CHECKOUT button, 277, 286
Checkout process, 224, 277, 286
checkSticky() function, 131, 136
chmod command, 32, 44, 58, 151, 221
CLEAR button, 290
client_email field, 144
Client-side processing, 15–17, 19–20, 177–193
Clocks, system, 200
cmd parameter, 82
COD orders, 243
Cold War, 13
Colon (:), 142
ColorHexer, 349
Color(s)
    background, 72, 130, 241, 275
    hexadecimal values for, 72, 130
    names of, 72, 130
    parameters, 53, 55
    of products, in PerlShop, 245, 266–267
Commas, 132, 142, 150, 151, 204, 208, 243, 292–293
Comments
    basic description of, 72, 73
    in Javascript, 183
    one-line, 183
Commerce Server Web server, 228
$company_name variable, 242

Compression, file, 343
Conditionals, 324
config_file field, 130
config_file parameter, 142, 144
Confirmation messages, 282
CONTINUE SHOPPING button, 277, 291
Control buttons, 244–245
Cookie mechanism, 227, 230, 234, 235, 256
$cookie_expires_days variable, 234
Copyrights, 10, 196–197, 232
Country codes, 243, 247, 286, 289, 293
cp command, 338
$create_page_log variable, 239
$create_search_long variable, 239
credit-card processing, 224, 228–229, 242–243, 286–292, 296
cron utility, 201
CSV (comma-separated-variable), 292
ctrl.html, 133
Curly braces ({}), 321–322, 323, 325
Currency formats, 244
Customer files, 224, 293–294
Cut-and-paste method, 184
Cut and try method, 153
CyberCash payments, 242, 286

D

Daemons, 12–13, 16
database_delimiter field, 169
database_name parameter, 142
Databases
 DBMS (database management system) and, 227, 229, 262
 formv script and, 178–193
 PerlShop and, 226, 227, 229–230, 294
Data files, in PerlShop, 230, 235
Data packets, 14
data_set parameter, 144
Data types, 319–322
Date stamps, 143
DBMS (database management system), 227, 229, 262. *See also* Databases
Debugging, 316. *See also* Errors
Deleting
 files, 38, 44, 296

 lines in scripts, 203
Demographic data, 178
Design of Everyday Things, The (Norman), 310
dice.html, 118
$digit_dir variable, 88
Directories
 cgi-bin directory, 57, 58, 89, 148, 151, 154, 205, 210, 211, 231, 232, 237, 252, 300
 cgi directory, 88–90, 151, 155, 231, 301
 creating, 38–44, 53, 57–58, 89, 151, 154, 231–232, 338
 formp.cgi script and, 144, 145, 151, 154
 ICE scripts and, 204, 207, 208–210, 217
 loading, into remote windows, 133
 master, 53
 PerlShop and, 237, 238, 252–253, 259, 296, 298–300
 pid.cgi script and, 115, 117
 remote script and, 127, 130, 132–133
 saving Javascript files in, 74
 specification of, in URLs, 88, 115
 Unix commands for, 337–339
 using the forward slash (/) character to separate, 115
 vcount.cgi and, 88, 89
@directories variable, 212
@Discount_Rates variable, 249
Discounts, 248–259
$discount_type variable, 248
dismiss button, 75
disp parameter, 83, 84, 90, 94
display_order_form subroutine, 281
DNS (Domain Name Service), 15, 17
Doblin Group, 313
Document Source option, 98
document.write method, 106
document.write parameter, 189
DOS (Disk Operating System), 38, 43, 45. *See also* MS-DOS
Dr. Dobb's Journal, 257
Drag 'n' Drop CGI CD-ROM, 6, 8, 28, 347–350
Drag 'n' Drop CGI Web site, 8, 37, 58, 213, 257, 313

Dr. Download Web site, 100–102, 112
Dumb terminals, 45

E

E-Cash, 286
echo_data parameter, 143, 169
E-mail, 27, 142. #SA# formp.cgi script
    addresses, at sign (@) in, 242
    addresses, for the authors of this book,
        308, 313
    client-side form validation and, 179, 185
    copies of invoice/orders, 291, 295
    formv script and, 179, 185
    guest-book forms and, 160, 166,
        168–170
    on-line test example and, 175
    PerlShop and, 242–244, 291, 295, 305
    request-for-information forms and, 160,
        161–166
    security and, 139, 305
    subject line, 142
$email_of_sender variable, 148
email_subject field, 130, 144
email_subject parameter, 142
Encryption, 228, 268, 298, 300, 303–306
END markers, 217–218
end-of-line characters, 43, 104
end-of-string markers, 54
Enter key, 103–104
ENTER parameter, 259
%ENV variable, 330
Environmental variables, 113, 330
Envision Graphics Web site, 68, 69
Error(s), 79, 90, 152, 316
    client-side form validation and, 179, 183,
        186, 187
    "No such file or directory," 61
    syntax, 53, 55, 76, 251
    when uploading files, 61–62
Event(s)
    basic description of, 70
    handlers, 70
    onBlur event, 179, 181, 187, 189, 190
    onClick event, 106, 127, 179, 187, 189
    OnFocus event, 70
    onLoad() event, 105, 135

onMouseOut event, 70, 75–76
onMouseOver event, 70, 75–76
onSubmit event, 179, 181
Exiting hints, 76
Explorer, Windows, 46
Expressions, regular, 322, 328–229
Extranet, 1, 4, 22, 311

F

Field(s). *See also* Fields (listed by name)
    hidden, 144
    names, 184
Fields (listed by name)
    ACTION field, 262, 270
    client_email field, 144
    config_file field, 130
    database_delimiter field, 169
    email_subject field, 130, 144
    html_error field, 173
    html_response field, 142
    include_blanks field, 164, 173
    mailto field, 130, 144, 164
    required_variables field, 142, 173
    response_url field, 169
    SUBMIT field, 262
    variable_order field, 141, 166, 169, 173
File(s). *See also* File extensions
    compression, 343
    deleting, 38, 44, 296
    formats, 53, 148–150
    -handles, 323
    locking, 147
    manipulation functions, 329–340
    -names, valid/invalid characters in, 89
    permissions, 38–39, 43, 44, 58, 61, 250
    size, changes in, 43
    Unix commands for, 337–339
File extensions
    .bat, 32
    .cgi, 37, 211
    .cnf, 37
    .dat, 37
    .exe, 32
    .htm, 30, 37
    .html, 30, 37
    .pl, 37

File extensions (*Cont.*)
  .shtml, 30, 82, 92
  .stm, 30
$file variable, 220
Firewalls, 288
firstcgi.cgi script
  basic description of, 52–63
  configuration of, 53–57
  HTML code to call, 56
firstcgi.html, 57, 59, 60, 62–63
FirstVirtual, 286, 288–289, 291
flock() command, 147
$flock_ok variable, 147, 155
focus groups, 312–313
FollowSymLinks option, 253
<FONT> tag, 130, 241
foreach statement, 327
formp.cgi script. *See also* Forms
  basic description of, 137–157
  configuration of, 144, 145–151, 152
  Data Accepted page, 140–141
  examples using, 159–176
  formv script and, 179, 186
  guest-book example, 160, 166–170
  how it works, 139–140
  installing, 145, 151–153
  online-test example, 160, 170–176
  request-for-information example, 160,
    161–166
  test-bed example, 153–156
  using, in your Web pages, 153–157
  why you would want to use, 138, 160
formp.cnf, 139
Forms. *See also* formp.cgi script; formv
    script
  client-side validation of, 177–193
  guest-book forms, 160, 166–170
  multi-item selection forms, 269–274
  online-test forms, 160, 170–176
  processing/responding to, with Perl,
    137–157
  request-for-information forms, 160,
    161–166
  single-item selection forms, 263–269
<FORM> tag, 154, 213, 257, 270, 281
formv script, 286. *See also* Forms

  basic description of, 177–193
  checking an entire form with, 190
  configuring, 181–185
  how it works, 178–180
  installing, 181, 185–186
  using, in your Web pages, 186–193
  why you would want to use, 178
formv.txt, 182
formvtst.htm, 178
for statements, 325–326
Forward slash (/), 72, 73, 104, 115, 183
Frequently Asked Questions list, 58
FrontPage (Microsoft), 33, 265
FTP (File Transfer Protocol), 27, 31–44, 89,
    151, 221
  anonymous, 34
  basic description of, 15, 34–44, 57–59
  directories, loading, into remote win-
    dows, 133
  PerlShop and, 231, 240, 250, 296, 302,
    304
  pid.cgi script and, 116–117
  uploading files with
  vcount.cgi script and, 89, 90
  WS_FTP, 35–36, 45, 58
Function(s). *See also* Functions (listed by
    name)
  basic description of, 322, 329–340
  file manipulation functions, 329–340
  libraries, 31, 147, 151, 152, 328
  methods and, 106
Functions (listed by name). *See also*
    Functions
  check_all() function, 179, 181, 184, 189,
    190
  check() function, 179, 184, 187–190
  checkSticky() function, 131, 136
  openRemote() function, 131, 133, 135,
    136
  REPLY function, 144
  required() function, 179, 181, 184,
    185–186
  Save As function, 218
  scroller() function, 104
  scrolloff() function, 105, 106
  submit function, 181

warn() function, 179, 181, 184, 185–186
Fusion (NetObjects), 350

G

Gateways, basic description of, 12, 16
Get method, 213
GET requests, 17–19, 81
GIF (Graphics Interchange Format) images, 112–113, 280
  scroller script and, 101
  vcount.cgi script and, 84, 89
Golden Gate Trading Company Web site, 226
Graphics. *See also* Color; Images
  changes to, automating, 109–124
  GIF (Graphics Interchange Format), 84, 89, 101, 112–113, 280
  logos, 280–281
  Web site search engines and, 196
Groups, of images, 111–112, 114–117, 120
  image picking rules and, 114
  name lines for, 115–116
gr parameter, 83, 84, 90
GUIs (graphical user interfaces), 16, 21, 335
gunzip command, 343
gzip command, 343

H

<H1....H6> tags, 207, 217
Hackers, 298, 303, 307–309
@Handling_table variable, 243
Hash arrays, 321, 323, 330
Hash-codes, 268
Hash tables, 321
Headers, 110–111, 113, 118–120
<HEAD> tag, 74, 76, 105, 182, 217
Help, for Unix, 341–342, 343
here document, 54–55
Hidden fields, 144
hintby variable, 73
hintdelay variable, 73
hint.html, 66
hint script, 348
  basic description of, 65–77
  configuring, 71–72
  installing of, 71, 74

scroller script and, 98, 102, 103, 107
  using, in your Web pages, 74–77
  why you would want to use, 66–67
hint.txt, 71–72
Hits, 80–81. *See also* vcount.cgi script
Holland Marketing, Inc. Web site, 19
HOME button, 278, 291
home.html, 70
$home_page variable, 238, 278
HREF parameter, 106
HTML (HyperText Markup Language). *See also* HTML tags
  editors, 33, 56, 72, 74, 103, 134, 143, 145, 221, 229, 265
  event handlers and, 70
  print statements and, 55
  "smart," 82
  -type remote, 127–128, 132, 133–134, 135
  Web site search engines and, 197, 221
html_error field, 173
html_error parameter, 143
html_response field, 142
html_response parameter, 143
HTML tags. *See also* HTML (HyperText Markup Language)
  <A> tag, 144, 257
  <BLINK> tag, 88
  <BODY> tag, 74, 76, 82, 130, 135–136, 143, 217, 220, 241, 263, 275, 280–281
  <FONT> tag, 130, 241
  <FORM> tag, 154, 213, 257, 270, 281
  <H1....H6> tags, 207, 217
  <HEAD> tag, 74, 76, 105, 182, 217
  <HTML> tag, 74, 263
  <IMG> tag, 88, 94, 110, 112, 116, 241
  <INPUT> tag, 105, 184, 187
  <META> tag, 74, 105, 120, 182
  <!MYURL!> tag, 258–259, 265, 273, 302
  <!MYWWW!> tag, 258–259, 273
  <PSTAG> tag, 275
  <SCRIPT> tag, 105, 134, 184
  <SELECT> tag, 144, 200
  <TD> tag, 88, 94, 281
  <TEXTAREA> tag, 184

HTML tags (*Cont.*)
    <TITLE> tag, 105, 130, 182, 198, 200, 217, 220
    <UL> tag, 219
HTTP (HyperText Transport Protocol), 11–13, 34, 56, 81, 288
    basic description of, 15–20
    daemons, 12–13, 16
    headers, 110–111, 113, 118–120
    PerlShop and, 224–226, 233–234, 252, 256, 288, 298, 302
httpd, 228, 229
HTTPS, 234, 252, 253
Hyperlinks. *See also* URLs (Uniform Resource Locators)
    counter reset, 84, 94
    formp.cgi script and, 143, 144
    formv script and, 188, 189
    hint script and, 67–69
    ICE script and, 198, 201–202, 220
    PerlShop and, 230, 259, 260–261, 269, 274–275, 276
    remote script and, 126, 127–129, 130, 131, 134
    scroller script and, 106
Hypertising Network Web site, The, 68

I

IBM (International Business Machines), 334
ice-form.cgi, 198, 200–201, 212–214
ice-form.pl, 205–212, 215–216
ice-idx.pl, 198–201, 203–212
ICE scripts
    basic description of, 197–222
    configuring, 202–210, 214–222
    installing, 202, 210–212
    search request forms, 215–216
    thesaurus files, 214
    using, in your Web pages, 212–222
    why you would want to use, 196–197
if statement, 220, 325
Image(s), 144, 275. *See also* Graphics
    banner images, 241, 263, 281
    caching, 121–122
    for control buttons, 244–245
    groups of, 111–112, 114–117, 120

    HTML tag for, 88, 94, 110, 112, 116, 241
    -maps, 127
    PerlShop and, 241, 244–245, 252
    picking rules for, 112, 114, 115, 116
    three ways to send, to a browser, 111
    thumbnail images, 126
$image_directory variable, 239, 245
$image_location variable, 239
<IMG> tag, 88, 94, 110, 112, 116, 241
include_blanks field, 164, 173
include_blanks parameter, 142
index.html, 298–299, 348
<INPUT> tag, 105, 184, 187
    Interactive Cardiac Health Assessment Questionnaire, 160
Internet
    brief history of, 13
    World Wide Web and, relationship of, 11–12
Internet *Explorer* browser (Microsoft), 10, 12, 21, 74, 230
    formv script and, 178, 181, 189
    hint script and, 70, 76, 69
    links and, 106
    pid.cgi script and, 121
    scroller script and, 106
    window options parameter and, 133
Intranets, 1, 4, 10, 12, 14, 27, 31, 32, 33, 196, 236, 311
Invoices, 291, 293, 294, 295–297
IP addresses, 14, 15, 17, 293
I/Pro, 80
ISO (International Standards Organization)
    country codes, 243, 247
    -Latin character set, 205
ISPs (Internet Service Providers), 3, 6, 20, 23, 26–36, 53–58
    how to determine if you can run CGI scripts with, 26–33
    ISP/SA questionnaire for, 32–33, 35–36, 40, 41, 47–48, 51, 54, 57–58, 60, 81, 87, 113, 145, 147, 204, 210, 232, 237, 348
    security and, 252–253, 300–301, 304, 342
    setting up, 35–36

ITEM_ID values, 265

J

Java, 1, 350
  basic description of, 12, 16, 21
  operating systems and, 22
Javascript, 1, 5, 7, 12, 307
  basic description of, 16, 21–22, 65–77
  books on, recommended, 314
  case-sensitivity and, 184
  client-side form validation with, 177–193
  remote control for all occasions using,
    125–136
  submit function and, 181
  using special character in, 183, 188
  Web site, 316
  Web sites with resources for, 316
  window options parameter and, 132–133

K

Keywords, 250

L

LANs (local-area networks), 27, 31, 32
  FTP and, 35, 40, 57
  Telnet and, 59
Lawhelper Web site, 85
$length parameter, 90–91
$length variable, 89
license agreements, 263
$line_length variable, 242, 295
Links. *See also* URLs (Uniform Resource
    Locators)
  counter reset, 84, 94
  formp.cgi script and, 143, 144
  formv script and, 188, 189
    hint script and, 67–69
    ICE script and, 198, 201–202, 220
    PerlShop and, 230, 259, 260–261, 269,
      274–275, 276
    remote script and, 126, 127–129, 130,
      131, 134
    scroller script and, 106
Linux, 334
Location methods, 127
Logging on, 36–37, 47, 51, 297

Logos, 280–281
ls command, 337, 341
lynx, 344

M

Macintosh, 21–22, 33, 89, 335
  FTP and, 35, 38, 39–44
  NCSA Telnet for, 50–52
  NetObjects Fusion 2.0 for, 350
  security and, 297
MacTCP, 50
$mail_orders_to variable, 295
$mail_program variable, 147, 155
Mailto field, 130, 144, 164
Mailto links, 163–164, 166, 242
Mailto parameter, 142
Main subroutines, 218
Man (Unix help facility), 341–342, 343
Marketing, 2–4, 178, 315–316
Matching expressions, 328
Memory, 233, 322
Menu bars, 132, 282
Merchant accounts, 286
META command, 118
<META> tag, 74, 105, 120, 182
Methods
  basic description of, 106
  document.write method, 106
  Get method, 213
  location methods, 127
  onClick method, 189
  POST method, 213
Military computer systems, 13, 298
MIME (Multipurpose Internet Mail Exten-
    sions), 15, 217
$MINLEN variable, 205
Minus sign (–), 185
Mission Hospital Regional Medical Center
    Web site, 128
Mkdir button, 38
Mkdir command, 151, 338
More command, 141, 338
Mosaic browser, 50
MS-DOS, 32, 59, 238, 304. *See also* DOS
    (Disk Operating System)
Muquit, Muhammed, 81

Mv command, 92, 338
<!MYURL!> tag, 258–259, 265, 273, 302
<!MYWWW!> tag, 258–259, 273

N

NAME parameter, 134, 141, 184–185, 190, 265
Navigating, the PerlShop site, 224, 274–275
NCSA Telnet for the MacOS, 50–52
NetCount, 80
NetObjects Fusion, 350
Netscape Communications, 228
Netscape Navigator browser, 10, 21, 69, 74, 307, 316
  cookies and, 230
  formv script and, 178, 181, 189
  FTP and, 34
  hint script and, 69
  links and, 106
  scroller script and, 98, 106
  support for Java, 12
  window options parameter and, 133
Neuss, Christian, 196–197
Neuss Web site, 196–197
Newton, Isaac, 197
Norman, Donald, 310
Numeric data type, 319

O

Object-oriented programming (OOP), 188
onBlur event, 179, 181, 187, 189, 190
onBlur parameter, 189
onClick event, 106, 127, 179, 187, 189
onClick method, 189
onClick parameter, 134
OnFocus event, 70
onLoad event, 105, 135
onLoad parameter, 136
onMouseOut event, 70, 75–76
onMouseOver event, 70, 75–76
onMouseOver parameter, 70
onSubmit event, 179, 181
open command, 305
openRemote function, 131, 133, 135, 136
Operators, 322, 323–324
Order data, 224, 281, 292–297

P

page name parameter, 83, 84
papers.html, 259–260
Parentheses, 72, 76, 250
Passwords, 36, 297
Paths, absolute, finding, 115
$Pay_checks_to variable, 243
Payment information, 224, 242–243. *See also* credit card processing
Percent sign (%), 87, 150, 217
Period (.), 73
Perl (Practical Extraction and Report Language), 5, 7–8
  associative arrays and, 150
  basic description of, 20–21, 317–322
  books on, recommended, 314–315
  choosing an ISP and, 31
  configuring files and, 54
  data types, 319–322
  errors and, 61–62, 152, 183, 217
  form processing examples, 159–176
  FTP and, 37
  installing, 29
  notes on, for nonprogrammers, 317–322
  operating systems and, 22
  print statements and, 55
  processing/responding to interactive forms with, 137–157
  subroutines, 215–217, 218
  using special character in, 53, 150–151, 152, 183, 217, 242
  Web site search engines based on, 195–202
  Web sites with resources for, 316
perllogo.gif, 280
perlre.htm, 276
PerlShop
  built-in search engine, 275–276
  configuring, 231–232
  customizing scripts for, 279–283
  driving the shopping in, 276–279
  entering the store with, 259–262
  how it works, 226
  installing, 223–254, 231
  introduction to, 225–230
  logo, 280–281

multi-item selection form, 269–274
processing pages with, 256–258
security and, 224, 228, 251–253, 268, 286–292, 297–303
server-independence tags, 258–259
setting up, 255–283
single-item selection forms, 263–269
system, overview of, 228–230
what you need to install, 224–225
perlshop.cgi, *see* PerlShop
permissions, 38, 43–44, 58, 60, 89, 116, 151, 165, 211, 221, 232, 250, 300, 302, 333, 337, 339–341
PGP (Pretty Good Privacy), 224, 304–306
pico, 343–344
pid.cgi script, 307
basic description of, 109–124
configuring, 113–116
dice-rolling example, 117–118
how it works, 111–112
installing, 113, 116–117
three modes of operation in, 111
timely greeting example, 119–121
using, in your Web pages, 117–123
why you would want to use, 110
PIN numbers, 288–289
ping, 238, 344
Pipe character (|), 141, 142
Pipes, 141, 305, 329
Pixels, 132
PLACE ORDER button, 291
Platform independence, 16
$post_image variable, 94
POST method, 213
Pound character (#), 148, 155, 318
Pragma: no-cache line, 121
$pre_image variable, 94
Print statements, 55, 217, 219, 280
Product options, 245–246
Protocols, 12, 14–17, 19
<PSTAG> tag, 275
pwd command, 338

Q

Questionnaires, ISP/SA, 32–33, 35–36, 40, 41, 47–48, 51, 54, 57–58, 60, 81, 87, 113, 145, 147, 204, 210, 232, 237, 348

QuickNet International, 49
Quote characters
" (double quotes), 53, 62, 73, 75, 76, 87, 104, 115, 183, 188, 219
' (single quote), 53, 204, 217, 242, 243, 320

R

Random rule, 112, 114, 116
Randomtimed rule, 112, 114, 115, 116
Readme files, 35, 50
readme.txt, 50
Regular expressions, 322, 328–329
remote.htm, 126, 127, 131, 135
remote script
basic description of, 125–136
configuring, 130–131
how it works, 127–129
installing, 130, 131
using, in your Web pages, 131–136
why you would want to use, 126
remote.txt, 130
remotebg variable, 130
REPLY function, 144
req_Text message, 183
require command, 328
required() function, 179, 181, 184, 185–186
required_variables field, 142, 173
required_variables parameter, 143
reset parameter, 83, 84, 91
Resizing windows, 132
response_title parameter, 143
response_url field, 169
$restricted_use variable, 148
return keyword, 70
return_link_name parameter, 144
return_link_url parameter, 143
$return_policy variable, 243–244
rm command, 338
rmdir command, 338
Robinson, Rick E., 313
Robots, 81
ROI (return on investment), 2, 80
rsrcs.html, 348, 349
rwintitle variable, 130

S

SAs (System Administrators), 6
  cgiwrap and, 300–301
  how to determine if you can run CGI
    scripts with, 26–33
  ISP/SA questionnaire, 32–33, 35–36, 40,
    41, 47–48, 51, 54, 57–58, 60, 81, 87,
    113, 145, 147, 204, 210, 232, 237, 348
  security and, 252–253, 304, 342
  setting up, 35–36
Save As function, 218
Saving
  bookmarks, 43
  files before uploading them, 59
  files as plain text files, 53
scalar variables
  $add_navigation variable, 234, 275
  $align variable, 241
  $allow_ssi_cgi variable, 235
  $background variable, 263
  $banner variable, 241, 263
  $button_image variable, 245
  $catalog_country variable, 247
  $catalog_directory variable, 259, 263,
    300
  $catalog_home variable, 238
  $cgi_directory variable, 237
  $cgiwrap_directory variable, 236–237,
    302
  $company_name variable, 242
  $cookie_expires_days variable, 234
  $create_page_log variable, 239
  $create_search_long variable, 239
  $current_dir variable, 239, 240
  $digit_dir variable, 88
  $discount_type variable, 248
  $email_of_sender variable, 148
  $file variable, 220
  $flock_ok variable, 147, 155
  $home_page variable, 238, 278
  $image_directory variable, 239, 245
  $image_location variable, 239
  $length variable, 89
  $line_length variable, 242, 295
  $mail_orders_to variable, 295
  $mail_program variable, 147, 155

$option2_caption variable, 265
$Pay_checks_to variable, 243
$post_image variable, 94
$pre_image variable, 94
$restricted_use variable, 148
$return_policy variable, 243–244
$secure_image_directory variable, 239,
  252
$secure_server_address variable, 236
$sendmail_loc variable, 238
$server_address variable, 236
$shipping_type variable, 247
$should_i_append_a_database variable,
  149
$should_i_mail variable, 149
$smtp_addr variable, 238
$stay_on_page variable, 250
$testing variable, 233
$text_color variable, 263
$title variable, 207, 218, 220
$type variable, 205
$use_cgiwrap variable, 233–234, 301
$use_cookies variable, 234
$use_secure_server variable, 234, 251
$wrong_server_error_message variable,
  149
$your_server_name variable, 149
Scheduled execution utilities, 201
Scripts. *See also* Scripts (listed by name)
  basic description of, 4–5, 16
  how to determine if you can run, 26–33
  testing, 61, 62, 90, 121–122, 221, 251
Scripts (listed by name). *See also* Scripts
  firstcgi.cgi script, 52–63
  formp.cgi script, 137–176
  formv script, 177–193, 286
  hint script, 65–77, 98, 102, 103, 107, 348
  ICE scripts, 197–222
  pid.cgi script, 109–124, 307
  remote script, 125–136
  scroller script, 97–107
  vcount.cgi script, 79–95
<SCRIPT> tag, 105, 134, 184
Scrollbars, 132
scroller() function, 104
scroller script. *See also* Scrolling text

basic description of, 97–107
configuring, 102–104
how it works, 101–102
installing, 102, 105
using, in your Web pages, 105–107
why would you want to use, 98–99
Scrolling text. *See also* Scroller script
effectiveness of, 98–99
letter-by-letter, 99, 101
remote windows and, 126
speed of, 107
in status lines, 99–100
stopping, 101, 105, 106
word-by-word, 99–100
scrolljs.htm, 107
scrolloff() function, 105, 106
scroll.txt, 102–104
@SEARCHDIRS variable, 204, 210, 212
Search engines, 81, 83, 126, 195–202,
275–276, 300
SECURE CHECK OUT button, 286
$secure_image_directory variable, 239, 252
SecureOrder system, 286, 289, 291
Secure server, 7, 223, 234, 251–253, 287,
298, 302
$secure_server_address variable, 236
SECURE SUBMIT button, 290
Security, 169, 173
cgiwrap and, 224, 233–234, 236–237,
300–304, 349
encryption, 228, 268, 298, 300, 303–306
file permissions, 38–39, 43, 44, 58, 61,
250
firewalls, 288
formp.cgi script and, 139, 148
increasing, 297–303
passwords, 36, 297
PerlShop and, 224, 228, 251–253, 268,
286–292, 297–303
PGP (Pretty Good Privacy) and, 224,
304–306
SHA (secure-hash-algorithm) and, 268
<SELECT> tag, 144, 200
Selena Sol Web site, 138
Semicolon (;), 54–55, 62, 87, 73, 76, 150,
151, 152, 183

send_confirmation subroutine, 282
send_header subroutine, 217, 218
send_index subroutine, 217
sendmail command, 31, 147, 237, 305
$sendmail_loc variable, 238
$server_address variable, 236
session IDs, 226–227, 230, 256–259, 268
SHA (secure-hash-algorithm), 268
Shareware licenses, 35
Shell accounts, 27
Shipping information, 224, 229, 246–248,
278–279, 282, 286–292
SHIPPING RATES button, 289, 291
@Shipping_Rates variable, 278, 282, 289
$shipping_type variable, 247
Shortcut tabs, 47
Shortcuts, 47
$should_i_append_a_database variable,
149
$should_i_mail variable, 149
Siggraph, 313
Silicon Graphics workstations, 21
Single quotes ('), 53, 204, 217, 242, 243,
320
SiteMill (Adobe), 33
SKUs (stock-keeping-units), 265
SMTP (Simple Mail Transport Protocol),
15, 31
$smtp_addr variable, 238
Spacer dots, 103, 104, 107
spacer variable, 104, 107
speed variable, 107
Square brackets ([]), 83, 323
SRC parameter, 110, 112, 116
SSI (Server-Side Includes) techniques, 30,
168, 169
basic description of, 82–83
image caching settings and, 121–122
pid.cgi script and, 110, 121–122
SSI (Server-Side Includes) techniques (*Cont.*)
vcount.cgi script and, 81–83, 91–92, 94
SSL (Secure Socket Layer), 228, 234
Statement(s)
basic description of, 73, 322, 324–327
foreach statement, 327
for statements, 325–326

Statement(s) (*Cont.*)
   if statement, 220, 325
   print statements, *55*, 217, 219, 280
   until statements, 326
   while statements, 326
Status lines, 75, 76, 132
$stay_on_page variable, 250
sticky parameter, 131, 133, 135
STOP button, 101, 105, 106
Strategic Internet Marketing (Vassos), 311
String(s)
   basic description of, 87
   character, 107
   data type, 319–320
   parameter, 132
   terminators, 152
SUBMIT buttons, 230, 262, 267, 290
SUBMIT field, 262
submit function, 181
Subroutines
   add_button_bar subroutine, 282
   add_company_footer subroutine, 280, 281
   add_menu_bar subroutine, 282
   add_search_screen subroutine, 282
   basic description of, 322, 327–328
   display_order_form subroutine, 281
   main subroutines, 218
   send_confirmation subroutine, 282
   send_header subroutine, 217, 218
   send_index subroutine, 217
   view_cart subroutine, 281
Substitution expressions, 328
Suite Software Web site, 180
Sun Microsystems, 16, 334
Symbols
   < (angle brackets), 54, 83, 107, 329
   * (asterisk), 73, 183
   @ (at sign), 87, 185, 217, 242, 250
   \ (backslash), 189, 217, 219, 221
   ! (bang character), 318
   ^ (caret), 107
   : (colon), 142
   , (comma), 132, 150, 151, 142, 204, 208, 243, 292–293
   {} (curly braces), 321–322, 323, 325

$ (dollar sign), 87, 150, 217
. (dots), 103, 104, 107
" (double quotes), 53, 62, 73, 75, 76, 87, 104, 115, 183, 188, 219
/ (forward slash), 72, 73, 104, 115, 183
– (minus sign), 185
() (parentheses), 72, 76, 250
% (percent sign), 87, 150, 217
. (period), 73
| (pipe character), 141, 142
(pound character), 148, 155, 318
; (semicolon), 54–55, 62, 73, 76, 87, 150, 151, 152, 183
' (single quote), 53, 204, 217, 242, 243, 320
[] (square brackets), 83, 323
_ (underline character), 107, 184

T

Tab character, 142
Tags
   <A> tag, 144, 257
   <BLINK> tag, 88
   <BODY> tag, 74, 76, 82, 130, 135–136, 143, 217, 220, 241, 263, 275, 280–281
   <FONT> tag, 130, 241
   <FORM> tag, 154, 213, 257, 270, 281
   <H1....H6> tags, 207, 217
   <HEAD> tag, 74, 76, 105, 182, 217
   <HTML> tag, 74, 263
   <IMG> tag, 88, 94, 110, 112, 116, 241
   <INPUT> tag, 105, 184, 187
   <META> tag, 74, 105, 120, 182
   <!MYURL!> tag, 258–259, 265, 273, 302
   <!MYWWW!> tag, 258–259, 273
   <PSTAG> tag, 275
   <SCRIPT> tag, 105, 134, 184
   <SELECT> tag, 144, 200
   <TD> tag, 88, 94, 281
   <TEXTAREA> tag, 184
   <TITLE> tag, 105, 130, 182, 198, 200, 217, 220
   <UL> tag, 219
tar command, 343
TARGET parameter, 134

Taussig, Edward, 225
Tax information, 224, 229, 249, 268, 294
@Tax_States variable, 268
TCP/IP (Transmission Control Protocol/
    Internet Protocol), 11, 14–17, 34, 181,
    335
    basic description of, 14–15
    ping and, 238
    Telnet and, 44–52
<TD> tag, 88, 94, 281
Telnet, 27, 31–32, 89, 92, 335
    basic description of, 15, 44–52, 59–63
    formp.cgi script and, 151, 152
    ICE script and, 211, 221
    PerlShop and, 231, 239, 250, 302
    pid.cgi script and, 116–117
telnet.exe, 46
Tera-Term, 48–50
Teranishi, Takashi, 48
Testing scripts, 61, 62, 90, 121–122, 221,
    251
<TEXTAREA> tag, 184
$text_color variable, 263
thesaurus file, 214
THISPAGE parameter, 259, 267, 274, 291
Thumbnail images, 126
Thumbprint matching, 298
ThumbsPlus, 349
Time
    stamps, 143
    universal coordinated, 200
time_stamp parameter, 143
Timed rule, 112, 114, 115, 116
Timers, calling window hints with, 75
Timex-Sinclair, 22
<TITLE> tag, 105, 130, 182, 198, 200, 217,
    220
$title variable, 207, 218, 220
Toad Suck Web site, 227
Toolbars, 132
Torvalds, Linus, 334
Translation expressions, 328–329
type parameter, 131
$Type variable, 205

U
<UL> tag, 219
Underline character (_), 107, 184
UNIX, 13, 20–23, 31, 147, 307, 318
    case-sensitivity and, 60, 89
    choosing an ISP and, 29–30, 32
    command format conventions, 336–337
    command reference, 333–345
    configuring files for, 54
    creating users in, 165–166
    directory/file commands, 337–339
    end-of-line characters, 43
    formp.cgi and, 165–166, 173
    FTP and, 38, 43, 44, 58
    help facility (man), 341–342, 343
    ICE script and, 200, 204
    introduction to, 334–335
    miscellaneous commands, 342
    mv command, 92, 338
    passwords, 297
    path name conventions, 336
    PerlShop and, 225, 251–252, 297, 300,
        301, 304–305
    pipes and, 141, 305, 329
    security and, 300, 301, 304, 339–341
    system clocks, 200
    Telnet and, 36, 45, 47, 49, 51, 59, 60
    testing scripts with, 61
    useful programs, 343–344
    vcount.cgi script and, 89, 91, 92
until statements, 326
unzip command, 343
UPDATE button, 277
URL parameter, 132
url_of_this_form parameter, 143
URLs (Uniform Resource Locators), 31, 34,
    88, 143. *See also* Links
    absolute paths in, 115
    favorite, in guest-book forms, 166, 168
    ICE script and, 201–202, 207–208, 220
    location methods and, 127
    PerlShop and, 230, 234, 237, 239,
        251–253, 257, 269, 286, 289,
        298–299, 301–302
    pid.cgi script and, 111, 114–115
    remote script and, 127, 129, 132–133

URLs (Uniform Resource Locators) (*Cont.*)
  server redirection and, 111
  specifying directories in, 88, 115
%urltopath variable, 209–210, 212
Usability testing, 312–313
use_cgiwrap variable, 233–234, 301
$use_cookies variable, 234
$use_secure_server variable, 234, 251
UTC (Universal Time Coordinated), 200

V

Validation, 177–193
VALUE parameter, 142
variable_order field, 141, 166, 169, 173
variable_order parameter, 142
Variables. *See also* Array variables; Scalar
    variables
  basic description of, 73, 87, 322, 323
  environmental variables, 113, 330
Vassos, Tom, 311
VBscript (Microsoft), 66
vcount.cgi script
  basic description of, 79–95
  configuring, 85–89
  graphical digit visit counter, 92–93
  how it works, 83–84
  installing, 85, 89–91
  pid.cgi script and, 110
  text visit counter example, 91–92
  using, in your Web pages, 91–95
  visit counter for multiple pages, 94–95
  why you would want to use, 80–81
view_cart subroutine, 281
view source command, 144
Visitor(s). *See also* vcount.cgi script
  counting, 79–95
  profiles, 178
  tracking, with PerlShop, 256–257

W

warn() function, 179, 181, 184, 185–186
warn_Text message, 183
Web browsers. *See also* Internet Explorer
    browser; Netscape Navigator browser
  basic description of, 12
  competition between, 69, 74, 189
  image caching settings for, 121–122
  non-Javascript, 105
  operating systems and, 22
  Save As functions for, 218
  sending images to, 111
Web-only accounts, 27
Webmasters, 2, 5, 165
Web site(s). *See also* Web sites (listed by
    name)
  design tips, 309–311
  maps of, 126
  recommended, 316
  search engines based on Perl, 195–202
Web sites (listed by name). *See also* Web
    sites
  Drag 'n' Drop CGI Web site, 8, 37, 58,
    213, 257, 313
  Dr. Download Web site, 100–102, 112
  Envision Graphics Web site, 68, 69
  Golden Gate Trading Company Web site,
    226
  Holland Marketing, Inc. Web site, 19
  Hypertising Network Web site, The, 68
  Javascript Web site, 316
  Lawhelper Web site, 85
  Mission Hospital Regional Medical Cen-
    ter Web site, 128
  Neuss Web site, 196–197
  Selena Sol Web site, 138
  Suite Software Web site, 180
  Toad Suck Web site, 227
Webtrends, (e.g. Software, Inc.), 80
Weight information, for products, 244, 245,
    266, 294
where command, 342
whereis command, 342
which command, 342
while statements, 326
window options parameter, 132–133
Windows 3.1 (Microsoft), 20, 22, 61, 297
  end-of-line characters, 43
  FTP and, 35
  Telnet and, 48–50
  Tera-Term for, 48–50
Windows 95 (Microsoft), 21, 61, 297, 350
  end-of-line characters, 43

filenames, 89
formv script and, 178
FTP and, 35, 36
Telnet and, 45, 46–48
Windows NT (Microsoft), 21–22, 29, 36,
    334, 350
  $mail_program variable and, 147
  configuring files and, 54
  filenames, 89
  FTP and, 35, 36, 38
  Telnet and, 45, 46–48
WingFlyer, 349–350
winhintdelay variable, 75
Word for Windows (Microsoft), 33, 53,
    318, 348
WordPerfect, 33
World Wide Web. *See also* Web browsers;
    Web sites
  introduction to, 11–17
  search engines for, 81, 83, 126, 195–202,
    275–276, 300

$wrong_server_error_message variable, 149
WS_FTP, 35–36, 45, 58
WYGIWYG (What You Get Is What You
    Get), 308
WYSIWYG (What You See Is What You
    Get), 265, 308

X
X Windows, 45, 335

Y
$your_server_name variable, 149

Z
Zimmerman, Phil, 304
ZIP archives, 343
zip command, 343
ZIP codes, 249, 286, 293